Ford Thunderbird & Mercury Cougar Automotive Repair Manual

by Ken Freund
and John H Haynes
Member of the Guild of Motoring Writers

Models covered:
All Ford Thunderbird and Mercury Cougar models
1989 and 1990

ABCDE
FGHIJ
KLMNO
P

Haynes Publishing Group
Sparkford Nr Yeovil
Somerset BA22 7JJ England

Haynes North America, Inc
861 Lawrence Drive
Newbury Park
California 91320 USA

Acknowledgements

We are grateful to the Ford Motor Company for assistance with technical information, certain illustrations and vehicle photos. The Champion Spark Plug Company supplied the illustrations of various spark plug conditions. Technical writers who contributed to this project include Robert Maddox, Larry Warren and Brian Styve.

A book in the **Haynes Automotive Repair Manual Series**

Printed in the U.S.A.

ISBN 1 85010 725 4

Library of Congress Catalog Card Number 90-85100

Contents

1989 Ford Thunderbird

About this manual

Its purpose

The purpose of this manual is to help you get the best value from your vehicle. It can do so in several ways. It can help you decide what work must be done, even if you choose to have it done by a dealer service department or a repair shop; it provides information and procedures for routine maintenance and servicing; and it offers diagnostic and repair procedures to follow when trouble occurs.

We hope you use the manual to tackle the work yourself. For many simpler jobs, doing it yourself may be quicker than arranging an appointment to get the vehicle into a shop and making the trips to leave it and pick it up. More importantly, a lot of money can be saved by avoiding the expense the shop must pass on to you to cover its labor and overhead costs. An added benefit is the sense of satisfaction and accomplishment that you feel after doing the job yourself.

Using the manual

The manual is divided into Chapters. Each Chapter is divided into numbered Sections, which are headed in bold type between horizontal lines. Each Section consists of consecutively numbered paragraphs.

At the beginning of each numbered Section you will be referred to any illustrations which apply to the procedures in that Section. The reference numbers used in illustration captions pinpoint the pertinent Section and the Step within that Section. That is, illustration 3.2 means the illustration refers to Section 3 and Step (or paragraph) 2 within that Section.

Procedures, once described in the text, are not normally repeated. When it's necessary to refer to another Chapter, the reference will be given as Chapter and Section number. Cross references given without use of the word "Chapter" apply to Sections and/or paragraphs in the same Chapter. For example, "see Section 8" means in the same Chapter.

References to the left or right side of the vehicle assume you are sitting in the driver's seat, facing forward.

Even though we have prepared this manual with extreme care, neither the publisher nor the author can accept responsibility for any errors in, or omissions from, the information given.

NOTE

A **Note** provides information necessary to properly complete a procedure or information which will make the procedure easier to understand.

CAUTION

A **Caution** provides a special procedure or special steps which must be taken while completing the procedure where the **Caution** is found. Not heeding a **Caution** can result in damage to the assembly being worked on.

WARNING

A **Warning** provides a special procedure or special steps which must be taken while completing the procedure where the **Warning** is found. Not heeding a **Warning** can result in personal injury.

Introduction to the Ford Thunderbird/Mercury Cougar

The Ford Thunderbird and Mercury Cougar have the conventional front engine/rear-wheel drive layout.

All models are equipped with a fuel-injected V6 engine. Some engines are supercharged.

Power from the engine is transferred through either a five-speed manual or four-speed automatic transmission to the frame-mounted differential by a tubular driveshaft incorporating universal joints. Halfshafts, incorporating constant velocity (CV) joints, carry power from the differential to the rear wheels.

Suspension is independent, both front and rear, with upper and lower control arms used to locate the knuckle assembly at each wheel. The front suspension uses strut/coil spring assemblies. The rear suspension features coil springs and conventional shock absorbers. Some models are equipped with Automatic Ride Control (ARC).

The rack and pinion steering unit is mounted in front of the suspension control arms. Power assist is standard.

The brakes are disc at the front and drum at the rear (some models are equipped with rear disc brakes) with vacuum assist standard. Some models are equipped an Anti-lock Braking System (ABS).

Vehicle identification numbers

Modifications are a continuing and unpublicized process in vehicle manufacturing. Since spare parts manuals and lists are compiled on a numerical basis, the individual vehicle numbers are essential to correctly identify the component required.

Vehicle Identification Number (VIN)

This very important identification number is stamped into a metal plate attached to the top of the driver's side of the dashboard. It is visible from outside the vehicle, looking through the windshield. The VIN also appears on the Vehicle Certificate of Title and Registration. It contains information such as where and when the vehicle was manufactured, the model year and the body style.

Vehicle Certification label

The Vehicle Certification label (VC label) is attached to the front of the left door lock pillar. The upper half of the label contains the name of the manufacturer, the month and year of production, the Gross Vehicle Weight Rating (GVWR), the Gross Axle weight rating (GAWR) and the certification statement **(see illustration)**.

The VC label also contains the VIN number, which is used for warranty identification of the vehicle, and provides such information as manufacturer, type of restraint system, body type, engine, transmission, model year and vehicle serial number.

Engine numbers

Labels containing the engine code, engine number and build date can be found on the valve cover **(see illustration)**. The engine number is also stamped into the engine block.

Manual transmission numbers

The manual transmission identification number and serial numbers can be found on a tag on the left side of the transmission.

Automatic transmission numbers

Metal tags with the automatic transmission serial number, build date and other information are attached with a bolt, usually at the extension housing.

Vehicle Emissions Control Information (VECI) label

This label is located in the engine compartment. It contains information on the emissions control equipment installed on the vehicle as well as tune-up specifications.

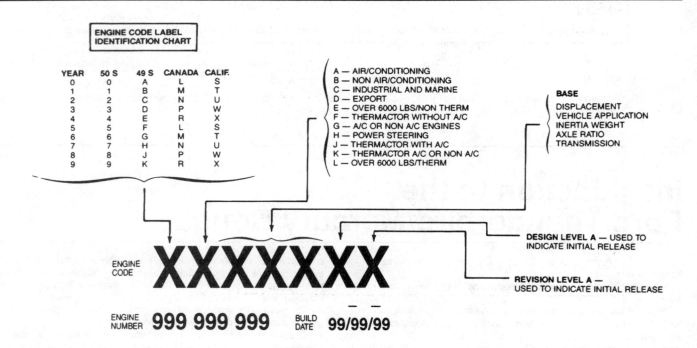

The engine code label, located on the valve cover, contains the engine code, engine number and build date

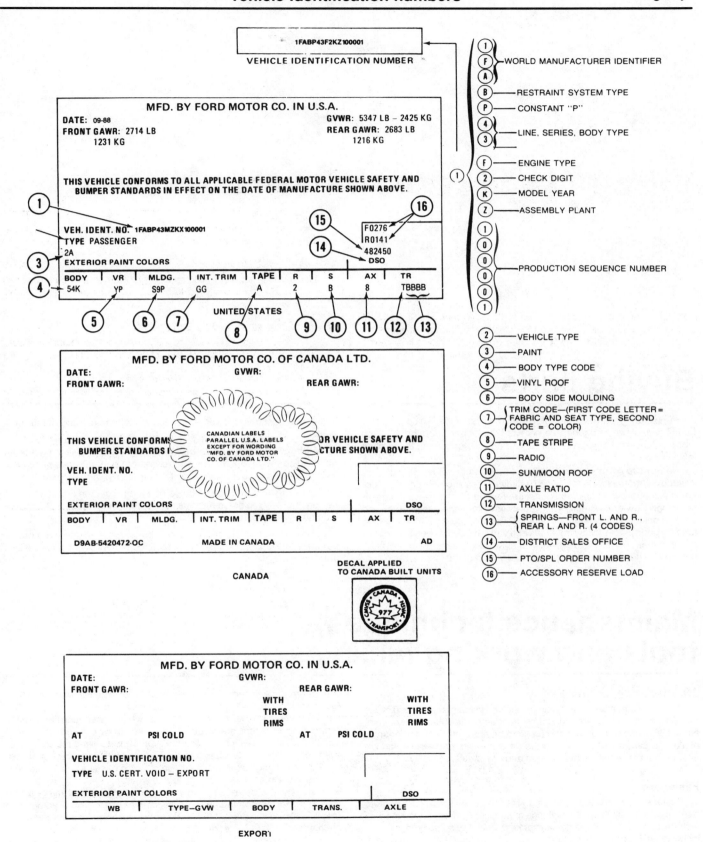

The Vehicle Certification label contains a variety of important information

Buying parts

Replacement parts are available from many sources, which generally fall into one of two categories – authorized dealer parts departments and independent retail auto parts stores. Our advice concerning these parts is as follows:

Retail auto parts stores: Good auto parts stores will stock frequently needed components which wear out relatively fast, such as clutch components, exhaust systems, brake parts, tune-up parts, etc. These stores often supply new or reconditioned parts on an exchange basis, which can save a considerable amount of money. Discount auto parts stores are often very good places to buy materials and parts needed for general vehicle maintenance such as oil, grease, filters, spark plugs, belts, touch-up paint, bulbs, etc. They also usually sell tools and general accessories, have con-

venient hours, charge lower prices and can often be found not far from home.

Authorized dealer parts department: This is the best source for parts which are unique to the vehicle and not generally available elsewhere (such as major engine parts, transmission parts, trim pieces, etc.).

Warranty information: If the vehicle is still covered under warranty, be sure that any replacement parts purchased – regardless of the source – do not invalidate the warranty!

To be sure of obtaining the correct parts, have engine and chassis numbers available and, if possible, take the old parts along for positive identification.

Maintenance techniques, tools and working facilities

Maintenance techniques

There are a number of techniques involved in maintenance and repair that will be referred to throughout this manual. Application of these techniques will enable the home mechanic to be more efficient, better organized and capable of performing the various tasks properly, which will ensure that the repair job is thorough and complete.

Fasteners

Fasteners are nuts, bolts, studs and screws used to hold two or more parts together. There are a few things to keep in mind when working with fasteners. Almost all of them use a locking device of some type, either a lockwasher, locknut, locking tab or thread adhesive. All threaded fasteners should be clean and straight, with undamaged threads and undamaged corners on the hex head where the wrench fits. Develop the habit of replacing all damaged nuts and bolts with new ones. Special locknuts

with nylon or fiber inserts can only be used once. If they are removed, they lose their locking ability and must be replaced with new ones.

Rusted nuts and bolts should be treated with a penetrating fluid to ease removal and prevent breakage. Some mechanics use turpentine in a spout-type oil can, which works quite well. After applying the rust penetrant, let it work for a few minutes before trying to loosen the nut or bolt. Badly rusted fasteners may have to be chiseled or sawed off or removed with a special nut breaker, available at tool stores.

If a bolt or stud breaks off in an assembly, it can be drilled and removed with a special tool commonly available for this purpose. Most automotive machine shops can perform this task, as well as other repair procedures, such as the repair of threaded holes that have been stripped out.

Flat washers and lockwashers, when removed from an assembly, should always be replaced exactly as removed. Replace any damaged washers with new ones. Never use a lockwasher on any soft metal surface (such as aluminum), thin sheet metal or plastic.

Fastener sizes

For a number of reasons, automobile manufacturers are making wider and wider use of metric fasteners. Therefore, it is important to be able to tell the difference between standard (sometimes called U.S. or SAE) and metric hardware, since they cannot be interchanged.

All bolts, whether standard or metric, are sized according to diameter, thread pitch and length. For example, a standard 1/2 – 13 x 1 bolt is 1/2 inch in diameter, has 13 threads per inch and is 1 inch long. An M12 – 1.75 x 25 metric bolt is 12 mm in diameter, has a thread pitch of 1.75 mm (the distance between threads) and is 25 mm long. The two bolts are nearly identical, and easily confused, but they are not interchangeable.

In addition to the differences in diameter, thread pitch and length, metric and standard bolts can also be distinguished by examining the bolt heads. To begin with, the distance across the flats on a standard bolt head is measured in inches, while the same dimension on a metric bolt is sized in millimeters (the same is true for nuts). As a result, a standard wrench should not be used on a metric bolt and a metric wrench should not be used on a standard bolt. Also, most standard bolts have slashes radiating out from the center of the head to denote the grade or strength of the bolt, which is an indication of the amount of torque that can be applied to it. The greater the number of slashes, the greater the strength of the bolt. Grades 0 through 5 are commonly used on automobiles. Metric bolts have a property class (grade) number, rather than a slash, molded into their heads to indicate bolt strength. In this case, the higher the number, the stronger the bolt. Property class numbers 8.8, 9.8 and 10.9 are commonly used on automobiles.

Strength markings can also be used to distinguish standard hex nuts from metric hex nuts. Many standard nuts have dots stamped into one side, while metric nuts are marked with a number. The greater the number of dots, or the higher the number, the greater the strength of the nut.

Metric studs are also marked on their ends according to property class (grade). Larger studs are numbered (the same as metric bolts), while smaller studs carry a geometric code to denote grade.

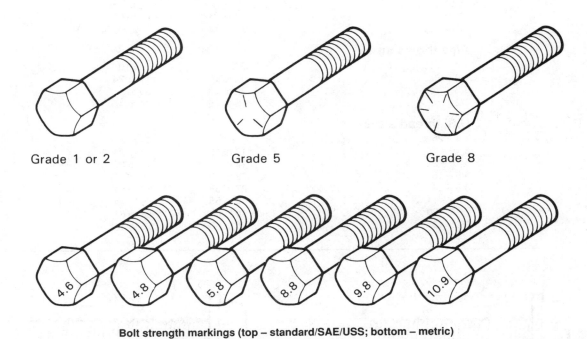

Grade 1 or 2   Grade 5   Grade 8

4.6   4.8   5.8   8.8   9.8   10.9

Bolt strength markings (top – standard/SAE/USS; bottom – metric)

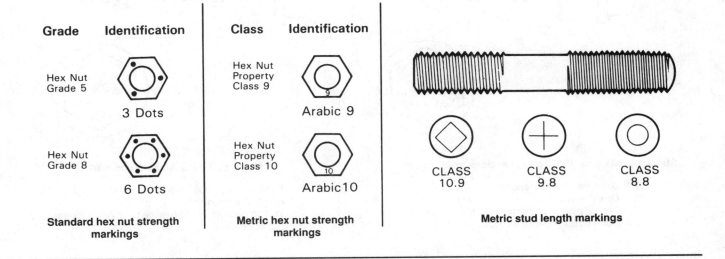

Grade	Identification
Hex Nut Grade 5	3 Dots
Hex Nut Grade 8	6 Dots

Standard hex nut strength markings

Class	Identification
Hex Nut Property Class 9	Arabic 9
Hex Nut Property Class 10	Arabic 10

Metric hex nut strength markings

CLASS 10.9   CLASS 9.8   CLASS 8.8

Metric stud length markings

It should be noted that many fasteners, especially Grades 0 through 2, have no distinguishing marks on them. When such is the case, the only way to determine whether it is standard or metric is to measure the thread pitch or compare it to a known fastener of the same size.

Standard fasteners are often referred to as SAE, as opposed to metric. However, it should be noted that SAE technically refers to a non-metric *fine thread* fastener only. Coarse thread non-metric fasteners are referred to as USS sizes.

Since fasteners of the same size (both standard and metric) may have different strength ratings, be sure to reinstall any bolts, studs or nuts removed from your vehicle in their original locations. Also, when replacing a fastener with a new one, make sure that the new one has a strength rating equal to or greater than the original.

Tightening sequences and procedures

Most threaded fasteners should be tightened to a specific torque value (torque is the twisting force applied to a threaded component such as a nut or bolt). Overtightening the fastener can weaken it and cause it to break, while undertightening can cause it to eventually come loose. Bolts, screws and studs, depending on the material they are made of and their thread diameters, have specific torque values, many of which are noted in the Specifications at the beginning of each Chapter. Be sure to follow the torque recommendations closely. For fasteners not assigned a specific torque, a general torque value chart is presented here as a guide. These torque values are for dry (unlubricated) fasteners threaded into steel or cast iron (not aluminum). As was previously mentioned, the size and grade of a fastener determine the amount of torque that can safely be

Metric thread sizes	Ft-lbs	Nm
M-6	6 to 9	9 to 12
M-8	14 to 21	19 to 28
M-10	28 to 40	38 to 54
M-12	50 to 71	68 to 96
M-14	80 to 140	109 to 154

Pipe thread sizes		
1/8	5 to 8	7 to 10
1/4	12 to 18	17 to 24
3/8	22 to 33	30 to 44
1/2	25 to 35	34 to 47

U.S. thread sizes		
1/4 – 20	6 to 9	9 to 12
5/16 – 18	12 to 18	17 to 24
5/16 – 24	14 to 20	19 to 27
3/8 – 16	22 to 32	30 to 43
3/8 – 24	27 to 38	37 to 51
7/16 – 14	40 to 55	55 to 74
7/16 – 20	40 to 60	55 to 81
1/2 – 13	55 to 80	75 to 108

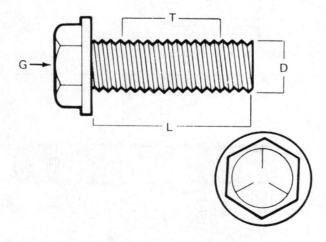

Standard (SAE and USS) bolt dimensions/grade marks

- G   Grade marks (bolt length)
- L   Length (in inches)
- T   Thread pitch (number of threads per inch)
- D   Nominal diameter (in inches)

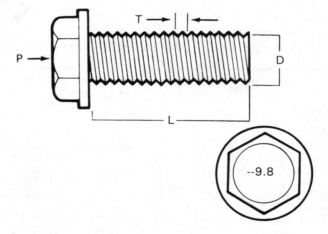

Metric bolt dimensions/grade marks

- P   Property class (bolt strength)
- L   Length (in millimeters)
- T   Thread pitch (distance between threads in millimeters)
- D   Diameter

applied to it. The figures listed here are approximate for Grade 2 and Grade 3 fasteners. Higher grades can tolerate higher torque values.

Fasteners laid out in a pattern, such as cylinder head bolts, oil pan bolts, differential cover bolts, etc., must be loosened or tightened in sequence to avoid warping the component. This sequence will normally be shown in the appropriate Chapter. If a specific pattern is not given, the following procedures can be used to prevent warping.

Initially, the bolts or nuts should be assembled finger-tight only. Next, they should be tightened one full turn each, in a criss-cross or diagonal pattern. After each one has been tightened one full turn, return to the first one and tighten them all one-half turn, following the same pattern. Finally, tighten each of them one-quarter turn at a time until each fastener has been tightened to the proper torque. To loosen and remove the fasteners, the procedure would be reversed.

Component disassembly

Component disassembly should be done with care and purpose to help ensure that the parts go back together properly. Always keep track of the sequence in which parts are removed. Make note of special characteristics or marks on parts that can be installed more than one way, such as a grooved thrust washer on a shaft. It is a good idea to lay the disassembled parts out on a clean surface in the order that they were removed. It may also be helpful to make sketches or take instant photos of components before removal.

When removing fasteners from a component, keep track of their locations. Sometimes threading a bolt back in a part, or putting the washers and nut back on a stud, can prevent mix-ups later. If nuts and bolts cannot be returned to their original locations, they should be kept in a compartmented box or a series of small boxes. A cupcake or muffin tin is ideal for this purpose, since each cavity can hold the bolts and nuts from a particular area (i.e. oil pan bolts, valve cover bolts, engine mount bolts, etc.). A pan of this type is especially helpful when working on assemblies with very small parts, such as the carburetor, alternator, valve train or interior dash and trim pieces. The cavities can be marked with paint or tape to identify the contents.

Whenever wiring looms, harnesses or connectors are separated, it is a good idea to identify the two halves with numbered pieces of masking tape so they can be easily reconnected.

Gasket sealing surfaces

Throughout any vehicle, gaskets are used to seal the mating surfaces between two parts and keep lubricants, fluids, vacuum or pressure contained in an assembly.

Many times these gaskets are coated with a liquid or paste-type gasket sealing compound before assembly. Age, heat and pressure can sometimes cause the two parts to stick together so tightly that they are very difficult to separate. Often, the assembly can be loosened by striking it with a soft-face hammer near the mating surfaces. A regular hammer can be used if a block of wood is placed between the hammer and the part. Do not hammer on cast parts or parts that could be easily damaged. With any particularly stubborn part, always recheck to make sure that every fastener has been removed.

Avoid using a screwdriver or bar to pry apart an assembly, as they can easily mar the gasket sealing surfaces of the parts, which must remain smooth. If prying is absolutely necessary, use an old broom handle, but keep in mind that extra clean up will be necessary if the wood splinters.

After the parts are separated, the old gasket must be carefully scraped off and the gasket surfaces cleaned. Stubborn gasket material can be soaked with rust penetrant or treated with a special chemical to soften it so it can be easily scraped off. A scraper can be fashioned from a piece of copper tubing by flattening and sharpening one end. Copper is recommended because it is usually softer than the surfaces to be scraped, which reduces the chance of gouging the part. Some gaskets can be removed with a wire brush, but regardless of the method used, the mating surfaces must be left clean and smooth. If for some reason the gasket surface is gouged, then a gasket sealer thick enough to fill scratches will have to be used during reassembly of the components. For most applications, a non-drying (or semi-drying) gasket sealer should be used.

Hose removal tips

Warning: *If the vehicle is equipped with air conditioning, do not disconnect any of the A/C hoses without first having the system depressurized by a dealer service department or a service station.*

Hose removal precautions closely parallel gasket removal precautions. Avoid scratching or gouging the surface that the hose mates against or the connection may leak. This is especially true for radiator hoses. Because of various chemical reactions, the rubber in hoses can bond itself to the metal spigot that the hose fits over. To remove a hose, first loosen the hose clamps that secure it to the spigot. Then, with slip-joint pliers, grab the hose at the clamp and rotate it around the spigot. Work it back and forth until it is completely free, then pull it off. Silicone or other lubricants will ease removal if they can be applied between the hose and the outside of the spigot. Apply the same lubricant to the inside of the hose and the outside of the spigot to simplify installation.

As a last resort (and if the hose is to be replaced with a new one anyway), the rubber can be slit with a knife and the hose peeled from the spigot. If this must be done, be careful that the metal connection is not damaged.

If a hose clamp is broken or damaged, do not reuse it. Wire-type clamps usually weaken with age, so it is a good idea to replace them with screw-type clamps whenever a hose is removed.

Tools

A selection of good tools is a basic requirement for anyone who plans to maintain and repair his or her own vehicle. For the owner who has few tools, the initial investment might seem high, but when compared to the spiraling costs of professional auto maintenance and repair, it is a wise one.

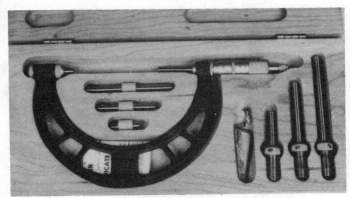

Micrometer set

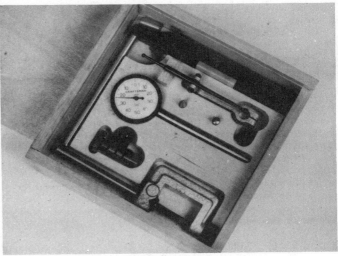

Dial indicator set

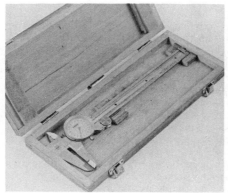

Dial caliper

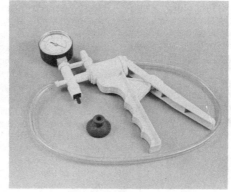

Hand-operated vacuum pump

Timing light

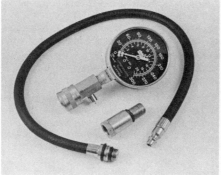

Compression gauge with spark plug
hole adapter

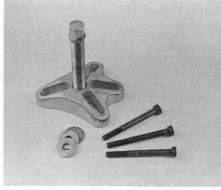

Damper/steering wheel puller

General purpose puller

Hydraulic lifter removal tool

Valve spring compressor

Valve spring compressor

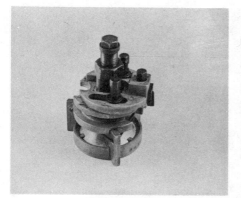

Ridge reamer

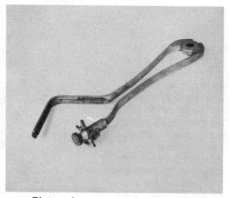

Piston ring groove cleaning tool

Ring removal/installation tool

Ring compressor

Cylinder hone

Brake hold-down spring tool

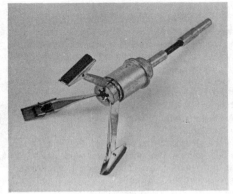

Brake cylinder hone

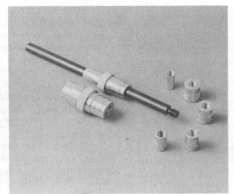

Clutch plate alignment tool

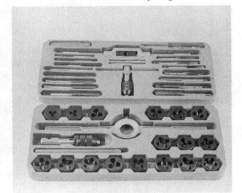

Tap and die set

To help the owner decide which tools are needed to perform the tasks detailed in this manual, the following tool lists are offered: *Maintenance and minor repair, Repair/overhaul* and *Special.*

The newcomer to practical mechanics should start off with the maintenance and minor repair tool kit, which is adequate for the simpler jobs performed on a vehicle. Then, as confidence and experience grow, the owner can tackle more difficult tasks, buying additional tools as they are needed. Eventually the basic kit will be expanded into the repair and overhaul tool set. Over a period of time, the experienced do-it-yourselfer will assemble a tool set complete enough for most repair and overhaul procedures and will add tools from the special category when it is felt that the expense is justified by the frequency of use.

Maintenance and minor repair tool kit

The tools in this list should be considered the minimum required for performance of routine maintenance, servicing and minor repair work. We recommend the purchase of combination wrenches (box-end and open-end combined in one wrench). While more expensive than open end wrenches, they offer the advantages of both types of wrench.

Combination wrench set (1/4-inch to 1 inch or 6 mm to 19 mm)
Adjustable wrench, 8 inch
Spark plug wrench with rubber insert
Spark plug gap adjusting tool
Feeler gauge set
Brake bleeder wrench
Standard screwdriver (5/16-inch x 6 inch)
Phillips screwdriver (No. 2 x 6 inch)
Combination pliers – 6 inch
Hacksaw and assortment of blades
Tire pressure gauge
Grease gun
Oil can
Fine emery cloth
Wire brush

Battery post and cable cleaning tool
Oil filter wrench
Funnel (medium size)
Safety goggles
Jackstands(2)
Drain pan

Note: *If basic tune-ups are going to be part of routine maintenance, it will be necessary to purchase a good quality stroboscopic timing light and combination tachometer/dwell meter. Although they are included in the list of special tools, it is mentioned here because they are absolutely necessary for tuning most vehicles properly.*

Repair and overhaul tool set

These tools are essential for anyone who plans to perform major repairs and are in addition to those in the maintenance and minor repair tool kit. Included is a comprehensive set of sockets which, though expensive, are invaluable because of their versatility, especially when various extensions and drives are available. We recommend the 1/2-inch drive over the 3/8-inch drive. Although the larger drive is bulky and more expensive, it has the capacity of accepting a very wide range of large sockets. Ideally, however, the mechanic should have a 3/8-inch drive set and a 1/2-inch drive set.

Socket set(s)
Reversible ratchet
Extension – 10 inch
Universal joint
Torque wrench (same size drive as sockets)
Ball peen hammer – 8 ounce
Soft-face hammer (plastic/rubber)
Standard screwdriver (1/4-inch x 6 inch)
Standard screwdriver (stubby – 5/16-inch)
Phillips screwdriver (No. 3 x 8 inch)
Phillips screwdriver (stubby – No. 2)

Pliers – vise grip
Pliers – lineman's
Pliers – needle nose
Pliers – snap-ring (internal and external)
Cold chisel – 1/2-inch
Scribe
Scraper (made from flattened copper tubing)
Centerpunch
Pin punches (1/16, 1/8, 3/16-inch)
Steel rule/straightedge – 12 inch
Allen wrench set (1/8 to 3/8-inch or 4 mm to 10 mm)
A selection of files
Wire brush (large)
Jackstands (second set)
Jack (scissor or hydraulic type)

Note: *Another tool which is often useful is an electric drill with a chuck capacity of 3/8-inch and a set of good quality drill bits.*

Special tools

The tools in this list include those which are not used regularly, are expensive to buy, or which need to be used in accordance with their manufacturer's instructions. Unless these tools will be used frequently, it is not very economical to purchase many of them. A consideration would be to split the cost and use between yourself and a friend or friends. In addition, most of these tools can be obtained from a tool rental shop on a temporary basis.

This list primarily contains only those tools and instruments widely available to the public, and not those special tools produced by the vehicle manufacturer for distribution to dealer service departments. Occasionally, references to the manufacturer's special tools are included in the text of this manual. Generally, an alternative method of doing the job without the special tool is offered. However, sometimes there is no alternative to their use. Where this is the case, and the tool cannot be purchased or borrowed, the work should be turned over to the dealer service department or an automotive repair shop.

Valve spring compressor
Piston ring groove cleaning tool
Piston ring compressor
Piston ring installation tool
Cylinder compression gauge
Cylinder ridge reamer
Cylinder surfacing hone
Cylinder bore gauge
Micrometers and/or dial calipers
Hydraulic lifter removal tool
Balljoint separator
Universal-type puller
Impact screwdriver
Dial indicator set
Stroboscopic timing light (inductive pick-up)
Hand operated vacuum/pressure pump
Tachometer/dwell meter
Universal electrical multimeter
Cable hoist
Brake spring removal and installation tools
Floor jack

Buying tools

For the do-it-yourselfer who is just starting to get involved in vehicle maintenance and repair, there are a number of options available when purchasing tools. If maintenance and minor repair is the extent of the work to be done, the purchase of individual tools is satisfactory. If, on the other hand, extensive work is planned, it would be a good idea to purchase a modest tool set from one of the large retail chain stores. A set can usually be bought at a substantial savings over the individual tool prices, and they often come with a tool box. As additional tools are needed, add–on sets, individual tools and a larger tool box can be purchased to expand the tool selection. Building a tool set gradually allows the cost of the tools to be spread over a longer period of time and gives the mechanic the freedom to choose only those tools that will actually be used.

Tool stores will often be the only source of some of the special tools that are needed, but regardless of where tools are bought, try to avoid cheap ones, especially when buying screwdrivers and sockets, because they won't last very long. The expense involved in replacing cheap tools will eventually be greater than the initial cost of quality tools.

Care and maintenance of tools

Good tools are expensive, so it makes sense to treat them with respect. Keep them clean and in usable condition and store them properly when not in use. Always wipe off any dirt, grease or metal chips before putting them away. Never leave tools lying around in the work area. Upon completion of a job, always check closely under the hood for tools that may have been left there so they won't get lost during a test drive.

Some tools, such as screwdrivers, pliers, wrenches and sockets, can be hung on a panel mounted on the garage or workshop wall, while others should be kept in a tool box or tray. Measuring instruments, gauges, meters, etc. must be carefully stored where they cannot be damaged by weather or impact from other tools.

When tools are used with care and stored properly, they will last a very long time. Even with the best of care, though, tools will wear out if used frequently. When a tool is damaged or worn out, replace it. Subsequent jobs will be safer and more enjoyable if you do.

Working facilities

Not to be overlooked when discussing tools is the workshop. If anything more than routine maintenance is to be carried out, some sort of suitable work area is essential.

It is understood, and appreciated, that many home mechanics do not have a good workshop or garage available, and end up removing an engine or doing major repairs outside. It is recommended, however, that the overhaul or repair be completed under the cover of a roof.

A clean, flat workbench or table of comfortable working height is an absolute necessity. The workbench should be equipped with a vise that has a jaw opening of at least four inches.

As mentioned previously, some clean, dry storage space is also required for tools, as well as the lubricants, fluids, cleaning solvents, etc. which soon become necessary.

Sometimes waste oil and fluids, drained from the engine or cooling system during normal maintenance or repairs, present a disposal problem. To avoid pouring them on the ground or into a sewage system, pour the used fluids into large containers, seal them with caps and take them to an authorized disposal site or recycling center. Plastic jugs, such as old antifreeze containers, are ideal for this purpose.

Always keep a supply of old newspapers and clean rags available. Old towels are excellent for mopping up spills. Many mechanics use rolls of paper towels for most work because they are readily available and disposable. To help keep the area under the vehicle clean, a large cardboard box can be cut open and flattened to protect the garage or shop floor.

Whenever working over a painted surface, such as when leaning over a fender to service something under the hood, always cover it with an old blanket or bedspread to protect the finish. Vinyl covered pads, made especially for this purpose, are available at auto parts stores.

Booster battery (jump) starting

Observe these precautions when using a booster battery to start a vehicle:

a) Before connecting the booster battery, make sure the ignition switch is in the Off position.

b) Turn off the lights, heater and other electrical loads.

c) Your eyes should be shielded. Safety goggles are a good idea.

d) Make sure the booster battery is the same voltage as the dead one in the vehicle.

e) The two vehicles MUST NOT TOUCH each other!

f) Make sure the transmission is in Neutral (manual) or Park (automatic).

g) If the booster battery is not a maintenance-free type, remove the vent caps and lay a cloth over the vent holes.

Connect the red jumper cable to the positive (+) terminals of each battery.

Connect one end of the black jumper cable to the negative (−) terminal of the booster battery. The other end of this cable should be connected to a good ground on the vehicle to be started, such as a bolt or bracket on the engine block (see illustration). Make sure the cable will not come into contact with the fan, drivebelts or other moving parts of the engine.

Start the engine using the booster battery, then, with the engine running at idle speed, disconnect the jumper cables in the reverse order of connection.

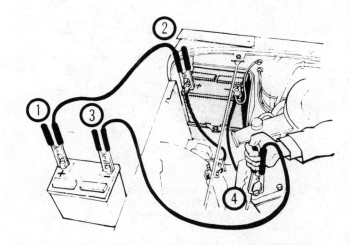

Make the booster battery cable connections in the numerical order shown (note that the negative cable of the booster battery is NOT attached to the negative terminal of the dead battery)

Jacking and towing

Jacking

Warning: *The jack supplied with the vehicle should only be used for changing a tire or placing jackstands under the frame. Never work under the vehicle or start the engine while this jack is being used as the only means of support.*

The vehicle should be on level ground. Place the shift lever in Park, if you have an automatic, or Reverse if you have a manual transmission. Block the wheel diagonally opposite the wheel being changed. Set the parking brake. Warning: When one rear wheel is lifted off the ground, neither the automatic nor the manual transmission will prevent the vehicle from moving and possibly slipping off the jack, even if it has been placed in Reverse or Park as described above. To prevent movement of the vehicle while changing a tire, always set the parking brake and block the wheel diagonally opposite the wheel being changed.

Remove the spare tire and jack from stowage. If equipped with anti-theft wire wheel covers, pry off the ornament and remove the bolt with the special key **(see illustration)**. Remove the wheel cover (if so equipped) with the tapered end of the lug nut wrench by inserting it and twisting the handle and then prying against the inner wheel cover flange. Loosen, but do not remove, the lug nuts (one-half turn is sufficient). If equipped with aluminum wheels, one of the lug nuts will be an anti-theft type (see Anti-theft wheel lug nuts below).

Place the scissors-type jack under the side of the vehicle and adjust the jack height with the jack handle so it fits into the notch in the vertical rocker panel flange nearest the wheel to be changed. There is a front and rear jacking notch on each side of the vehicle **(see illustration)**. When lifting the vehicle in any other way, special care must be exercised to avoid damage to the fuel tank, filler neck, exhaust system and underbody. Caution: Do not raise the vehicle with a bumper jack. The bumper could be damaged. Also, jack slippage may occur, causing personal injury.

Turn the jack handle clockwise until the tire clears the ground. Remove the lug nuts and the wheel. Pull the wheel off and replace it with the spare.

Replace the lug nuts with the beveled edges facing in. Tighten them snugly. Don't attempt to tighten them completely until the vehicle is lowered or it could slip off the jack.

Turn the jack handle counterclockwise to lower the vehicle. Remove the jack and tighten the lug nuts in a criss-cross pattern.

Align the wheel cover (if so equipped) with the valve stem extension matching the hole in the cover. Install the cover and be sure that it's snapped in place all the way around. Stow the tire, jack and wrench. Unblock the wheels.

Anti-theft wheel lug nuts

If your vehicle is equipped with aluminum wheels, they have anti-theft wheel lug nuts (one per wheel). The key and your registration card are attached to the lug wrench stowed with the spare tire. Don't lose the registration card. You must send it to the manufacturer, not the dealer, to get a replacement key if yours is lost. To remove or install the anti-theft lug nut, insert the key into the slot in the lug nut. Place the lug nut wrench on the key and, while applying pressure on the key, remove or install the lug nut. Mark the anti-theft lug nut location on the wheel before removing it. This will allow you to install it in the same location.

Towing

As a general rule, the vehicle should be towed with the rear (drive) wheels off the ground. If they can't be raised, either place them on a dolly or disconnect the driveshaft from the differential. When a vehicle is towed with the rear wheels raised, the steering wheel must be clamped in the straight ahead position with a special device designed for use during towing. Warning: Don't use the steering column lock to keep the front wheels pointed straight ahead. It's not strong enough for this purpose.

Vehicles can be towed with all four wheels on the ground, provided that speeds don't exceed 35 mph and, on models with automatic transmissions, the distance is not over 50 miles (there is no distance limit for models with manual tranmissions). When the rear wheels are off the ground there's no distance limitation, but don't exceed 50 mph.

Equipment specifically designed for towing should be used. It should be attached to the main structural members of the vehicle, not the bumpers or brackets.

Safety is a major consideration when towing and all applicable state and local laws must be obeyed. A safety chain system must be used at all times.

While towing, the parking brake should be released and the transmission must be in Neutral. The steering must be unlocked (ignition switch in the Off position). Remember that power steering and power brakes will not work with the engine off.

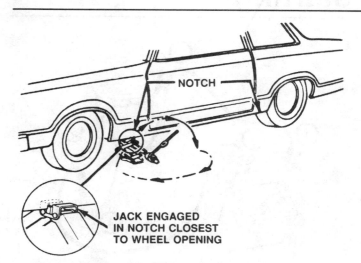

Place the jack so it engages the vertical rocker panel flange nearest the wheel that will be raised

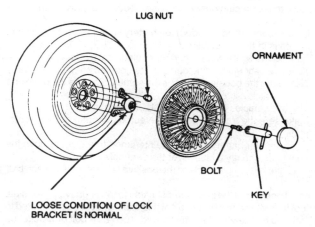

An exploded view of an anti-theft wire wheel cover

Automotive chemicals and lubricants

A number of automotive chemicals and lubricants are available for use during vehicle maintenance and repair. They include a wide variety of products ranging from cleaning solvents and degreasers to lubricants and protective sprays for rubber, plastic and vinyl.

Cleaners

Carburetor cleaner and choke cleaner is a strong solvent for gum, varnish and carbon. Most carburetor cleaners leave a dry-type lubricant film which will not harden or gum up. Because of this film it is not recommended for use on electrical components.

Brake system cleaner is used to remove grease and brake fluid from the brake system, where clean surfaces are absolutely necessary. It leaves no residue and often eliminates brake squeal caused by contaminants.

Electrical cleaner removes oxidation, corrosion and carbon deposits from electrical contacts, restoring full current flow. It can also be used to clean spark plugs, carburetor jets, voltage regulators and other parts where an oil-free surface is desired.

Demoisturants remove water and moisture from electrical components such as alternators, voltage regulators, electrical connectors and fuse blocks. They are non-conductive, non-corrosive and non-flammable.

Degreasers are heavy-duty solvents used to remove grease from the outside of the engine and from chassis components. They can be sprayed or brushed on and, depending on the type, are rinsed off either with water or solvent.

Lubricants

Motor oil is the lubricant formulated for use in engines. It normally contains a wide variety of additives to prevent corrosion and reduce foaming and wear. Motor oil comes in various weights (viscosity ratings) from 5 to 80. The recommended weight of the oil depends on the season, temperature and the demands on the engine. Light oil is used in cold climates and under light load conditions. Heavy oil is used in hot climates and where high loads are encountered. Multi-viscosity oils are designed to have characteristics of both light and heavy oils and are available in a number of weights from 5W-20 to 20W-50.

Gear oil is designed to be used in differentials, manual transmissions and other areas where high-temperature lubrication is required.

Chassis and wheel bearing grease is a heavy grease used where increased loads and friction are encountered, such as for wheel bearings, balljoints, tie-rod ends and universal joints.

High-temperature wheel bearing grease is designed to withstand the extreme temperatures encountered by wheel bearings in disc brake equipped vehicles. It usually contains molybdenum disulfide (moly), which is a dry-type lubricant.

White grease is a heavy grease for metal-to-metal applications where water is a problem. White grease stays soft under both low and high temperatures (usually from −100 to +190-degrees F), and will not wash off or dilute in the presence of water.

Assembly lube is a special extreme pressure lubricant, usually containing moly, used to lubricate high-load parts (such as main and rod bearings and cam lobes) for initial start-up of a new engine. The assembly lube lubricates the parts without being squeezed out or washed away until the engine oiling system begins to function.

Silicone lubricants are used to protect rubber, plastic, vinyl and nylon parts.

Graphite lubricants are used where oils cannot be used due to contamination problems, such as in locks. The dry graphite will lubricate metal parts while remaining uncontaminated by dirt, water, oil or acids. It is electrically conductive and will not foul electrical contacts in locks such as the ignition switch.

Moly penetrants loosen and lubricate frozen, rusted and corroded fasteners and prevent future rusting or freezing.

Heat-sink grease is a special electrically non-conductive grease that is used for mounting electronic ignition modules where it is essential that heat is transferred away from the module.

Sealants

RTV sealant is one of the most widely used gasket compounds. Made from silicone, RTV is air curing, it seals, bonds, waterproofs, fills surface irregularities, remains flexible, doesn't shrink, is relatively easy to remove, and is used as a supplementary sealer with almost all low and medium temperature gaskets.

Anaerobic sealant is much like RTV in that it can be used either to seal gaskets or to form gaskets by itself. It remains flexible, is solvent resistant and fills surface imperfections. The difference between an anaerobic sealant and an RTV-type sealant is in the curing. RTV cures when exposed to air, while an anaerobic sealant cures only in the absence of air. This means that an anaerobic sealant cures only after the assembly of parts, sealing them together.

Thread and pipe sealant is used for sealing hydraulic and pneumatic fittings and vacuum lines. It is usually made from a teflon compound, and comes in a spray, a paint-on liquid and as a wrap-around tape.

Chemicals

Anti-seize compound prevents seizing, galling, cold welding, rust and corrosion in fasteners. High-temperature anti-seize, usually made with copper and graphite lubricants, is used for exhaust system and exhaust manifold bolts.

Anaerobic locking compounds are used to keep fasteners from vibrating or working loose and cure only after installation, in the absence of air. Medium strength locking compound is used for small nuts, bolts and screws that may be removed later. High-strength locking compound is for large nuts, bolts and studs which aren't removed on a regular basis.

Oil additives range from viscosity index improvers to chemical treatments that claim to reduce internal engine friction. It should be noted that most oil manufacturers caution against using additives with their oils.

Gas additives perform several functions, depending on their chemical makeup. They usually contain solvents that help dissolve gum and varnish that build up on carburetor, fuel injection and intake parts. They also serve to break down carbon deposits that form on the inside surfaces of the combustion chambers. Some additives contain upper cylinder lubricants for valves and piston rings, and others contain chemicals to remove condensation from the gas tank.

Miscellaneous

Brake fluid is specially formulated hydraulic fluid that can withstand the heat and pressure encountered in brake systems. Care must be taken so this fluid does not come in contact with painted surfaces or plastics. An opened container should always be resealed to prevent contamination by water or dirt.

Weatherstrip adhesive is used to bond weatherstripping around doors, windows and trunk lids. It is sometimes used to attach trim pieces.

Undercoating is a petroleum-based, tar-like substance that is designed to protect metal surfaces on the underside of the vehicle from corrosion. It also acts as a sound-deadening agent by insulating the bottom of the vehicle.

Waxes and polishes are used to help protect painted and plated surfaces from the weather. Different types of paint may require the use of different types of wax and polish. Some polishes utilize a chemical or abrasive cleaner to help remove the top layer of oxidized (dull) paint on older vehicles. In recent years many non-wax polishes that contain a wide variety of chemicals such as polymers and silicones have been introduced. These non-wax polishes are usually easier to apply and last longer than conventional waxes and polishes.

Safety first!

Regardless of how enthusiastic you may be about getting on with the job at hand, take the time to ensure that your safety is not jeopardized. A moment's lack of attention can result in an accident, as can failure to observe certain simple safety precautions. The possibility of an accident will always exist, and the following points should not be considered a comprehensive list of all dangers. Rather, they are intended to make you aware of the risks and to encourage a safety conscious approach to all work you carry out on your vehicle.

Essential DOs and DON'Ts

DON'T rely on a jack when working under the vehicle. Always use approved jackstands to support the weight of the vehicle and place them under the recommended lift or support points.

DON'T attempt to loosen extremely tight fasteners (i.e. wheel lug nuts) while the vehicle is on a jack – it may fall.

DON'T start the engine without first making sure that the transmission is in Neutral (or Park where applicable) and the parking brake is set.

DON'T remove the radiator cap from a hot cooling system – let it cool or cover it with a cloth and release the pressure gradually.

DON'T attempt to drain the engine oil until you are sure it has cooled to the point that it will not burn you.

DON'T touch any part of the engine or exhaust system until it has cooled sufficiently to avoid burns.

DON'T siphon toxic liquids such as gasoline, antifreeze and brake fluid by mouth, or allow them to remain on your skin.

DON'T inhale brake lining dust – it is potentially hazardous (see *Asbestos* below)

DON'T allow spilled oil or grease to remain on the floor – wipe it up before someone slips on it.

DON'T use loose fitting wrenches or other tools which may slip and cause injury.

DON'T push on wrenches when loosening or tightening nuts or bolts. Always try to pull the wrench toward you. If the situation calls for pushing the wrench away, push with an open hand to avoid scraped knuckles if the wrench should slip.

DON'T attempt to lift a heavy component alone – get someone to help you.

DON'T rush or take unsafe shortcuts to finish a job.

DON'T allow children or animals in or around the vehicle while you are working on it.

DO wear eye protection when using power tools such as a drill, sander, bench grinder, etc. and when working under a vehicle.

DO keep loose clothing and long hair well out of the way of moving parts.

DO make sure that any hoist used has a safe working load rating adequate for the job.

DO get someone to check on you periodically when working alone on a vehicle.

DO carry out work in a logical sequence and make sure that everything is correctly assembled and tightened.

DO keep chemicals and fluids tightly capped and out of the reach of children and pets.

DO remember that your vehicle's safety affects that of yourself and others. If in doubt on any point, get professional advice.

Asbestos

Certain friction, insulating, sealing, and other products – such as brake linings, brake bands, clutch linings, torque converters, gaskets, etc. – contain asbestos. *Extreme care must be taken to avoid inhalation of dust from such products, since it is hazardous to health.* If in doubt, assume that they *do* contain asbestos.

Fire

Remember at all times that gasoline is highly flammable. Never smoke or have any kind of open flame around when working on a vehicle. But the risk does not end there. A spark caused by an electrical short circuit, by two metal surfaces contacting each other, or even by static electricity built up in your body under certain conditions, can ignite gasoline vapors, which in a confined space are highly explosive. Do not, under any circumstances, use gasoline for cleaning parts. Use an approved safety solvent.

Always disconnect the battery ground (–) cable *at the battery* before working on any part of the fuel system or electrical system. Never risk spilling fuel on a hot engine or exhaust component.

It is strongly recommended that a fire extinguisher suitable for use on fuel and electrical fires be kept handy in the garage or workshop at all times. Never try to extinguish a fuel or electrical fire with water.

Fumes

Certain fumes are highly toxic and can quickly cause unconsciousness and even death if inhaled to any extent. Gasoline vapor falls into this category, as do the vapors from some cleaning solvents. Any draining or pouring of such volatile fluids should be done in a well ventilated area.

When using cleaning fluids and solvents, read the instructions on the container carefully. Never use materials from unmarked containers.

Never run the engine in an enclosed space, such as a garage. Exhaust fumes contain carbon monoxide, which is extremely poisonous. If you need to run the engine, always do so in the open air, or at least have the rear of the vehicle outside the work area.

If you are fortunate enough to have the use of an inspection pit, never drain or pour gasoline and never run the engine while the vehicle is over the pit. The fumes, being heavier than air, will concentrate in the pit with possibly lethal results.

The battery

Never create a spark or allow a bare light bulb near a battery. They normally give off a certain amount of hydrogen gas, which is highly explosive.

Always disconnect the battery ground (–) cable *at the battery* before working on the fuel or electrical systems.

If possible, loosen the filler caps or cover when charging the battery from an external source (this does not apply to sealed or maintenancefree batteries). Do not charge at an excessive rate or the battery may burst.

Take care when adding water to a non maintenance–free battery and when carrying a battery. The electrolyte, even when diluted, is very corrosive and should not be allowed to contact clothing or skin.

Always wear eye protection when cleaning the battery to prevent the caustic deposits from entering your eyes.

Household current

When using an electric power tool, inspection light, etc., which operates on household current, always make sure that the tool is correctly connected to its plug and that, where necessary, it is properly grounded. Do not use such items in damp conditions and, again, do not create a spark or apply excessive heat in the vicinity of fuel or fuel vapor.

Secondary ignition system voltage

A severe electric shock can result from touching certain parts of the ignition system (such as the spark plug wires) when the engine is running or being cranked, particularly if components are damp or the insulation is defective. In the case of an electronic ignition system, the secondary system voltage is much higher and could prove fatal.

Conversion factors

Length (distance)

Inches (in)	X	25.4	= Millimetres (mm)	X 0.0394	= Inches (in)
Feet (ft)	X	0.305	= Metres (m)	X 3.281	= Feet (ft)
Miles	X	1.609	= Kilometres (km)	X 0.621	= Miles

Volume (capacity)

Cubic inches (cu in; in^3)	X	16.387	= Cubic centimetres (cc; cm^3)	X 0.061	= Cubic inches (cu in; in^3)
Imperial pints (Imp pt)	X	0.568	= Litres (l)	X 1.76	= Imperial pints (Imp pt)
Imperial quarts (Imp qt)	X	1.137	= Litres (l)	X 0.88	= Imperial quarts (Imp qt)
Imperial quarts (Imp qt)	X	1.201	= US quarts (US qt)	X 0.833	= Imperial quarts (Imp qt)
US quarts (US qt)	X	0.946	= Litres (l)	X 1.057	= US quarts (US qt)
Imperial gallons (Imp gal)	X	4.546	= Litres (l)	X 0.22	= Imperial gallons (Imp gal)
Imperial gallons (Imp gal)	X	1.201	= US gallons (US gal)	X 0.833	= Imperial gallons (Imp gal)
US gallons (US gal)	X	3.785	= Litres (l)	X 0.264	= US gallons (US gal)

Mass (weight)

Ounces (oz)	X	28.35	= Grams (g)	X 0.035	= Ounces (oz)
Pounds (lb)	X	0.454	= Kilograms (kg)	X 2.205	= Pounds (lb)

Force

Ounces-force (ozf; oz)	X	0.278	= Newtons (N)	X 3.6	= Ounces-force (ozf; oz)
Pounds-force (lbf; lb)	X	4.448	= Newtons (N)	X 0.225	= Pounds-force (lbf; lb)
Newtons (N)	X	0.1	= Kilograms-force (kgf; kg)	X 9.81	= Newtons (N)

Pressure

Pounds-force per square inch (psi; lbf/in^2; lb/in^2)	X	0.070	= Kilograms-force per square centimetre (kgf/cm^2; kg/cm^2)	X 14.223	= Pounds-force per square inch (psi; lbf/in^2; lb/in^2)
Pounds-force per square inch (psi; lbf/in^2; lb/in^2)	X	0.068	= Atmospheres (atm)	X 14.696	= Pounds-force per square inch (psi; lbf/in^2; lb/in^2)
Pounds-force per square inch (psi; lbf/in^2; lb/in^2)	X	0.069	= Bars	X 14.5	= Pounds-force per square inch (psi; lbf/in^2; lb/in^2)
Pounds-force per square inch (psi; lbf/in^2; lb/in^2)	X	6.895	= Kilopascals (kPa)	X 0.145	= Pounds-force per square inch (psi; lbf/in^2; lb/in^2)
Kilopascals (kPa)	X	0.01	= Kilograms-force per square centimetre (kgf/cm^2; kg/cm^2)	X 98.1	= Kilopascals (kPa)

Torque (moment of force)

Pounds-force inches (lbf in; lb in)	X	1.152	= Kilograms-force centimetre (kgf cm; kg cm)	X 0.868	= Pounds-force inches (lbf in; lb in)
Pounds-force inches (lbf in; lb in)	X	0.113	= Newton metres (Nm)	X 8.85	= Pounds-force inches (lbf in; lb in)
Pounds-force inches (lbf in; lb in)	X	0.083	= Pounds-force feet (lbf ft; lb ft)	X 12	= Pounds-force inches (lbf in; lb in)
Pounds-force feet (lbf ft; lb ft)	X	0.138	= Kilograms-force metres (kgf m; kg m)	X 7.233	= Pounds-force feet (lbf ft; lb ft)
Pounds-force feet (lbf ft; lb ft)	X	1.356	= Newton metres (Nm)	X 0.738	= Pounds-force feet (lbf ft; lb ft)
Newton metres (Nm)	X	0.102	= Kilograms-force metres (kgf m; kg m)	X 9.804	= Newton metres (Nm)

Power

Horsepower (hp)	X	745.7	= Watts (W)	X 0.0013	= Horsepower (hp)

Velocity (speed)

Miles per hour (miles/hr; mph)	X	1.609	= Kilometres per hour (km/hr; kph)	X 0.621	= Miles per hour (miles/hr; mph)

Fuel consumption*

Miles per gallon, Imperial (mpg)	X	0.354	= Kilometres per litre (km/l)	X 2.825	= Miles per gallon, Imperial (mpg)
Miles per gallon, US (mpg)	X	0.425	= Kilometres per litre (km/l)	X 2.352	= Miles per gallon, US (mpg)

Temperature

Degrees Fahrenheit = (°C x 1.8) + 32   Degrees Celsius (Degrees Centigrade; °C) = (°F - 32) x 0.56

*It is common practice to convert from miles per gallon (mpg) to litres/100 kilometres (l/100km), where mpg (Imperial) x l/100 km = 282 and mpg (US) x l/100 km = 235

Troubleshooting

Contents

This section provides an easy reference guide to the more common problems which may occur during the operation of your vehicle. These problems and possible causes are grouped under various components or systems, such as Engine, Cooling system, etc., and also refer to the Chapter and/or Section which deals with the problem.

Remember that successful troubleshooting is not a mysterious black art practiced only by professional mechanics. It's simply the result of a bit of knowledge combined with an intelligent, systematic approach to the problem. Always work by a process of elimination, starting with the simplest solution and working through to the most complex – and never overlook the obvious. Anyone can forget to fill the gas tank or leave the lights on overnight, so don't assume that you are above such oversights.

Finally, always get clear in your mind why a problem has occurred and take steps to ensure that it doesn't happen again. If the electrical system fails because of a poor connection, check all other connections in the system to make sure that they don't fail as well. If a particular fuse continues to blow, find out why – don't just go on replacing fuses. Remember, failure of a small component can often be indicative of potential failure or incorrect functioning of a more important component or system.

Engine

1 Engine will not rotate when attempting to start

1 Battery terminal connections loose or corroded. Check the cable terminals at the battery. Tighten the cable or remove corrosion as necessary.
2 Battery discharged or faulty. If the cable connections are clean and tight on the battery posts, turn the key to the On position and switch on the headlights and/or windshield wipers. If they fail to function, the battery is discharged.
3 Automatic transmission not completely engaged in Park or clutch not completely depressed.
4 Broken, loose or disconnected wiring in the starting circuit. Inspect all wiring and connectors at the battery, starter solenoid and ignition switch.
5 Starter motor pinion jammed in flywheel ring gear. If equipped with a manual transmission, place the transmission in gear and rock the vehicle to manually turn the engine. Remove the starter and inspect the pinion and flywheel at earliest convenience.
6 Starter solenoid faulty (Chapter 5).
7 Starter motor faulty (Chapter 5).
8 Ignition switch faulty (Chapter 12).

2 Engine rotates but will not start

1 Fuel tank empty.
2 Battery discharged (engine rotates slowly). Check the operation of electrical components as described in previous Section.
3 Battery terminal connections loose or corroded. See previous Section.
4 Fuel injection system or fuel pump faulty (Chapter 4).
5 No power to fuel pump (Chapter 4).
6 Worn, faulty or incorrectly gapped spark plugs (Chapter 1).
7 Broken, loose or disconnected wiring in the starting circuit (see previous Section).
8 Distributor loose, causing ignition timing to change. Turn the distributor as necessary to start the engine, then set the ignition timing as soon as possible (Chapter 5).
9 Broken, loose or disconnected wires at the ignition coil or faulty coil (Chapter 5).
10 Other fault in the ignition system (Chapter 5).

3 Starter motor operates without rotating engine

1 Starter pinion sticking. Remove the starter (Chapter 5) and inspect.
2 Starter pinion or flywheel teeth worn or broken. Remove the cover at the rear of the engine and inspect.

4 Engine hard to start when cold

1 Battery discharged or low. Check as described in Section 1.
2 Fuel supply not reaching the fuel rail (Chapter 4).
3 Fault in the fuel injection system (Chapter 4).
4 Distributor rotor carbon tracked and/or damaged (Chapter 1).
5 Other fault in the ignition system (Chapter 5).

5 Engine hard to start when hot

1 Air filter clogged (Chapter 1).
2 Fuel not reaching the fuel rail (Chapter 4).
3 Corroded electrical leads at the battery (Chapter 1).
4 Bad engine ground (Chapter 12).
5 Starter worn (Chapter 5).
6 Corroded electrical leads at the fuel injectors (Chapter 4).

6 Starter motor noisy or excessively rough in engagement

1 Pinion or flywheel gear teeth worn or broken. Remove the cover at the rear of the engine (if so equipped) and inspect.
2 Starter motor mounting bolts loose or missing.

7 Engine starts but stops immediately

1 Loose or faulty electrical connections in the ignition system (Chapter 5).
2 Insufficient fuel reaching the fuel rail (Chapter 4).
3 Vacuum leak (likely at the gasket surfaces of the throttle body) – see the next Section. Make sure that all mounting bolts/nuts are tightened securely and that all vacuum hoses connected to the throttle body are positioned properly and in good condition.

8 Engine lopes while idling or idles erratically

1 Vacuum leakage. Check mounting bolts/nuts at the throttle body and intake manifold for tightness. Make sure that all vacuum hoses are connected and in good condition. Use a stethoscope or a length of fuel hose held against your ear to listen for vacuum leaks while the engine is running. A hissing sound will be heard. Check the throttle body and intake manifold gasket surfaces.
2 Leaking EGR valve or plugged PCV valve (see Chapters 1 and 6).
3 Air filter clogged (Chapter 1).
4 Fuel pump not delivering sufficient fuel to the fuel rail (see Section 7).
5 Fuel injection system malfunctioning or out of adjustment (Chapter 4).
6 Leaking head gasket. If this is suspected, take the vehicle to a repair shop or dealer where the engine can be pressure checked.
7 Timing chain and/or gears worn (Chapter 2).
8 Camshaft lobes worn (Chapter 2).

9   Engine misses at idle speed

1   Spark plugs worn or not gapped properly (Chapter 1).
2   Faulty spark plug wires (Chapter 1).
3   Sticking or faulty emissions system components (Chapter 6).
4   Clogged fuel filter and/or foreign matter in fuel. Remove the fuel filter (Chapter 1) and inspect.
5   Vacuum leaks at the intake manifold or at hose connections. Check as described in the previous Section.
6   Incorrect ignition timing (Chapter 5).
7   Uneven or low cylinder compression. Check compression as described in Chapter 2.

10   Engine misses throughout driving speed range

1   Fuel filter clogged and/or impurities in the fuel system (Chapter 1). Also check fuel pressure (see Chapter 4).
2   Faulty or incorrectly gapped spark plugs (Chapter 1).
3   Incorrect ignition timing (Chapter 5).
4   On models with a standard ignition system, check for cracked distributor cap, disconnected distributor wires and damaged distributor components (Chapter 1). On models with DIS, check the coil pack (Chapter 5).
5   Leaking spark plug wires (Chapter 1).
6   Faulty emissions system components (Chapter 6).
7   Low or uneven cylinder compression pressures. Remove the spark plugs and test the compression with gauge (Chapter 2).
8   Weak or faulty ignition system (Chapter 5).
9   Vacuum leaks at the throttle body or vacuum hoses (see Section 8).

11   Engine stalls

1   Fuel filter clogged and/or water and impurities in the fuel system (Chapter 1).
2   Incorrect ignition timing (see Chapter 5).
3   Ignition system components damp or damaged (Chapter 5).
4   Faulty emissions system components (Chapter 6).
5   Faulty or incorrectly gapped spark plugs (Chapter 1). Also check spark plug wires (Chapter 1).
6   Vacuum leak at the throttle body or vacuum hoses. Check as described in Section 8.

12   Engine lacks power

1   Incorrect ignition timing (Chapter 5).
2   On models with standard ignition systems, excessive play in distributor shaft. At the same time, check for worn rotor, faulty distributor cap, wires, etc. (Chapters 1 and 5).
3   Faulty or incorrectly gapped spark plugs (Chapter 1).
4   Fuel injection system not adjusted properly or excessively worn (Chapter 4).
5   Faulty coil or other ignition system component (Chapter 5).
6   Brakes binding (Chapter 1).
7   Automatic transmission fluid level incorrect (Chapter 1).
8   Clutch slipping (Chapter 8).
9   Fuel filter clogged and/or impurities in the fuel system (Chapter 1).
10   Emissions control system not functioning properly (Chapter 6).
11   Use of substandard fuel. Fill tank with proper octane fuel.
12   Low or uneven cylinder compression pressures. Test with compression tester, which will detect leaking valves and/or blown head gasket (Chapter 2).

13   Engine backfires

1   Emissions system not functioning properly (Chapter 6).
2   Faulty secondary ignition system (cracked spark plug insulator, faulty plug wires, distributor cap and/or rotor) (Chapters 1 and 5).
3   Fuel injection system in need of adjustment or worn excessively (Chapter 4).
4   Vacuum leak at the throttle body or vacuum hoses. Check as described in Section 8.
5   Valves sticking (Chapter 2).
6   Incorrectly routed spark plug wires (Chapter 1).

14   Pinging or knocking engine sounds during acceleration or uphill

1   Incorrect grade of fuel. Fill tank with fuel of the proper octane rating.
2   Ignition timing incorrect (Chapter 5).
3   Fuel-injection system in need of adjustment (Chapter 4).
4   Improper spark plugs. Check plug type against Emissions Control Information label located under hood. Also check plugs and wires for damage (Chapter 1).
5   Worn or damaged distributor or DIS system components (Chapter 5).
6   Faulty emissions system (Chapter 6).
7   Vacuum leak. Check as described in Section 8.
8   Excessive carbon build-up on piston head or on cylinder head.

15   Engine diesels (continues to run) after switching off

1   Ignition timing incorrectly adjusted (Chapter 5).
2   Excessive engine operating temperature. Probable causes of this are malfunctioning thermostat, clogged radiator, faulty water pump (Chapter 3).
3   Malfunctioning fuel injection system (Chapter 4).

Engine electrical system

16   Battery will not hold a charge

1   Alternator drivebelt defective or not adjusted properly (Chapter 1).
2   Electrolyte level low or battery discharged (Chapter 1).
3   Battery terminals loose or corroded (Chapter 1).
4   Alternator not charging properly (Chapter 5).
5   Loose, broken or faulty wiring in the charging circuit (Chapter 5).
6   Short in vehicle wiring causing a continual drain on battery.
7   Battery defective internally.

17   Alternator light stays on

1   Fault in alternator or charging circuit (Chapter 5).
2   Alternator drivebelt defective or not properly adjusted (Chapter 1).

18   Alternator light fails to come on when key is turned on

1   Warning light bulb defective (Chapter 12).
2   Alternator faulty (Chapter 5).
3   Fault in the printed circuit, dash wiring or bulb holder (Chapter 12).

19 Check engine light comes on

Take the vehicle to a dealer service department for further diagnosis.

Fuel system

20 Excessive fuel consumption

1 Dirty or clogged air filter element (Chapter 1).
2 Incorrectly set ignition timing (Chapter 5).
3 Emissions system not functioning properly (Chapter 6).
4 Fuel injection system parts excessively worn or damaged (Chapter 4).
5 Low tire pressure or incorrect tire size (Chapter 1).

21 Fuel leakage and/or fuel odor

1 Leak in a fuel feed or vent line (Chapter 4).
2 Tank overfilled. Fill only to automatic shut-off.
3 Emissions system clogged or damaged (Chapter 6).
4 Vapor leaks from fuel system lines (Chapter 4).

Cooling system

22 Overheating

1 Insufficient coolant in system (Chapter 1).
2 Water pump drivebelt defective or not adjusted properly (Chapter 1).
3 Radiator core blocked or radiator grille dirty and restricted (Chapter 3).
4 Thermostat faulty (Chapter 3).
5 Fan blades broken or cracked (Chapter 3).
6 Radiator cap not maintaining proper pressure. Have cap pressure tested by gas station or repair shop.
7 Ignition timing incorrect (Chapter 5).

23 Overcooling

1 Thermostat faulty (Chapter 3).
2 Inaccurate temperature gauge (Chapter 12)

24 External coolant leakage

1 Deteriorated or damaged hoses or loose clamps. Replace hoses and/or tighten clamps at hose connections (Chapter 1).
2 Water pump seals defective. If this is the case, water will drip from the weep hole in the water pump body (Chapter 3).
3 Leakage from radiator core or header tank. This will require the radiator to be professionally repaired (see Chapter 3 for removal procedures).
4 Engine drain plugs or water jacket core plugs leaking (see Chapter 2).

25 Internal coolant leakage

Note: *Internal coolant leaks can usually be detected by examining the oil. Check the dipstick and inside of the rocker arm cover(s) for water deposits and an oil consistency like that of a milkshake.*

1 Leaking cylinder head gasket. Have the cooling system pressure tested.
2 Cracked cylinder bore or cylinder head. Dismantle engine and inspect (Chapter 2).

26 Coolant loss

1 Too much coolant in system (Chapter 1).
2 Coolant boiling away due to overheating (see Section 22).
3 Internal or external leakage (see Sections 24 and 25).
4 Faulty radiator cap. Have the cap pressure tested.

27 Poor coolant circulation

1 Inoperative water pump. A quick test is to pinch the top radiator hose closed with your hand while the engine is idling, then let it loose. You should feel the surge of coolant if the pump is working properly (Chapter 3).
2 Restriction in cooling system. Drain, flush and refill the system (Chapter 1). If necessary, remove the radiator (Chapter 3) and have it reverse flushed.
3 Water pump drivebelt defective or not adjusted properly (Chapter 1).
4 Thermostat sticking (Chapter 3).

Clutch

28 Fails to release (pedal pressed to the floor – shift lever does not move freely in and out of Reverse)

1 Clutch fork off ball stud. Look under the vehicle, on the left side of transmission.
2 Clutch plate warped or damaged (Chapter 8).
3 Clutch hydraulic system low or has air in system and needs to be bled (Chapter 8).

29 Clutch slips (engine speed increases with no increase in vehicle speed)

1 Clutch plate oil soaked or lining worn. Remove clutch (Chapter 8) and inspect.
2 Clutch plate not seated. It may take 30 or 40 normal starts for a new one to seat.
3 Pressure plate worn (Chapter 8).

30 Grabbing (chattering) as clutch is engaged

1 Oil on clutch plate lining. Remove (Chapter 8) and inspect. Correct any leakage source.
2 Worn or loose engine or transmission mounts. These units move slightly when clutch is released. Inspect mounts and bolts.
3 Worn splines on clutch plate hub. Remove clutch components (Chapter 8) and inspect.
4 Warped pressure plate or flywheel. Remove clutch components and inspect.

31   Squeal or rumble with clutch fully engaged (pedal released)

1   Release bearing binding on transmission bearing retainer. Remove clutch components (Chapter 8) and check bearing. Remove any burrs or nicks, clean and relubricate before reinstallation.
2   Weak linkage return spring. Replace the spring.

32   Squeal or rumble with clutch fully disengaged (pedal depressed)

1   Worn, defective or broken release bearing (Chapter 8).
2   Worn or broken pressure plate springs (or diaphragm fingers) (Chapter 8).
3   Air in hydraulic line (Chapter 8).

33   Clutch pedal stays on floor when disengaged

1   Bind in linkage or release bearing. Inspect linkage or remove clutch components as necessary.
2   Clutch hydraulic cylinder faulty or there is air in the system.

Manual transmission

Note: *All the following references are to Chapter 7, unless otherwise noted.*

34   Noisy in Neutral with engine running

1   Input shaft bearing worn.
2   Damaged main drive gear bearing.
3   Worn countershaft bearings.
4   Worn or damaged countershaft end play shims.

35   Noisy in all gears

1   Any of the above causes, and/or:
2   Insufficient lubricant (see checking procedures in Chapter 1).

36   Noisy in one particular gear

1   Worn, damaged or chipped gear teeth for that particular gear.
2   Worn or damaged synchronizer for that particular gear.

37   Slips out of high gear

1   Transmission mounting bolts loose.
2   Shift rods not working freely.
3   Damaged mainshaft pilot bushing.
4   Dirt between transmission case and engine or misalignment of transmission.

38   Difficulty in engaging gears

1   Loose, damaged or out-of-adjustment shift linkage. Make a thorough inspection, replacing parts as necessary.
2   Air in hydraulic system (Chapter 8)

39   Oil leakage

1   Excessive amount of lubricant in transmission (see Chapter 1 for correct checking procedures). Drain lubricant as required.
2   Side cover loose or gasket damaged.
3   Rear oil seal or speedometer oil seal in need of replacement.
4   Clutch hydraulic system leaking (Chapter 8).

Automatic transmission

Note: *Due to the complexity of the automatic transmission, it is difficult for the home mechanic to properly diagnose and service this component. For problems other than the following, the vehicle should be taken to a dealer or reputable repair shop.*

40   General shift mechanism problems

1   Chapter 7 deals with checking and adjusting the shift linkage on automatic transmissions. Common problems which may be attributed to poorly adjusted linkage are:
    Engine starting in gears other than Park or Neutral
    Indicator on shifter pointing to a gear other than the one actually being used
    Vehicle moves when in Park
2   Refer to Chapter 7 to adjust the linkage.

41   Transmission will not downshift with accelerator pedal pressed to the floor

    Chapter 7 deals with adjusting the TV cable to enable the transmission to downshift properly.

42   Transmission slips, shifts rough, is noisy or has no drive in forward or reverse gears

1   There are many probable causes for the above problems, but the home mechanic should be concerned with only one possibility – fluid level.
2   Before taking the vehicle to a repair shop, check the level and condition of the fluid as described in Chapter 1. Correct fluid level as necessary or change the fluid and filter if needed. If the problem persists, have a professional diagnose the probable cause.

43   Fluid leakage

1   Automatic transmission fluid is a deep red color. Fluid leaks should not be confused with engine oil, which can easily be blown by air flow to the transmission.
2   To pinpoint a leak, first remove all built-up dirt and grime from around the transmission. Degreasing agents and/or steam cleaning will achieve this. With the underside clean, drive the vehicle at low speeds so air flow will not blow the leak far from its source. Raise the vehicle and determine where the leak is coming from. Common areas of leakage are:
    a)   **Pan:** Tighten mounting bolts and/or replace pan gasket as necessary (see Chapters 1 and 7).
    b)   **Filler pipe:** Replace the rubber seal where pipe enters transmission case.
    c)   **Transmission oil lines:** Tighten connectors where lines enter transmission case and/or replace lines.
    d)   **Vent pipe:** Transmission overfilled and/or water in fluid (see checking procedures, Chapter 1).
    e)   **Speedometer connector:** Replace the O-ring where speedometer cable enters transmission case (Chapter 7).

Driveshaft

44   Oil leak at front of driveshaft

Defective transmission rear oil seal. See Chapter 7 for replacement procedures. While this is done, check the splined yoke for burrs or a rough condition which may be damaging the seal. Burrs can be removed with crocus cloth or a fine whetstone.

45   Knock or clunk when the transmission is under initial load (just after transmission is put into gear)

1   Loose or disconnected rear suspension components. Check all mounting bolts, nuts and bushings (Chapter 10).
2   Loose driveshaft bolts. Inspect all bolts and nuts and tighten them to the specified torque.
3   Worn or damaged universal joint bearings. Check for wear (Chapter 8).
4   Worn or damaged halfshaft CV joints (Chapter 8).

46   Metallic grating sound consistent with vehicle speed

Pronounced wear in the universal joint bearings. Check as described in Chapter 8.

47   Vibration

Note: *Before assuming that the driveshaft is at fault, make sure the tires are perfectly balanced and perform the following test.*

1   Install a tachometer inside the vehicle to monitor engine speed as the vehicle is driven. Drive the vehicle and note the engine speed at which the vibration (roughness) is most pronounced. Now shift the transmission to a different gear and bring the engine speed to the same point.
2   If the vibration occurs at the same engine speed (rpm) regardless of which gear the transmission is in, the driveshaft is NOT at fault since the driveshaft speed varies.
3   If the vibration decreases or is eliminated when the transmission is in a different gear at the same engine speed, refer to the following probable causes.
4   Bent or dented driveshaft. Inspect and replace as necessary (Chapter 8).
5   Undercoating or built-up dirt, etc. on the driveshaft. Clean the shaft thoroughly and recheck.
6   Worn universal joint bearings. Remove and inspect (Chapter 8).
7   Driveshaft and/or companion flange out-of-balance. Check for missing weights on the shaft. Remove the driveshaft (Chapter 8) and reinstall 180-degrees from original position, then retest. Have the driveshaft professionally balanced if the problem persists.
8   Worn or damaged halfshaft CV joints (Chapter 8).

Halfshafts

48   Noise

1   Road noise. No corrective procedures available.
2   Tire noise. Inspect the tires and check tire pressures (Chapter 1).
3   Rear wheel bearings loose, worn or damaged (Chapter 8).
4   Halfshaft CV joints worn or damaged (see noises listed under Driveshaft above).

49   Vibration

See probable causes under Driveshaft. Proceed under the guidelines listed for the driveshaft. If the problem persists, check the rear wheel bearings by raising the rear of the vehicle and spinning the wheels by hand. Listen for evidence of rough (noisy) bearings. Remove and inspect (Chapter 8).

50   Oil leakage

1   Pinion seal damaged (Chapter 8).
2   Differential side oil seals damaged (Chapter 8).
3   Differential inspection cover leaking. Tighten the bolts or replace the gasket as required (Chapters 1 and 8).
4   Torn CV joint boot (Chapter 8).

Brakes

Note: *Before assuming that a brake problem exists, make sure that the tires are in good condition and inflated properly (see Chapter 1), that the front end alignment is correct and that the vehicle is not loaded with weight in an unequal manner.*

51   Vehicle pulls to one side during braking

1   Defective, damaged or oil contaminated brake pads or shoes on one side. Inspect as described in Chapter 9.
2   Excessive wear of brake shoe or pad material or drum/disc on one side. Inspect and correct as necessary.
3   Loose or disconnected front suspension components. Inspect and tighten all bolts to the specified torque (Chapter 10).
4   Defective drum brake or caliper assembly. Remove the drum or caliper and inspect for a stuck piston or other damage (Chapter 9).

52   Noise (high-pitched squeal with the brakes applied)

Disc brake pads worn out. The noise comes from the wear sensor rubbing against the disc. Replace the pads with new ones immediately (Chapter 9).

53   Excessive brake pedal travel

1   Partial brake system failure. Inspect the entire system (Chapter 9) and correct as required.
2   Insufficient fluid in the master cylinder. Check (Chapter 1), add fluid and bleed the system if necessary (Chapter 9).
3   Brakes not adjusting properly. Make a series of starts and stops with the vehicle is in Reverse. If this does not correct the situation, remove the drums and inspect the self-adjusters (Chapter 9).

54   Brake pedal feels spongy when depressed

1   Air in the hydraulic lines. Bleed the brake system (Chapter 9).
2   Faulty flexible hoses. Inspect all system hoses and lines. Replace parts as necessary.
3   Master cylinder mounting bolts/nuts loose.
4   Master cylinder defective (Chapter 9).

55   Excessive effort required to stop vehicle

1   Power brake booster not operating properly (Chapter 9).
2   Excessively worn linings or pads. Inspect and replace if necessary (Chapters 1 and 9).
3   One or more caliper pistons or wheel cylinders seized or sticking. Inspect and rebuild as required (Chapter 9).
4   Brake linings or pads contaminated with oil or grease. Inspect and replace as required (Chapters 1 and 9).
5   New pads or shoes installed and not yet seated. It will take a while for the new material to seat against the drum (or rotor).

56   Pedal travels to the floor with little resistance

Little or no fluid in the master cylinder reservoir caused by leaking wheel cylinder(s), leaking caliper piston(s), loose, damaged or disconnected brake lines. Inspect the entire system and correct as necessary.

57   Brake pedal pulsates during brake application

1   Wheel bearings not adjusted properly or in need of replacement (Chapter 1).
2   Caliper not sliding properly due to improper installation or obstructions. Remove and inspect (Chapter 9).
3   Rotor or drum defective. Remove the rotor or drum (Chapter 9) and check for excessive lateral runout, out-of-round and parallelism. Have the drum or rotor resurfaced or replace it with a new one.

Suspension and steering systems

58   Vehicle pulls to one side

1   Tire pressures uneven (Chapter 1).
2   Defective tire (Chapter 1).
3   Excessive wear in suspension or steering components (Chapter 10).
4   Wheels out of alignment.
5   Front brakes dragging. Inspect the brakes as described in Chapter 9.

59   Shimmy, shake or vibration

1   Tire or wheel out-of-balance or out-of-round. Have professionally balanced.
2   Loose, worn or out-of-adjustment wheel bearings (Chapters 1 and 8).
3   Shock absorbers and/or suspension components worn or damaged (Chapter 10).

60   Excessive pitching and/or rolling around corners or during braking

1   Defective shock absorbers. Replace as a set (Chapter 10).

2   Broken or weak springs and/or suspension components. Inspect as described in Chapter 10.

61   Excessively stiff steering

1   Lack of fluid in power steering fluid reservoir (Chapter 1).
2   Incorrect tire pressures (Chapter 1).
3   Lack of lubrication at steering joints (Chapter 1).
4   Front end out of alignment.
5   See Section 63.

62   Excessive play in steering

1   Loose front wheel bearings (Chapter 1).
2   Excessive wear in suspension or steering components (Chapter 10).
3   Steering gear out of adjustment (Chapter 10).

63   Lack of power assistance

1   Steering pump drivebelt faulty or not adjusted properly (Chapter 1).
2   Fluid level low (Chapter 1).
3   Hoses or lines restricted. Inspect and replace parts as necessary.
4   Air in power steering system. Bleed the system (Chapter 10).

64   Excessive tire wear (not specific to one area)

1   Incorrect tire pressures (Chapter 1).
2   Tires out-of-balance. Have professionally balanced.
3   Wheels damaged. Inspect and replace as necessary.
4   Suspension or steering components excessively worn (Chapter 10).

65   Excessive tire wear on outside edge

1   Inflation pressures incorrect (Chapter 1).
2   Excessive speed in turns.
3   Wheel alignment incorrect (excessive toe-in). Have professionally aligned.
4   Suspension arm bent or twisted (Chapter 10).

66   Excessive tire wear on inside edge

1   Inflation pressures incorrect (Chapter 1).
2   Wheel alignment incorrect (toe-out). Have professionally aligned.
3   Loose or damaged steering components (Chapter 10).

67   Tire tread worn in one place

1   Tires out-of-balance.
2   Damaged or buckled wheel. Inspect and replace if necessary.
3   Defective tire (Chapter 1).

Chapter 1 Tune-up and routine maintenance

Contents

Air and PCV filter replacement 15
Automatic transmission control linkage lubrication 24
Automatic transmission fluid and filter change 30
Automatic transmission fluid level check 7
Battery check and maintenance 13
Brake system check 23
Chassis lubrication 32
Cooling system check 19
Cooling system servicing (draining, flushing and refilling) 31
Drivebelt check and replacement 10
Engine oil and filter change 8
Exhaust system check 20
Fluid level checks 4
Fuel filter replacement 18
Fuel system check 17
Introduction 2
Maintenance schedule 1
Manual transmission lubricant level check 25
Neutral safety switch check 11
PCV valve check 16
Power steering fluid level check 6
Rear axle (differential) lubricant change 33
Rear axle (differential) lubricant level check 26
Seat belt check 12
Spark plug replacement 27
Spark plug wire, distributor cap and rotor
    check and replacement 28
Steering and suspension check 22
Supercharger lubricant level check 29
Tire and tire pressure checks 5
Tire rotation 21
Tune-up sequence 3
Underhood hose check and replacement 9
Windshield wiper blade check and replacement 14

***

Specifications

Recommended lubricants and fluids

Engine oil
  Type .... API grade SG or SG/CC multigrade and fuel efficient oil
  Viscosity .... See accompanying chart

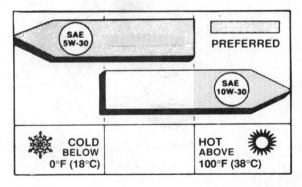

For best fuel economy and cold starting, select the lowest SAE viscosity grade oil for the expected temperature range

Recommended lubricants and fluids (continued)

Engine oil capacity (all)	5.0 qts
Brake fluid type	DOT 3 heavy duty brake fluid
Power steering fluid type	Motorcraft Type F automatic transmission fluid (part no. XT-1-QF)
Automatic transmission fluid type	Motorcraft MERCON automatic transmission fluid (part no. XT-2-QDX)
Manual transmission lubricant type	Motorcraft MERCON automatic transmission fluid (part no. XT-2-QDX)
Supercharger lubricant type	Ford Synthetic Supercharger Fluid (part no. E95Z-19577-A)
Coolant type	Ethylene glycol-based antifreeze and water
Cooling system capacity (approximate)	11.8 qts
Chassis grease	Motorcraft multi-purpose grease (part no. C1AZ-19590-B)
Differential oil*	Hypoid lubricant (part no. EOAZ-19580-AA)

* Trak-Lok axles add 4 oz. of friction modifier (part no. C8AZ-19B546-A) when oil is changed.

General

Radiator cap pressure
Standard	16 psi
Lower limit (must hold pressure)	13 psi
Upper limit (must relieve pressure)	18 psi

Brakes

Disc brake pad thickness (minimum)	1/8 in
Drum brake shoe lining thickness (minimum)	1/8 in

Ignition system

Recommended spark plugs	Refer to Vehicle Emission Control Information label
Spark plug gap	Refer to Vehicle Emission Control Information label
Idle speed	Refer to Vehicle Emission Control Information label
Firing order	1-4-2-5-3-6

Torque specifications

Ft-lbs (unless otherwise noted)

Wheel lug nuts	85 to 105
Spark plugs	7 to 15
Oil pan drain plug	15 to 25
Engine block drain plug	5 to 8
Automatic transmission pan bolts	72 to 120 in-lbs
Automatic transmission filter bolt	80 to 120 in-lbs

CYLINDER NUMBERING AND DISTRIBUTOR LOCATION

FRONT OF VEHICLE

DISTRIBUTOR

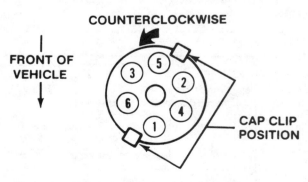

FIRING ORDER AND ROTATION

COUNTERCLOCKWISE

FRONT OF VEHICLE

CAP CLIP POSITION

FIRING ORDER — 1-4-2-5-3-6
3.8L ENGINE

Ford Thunderbird & Mercury Cougar
Maintenance schedule

The following maintenance intervals are based on the assumption that the vehicle owner will be doing the maintenance or service work, as opposed to having a dealer service department do the work. Although the time/mileage intervals are loosely based on factory recommendations, most have been shortened to ensure, for example, that such items as lubricants and fluids are checked/changed at intervals that promote maximum engine/driveline service life. Also, subject to the preference of the individual owner interested in keeping his or her vehicle in peak condition at all times, and with the vehicle's ultimate resale in mind, many of the maintenance procedures may be performed more often than recommended in the following schedule. We encourage such owner initiative.

When the vehicle is new it should be serviced initially by a factory authorized dealer service department to protect the factory warranty. In many cases the initial maintenance check is done at no cost to the owner (check with your dealer service department for more information).

Every 250 miles or weekly, whichever comes first

Check the engine oil level (Section 4)
Check the engine coolant level (Section 4)
Check the windshield washer fluid level (Section 4)
Check the brake fluid level (Section 4)
Check the tires and tire pressures (Section 5)

Every 3000 miles or 3 months, whichever comes first

All items listed above plus :
Check the power steering fluid level (Section 6)
Check the automatic transmission fluid
    level (Section 7)
Change the engine oil and oil filter (Section 8)

Every 6000 miles or 6 months, whichever comes first

All items listed above plus:
Inspect/replace the underhood hoses (Section 9)
Check the drivebelt (Section 10)

Check the operation of the neutral safety
    switch (Section 11)
Check the seatbelt operation (Section 12)
Check/service the battery (Section 13)
Rotate the tires (Section 21)

Every 24,000 miles or 24 months, whichever comes first

All items listed above plus:
Inspect/replace the windshield wiper blades
    (Section 14)
Replace the air filter (Section 15)*
Check the PCV valve (Section 16)
Check the fuel system (Section 17)
Replace the fuel filter (Section 18)
Inspect the cooling system (Section 19)
Inspect the exhaust system (Section 20)
Inspect the steering and suspension
    components (Section 22)
Inspect the brakes (Section 23)
Lubricate the automatic transmission control
    linkage (Section 24)
Check/replenish the manual transmission
    lubricant (Section 25)
Check the rear axle (differential) oil
    level (Section 26)
Replace the spark plugs (Section 27)
Check/replace the spark plug wires, distributor cap
    and rotor (Section 28)
Check the supercharger lubricant level (Section 29)
Change the automatic transmission fluid and
    filter (Section 30)**
Service the cooling system (drain, flush and
    refill) (Section 31)

Every 30,000 miles or 30 months, whichever comes first

Lubricate the chassis components (Section 32)
Change the rear axle (differential) oil (Section 33)

* Replace more often is the vehicle is driven in dusty areas
** If the vehicle is operated in continuous stop-and-go driving or in mountainous areas, change at 15,000 miles

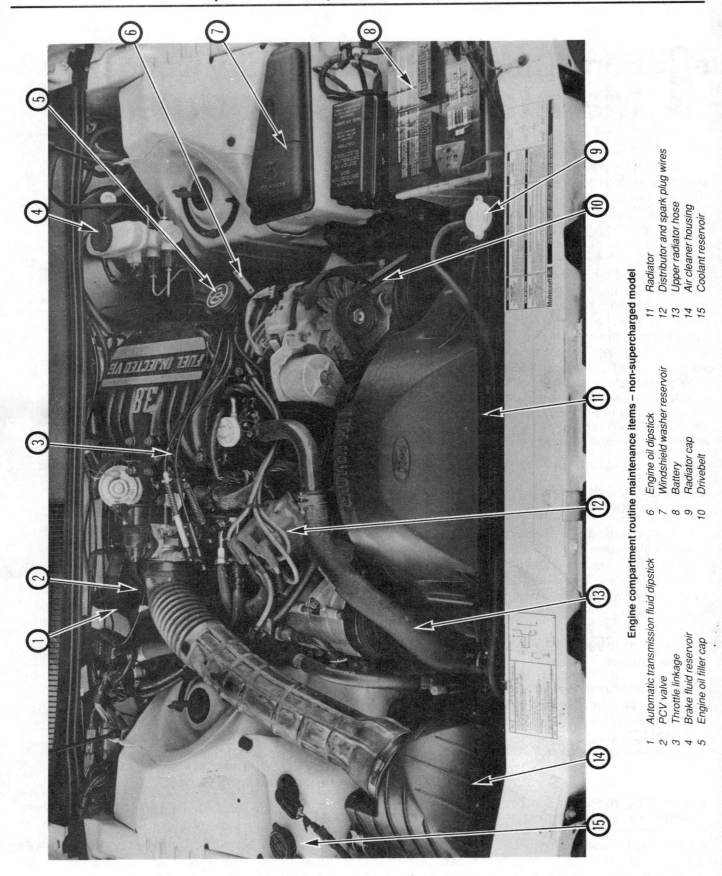

Engine compartment routine maintenance items – non-supercharged model

1   Automatic transmission fluid dipstick
2   PCV valve
3   Throttle linkage
4   Brake fluid reservoir
5   Engine oil filler cap

6   Engine oil dipstick
7   Windshield washer reservoir
8   Battery
9   Radiator cap
10   Drivebelt

11   Radiator
12   Distributor and spark plug wires
13   Upper radiator hose
14   Air cleaner housing
15   Coolant reservoir

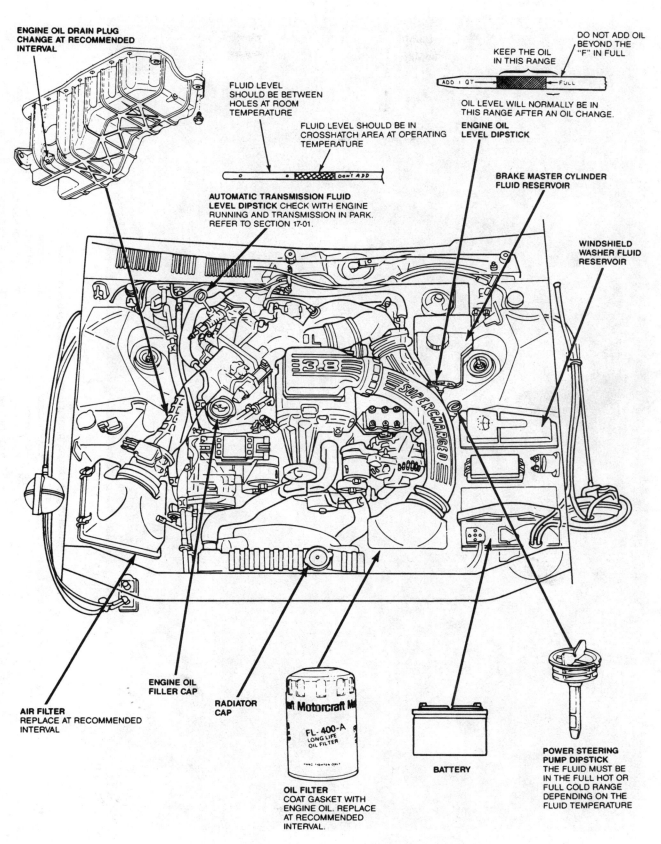

ENGINE OIL DRAIN PLUG
CHANGE AT RECOMMENDED
INTERVAL

FLUID LEVEL
SHOULD BE BETWEEN
HOLES AT ROOM
TEMPERATURE

FLUID LEVEL SHOULD BE IN
CROSSHATCH AREA AT OPERATING
TEMPERATURE

AUTOMATIC TRANSMISSION FLUID
LEVEL DIPSTICK CHECK WITH ENGINE
RUNNING AND TRANSMISSION IN PARK.
REFER TO SECTION 17-01.

DO NOT ADD OIL
BEYOND THE
"F" IN FULL

KEEP THE OIL
IN THIS RANGE

OIL LEVEL WILL NORMALLY BE IN
THIS RANGE AFTER AN OIL CHANGE.

ENGINE OIL
LEVEL DIPSTICK

BRAKE MASTER CYLINDER
FLUID RESERVOIR

WINDSHIELD
WASHER FLUID
RESERVOIR

1

AIR FILTER
REPLACE AT RECOMMENDED
INTERVAL

ENGINE OIL
FILLER CAP

RADIATOR
CAP

OIL FILTER
COAT GASKET WITH
ENGINE OIL. REPLACE
AT RECOMMENDED
INTERVAL.

BATTERY

POWER STEERING
PUMP DIPSTICK
THE FLUID MUST BE
IN THE FULL HOT OR
FULL COLD RANGE
DEPENDING ON THE
FLUID TEMPERATURE

Engine compartment routine maintenance items – supercharged model

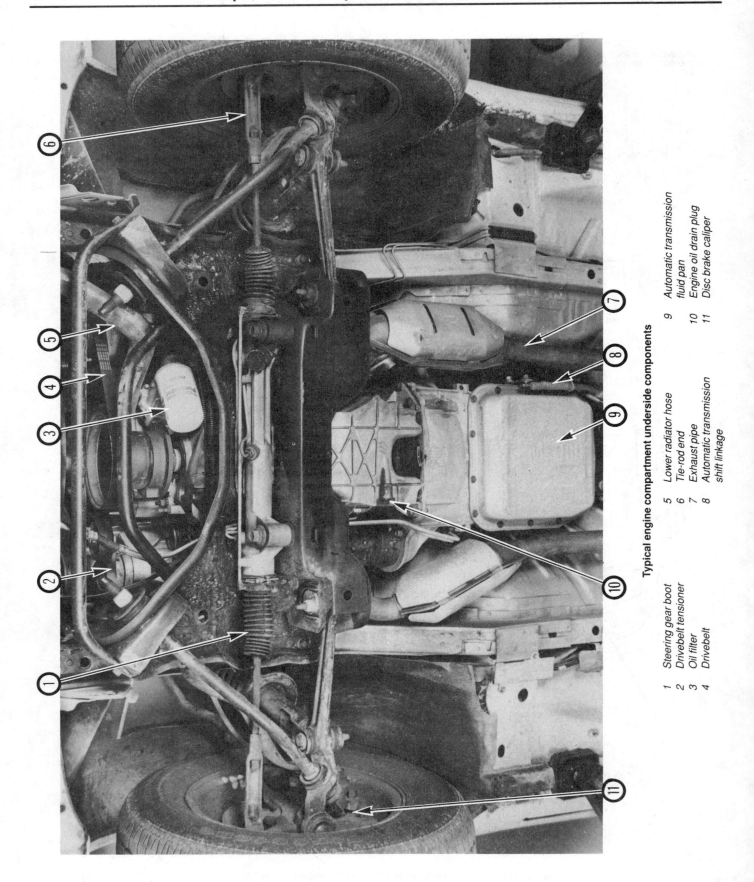

Typical engine compartment underside components

1   Steering gear boot
2   Drivebelt tensioner
3   Oil filter
4   Drivebelt

5   Lower radiator hose
6   Tie-rod end
7   Exhaust pipe
8   Automatic transmission
    shift linkage

9   Automatic transmission
    fluid pan
10 Engine oil drain plug
11 Disc brake caliper

Typical rear underside components

1	Rear brake	5 Driveaxle CV joint boot
2	Fuel tank	6 Differential fill plug
3	Parking brake cable	
4	Exhaust pipe	

2   Introduction

This Chapter is designed to help the home mechanic maintain the Ford Thunderbird/Mercury Cougar with the goals of maximum performance, economy, safety and reliability in mind.

Included is a master maintenance schedule (page xx), followed by procedures dealing specifically with each item on the schedule. Visual checks, adjustments, component replacement and other helpful items are included. Refer to the accompanying illustrations of the engine compartment and the underside of the vehicle for the locations of various components.

Servicing the vehicle, in accordance with the mileage/time maintenance schedule and the step-by-step procedures will result in a planned maintenance program that should produce a long and reliable service life. Keep in mind that it is a comprehensive plan, so maintaining some items but not others at the specified intervals will not produce the same results.

As you service the vehicle, you will discover that many of the procedures can – and should – be grouped together because of the nature of the particular procedure you're performing or because of the close proximity of two otherwise unrelated components to one another.

For example, if the vehicle is raised for chassis lubrication, you should inspect the exhaust, suspension, steering and fuel systems while you're under the vehicle. When you're rotating the tires, it makes good sense to check the brakes since the wheels are already removed. Finally, let's suppose you have to borrow or rent a torque wrench. Even if you only need it to tighten the spark plugs, you might as well check the torque of as many critical fasteners as time allows.

The first step in this maintenance program is to prepare yourself before the actual work begins. Read through all the procedures you're planning to do, then gather up all the parts and tools needed. If it looks like you might run into problems during a particular job, seek advice from a mechanic or an experienced do-it-yourselfer.

3   Tune-up sequence

The term tune-up is used in this manual to represent a combination of individual operations rather than one specific procedure.

If, from the time the vehicle is new, the routine maintenance schedule is followed closely and frequent checks are made of fluid levels and high wear items, as suggested throughout this manual, the engine will be kept in relatively good running condition and the need for additional work will be minimized.

More likely than not, however, there will be times when the engine is running poorly due to lack of regular maintenance. This is even more likely if a used vehicle, which has not received regular and frequent maintenance checks, is purchased. In such cases, an engine tune-up will be needed outside of the regular routine maintenance intervals.

The first step in any tune-up or diagnostic procedure to help correct a poor running engine is a cylinder compression check. A compression check (see Chapter 2) will help determine the condition of internal engine components and should be used as a guide for tune-up and repair procedures. If, for instance, a compression check indicates serious internal engine wear, a conventional tune-up will not improve the performance of the engine and would be a waste of time and money. Because of its importance, the compression check should be done by someone with the right equipment and the knowledge to use it properly.

The following procedures are those most often needed to bring a generally poor running engine back into a proper state of tune.

Minor tune-up

Clean, inspect and test the battery (Section 13)
Check all engine related fluids (Section 4)
Check the drivebelt (Section 10)
Replace the spark plugs (Section 27)
Inspect the distributor cap and rotor (Section 28)
Inspect the spark plug and coil wires (Section 28)
Check the PCV valve (Section 16)
Check the air filter (Section 15)

Check the cooling system (Section 19)
Check all underhood hoses (Section 9)

Major tune-up

All items listed under Minor tune-up, plus . . .
Check the EGR system (Chapter 6)
Check the ignition system (Chapter 5)
Check the charging system (Chapter 5)
Check the fuel system (Chapter 4)
Replace the air filter (Section 15)
Replace the distributor cap and rotor (Section 28)
Replace the spark plug wires (Section 28)

4   Fluid level checks

Note: *The following are fluid level checks to be done on a 250 mile or weekly basis. Additional fluid level checks can be found in specific maintenance procedures which follow. Regardless of intervals, be alert to fluid leaks under the vehicle which would indicate a fault to be corrected immediately.*

1   Fluids are an essential part of the lubrication, cooling, brake and windshield washer systems. Because the fluids gradually become depleted and/or contaminated during normal operation of the vehicle, they must be periodically replenished. See Recommended lubricants and fluids at the beginning of this Chapter before adding fluid to any of the following components. **Note:** *The vehicle must be on level ground when fluid levels are checked.*

Engine oil

Refer to illustrations 4.2, 4.4 and 4.6

2   The oil level is checked with a dipstick, which is located on the left (driver's) side of the engine **(see illustration)**. The dipstick extends through a metal tube down into the oil pan.

4.2   The oil dipstick is located at the left (driver's side) front corner of the engine and is clearly marked

4.4   The engine oil level should be in the hatched area of the dipstick – if it is below the ADD line, add enough oil to bring the level into the SAFE range (DO NOT add more oil if the level is at the FULL line)

4.6 The oil is added to the engine after turning the filler cap on the valve cover half a turn and lifting it

4.9 Flip the cap up to add coolant to the reservoir

4.15a The brake fluid level should be kept between the MIN and MAX lines on the translucent plastic reservoir

3   The oil level should be checked before the vehicle has been driven, or about 15 minutes after the engine has been shut off. If the oil is checked immediately after driving the vehicle, some of the oil will remain in the upper part of the engine, resulting in an inaccurate reading on the dipstick.

4   Pull the dipstick out of the tube and wipe all the oil from the end with a clean rag or paper towel. Insert the clean dipstick all the way back into the tube and pull it out again. Note the oil at the end of the dipstick. At its highest point, the level should be above the ADD mark, within the hatched marked section of the dipstick **(see illustration)**.

5   It takes one quart of oil to raise the level from the ADD mark to the FULL mark on the dipstick. Do not allow the level to drop below the ADD mark or oil starvation may cause engine damage. Conversely, overfilling the engine (adding oil above the FULL mark) may cause oil fouled spark plugs, oil leaks or oil seal failures.

6   To add oil, remove the filler cap located on valve cover **(see illustration)**. After adding oil, wait a few minutes to allow the level to stabilize, then pull out the dipstick and check the level again. Add more oil if required. Install the filler cap and tighten it by hand only.

7   Checking the oil level is an important preventive maintenance step. A consistently low oil level indicates oil leakage through damaged seals, defective gaskets or past worn rings or valve guides. If the oil looks milky in color or has water droplets in it, the cylinder head gasket(s) may be blown or the head(s) or block may be cracked. The engine should be noted immediately. The condition of the oil should also be noted. Whenever you check the oil level, slide your thumb and index finger up the dipstick before wiping off the oil. If you see small dirt or metal particles clinging to the dipstick, the oil should be changed (Section 8).

Engine coolant

Refer to illustration 4.9

Warning: *Do not allow antifreeze to come in contact with your skin or painted surfaces of the vehicle. Flush contaminated areas immediately with plenty of water. Do not store new coolant or leave old coolant lying around where it's accessible to children or pets – they are attracted by its sweet taste. Ingestion of even a small amount of coolant can be fatal! Wipe up garage floor and drip pan coolant spills. Keep antifreeze containers covered and repair leaks in your cooling system immediately.*

8   All vehicles covered by this manual are equipped with a pressurized coolant recovery system. A white plastic coolant reservoir located at the front of the engine compartment is connected by a hose to the radiator filler neck. If the engine overheats, coolant escapes through a valve in the radiator cap and travels through the hose into the reservoir. As the engine cools, the coolant is automatically drawn back into the cooling system to maintain the correct level.

9   The coolant level in the reservoir should be checked regularly. **Warning:** *Do not remove the radiator cap to check the coolant level when the engine is warm!* The level in the reservoir varies with the temperature of

the engine. When the engine is cold, the coolant level should be at or slightly above the FULL COLD mark on the reservoir. Once the engine has warmed up, the level should be at or near the FULL HOT mark. If it isn't, allow the engine to cool, then remove the cap from the reservoir and add a 50/50 mixture of ethylene glycol based antifreeze and water **(see illustration)**.

10   Drive the vehicle and recheck the coolant level. Don't use rust inhibitors or additives. If only a small amount of coolant is required to bring the system up to the proper level, water can be used. However, repeated additions of water will dilute the antifreeze and water solution. In order to maintain the proper ratio of antifreeze and water, always top up the coolant level with the correct mixture. An empty plastic milk jug or bleach bottle makes an excellent container for mixing coolant.

11   If the coolant level drops consistently, there may be a leak in the system. Inspect the radiator, hoses, filler cap, drain plugs and water pump (see Section 19). If no leaks are noted, have the radiator cap pressure tested by a service station.

12   If you have to remove the radiator cap, wait until the engine has cooled completely, then wrap a thick cloth around the cap and turn it to the first stop. If coolant or steam escapes, let the engine cool down longer, then remove the cap.

13   Check the condition of the coolant as well. It should be relatively clear. If it's brown or rust colored, the system should be drained, flushed and refilled. Even if the coolant appears to be normal, the corrosion inhibitors wear out, so it must be replaced at the specified intervals.

Brake fluid

Refer to illustrations 4.15a and 4.15b

14   The brake fluid level is checked by looking through the plastic reservoir mounted on the master cylinder. The master cylinder is mounted on the front of the power booster unit in the left rear corner of the engine compartment.

15   The fluid level should be between the MAX and MIN lines on the side of the reservoir **(see illustration)**. On ABS-equipped models, pump the brake pedal approximately 20 times, or until the brake pedal feels hard, turn the ignition key on and wait one minute to let the fluid level stabilize before checking it **(see illustration)**.

16   If the fluid level is low, wipe the top of the reservoir and the cap with a clean rag to prevent contamination of the system as the cap is unscrewed.

17   Add only the specified brake fluid to the reservoir (refer to Recommended lubricants and fluids at the front of this Chapter or your owner's manual). Mixing different types of brake fluid can damage the system. Fill the reservoir to the MAX line. **Warning:** *Brake fluid can harm your eyes and damage painted surfaces, so use extreme caution when handling or pouring it. Do not use brake fluid that has been standing open or is more than one year old. Brake fluid absorbs moisture from the air, which can cause a dangerous loss of braking effectiveness.*

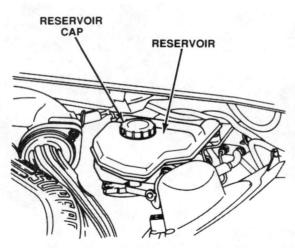

4.15b   ABS-equipped vehicles require a special fluid level checking procedure (refer to the text)

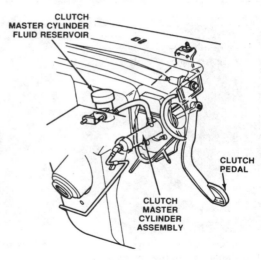

4.22   Location of the clutch fluid reservoir

4.24   Add windshield washer fluid to the reservoir after flipping the cap up

18   While the reservoir cap is off, check the master cylinder reservoir for contamination. If rust deposits, dirt particles or water droplets are present, the system should be drained and refilled by a dealer service department or repair shop.

19   After filling the reservoir to the proper level, make sure the cap is seated to prevent fluid leakage and/or contamination.

20   The fluid level in the master cylinder will drop slightly as the brake shoes or pads at each wheel wear down during normal operation. If the brake fluid level drops consistently, check the entire system for leaks immediately. Examine all brake lines, hoses and connections, along with the calipers, wheel cylinders and master cylinder (see Section 23).

21   When checking the fluid level, if you discover one or both reservoirs empty or nearly empty, the brake system should be bled (see Chapter 9).

Clutch fluid

Refer to illustration 4.22

22   Manual transmission-equipped vehicles have a hydraulic clutch with a fluid reservoir connected by a tube to the clutch master cylinder **(see illustration)**.

23   The clutch fluid level is checked in the same manner as the brake fluid.

Windshield washer fluid

Refer to illustration 4.24

24   Fluid for the windshield washer system is stored in a plastic reservoir located at the left (driver's) side of the engine compartment **(see illustration)**.

25   In milder climates, plain water can be used in the reservoir, but it should be kept no more than 2/3 full to allow for expansion if the water freezes. In colder climates, use windshield washer system antifreeze, available at any auto parts store, to lower the freezing point of the fluid. Mix the antifreeze with water in accordance with the manufacturer's directions on the container. **Caution:** *Do not use cooling system antifreeze – it will damage the vehicle's paint.*

---

5   Tire and tire pressure checks

Refer to illustrations 5.2, 5.3, 5.4a, 5.4b and 5.8

1   Periodic inspection of the tires may spare you the inconvenience of being stranded with a flat tire. It can also provide you with vital information regarding possible problems in the steering and suspension systems before major damage occurs.

2   The original tires on this vehicle are equipped with 1/2-inch side bands that will appear when tread depth reaches 1/16-inch, but they don't appear until the tires are worn out. Tread wear can be monitored with a

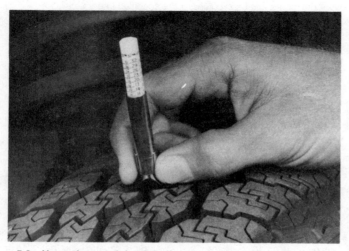

5.2   Use a tire tread depth indicator to monitor tire wear – they are available at auto parts stores and service stations and cost very little

Condition	Probable cause	Corrective action	Condition	Probable cause	Corrective action
Shoulder wear	• Underinflation (both sides wear) • Incorrect wheel camber (one side wear) • Hard cornering • Lack of rotation	• Measure and adjust pressure. • Repair or replace axle and suspension parts. • Reduce speed. • Rotate tires.	Feathered edge **Toe wear**	• Incorrect toe	• Adjust toe-in.
Center wear	• Overinflation • Lack of rotation	• Measure and adjust pressure. • Rotate tires.	**Uneven wear**	• Incorrect camber or caster • Malfunctioning suspension • Unbalanced wheel • Out-of-round brake drum • Lack of rotation	• Repair or replace axle and suspension parts. • Repair or replace suspension parts. • Balance or replace. • Turn or replace. • Rotate tires.

5.3   This chart will help you determine the condition of the tires, the probable cause(s) of abnormal wear and the corrective action necessary

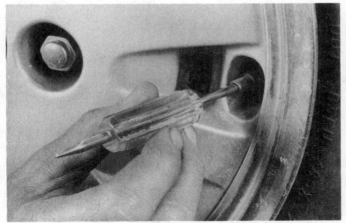

5.4a   If a tire loses air on a steady basis, check the valve core first to make sure it's snug (special inexpensive wrenches are commonly available at auto parts stores)

5.4b   If the valve core is tight, raise the corner of the vehicle with the low tire and spray a soapy water solution onto the tread as the tire is turned slowly – leaks will cause small bubbles to appear

simple, inexpensive device known as a tread depth indicator (**see illustration**).

3   Note any abnormal tread wear (**see illustration**). Tread pattern irregularities such as cupping, flat spots and more wear on one side than the other are indications of front end alignment and/or balance problems. If any of these conditions are noted, take the vehicle to a tire shop or service station to correct the problem.

4   Look closely for cuts, punctures and embedded nails or tacks. Sometimes a tire will hold air pressure for a short time or leak down very slowly after a nail has embedded itself in the tread. If a slow leak persists, check the valve stem core to make sure it is tight (**see illustration**). Examine the tread for an object that may have embedded itself in the tire or for a "plug" that may have begun to leak (radial tire punctures are repaired with a plug that is installed in a puncture). If a puncture is suspected, it can be easily verified by spraying a solution of soapy water onto the puncture area (**see illustration**). The soapy solution will bubble if there is a leak. Unless the puncture is unusually large, a tire shop or service station can usually repair the tire.

5   Carefully inspect the inner sidewall of each tire for evidence of brake fluid leakage. If you see any, inspect the brakes immediately.

6   Correct air pressure adds miles to the lifespan of the tires, improves mileage and enhances overall ride quality. Tire pressure cannot be accurately estimated by looking at a tire, especially if it's a radial. A tire pressure gauge is essential. Keep an accurate gauge in the glove compartment. The pressure gauges attached to the nozzles of air hoses at gas stations are often inaccurate.

7   Always check tire pressure when the tires are cold. Cold, in this case, means the vehicle has not been driven over a mile in the three hours preceding a tire pressure check. A pressure rise of four to eight pounds is not uncommon once the tires are warm.

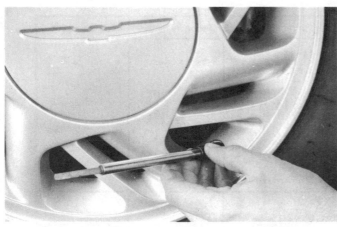

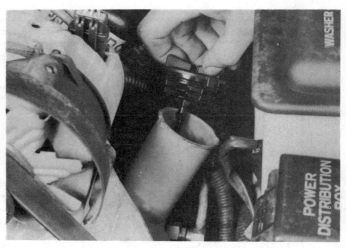

5.8   To extend the life of the tires, check the air pressure at least once a week with an accurate gauge (don't forget the spare!)

6.5a   Once the engine is properly warmed up and the wheel has been turned back-and-forth a few times to rid the system of bubbles, pull the dipstick out and wipe it off, reinsert it and verify that the power steering fluid level is in the proper range – if it isn't, add enough fluid to bring the level between the two lines

6.5b   The dipstick is marked on both sides so the fluid can be checked hot . . .

6.5c   . . . or cold

8   Unscrew the valve cap protruding from the wheel or hubcap and push the gauge firmly onto the valve stem **(see illustration)**. Note the reading on the gauge and compare the figure to the recommended tire pressure shown on the tire placard on the driver's side door. Be sure to reinstall the valve cap to keep dirt and moisture out of the valve stem mechanism. Check all four tires and, if necessary, add enough air to bring them up to the recommended pressure.

9   Don't forget to keep the spare tire inflated to the specified pressure (refer to your owner's manual or the decal attached to the right door pillar). Note that the pressure recommended for the Temporal (mini) spare is higher than for the tires on the vehicle.

---

6   Power steering fluid level check

Refer to illustrations 6.5a, 6.5b and 6.5c

1   Check the power steering fluid level periodically to avoid steering system problems, such as damage to the pump. **Caution:** *DO NOT hold the steering wheel against either stop (extreme left or right turn) for more than five seconds. If you do, the power steering pump could be damaged.*
2   The power steering pump, located at the front corner of the engine, is equipped with a twist-off cap with an integral fluid level dipstick.
3   Park the vehicle on level ground and apply the parking brake.
4   Run the engine until it has reached normal operating temperature. With the engine at idle, turn the steering wheel back-and-forth several

times to get any air out of the steering system. Shut the engine off, remove the cap by turning it counterclockwise, wipe the dipstick clean and reinstall the cap. (Make sure it is seated).
5   Remove the cap again and note the fluid level. It must be between the two lines designating the FULL HOT or FULL COLD range **(see illustration)**. Be sure to use the proper temperature range on the dipstick when checking the fluid level – the FULL COLD lines on the reverse side of the dipstick are only usable when the engine is cold **(see illustrations)**.
6   Add small amounts of fluid until the level is correct. **Caution:** *Do not overfill the pump. If too much fluid is added, remove the excess with a clean syringe or suction pump.*
7   Check the power steering hoses and connections for leaks and wear (see Section 9).
8   Check the condition and tension of the power steering pump drivebelt (see Section 10).

---

7   Automatic transmission fluid level check

Refer to illustrations 7.4 and 7.6

1   The automatic transmission fluid level should be carefully maintained. Low fluid level can lead to slipping or loss of drive, while overfilling

7.4   The automatic transmission dipstick (arrow) is located at the rear of the engine compartment, on the passenger side of the vehicle

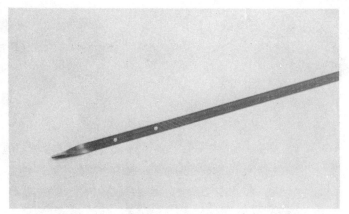

7.6   If the automatic transmission fluid is cold, the level should be between the two holes in the dipstick; if it's at operating temperature, it should be in the hatched area

can cause foaming and loss of fluid. Either condition can cause transmission damage.

2   Since transmission fluid expands as it heats up, the fluid level should only be checked when the transmission is warm (at normal operating temperature). If the vehicle has just been driven over 20 miles (32 km), the transmission can be considered warm. **Caution:** *If the vehicle has just been driven for a long time at high speed or in city traffic in hot weather, or if it has been pulling a trailer, an accurate fluid level reading cannot be obtained. Allow the transmission to cool down for about 30 minutes. You can also check the transmission fluid level when the transmission is cold. If the vehicle has not been driven for over five hours and the fluid is about room temperature (70 to 95-degrees F), the transmission is cold. However, the fluid level is normally checked with the transmission warm to ensure accurate results.*

3   Immediately after driving the vehicle, park it on a level surface, set the parking brake and start the engine. While the engine is idling, depress the brake pedal and move the selector lever through all the gear ranges, beginning and ending in Park.

4   Locate the automatic transmission dipstick tube in the engine compartment **(see illustration)**.

5   With the engine still idling, pull the dipstick from the tube, wipe it off with a clean rag, push it all the way back into the tube and withdraw it again, then note the fluid level.

6   If the transmission is cold, the level should be in the room temperature range on the dipstick (between the two holes); if it's warm, the fluid level should be in the operating temperature range (in the hatched area) **(see illustration)**. If the level is low, add the specified automatic transmission fluid through the dipstick tube – use a funnel to prevent spills.

7   Add just enough of the recommended fluid to fill the transmission to the proper level. It takes about one pint to raise the level from the low mark to the high mark when the fluid is hot, so add the fluid a little at a time and keep checking the level until it's correct.

8   The condition of the fluid should also be checked along with the level. If the fluid is black or a dark reddish-brown color, or if it smells burned, it should be changed (Section 30). If you are in doubt about its condition, purchase some new fluid and compare the two for color and smell.

---

8   Engine oil and filter change

Refer to illustrations 8.2, 8.7, 8.12 and 8.16

1   Frequent oil changes are the most important preventive maintenance procedures that can be done by the home mechanic. As engine oil ages, in becomes diluted and contaminated, which leads to premature engine wear.

2   Make sure that you have all the necessary tools before you begin this procedure **(see illustration)**. You should also have plenty of rags or newspapers handy for mopping up oil spills.

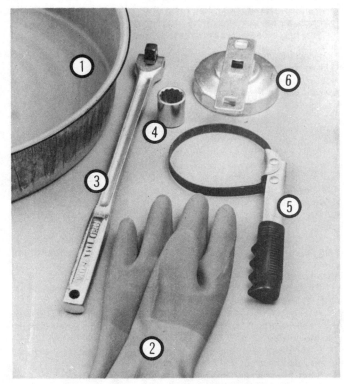

8.2   These tools are required when changing the engine oil and filter

1   **Drain pan** – *It should be fairly shallow in depth, but wide to prevent spills*
2   **Rubber gloves** – *When removing the drain plug and filter, you will get oil on your hands (the gloves will prevent burns)*
3   **Breaker bar** – *Sometimes the oil drain plug is tight and a long breaker bar is needed to loosen it*
4   **Socket** – *To be used with the breaker bar or a ratchet (must be the correct size to fit the drain plug – six-point preferred)*
5   **Filter wrench** – *This is a metal band-type wrench, which requires clearance around the filter to be effective*
6   **Filter wrench** – *This type fits on the bottom of the filter and can be turned with a ratchet or breaker bar (different size wrenches are available for different types of filters)*

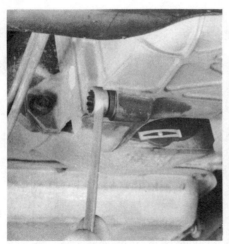

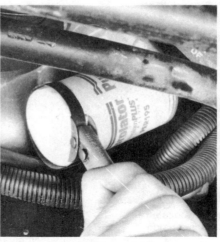

8.7   The oil drain plug is located at the bottom edge of the pan and should be removed with a socket or box-end wrench – DO NOT used an open end wrench, as the corners of the plug head can be easily rounded off

8.12   The oil filter is usually on very tight and will require a special wrench for removal – DO NOT use the wrench to tighten the new filter

8.16   Lubricate the oil filter gasket with clean engine oil before installing the filter on the engine

3   Access to the oil drain plug and filter will be improved if the vehicle can be lifted on a hoist, driven onto ramps or supported by jackstands. **Warning:** *Do not work under a vehicle supported only by a bumper, hydraulic or scissors-type jack – always use jackstands!*

4   If you haven't changed the oil on this vehicle before, get under it and locate the oil drain plug and the oil filter. The exhaust components will be warm as you work, so note how they are routed to avoid touching them when you are under the vehicle.

5   Start the engine and allow it to reach normal operating temperature – oil and sludge will flow out more easily when warm. If new oil, a filter or tools are needed, use the vehicle to go get them and warm up the engine/oil at the same time. Park on a level surface and shut off the engine when it's warmed up. Remove the oil filler cap from the valve cover.

6   Raise the vehicle and support it on jackstands. Make sure it is safely supported!

7   Being careful not to touch the hot exhaust components, position a drain pan under the plug in the bottom of the engine **(see illustration)**, then remove the plug. It's a good idea to wear an old glove while unscrewing the plug the final few turns to avoid being scalded by hot oil.

8   It may be necessary to move the drain pan slightly as oil flow slows to a trickle. Inspect the old oil for the presence of metal particles.

9   After all the oil has drained, wipe off the drain plug with a clean rag. Any small metal particles clinging to the plug would immediately contaminate the new oil.

10   Clean the area around the drain plug opening, reinstall the plug and tighten it securely, but don't strip the threads.

11   Move the drain pan into position under the oil filter.

12   Loosen the oil filter by turning it counterclockwise with a filter wrench **(see illustration)**. Any standard filter wrench will work.

13   Sometimes the oil filter is screwed on so tightly that it can't be loosened. If it is, punch a metal bar or long screwdriver directly through it, as close to the engine as possible, and use it as a T-bar to turn the filter. Be prepared for oil to spurt out of the canister as it's punctured.

14   Once the filter is loose, use your hands to unscrew it from the block. Just as the filter is detached from the block, immediately tilt the open end up to prevent the oil inside the filter from spilling out.

15   Using a clean rag, wipe off the mounting surface on the block. Also, make sure that none of the old gasket remains stuck to the mounting surface. It can be removed with a scraper if necessary.

16   Compare the old filter with the new one to make sure they are the same type. Smear some engine oil on the rubber gasket of the new filter and screw it into place **(see illustration)**. Overtightening the filter will damage the gasket, so don't use a filter wrench. Most filter manufacturers recommend tightening the filter by hand only. Normally they should be

tightened 3/4-turn after the gasket contacts the block, but be sure to follow the directions on the filter or container.

17   Remove all tools and materials from under the vehicle, being careful not to spill the oil in the drain pan, then lower the vehicle.

18   Add new oil to the engine through the oil filler cap in the valve cover. Use a funnel to prevent oil from spilling onto the top of the engine. Pour four quarts of fresh oil into the engine. Wait a few minutes to allow the oil to drain into the pan, then check the level on the dipstick (see Section 4 if necessary). If the oil level is in the SAFE range (hatched area), install the filler cap.

19   Start the engine and run it for about a minute. While the engine is running, look under the vehicle and check for leaks at the oil pan drain plug and around the oil filter. If either one is leaking, stop the engine and tighten the plug or filter slightly.

20   Wait a few minutes, then recheck the level on the dipstick. Add oil as necessary to bring the level into the SAFE range.

21   During the first few trips after an oil change, make it a point to check frequently for leaks and proper oil level.

22   The old oil drained from the engine cannot be reused in its present state and should be discarded. Oil reclamation centers, auto repair shops and gas stations will normally accept the oil, which can be recycled. After the oil has cooled, it can be drained into a container (plastic jugs, bottles, milk cartons, etc.) for transport to a disposal site.

---

9   Underhood hose check and replacement

Caution: *Replacement of air conditioning hoses must be left to a dealer service department or air conditioning shop that has the equipment to depressurize the system safely. Never remove air conditioning components or hoses until the system has been depressurized.*

General

1   High temperatures under the hood can cause deterioration of the rubber and plastic hoses used for engine, accessory and emission systems operation. Periodic inspection should be made for cracks, loose clamps, material hardening and leaks.

2   Information specific to the cooling system hoses can be found in Section 19.

3   Most (but not all) hoses are secured to the fittings with clamps. Where clamps are used, check to be sure they haven't lost their tension, allowing the hose to leak. If clamps aren't used, make sure the hose has not expanded and/or hardened where it slips over the fitting, allowing it to leak.

PCV system hose

4   To reduce hydrocarbon emissions, crankcase blow-by gas is vented through the PCV valve in the rocker arm cover to the intake manifold via a rubber hose on most models. The blow-by gases mix with incoming air in the intake manifold before being burned in the combustion chambers.

5   Check the PCV hose for cracks, leaks and other damage. Disconnect it from the valve cover and the intake manifold and check the inside for obstructions. If it's clogged, clean it out with solvent.

Vacuum hoses

6   It's quite common for vacuum hoses, especially those in the emissions system, to be color coded or identified by colored stripes molded into them. Various systems require hoses with different wall thicknesses, collapse resistance and temperature resistance. When replacing hoses, be sure the new ones are made of the same material.

7   Often the only effective way to check a hose is to remove it completely from the vehicle. If more than one hose is removed, be sure to label the hoses and fittings to ensure correct installation.

8   When checking vacuum hoses, be sure to include any plastic T-fittings in the check. Inspect the fittings for cracks and the hose where it fits over each fitting for distortion, which could cause leakage.

9   A small piece of vacuum hose (1/4-inch inside diameter) can be used as a stethoscope to detect vacuum leaks. Hold one end of the hose to your ear and probe around vacuum hoses and fittings, listening for the "hissing" sound characteristic of a vacuum leak. **Warning:** *When probing with the vacuum hose stethoscope, be careful not to come into contact with moving engine components such as drivebelts, the cooling fan, etc.*

Fuel hose

Warning: *Gasoline is extremely flammable, so take extra precautions when you work on any part of the fuel system. Don't smoke or allow open flames or bare light bulbs near the work area, and don't work in a garage where a natural gas-type appliance (such as a water heater or clothes dryer) with a pilot light is present. If you spill any fuel on your skin, rinse it off immediately with soap and water. When you perform any kind of work on the fuel system, wear safety glasses and have a Class B type fire extinguisher on hand.*

10   The fuel lines are usually under pressure, so if any fuel lines are to be disconnected be prepared to catch spilled fuel. **Warning:** *Your vehicle is equipped with fuel injection and you must relieve the fuel system pressure before servicing the fuel lines. Refer to Chapter 4 for the fuel system pressure relief procedure.*

11   Check all rubber fuel lines for deterioration and chafing. Check especially for cracks in areas where the hose bends and just before fittings, such as where a hose attaches to the fuel pump, fuel filter and fuel injection unit.

12   High quality fuel line, usually identified by the word Fluroelastomer printed on the hose, should be used for fuel line replacement. Never, under any circumstances, use unreinforced vacuum line, clear plastic tubing or water hose for fuel lines.

13   Spring-type clamps are commonly used on fuel lines. These clamps often lose their tension over a period of time, and can be "sprung" during removal. Replace all spring-type clamps with screw clamps whenever a hose is replaced. Some fuel lines use spring-lock type couplings, which require a special tool to disconnect. See Chapter 4 for more information on these type of couplings.

Metal lines

14   Sections of metal line are often used for fuel line between the fuel pump and the fuel injection unit. Check carefully to make sure the line isn't bent, crimped or cracked.

15   If a section of metal fuel line must be replaced, use seamless steel tubing only, since copper and aluminum tubing do not have the strength necessary to withstand vibration caused by the engine.

16   Check the metal brake lines where they enter the master cylinder and brake proportioning unit (if used) for cracks in the lines and loose fittings. Any sign of brake fluid leakage calls for an immediate thorough inspection of the brake system.

---

10   Drivebelt check and replacement

Refer to illustration 10.4

1   A single serpentine drivebelt is located at the front of the engine and plays an important role in the overall operation of the engine and its components. Due to its function and material make up, the belt is prone to wear and should be periodically inspected. The serpentine belt drives the alternator, power steering pump, water pump and air conditioning compressor (if equipped).

Check

2   With the engine off, open the hood and use your fingers (and a flashlight if necessary), to move along the belt checking for cracks and separation of the belt plies. Also check for fraying and glazing, which gives the belt a shiny appearance. Both sides of the belt should be inspected, which means you will have to twist the belt to check the underside.

3   Check the ribs on the underside of the belt. They should all be the same depth, with none of the surface uneven.

4   The tension of the belt is checked visually. Locate the belt tensioner at the front of the engine on the right (passenger) side, adjacent to the lower crankshaft pulley, then find the tensioner operating marks (**see illustration**). If the indicator mark is outside the operating range, the belt should be replaced.

Replacement

5   To replace the belt, lift the tensioner at the bolt. The tensioner will swing down once the tension of the belt is released.

6   Remove the belt from the auxiliary components and carefully release the tensioner.

7   Route the new belt over the various pulleys, again rotating the tensioner to allow the belt to be installed, then release the belt tensioner. Make sure the belt fits properly into the pulley grooves – it must be completely engaged. **Note:** *Most models have a drivebelt routing decal on the upper radiator panel to help during drivebelt installation.*

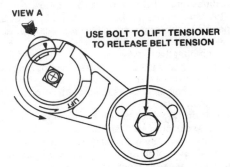

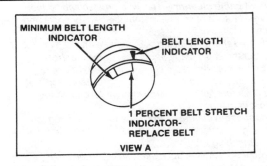

10.4   The serpentine drivebelt is automatically tensioned and requires no service as long as it is in good condition and the indicator is in the proper range

11   Neutral safety switch check

Warning: *During the following checks there's a possibility the vehicle could lunge forward, possibly causing damage or injuries. Allow plenty of room around the vehicle, apply the parking brake and hold down the service brake pedal during the checks.*

1   Try to start the engine in each gear. The engine should crank only when the clutch pedal is depressed (manual) or in Park or Neutral (automatic).
2   Make sure the steering column lock allows the key to go into the Lock position only when the shift lever is in Park.
3   The ignition key should come out only in the Lock position.

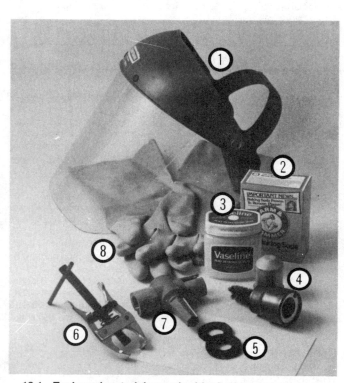

13.1   Tools and materials required for battery maintenance

1   *Face shield/safety goggles* – *When removing corrosion with a brush, the acidic particles can easily fly up into your eyes*
2   *Baking soda* – *A solution of baking soda and water can be used to neutralize corrosion*
3   *Petroleum jelly* – *A layer of this on the battery posts will help prevent corrosion*
4   *Battery post/cable cleaner* – *This wire brush cleaning tool will remove all traces of corrosion from the battery posts and cable clamps*
5   *Treated felt washers* – *Placing one of these on each post, directly under the cable clamps, will help prevent corrosion*
6   *Puller* – *Sometimes the cable clamps are very difficult to pull off the posts, even after the nut/bolt has been completely loosened. This tool pulls the clamp straight up and off the post without damage*
7   *Battery post/cable cleaner* – *Here is another cleaning tool which is a slightly different version of number 4 above, but it does the same thing*
8   *Rubber gloves* – *Another safety item to consider when servicing the battery; remember that's acid inside the battery!*

12   Seat belt check

1   Check seat belts, buckles, latch plates and guide loops for obvious damage and signs of wear.
2   See if the seat belt reminder light comes on when the key is turned to the Run or Start position. A chime should also sound. On passive restraint systems, the shoulder belt should move into position in the A-pillar.
3   The seat belts are designed to lock up during a sudden stop or impact, yet allow free movement during normal driving. Make sure the retractors return the belt against your chest while driving and rewind the belt fully when the buckle is unlatched.
4   If any of the above checks reveal problems with the seat belt system, replace parts as necessary.

13   Battery check and maintenance

Refer to illustrations 13.1, 13.8a, 13.8b, 13.8c and 13.8d
Warning: *Certain precautions must be followed when checking and servicing the battery. Hydrogen gas, which is highly flammable, is always present in the battery cells, so keep cigarettes and all other open flames and sparks away from it. The electrolyte inside the battery is actually dilute sulfuric acid, which will cause injury if splashed on your skin or in your eyes. It will also ruin clothes and painted surfaces. When removing the battery cables, always detach the negative cable first and hook it up last!*

1   Battery maintenance is an important procedure which will help ensure that you are not stranded because of a dead battery. Several tools are required for this procedure **(see illustration)**.
2   Before servicing the battery, always turn the engine and all accessories off and disconnect the cable from the negative terminal of the battery.
3   A sealed (sometimes called maintenance-free) battery is standard equipment on these models. The cell caps cannot be removed, no electrolyte checks are required and water cannot be added to the cells. However, if an aftermarket battery has been installed and it is a type that requires regular maintenance, the following procedure can be used.
4   Check the electrolyte level in each of the battery cells. It must be above the plates. There's usually a split-ring indicator in each cell to indicate the correct level. If the level is low, add distilled water only, then install the cell caps. **Caution:** *Overfilling the cells may cause electrolyte to spill over during periods of heavy charging, causing corrosion and damage to nearby components.*
5   If the positive terminal and cable clamp on your vehicle's battery is equipped with a rubber protector, make sure that it's not torn or damaged. It should completely cover the terminal.
6   The external condition of the battery should be checked periodically. Look for damage such as a cracked case.
7   Check the tightness of the battery cable clamps to ensure good electrical connections and inspect the entire length of each cable, looking for cracked or abraded insulation and frayed conductors.
8   If corrosion (visible as white, fluffy deposits) is evident, remove the cables from the terminals, clean them with a battery brush and reinstall them **(see illustrations)**. Corrosion can be kept to a minimum by installing specially treated washers available at auto parts stores or by applying a layer of petroleum jelly or grease to the terminals and cable clamps after they are assembled.
9   Make sure that the battery carrier is in good condition and that the hold-down clamp bolt is tight. If the battery is removed (see Chapter 5 for the removal and installation procedure), make sure that no parts remain in the bottom of the carrier when it's reinstalled. When reinstalling the hold-down clamp, don't overtighten the bolt.
10   Corrosion on the carrier, battery case and surrounding areas can be removed with a solution of water and baking soda. Apply the mixture with a small brush, let it work, then rinse it off with plenty of clean water.
11   Any metal parts of the vehicle damaged by corrosion should be coated with a zinc-based primer, then painted.
12   Additional information on the battery, charging and jump starting can be found in Chapter 5 and at the front of this manual.

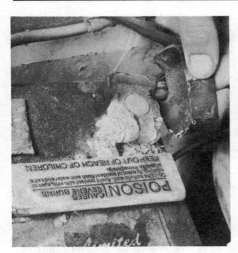

13.8a Battery terminal corrosion usually appears as light, fluffy powder

13.8b Removing the cable from a battery post with a wrench – sometimes a special battery pliers is required for this procedure if corrosion has caused deterioration of the nut hex (always remove the ground cable first and hook it up last!)

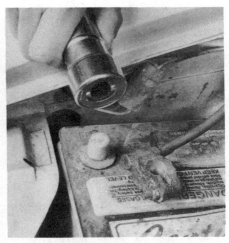

13.8c Regardless of the type of tool used on the battery posts, a clean, shiny surface should be the result

1

13.8d When cleaning the cable clamps, all corrosion must be removed (the inside of the clamp is tapered to match the taper on the post, so don't remove too much material)

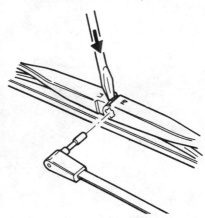

14.4 Press down on the spring with a screwdriver blade as shown to release the wiper blade assembly from the arm

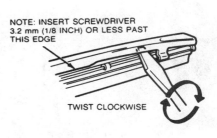

NOTE: INSERT SCREWDRIVER 3.2 mm (1/8 INCH) OR LESS PAST THIS EDGE

TWIST CLOCKWISE

14.6 Pry between the wiper frame and the element backing strip by twisting the screwdriver tip clockwise to disengage the element

14 Windshield wiper blade check and replacement

Refer to illustrations 14.4, 14.6, 14.8a and 14.8b
1   Road film can build up on the wiper blades and affect their efficiency, so they should be washed regularly with a mild detergent solution.

Check

2   The windshield wiper and blade assembly should be inspected periodically. Even if you don't use your wipers, the sun and elements will dry out the rubber portions, causing them to crack and break apart. If inspection reveals hardened or cracked rubber, replace the wiper blades. If inspection reveals nothing unusual, wet the windshield, turn the wipers on, allow them to cycle several times, then shut them off. An uneven wiper pattern across the glass or streaks over clean glass indicate that the blades should be replaced.
3   The operation of the wiper mechanism can loosen the fasteners, so they should be checked and tightened, as necessary, at the same time the wiper blades are checked (see Chapter 12 for further information regarding the wiper mechanism).

Blade assembly replacement

4   Cycle the wiper assembly to a position on the windshield where removal of the blade assembly can be performed without difficulty. Turn the ignition key off at the desired position. With the blade assembly resting on the windshield, insert a small screwdriver into the release spring at the center of the blade and push down on the spring. While pressing down with the screwdriver, pull the wiper blade off the wiper arm pin (**see illustration**).
5   To install the blade assembly, push it onto the pin until it snaps into place. Be sure that the blade assembly is securely attached to the wiper arm.

Blade element replacement

6   At one end of the rubber blade element, insert a small screwdriver between the blade and the metal backing strip (**see illustration**). Press down and in, then twist the screwdriver clockwise to release the element from the retaining claw.
7   Slide the blade element out of the retaining claws until the element is completely detached from the frame.

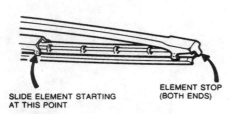

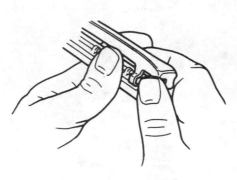

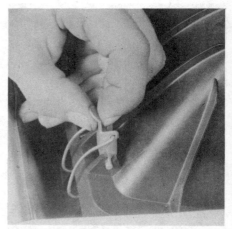

14.8a   Slide the element into the wiper frame claws up to the stops, starting at the second claw

14.8b   Lock the end of the element backing strip by twisting it into the end claw

15.2   The filter housing cover clips can be released by hand

15.3   Lift the filter out, noting the direction in which it faces

15.5   After detaching the PCV filter hose, slide the clip off and remove the filter element from the housing

15.7   Seat the tabs in the housing and rotate the cover into place

16.1   The PCV valve is located in the valve cover at the right (passenger) rear corner of the engine compartment

18.2a   Remove the bolts (arrows) and rotate the fuel filter bracket down

18.2b   Use a screwdriver to loosen the screw clamp and detach the bracket from the filter

8   To install the element, slide the metal backing strip into the retaining claws starting with the second claw from either end **(see illustration)**. Continue sliding the element up to the element stops, then secure the element by twisting the backing strip into the end claws **(see illustration)**.
9   Make sure that all the claws are locked onto the metal backing strip before installing the blade on the wiper arm.

15   Air and PCV filter replacement

Refer to illustrations 15.2, 15.3, 15.5 and 15.7
1   Purchase a new filter element and (if equipped) PCV filter for your specific engine type.
2   Detach the clips and lift the filter housing cover off **(see illustration)**.
3   Remove the filter element **(see illustration)**
4   Wipe the inside of the air cleaner housing with a clean cloth.
5   Some models are equipped with a PCV filter which should be replaced at the same time as the air filter. Detach the hose from PCV filter element, slide the clip off and remove the element **(see illustration)**. Place the new filter in the housing, secure it with the clip and connect the hose.
6   Place the new air filter element in the housing. If the element is marked TOP be sure the marked side faces up.
7   Seat the tabs, rotate the cover into place and secure it with the clips **(see illustration)**.

16   PCV valve check

Refer to illustration 16.1
Note: *To maintain efficient operation of the PCV system, clean the hoses and check the PCV valve at the intervals recommended in the maintenance schedule. For additional information on the PCV system, refer to Chapter 6.*
1   Locate the PCV valve **(see illustration)**.
2   Check the valve by first pulling it out of the valve cover. Shake it – if it rattles, reinstall it in the cover.
3   Start the engine and allow it to idle, then disconnect the PCV hose from the air cleaner housing and feel for vacuum at the hose. If vacuum is felt, the PCV valve/system is working properly (see Chapter 6 for additional PCV system information).
4   If no vacuum is felt, the oil filler cap, hoses or valve cover gasket may be leaking or the PCV valve may be bad. Check for vacuum leaks at the valve, filler cap and all hoses.
5   Pull straight up on the valve to remove it. Check the rubber grommet in the rocker arm cover for cracks and distortion. If it's damaged, replace it.
6   If the valve is clogged, the hose is also probably plugged. Remove the hose between the valve and the intake manifold and clean it with solvent.
7   After cleaning the hose, inspect it for damage, wear and deterioration. Make sure it fits snugly on the fittings.
8   If necessary, install a new PCV valve. **Note:** *The elbow is not part of the PCV valve. A new valve will not include the elbow. The original must be transferred to the new valve. If a new elbow is purchased, it may be necessary to soak it in warm water for up to an hour to slip it onto the new valve. Do not attempt to force the elbow onto the valve or it will break.*
9   Install the clean PCV system hose. Make sure that the PCV valve and hose are secure.

17   Fuel system check

Warning: *Gasoline is extremely flammable, so take extra precautions when you work on any part of the fuel system. Don't smoke or allow open flames or bare light bulbs near the work area, and don't work in a garage where a natural gas-type appliance (such as a water heater or clothes dryer) with a pilot light is present. If you spill any fuel on your skin, rinse it off immediately with soap and water. When you perform any kind of work on*

the fuel system, wear safety glasses and have a Class B type fire extinguisher on hand.
1   If you smell gasoline while driving or after the vehicle has been sitting in the sun, inspect the fuel system immediately.
2   Remove the gas filler cap and inspect if for damage and corrosion. The gasket should have an unbroken sealing imprint. If the gasket is damaged or corroded, install a new cap.
3   Inspect the fuel feed and return lines for cracks. Make sure that the connections between the fuel lines and the fuel injection system and between the fuel lines and the in-line fuel filter are tight. **Warning:** *Your vehicle is fuel injected, so you must relieve the fuel system pressure before servicing fuel system components. The fuel system pressure relief procedure is outlined in Chapter 4.*
4   Since some components of the fuel system – the fuel tank and part of the fuel feed and return lines, for example – are underneath the vehicle, they can be inspected more easily with the vehicle raised on a hoist. If that's not possible, raise the vehicle and support it on jackstands.
5   With the vehicle raised and safely supported, inspect the gas tank and filler neck for punctures, cracks and other damage. The connection between the filler neck and the tank is particularly critical. Sometimes a rubber filler neck will leak because of loose clamps or deteriorated rubber. Inspect all fuel tank mounting brackets and straps to be sure that the tank is securely attached to the vehicle. **Warning:** *Do not, under any circumstances, try to repair a fuel tank (except rubber components). A welding torch or any open flame can easily cause fuel vapors inside the tank to explode.*
6   Carefully check all rubber hoses and metal lines leading away from the fuel tank. Check for loose connections, deteriorated hoses, crimped lines and other damage. Repair or replace damaged sections as necessary (see Chapter 4).

18   Fuel filter replacement

Refer to illustrations 18.2a, 18.2b and 18.3
Warning: *Gasoline is extremely flammable, so take extra precautions when you work on any part of the fuel system. Don't smoke or allow open flames or bare light bulbs near the work area, and don't work in a garage where a natural gas-type appliance (such as a water heater or clothes dryer) with a pilot light is present. If you spill any fuel on your skin, rinse it off immediately with soap and water. When you perform any kind of work on the fuel system, wear safety glasses and have a Class B type fire extinguisher on hand. Before removing the fuel filter, the fuel system pressure must be relieved. See Chapter 4.*
1   The fuel filter is located under the vehicle on the outside of the right frame rail.
2   Remove the two retaining bolts, loosen the screw clamp and remove the filter cover **(see illustrations)**. Inspect the hose fittings at both ends of the filter to see if they're clean. If more than a light coating of dust is present, clean the fittings before proceeding.

18.3   If the new filter included new fuel line clips, the old ones can be disengaged with small screwdriver – don't use a tool for this procedure if the original clips must be reused

3   Relieve the fuel system pressure (see Chapter 4). Removal of the
hairpin clip from each fitting is a two-stage procedure. First, spread the two
clip legs apart about 1/8-inch to disengage them, then push in on them.
Pull on the other end of the clip to detach it from the fitting **(see illustration)**. **Caution:** *If the new filter doesn't include new clips, don't use any
tools or you may damage the plastic clips, which will have to be reused.
Use your fingers only.*
4   Once both hairpin clips are released, grasp the fuel hoses, one at a
time, and pull them straight off the filter. Be prepared for fuel spillage.
5   After the hoses have been detached, check the clips for damage and
distortion. If they were damaged in any way during removal, new ones
must be used when the hoses are reattached to the new filter (if new clips
are packaged with the filter, be sure to use them in place of the originals).
6   Note which way the arrow on the filter is pointing – the new filter must
be installed the same way.
7   Install the new filter with the arrow pointing the right direction.
8   Carefully push each hose onto the filter until it's seated against the
collar on the fitting, then install the hairpin clips. The triangular shaped side
of each clip must point away from the filter. Make sure the clips are securely attached to the hose fittings – if they come off, the hoses could back off
the filter and a fire could result!
9   Place the filter in the bracket and secure it with the screw clamp. Place
the bracket and filter assembly in position and install the retaining bolts.
10   Start the engine and check for fuel leaks.

19   Cooling system check

Refer to illustration 19.4

1   Many major engine failures can be attributed to a faulty cooling system. If the vehicle is equipped with an automatic transmission, the cooling
system also plays an important role in prolonging transmission life because it cools the fluid.
2   The engine should be cold for the cooling system check, so perform
the following procedure before the vehicle is driven for the day or after it
has been shut off for at least three hours.
3   Remove the radiator cap and clean it thoroughly, inside and out, with
clean water. Also clean the filler neck on the radiator. The presence of rust
or corrosion in the filler neck means the coolant should be changed (Section 31). The coolant inside the radiator should be relatively clean and
transparent. If it's rust colored, drain the system and refill it with new coolant.
4   Carefully check the radiator hoses and the smaller diameter heater
hoses **(see illustration)**. Inspect each coolant hose along its entire
length, replacing any hose which is cracked, swollen or deteriorated.
Cracks will show up better if the hose is squeezed. Pay close attention to
hose clamps that secure the hoses to cooling system components. Hose
clamps can pinch and puncture hoses, resulting in coolant leaks.
5   Make sure that all hose connections are tight. A leak in the cooling
system will usually show up as white or rust colored deposits on the area
adjoining the leak. If wire-type clamps are used on the hoses, it may be a
good idea to replace them with screw-type clamps.
6   Clean the front of the radiator and air conditioning condenser with
compressed air, if available, or a soft brush. Remove all bugs, leaves, etc.
embedded in the radiator fins. Be extremely careful not to damage the
cooling fins or cut your fingers on them.
7   If the coolant level has been dropping consistently and no leaks are
detectable, have the radiator cap and cooling system pressure checked at
a service station.

20   Exhaust system check

Refer to illustration 20.2

1   With the engine cold (at least three hours after the vehicle has been
driven), check the complete exhaust system from the engine to the end of
the tailpipe. Ideally, the inspection should be done with the vehicle on a
hoist to permit unrestricted access. If a hoist isn't available, raise the ve-

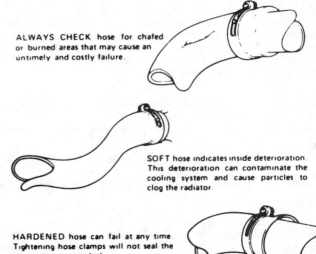

ALWAYS CHECK hose for chafed
or burned areas that may cause an
untimely and costly failure.

SOFT hose indicates inside deterioration.
This deterioration can contaminate the
cooling system and cause particles to
clog the radiator.

HARDENED hose can fail at any time.
Tightening hose clamps will not seal the
connection or stop leaks.

SWOLLEN hose or oil soaked ends indicate danger and possible failure from
oil or grease contamination. Squeeze
the hose to locate cracks and breaks
that cause leaks.

**19.4   Hoses, like drivebelts, have a habit of failing at
the worst possible time – to prevent the inconvenience
of a blown radiator or heater hose, inspect them
carefully as shown here**

hicle and support it securely on jackstands.
2   Check the exhaust pipes and connections for evidence of leaks, severe corrosion and damage. Make sure that all brackets and hangers are
in good condition and tight **(see illustration)**.
3   At the same time, inspect the underside of the body for holes, corrosion, open seams, etc. which may allow exhaust gases to enter the passenger compartment. Seal all body openings with silicone or body putty.
4   Rattles and other noises can often be traced to the exhaust system,
especially the mounts and hangers. Try to move the pipes, muffler and catalytic converter. If the components can come in contact with the body or
suspension parts, secure the exhaust system with new mounts.
5   Check the running condition of the engine by inspecting inside the end
of the tailpipe. The exhaust deposits here are an indication of engine state-
of-tune. If the pipe is black and sooty or coated with white deposits, the
engine may need a tune-up, including a thorough fuel system inspection
and adjustment.

21   Tire rotation

Refer to illustration 21.2

1   The tires should be rotated at the specified intervals and whenever
uneven wear is noticed. Since the vehicle will be raised and the tires removed anyway, check the brakes also (see Section 23).
2   Radial tires and the unidirectional tires used on some models must be
rotated in a specific pattern **(see illustration)**.
3   Refer to the information in Jacking and towing at the front of this manual for the proper procedure to follow when raising the vehicle and changing a tire. If the brakes must be checked, don't apply the parking brake as
stated.

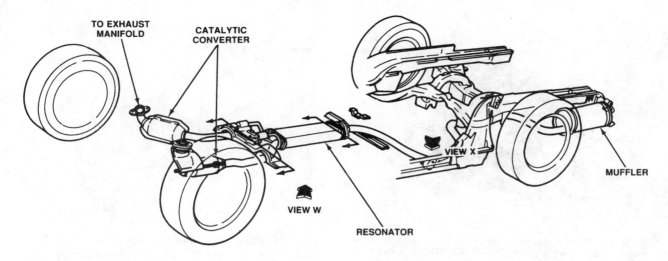

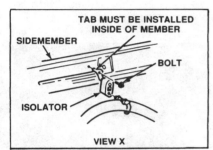
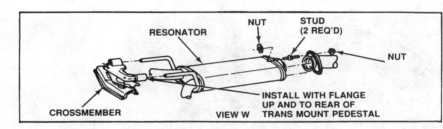

20.2 Inspect the exhaust system and hangers for damage, corrosion and loose components

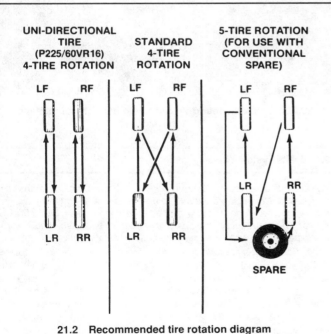

21.2 Recommended tire rotation diagram

4   The vehicle must be raised on a hoist or supported on jackstands to get all four wheels off the ground. Make sure the vehicle is safely supported!

5   After the rotation procedure is finished, check and adjust the tire pressures as necessary and be sure to check the lug nut tightness.

22   Steering and suspension check

Refer to illustrations 22.10, 22.11a, 22.11b and 22.12

Note: *The steering linkage and suspension components should be checked periodically. Worn or damaged suspension and steering linkage components can result in excessive and abnormal tire wear, poor ride quality and vehicle handling and reduced fuel economy. For detailed illustrations of the steering and suspension components, refer to Chapter 10.*

Shock absorber check

1   Park the vehicle on level ground, turn the engine off and set the parking brake. Check the tire pressures.

2   Push down at one corner of the vehicle, then release it while noting the movement of the body. It should stop moving and come to rest in a level position within one or two bounces.

3   If the vehicle continues to move up-and-down or if it fails to return to its original position, a worn or weak shock absorber is probably the reason.

4   Repeat the above check at each of the three remaining corners of the vehicle.

5   Raise the vehicle and support it on jackstands.

6   Check the shock absorbers for evidence of fluid leakage. A light film of fluid is no cause for concern. Make sure that any fluid noted is from the shocks and not from some other source. If leakage is noted, replace the shocks as a set.

7   Check the shock absorbers to be sure that they are securely mounted and undamaged. Check the upper mounts for damage and wear. If damage or wear is noted, replace the shock absorbers as a set (front or rear).

8   If the shock absorbers must be replaced, refer to Chapter 10 for the procedure.

22.10   Check the suspension balljoints by trying to move the lower edge of each front tire in-and-out while watching/feeling for movement at the top of the tire and balljoints

22.11a   Grasp each front tire as shown and try to move it back-and-forth – if play is noted, check the steering gear mounts and make sure that they're tight; if either tie-rod is worn or bent, replace it

22.11b   Push on the steering gear boots to check for cracks or leaking grease

22.12   Check the rear driveaxle CV joint boots for damage and leaks

Steering and suspension check

9   Visually inspect the steering system components for damage and distortion. Look for leaks and damaged seals, boots and fittings.

10   Clean the lower end of the steering knuckle. Have an assistant grasp the lower edge of the tire and move the wheel in-and-out **(see illustration)** while you look for movement at the steering knuckle-to-control arm joint. If there is any movement the suspension balljoint(s) must be replaced.

11   Grasp each front tire at the front and rear edges, push in at the front, pull out at the rear and feel for play in the steering system components **(see illustration)**. If any freeplay is noted, check the steering gear mounts and the tie-rod balljoints for looseness. If the steering gear mounts are loose, tighten them. If the tie-rods are loose, the balljoints may be worn (check to make sure the nuts are tight). Make sure the steering gear rack and pinion boots are kept clean and are not damaged **(see illustration)**. Additional steering and suspension system information and illustrations can be found in Chapter 10.

Rear driveaxle CV joint boot check

12   While the vehicle is raised, check the rear driveaxle constant velocity (CV) joint boots for damage or leaking grease **(see illustration)**. Refer to Chapter 8 for more information on the rear driveaxles.

23   Brake system check

Warning: *Brake system dust may contain asbestos, which is harmful to your health. Never blow it out with compressed air and don't inhale any of it. An approved filtering mask should be worn when working on the brakes. Do not, under any circumstances, use petroleum-based solvents to clean brake parts. Use brake cleaner or denatured alcohol only!*

Note: *For detailed photographs of the brake system, refer to Chapter 9.*

1   In addition to the specified intervals, the brake system should be inspected each time the wheels are removed or a malfunction is suspected. Raise the vehicle and support it securely on jackstands. Remove the wheels (see Jacking and towing at the front of this book, or refer to your owner's manual, if necessary).

Disc brakes

Refer to illustration 23.4

2   Disc brakes are used at the front, and on some models, the rear of these vehicles. Extensive rotor damage can occur if the pads are not replaced when needed.

3   The disc brake calipers, which contain the pads, are now visible. Each caliper has an outer and an inner pad – all pads should be checked.

23.4   Disc brake pad thickness can be checked through the caliper inspection hole

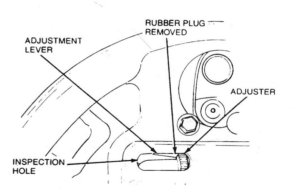

23.10   Remove the rubber plug from the backing plate, push the self-adjusting lever aside and turn the adjuster wheel

23.11   Measure the thickness of the remaining brake shoe material

23.13   Carefully peel back the rubber cup on each end of the wheel cylinder – if the exposed area is covered with brake fluid, or if fluid runs out, the wheel cylinder must be overhauled or replaced

4   Each caliper has an opening to inspect the pads **(see illustration)**. If the pad material has worn to about 1/8-inch thick or less, the pads should be replaced.

5   If you're unsure about the exact thickness of the remaining lining material, remove the pads for further inspection or replacement (refer to Chapter 9).

6   Before installing the wheels, check for leakage and/or damage at the brake hoses and connections. Replace the hose or fittings as necessary, referring to Chapter 9.

7   Check the condition of the brake disc. Look for score marks, deep scratches and overheated areas (they will appear blue or discolored). If damage or wear is noted, the disc can be removed and resurfaced by an automotive machine shop or replaced with a new one. Refer to Chapter 9 for more detailed inspection and repair procedures.

Drum brakes

Refer to illustrations 23.10, 23.11 and 23.13

8   Using a scribe or chalk, mark the drums and hub so the drum can be reinstalled in the same position on the hub.

9   Pull the brake drum off the hub and brake assembly. If this proves difficult, make sure the parking brake is released, then squirt some penetrating oil around the center hub area. Allow the oil to soak in and try to pull the drum off again.

10   If the drum still cannot be pulled off, the brake shoes will have to be retracted. This is done by first removing the rubber plug in the backing

plate. Pull the self-adjusting lever off the star wheel and use a small screwdriver to turn the adjuster wheel, which will move the shoes away from the drum **(see illustration)**. With the drum removed, carefully brush away the accumulations of dirt and dust (see Warning above).

11   Note the thickness of the lining material on the brake shoes. If the material is worn to within 1/16-inch of the recessed rivets or metal backing, the shoes should be replaced **(see illustration)**. The shoes should also be replaced if they are cracked, glazed, (shiny surface) or contaminated with brake fluid.

12   Check to make sure all the brake assembly springs are connected and in good condition.

13   Check the brake components for signs of fluid leakage. Carefully pry back the rubber cups on the wheel cylinder, located on the top of the backing plate **(see illustration)**. Any leakage is an indication that the wheel cylinders should be replaced or overhauled immediately (see Chapter 9). Also check the hoses and connections for signs of leakage.

14   Wipe the inside of the drum with a clean rag and brake cleaner or denatured alcohol.

15   Check the inside of the drum for cracks, score marks, deep scratches and hard spots, which will appear as small discolored areas. If imperfections cannot be removed with emery cloth or sandpaper, the drums must be taken to an automotive machine shop for resurfacing.

16   After the inspection process is complete, and if all the components are in good condition, reinstall the brake drums.

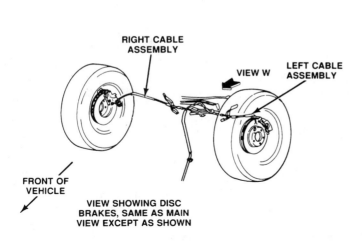

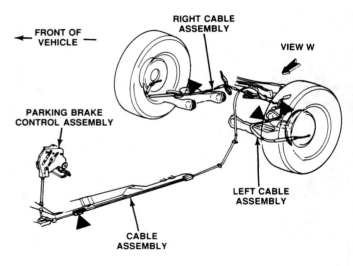

▲ LUBRICATION POINT

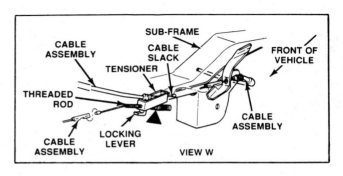

23.18   Lubricate the parking brake components at the points shown here

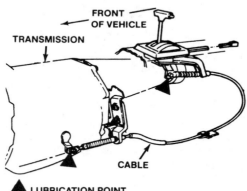

▲ LUBRICATION POINT

24.3   Automatic transmission control linkage lubrication points

Parking brake

Lubrication

Refer to illustration 23.18

17   Apply the parking brake.

18   Apply multi-purpose grease to the parking brake linkage, adjuster assembly, connectors and the areas of the parking brake cable that come in contact with other parts of the vehicle **(see illustration)**.

19   Release the parking brake and repeat the lubrication procedure.

20   Install the wheels and lower the vehicle to the ground.

Check

21   The parking brake is operated by a hand lever and locks the rear brake system. The easiest, and perhaps most obvious, method of periodically checking the parking brake is to park the vehicle on a steep hill with the parking brake set and the transmission in Neutral (remain in the car while performing this check). If the parking brake doesn't prevent the vehicle from rolling, it is in need of adjustment (see Chapter 9).

24   Automatic transmission control linkage lubrication

Refer to illustration 24.3

1   Open the hood and locate the shift cable and rod contact points.

2   Clean the linkage and pivot points.

3   Lubricate the shift linkage and pivot points with multi-purpose grease **(see illustration)**.

25   Manual transmission lubricant level check

Refer to illustration 25.1

Note: *The transmission lubricant level and quality should not deteriorate under normal driving conditions. However, it's recommended that you check the level occasionally. The most convenient time would be when the vehicle is raised for another reason, such as an engine oil change.*

CARBON DEPOSITS

Symptoms: Dry sooty deposits indicate a rich mixture or weak ignition. Causes misfiring, hard starting and hesitation.

Recommendation: Check for a clogged air cleaner, high float level, sticky choke and worn ignition points. Use a spark plug with a longer core nose for greater anti-fouling protection.

OIL DEPOSITS

Symptoms: Oily coating caused by poor oil control. Oil is leaking past worn valve guides or piston rings into the combustion chamber. Causes hard starting, misfiring and hesition.

Recommendation: Correct the mechanical condition with necessary repairs and install new plugs.

TOO HOT

Symptoms: Blistered, white insulator, eroded electrode and absence of deposits. Results in shortened plug life.

Recommendation: Check for the correct plug heat range, over-advanced ignition timing, lean fuel mixture, intake manifold vacuum leaks and sticking valves. Check the coolant level and make sure the radiator is not clogged.

PREIGNITION

Symptoms: Melted electrodes. Insulators are white, but may be dirty due to misfiring or flying debris in the combustion chamber. Can lead to engine damage.

Recommendation: Check for the correct plug heat range, over-advanced ignition timing, lean fuel mixture, clogged cooling system and lack of lubrication.

HIGH SPEED GLAZING

Symptoms: Insulator has yellowish, glazed appearance. Indicates that combustion chamber temperatures have risen suddenly during hard acceleration. Normal deposits melt to form a conductive coating. Causes misfiring at high speeds.

Recommendation: Install new plugs. Consider using a colder plug if driving habits warrant.

GAP BRIDGING

Symptoms: Combustion deposits lodge between the electrodes. Heavy deposits accumulate and bridge the electrode gap. The plug ceases to fire, resulting in a dead cylinder.

Recommendation: Locate the faulty plug and remove the deposits from between the electrodes.

NORMAL

Symptoms: Brown to grayish-tan color and slight electrode wear. Correct heat range for engine and operating conditions.

Recommendation: When new spark plugs are installed, replace with plugs of the same heat range.

ASH DEPOSITS

Symptoms: Light brown deposits encrusted on the side or center electrodes or both. Derived from oil and/or fuel additives. Excessive amounts may mask the spark, causing misfiring and hesitation during acceleration.

Recommendation: If excessive deposits accumulate over a short time or low mileage, install new valve guide seals to prevent seepage of oil into the combustion chambers. Also try changing gasoline brands.

WORN

Symptoms: Rounded electrodes with a small amount of deposits on the firing end. Normal color. Causes hard starting in damp or cold weather and poor fuel economy.

Recommendation: Replace with new plugs of the same heat range.

DETONATION

Symptoms: Insulators may be cracked or chipped. Improper gap setting techniques can also result in a fractured insulator tip. Can lead to piston damage.

Recommendation: Make sure the fuel anti-knock values meet engine requirements. Use care when setting the gaps on new plugs. Avoid lugging the engine.

SPLASHED DEPOSITS

Symptoms: After long periods of misfiring, deposits can loosen when normal combustion temperature is restored by an overdue tune-up. At high speeds, deposits flake off the piston and are thrown against the hot insulator, causing misfiring.

Recommendation: Replace the plugs with new ones or clean and reinstall the originals.

MECHANICAL DAMAGE

Symptoms: May be caused by a foreign object in the combustion chamber or the piston striking an incorrect reach (too long) plug. Causes a dead cylinder and could result in piston damage.

Recommendation: Remove the foreign object from the engine and/or install the correct reach plug.

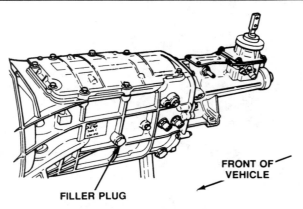

25.1   Manual transmission filler plug location

FRONT OF VEHICLE

FILLER PLUG

1   The transmission has an inspection and filler plug which must be removed to check the lubricant level **(see illustration)**. If the vehicle is raised to gain access to the plug, be sure to support it safely on jackstands – DO NOT crawl under a vehicle which is supported only by a jack!
2   Remove the plug from the transmission and use your little finger to reach inside the housing and feel the lubricant level. It should be at or very near the bottom of the plug hole.
3   If it isn't, add the recommended lubricant through the plug hole with a syringe or squeeze bottle.
4   Install and tighten the plug securely and check for leaks after the first few miles of driving.

26   Rear axle (differential) lubricant level check

Refer to illustration 26.2
1   The differential has a check/fill plug which must be removed to check the lubricant level. If the vehicle is raised to gain access to the plug, be sure to support it safely on jackstands – DO NOT crawl under the vehicle when it's supported only by the jack!
2   Remove the check/fill plug from the differential **(see illustration)**.
3   Use your little finger as a dipstick to make sure the lubricant level is even with the bottom of the plug hole. If not, use a syringe to add the recommended lubricant until it just starts to run out of the opening. On some models a tag is located in the area of the plug which gives information regarding lubricant type, particularly on models equipped with a limited slip differential.
4   Install the plug and tighten it securely.

27   Spark plug replacement

Refer to illustrations 27.2, 27.5a, 27.5b, 27.6 and 27.10
1   The spark plugs are located on the sides of the engine.
2   In most cases, the tools necessary for spark plug replacement include a spark plug socket which fits onto a ratchet (spark plug sockets are padded inside to prevent damage to the porcelain insulators on the new plugs), various extensions and a gap gauge to check and adjust the gaps on the new plugs **(see illustration)**. A special plug wire removal tool is available for separating the wire boots from the spark plugs, but it isn't absolutely necessary. A torque wrench should be used to tighten the new plugs.
3   The best approach when replacing the spark plugs is to purchase the new ones in advance, adjust them to the proper gap and replace the plugs one at a time. When buying the new spark plugs, be sure to obtain the correct plug type for your particular engine. This information can be found on the Emission Control Information label located under the hood and in the factory owner's manual. If differences exist between the plug specified on

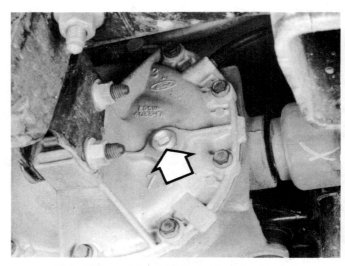

26.2   Differential check/fill plug location (arrow)

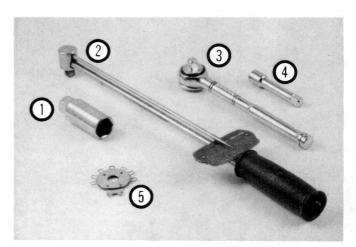

27.2   Tools required for changing spark plugs

1   *Spark plug socket* – This will have special padding inside to protect the spark plug's porcelain insulator
2   *Torque wrench* – Although not mandatory, using this tool is the best way to ensure the plugs are tightened properly
3   *Ratchet* – Standard hand tool to fit the spark plug socket
4   *Extension* – Depending on model and accessories, you may need special extensions and universal joints to reach one or more of the plugs
5   *Spark plug gap gauge* – This gauge for checking the gap comes in a variety of styles. Make sure the gap for your engine is included.

the emissions label and in the owner's manual, assume that the emissions label is correct.
4   Allow the engine to cool completely before attempting to remove any of the plugs. These models have aluminum cylinder heads, which can be damaged if the spark plugs are removed when the engine is hot. While you are waiting for the engine to cool, check the new plugs for defects and adjust the gaps.
5   The gap is checked by inserting the proper thickness gauge between the electrodes at the tip of the plug **(see illustration)**. The gap between the electrodes should be the same as the one specified on the Emissions Control Information label. The wire should just slide between the electrodes with a slight amount of drag. If the gap is incorrect, use the adjuster on the gauge body to bend the curved side electrode slightly until the specified gap is obtained **(see illustration)**. If the side electrode is not exactly

27.5a   Spark plug manufacturers recommend using a wire type gauge when checking the gap – if the wire does not slide between the electrodes with a slight drag, adjustment is required

27.5b   To change the gap, bend the *side* electrode only, as indicated by the arrows, and be very careful not to crack or chip the porcelain insulator surrounding the center electrode

1

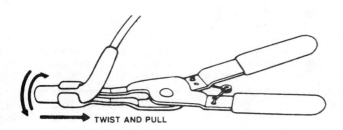

TWIST AND PULL

27.6   When removing the spark plug wires, pull only on the boot and twist it back-and-forth

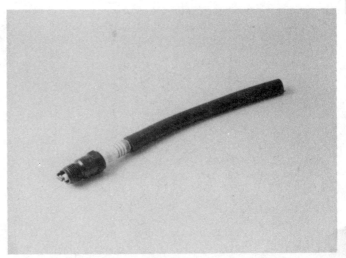

27.10   A length of 3/16-inch ID rubber hose will save time and prevent damaged threads when installing the spark plugs

over the center electrode, bend it with the adjuster until it is. Check for cracks in the porcelain insulator (if any are found, the plug should not be used).

6   With the engine cool, remove the spark plug wire from one spark plug. Pull only on the boot at the end of the wire – do not pull on the wire. A plug wire removal tool should be used if available **(see illustration)**.

7   If compressed air is available, use it to blow any dirt or foreign material away from the spark plug hole. A common bicycle pump will also work. The idea here is to eliminate the possibility of debris falling into the cylinder as the spark plug is removed.

8   Place the spark plug socket over the plug and remove it from the engine by turning it in a counterclockwise direction.

9   Compare the spark plug to those shown in the accompanying color photos to get an indication of the general running condition of the engine.

10   Thread one of the new plugs into the hole until you can no longer turn it with your fingers, then tighten it with a torque wrench (if available) or the ratchet. It might be a good idea to slip a short length of rubber hose over the end of the plug to use as a tool to thread it into place, particularly since the head is made of aluminum **(see illustration)**. The hose will grip the plug well enough to turn it, but will start to slip if the plug begins to cross-thread in the hole – this will prevent damaged threads and the accompanying repair costs.

11   Before pushing the spark plug wire onto the end of the plug, inspect it following the procedures outlined in Section 28.

12   Attach the plug wire to the new spark plug, again using a twisting motion on the boot until it is seated on the spark plug.

13   Repeat the procedure for the remaining spark plugs, replacing them one at a time to prevent mixing up the spark plug wires.

28   Spark plug wire, distributor cap and rotor check and replacement

Refer to illustrations 28.11 and 28.12

Spark plug wires

Note: *Every time a spark plug wire is detached from a spark plug, the distributor cap or the coil, silicone dielectric compound (a white grease available at auto parts stores) must be applied to the inside of each boot before reconnection. Use a small standard screwdriver to coat the entire inside surface of each boot with a thin layer of the compound.*

1   The spark plug wires should be checked and, if necessary, replaced at the same time new spark plugs are installed.

2   The easiest way to identify bad wires is to make a visual check while the engine is running. In a dark, well-ventilated garage, start the engine and look at each plug wire. Be careful not to come into contact with any moving engine parts. If there is a break in the wire, you will see arcing or a small spark at the damaged area. If arcing is noticed, make a note to obtain new wires.

3   The spark plug wires should be inspected one at a time, beginning with the spark plug for the number one cylinder, (the cylinder closest to the

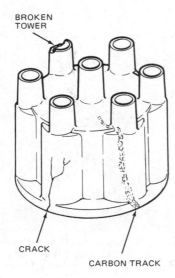

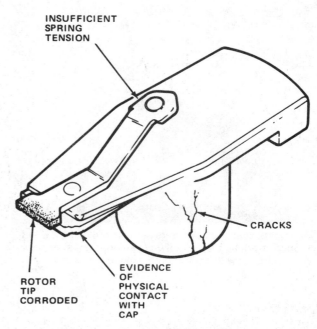

28.12   The ignition rotor should be checked for wear and corrosion as indicated here (if in doubt about its condition, buy a new one)

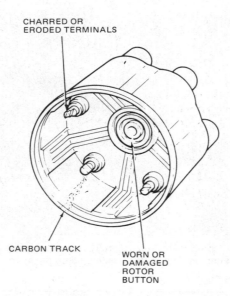

28.11   Shown here are some of the common defects to look for when inspecting the distributor cap (if in doubt about its condition, install a new one)

radiator on the right bank), to prevent confusion. Clearly label each original plug wire with a piece of tape marked with the correct number. The plug wires must be reinstalled in the correct order to ensure proper engine operation.

4   Disconnect the plug wire from the first spark plug. A removal tool can be used **(see illustration 27.6)**, or you can grab the wire boot, twist it slightly and pull the wire free. Do not pull on the wire itself, only on the rubber boot.

5   Push the wire and boot back onto the end of the spark plug. It should fit snugly. If it doesn't, detach the wire and boot once more and use a pair of pliers to carefully crimp the metal connector inside the wire boot until it does.

6   Using a clean rag, wipe the entire length of the wire to remove built-up dirt and grease.

7   Once the wire is clean, check for burns, cracks and other damage. Do not bend the wire sharply or you might break the conductor.

8   Disconnect the wire from the distributor. Again, pull only on the rubber boot. Check for corrosion and a tight fit. Replace the wire in the distributor.

9   Inspect each of the remaining spark plug wires, making sure that each one is securely fastened at the distributor and spark plug when the check is complete.

10   If new spark plug wires are required, purchase a set for your specific engine model. Pre-cut wire sets with the boots already installed are available. Remove and replace the wires one at a time to avoid mixups in the firing order.

Distributor cap and rotor

Note: *It's common practice to install a new distributor cap and rotor each time new spark plug wires are installed. If you're planning to install new wires, install a new cap and rotor also. But if you're planning to reuse the existing wires, be sure to inspect the cap and rotor to make sure that they are in good condition. Models equipped with the DIS ignition system do not have a distributor or rotor.*

11   Remove the mounting screws and detach the cap from the distributor. Check it for cracks, carbon tracks and worn, burned or loose terminals **(see illustration)**

12   Check the rotor for cracks and carbon tracks. Make sure the center terminal spring tension is adequate and look for corrosion and wear on the rotor tip **(see illustration)**.

13   Replace the cap and rotor if damage or defects are found. Note that the rotor is indexed so it can only be installed one way. Before installing the cap, apply silicone dielectric compound to the rotor tip (see Note at beginning of this Section).

14   When installing a new cap, remove the wires from the old cap one at a time and attach them to the new cap in the exact same location – do not simultaneously remove all the wires from the old cap or firing order mixups may occur.

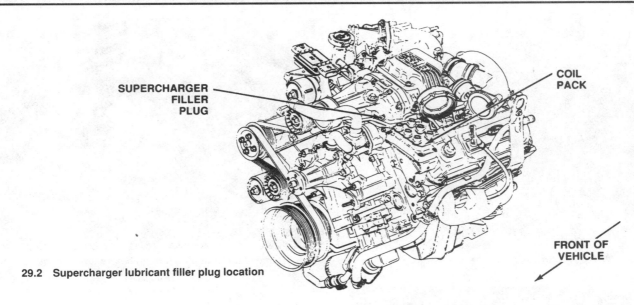

29.2 Supercharger lubricant filler plug location

1

30.7 Pry the pan free of the gasket and allow the fluid to drain

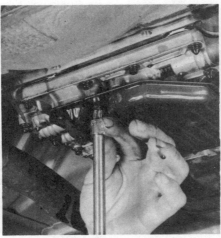

30.10 Use a socket and extension to remove the filter bolts

30.11a Install a new filter seal on the transmission . . .

29 Supercharger lubricant level check

Refer to illustration 29.2

1   The supercharger has a self-contained lubrication system. The system lubricant level must be checked periodically, at the specified intervals.
2   Use an Allen wrench to remove the filler plug from the supercharger (the vehicle must be parked on level ground, with the engine off and cold) **(see illustration)**.
3   The lubricant level should be at the bottom of the filler plug threads. If the level is low, add the lubricant specified at the beginning of this Chapter.

30 Automatic transmission fluid and filter change

Refer to illustrations 30.7, 30.10, 30.11a, 30.11b and 30.12

1   At the specified intervals, the transmission fluid should be drained and replaced. Since the fluid will remain hot long after driving, perform this procedure only after the engine has cooled down completely.

2   Before beginning work, purchase the transmission fluid specified in Recommended lubricants and fluids at the front of this Chapter, a new filter and gaskets. Never reuse the old filter or gasket!
3   Other tools necessary for this job include jackstands to support the vehicle in a raised position, a drain pan capable of holding at least eight quarts, newspapers and clean rags.
4   Raise the vehicle and support it securely on jackstands.
5   With the drain pan in place, remove the front and side transmission pan mounting bolts.
6   Loosen the rear pan bolts approximately four turns.
7   Carefully pry the transmission pan loose with a screwdriver, allowing the fluid to drain **(see illustration)**. Don't damage the pan or transmission gasket surfaces or leaks could develop.
8   Remove the remaining bolts, pan and gasket. Carefully clean the gasket surface of the transmission to remove all traces of the old gasket and sealant.
9   Drain the fluid from the transmission pan, clean it with solvent and dry it with compressed air.
10   Remove the filter from the mount inside the transmission **(see illustration)**.
11   Install a new seal, gasket and filter **(see illustrations)**. Tighten the mounting bolts securely.

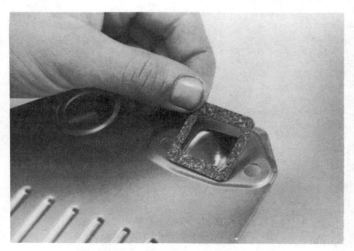

30.11b . . . and gasket on the filter itself

31.3   Remove the vent plug (arrow) before draining the coolant

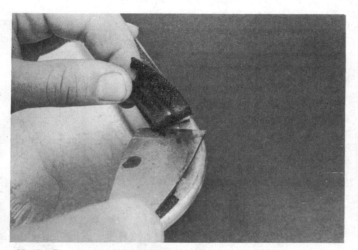

30.12   Be sure to clean all traces of the old gasket from the pan before installing a new one

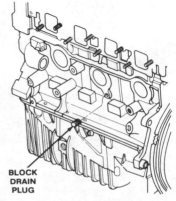

BLOCK DRAIN PLUG

31.5   Drain plugs are located just below the exhaust manifolds on both sides of the engine block

12   Make sure the gasket surface on the transmission pan is clean, then install a new gasket **(see illustration)**. Put the pan in place against the transmission and install the bolts. Working around the pan, tighten each bolt a little at a time until the final torque figure is reached. Don't overtighten the bolts!

13   Lower the vehicle and add about four or five pints of automatic transmission fluid through the filler tube (Section 7).

14   With the transmission in Park and the parking brake set, run the engine at a fast idle, but don't race it.

15   Move the gear selector through each range and back to Park. Check the fluid level. Add fluid if needed to reach the correct level.

16   Check under the vehicle for leaks during the first few trips.

---

31   Cooling system servicing (draining, flushing and refilling)

Refer to illustrations 31.3 and 31.5

Warning: *Do not allow antifreeze to come in contact with your skin or painted surfaces of the vehicle. Rinse off spills immediately with plenty of water. Antifreeze is highly toxic if ingested. Never leave antifreeze lying around in an open container or in puddles on the floor; children and pets are attracted by it's sweet smell and may drink it. Check with local authorities about disposing of used antifreeze. Many communities have collection centers which will see that antifreeze is disposed of safely.*

1   Periodically, the cooling system should be drained, flushed and re-filled to replenish the antifreeze mixture and prevent formation of rust and corrosion, which can impair the performance of the cooling system and cause engine damage. When the cooling system is serviced, all hoses and the radiator cap should be checked and replaced if necessary.

Draining

2   Apply the parking brake and block the wheels. If the vehicle has just been driven, wait several hours to allow the engine to cool down before beginning this procedure.

3   Once the engine is completely cool, remove the vent plug and the radiator cap **(see illustration)**.

4   Move a large container under the radiator drain to catch the coolant. Attach a 3/8-inch diameter hose to the drain fitting to direct the coolant into the container, then open the drain fitting (a pair of pliers may be required to turn it).

5   After the coolant stops flowing out of the radiator, move the container under the engine block drain plugs. Remove the plugs and allow the coolant in the block to drain **(see illustration)**.

6   While the coolant is draining, check the condition of the radiator hoses, heater hoses and clamps (refer to Section 19 if necessary).

7   Replace any damaged clamps or hoses (refer to Chapter 3 for detailed replacement procedures).

Flushing

8   Once the system is completely drained, flush the radiator with fresh water from a garden hose until water runs clear at the drain. The flushing

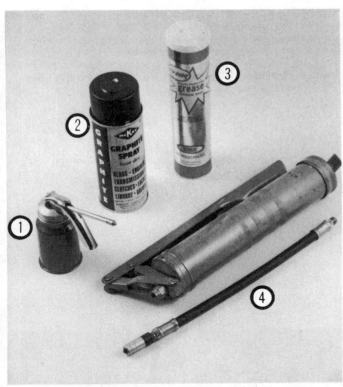

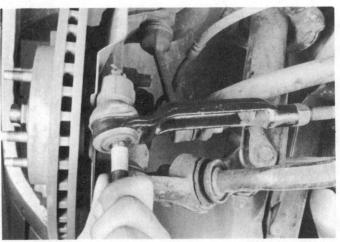

32.6   After cleaning the grease fitting, push the gun nozzle firmly into place and pump the grease into the component (usually about two pumps will be sufficient)

32.1   Materials required for chassis and body lubrication

1   *Engine oil* – Light engine oil in a can like this can be used for door and hood hinges
2   *Graphite spray* – Used to lubricate lock cylinders
3   *Grease* – Grease, in a variety of types and weights, is available for use in a grease gun. Check the Specifications for your requirements.
4   *Grease gun* – A common grease gun, shown here with a detachable hose and nozzle, is needed for chassis lubrication. After use, clean it thoroughly!

action of the water will remove sediments from the radiator but will not remove rust and scale from the engine and cooling tube surfaces.
9   These deposits can be removed by the chemical action of a cleaner such as Ford Cooling System Fast Flush. Follow the procedure outlined in the manufacturer's instructions. If the radiator is severely corroded, damaged or leaking, it should be removed (see Chapter 3) and taken to a radiator repair shop.
10   Remove the overflow hose from the coolant recovery reservoir. Drain the reservoir and flush it with clean water, then reconnect the hose.

Refilling

11   Close and tighten the radiator drain. Install and tighten the block drain plugs.
12   Place the heater temperature control in the maximum heat position.
13   Slowly add new coolant (a 50/50 mixture of water and antifreeze) to the radiator until it is full. Add coolant to the reservoir up to the lower mark. Install the vent plug.
14   Leave the radiator cap off and run the engine in a well-ventilated area until the thermostat opens (coolant will begin flowing through the radiator and the upper radiator hose will become hot).
15   Turn the engine off and let it cool. Add more coolant mixture to bring the level back up to the lip on the radiator filler neck.
16   Squeeze the upper radiator hose to expel air, then add more coolant mixture if necessary. Replace the radiator cap.
17   Start the engine, allow it to reach normal operating temperature and check for leaks.

32   Chassis lubrication

Refer to illustrations 32.1 and 32.6
1   Refer to Recommended lubricants and fluids at the front of this Chapter to obtain the necessary grease, etc. You'll also need a grease gun **(see illustration)**. Occasionally plugs will be installed rather than grease fittings. If so, grease fittings will have to be purchased and installed.
2   Look under the vehicle and see if grease fittings or plugs are installed in the tie-rod ends. If there are plugs, remove them and buy grease fittings, which will thread into the component. A dealer or auto parts store will be able to supply the correct fittings. Straight, as well as angled, fittings are available.
3   For easier access under the vehicle, raise it with a jack and place jack-stands under the frame. Make sure it's safely supported by the stands. If the wheels are to be removed at this interval for tire rotation or brake inspection, loosen the lug nuts slightly while the vehicle is still on the ground.
4   Before beginning, force a little grease out of the nozzle to remove any dirt from the end of the gun. Wipe the nozzle clean with a rag.
5   With the grease gun and plenty of clean rags, crawl under the vehicle.
6   Wipe the tie-rod end grease fitting nipple clean and push the nozzle firmly over it. Squeeze the trigger on the grease gun to force grease into the component **(see illustration)**. They should be lubricated until the rubber seal is firm to the touch. Don't pump too much grease into the fitting as it could rupture the seal. If grease escapes around the grease gun nozzle, the nipple is clogged or the nozzle is not completely seated on the fitting. Resecure the gun nozzle to the fitting and try again. If necessary, replace the fitting with a new one.
7   Wipe the excess grease from the components and the grease fitting. Repeat the procedure for the remaining fitting.
8   While you're under the vehicle, clean and lubricate the parking brake cable, along with the cable guides and levers. This can be done by smearing some of the chassis grease onto the cable and its related parts with your fingers.
9   Open the hood and smear a little chassis grease on the hood latch mechanism. Have an assistant pull the hood release lever from inside the vehicle as you lubricate the cable at the latch.
10   Lubricate all the hinges (door, hood, etc.) with engine oil to keep them in proper working order.
11   The key lock cylinders can be lubricated with spray graphite or silicone lubricant, which is available at auto parts stores.
12   Lubricate the door weatherstripping with silicone spray. This will reduce chafing and retard wear.

33   Rear axle (differential) lubricant change

1   There is no drain plug on these models, so a hand suction pump must be used to remove the differential lubricant through the filler hole.

2   Raise the vehicle and support it securely on jackstands. Move a drain pan, rags, newspapers and the tools you will need under the vehicle.

3   Remove the check/fill plug from the differential (see illustration 26.2).

4   Insert the suction pump flexible hose. Work the hose down to the bottom of the differential housing and pump the oil out.

5   Use a hand pump, syringe or funnel to fill the differential housing with the specified lubricant until it's level with the bottom of the plug hole.

6   Install the check/fill plug and tighten it securely.

Chapter 2 Part A   Engine

Contents

Specifications

General

Displacement	3.8 liters
Cylinder numbers (front-to-rear)	
Left (driver's) side	4–5–6
Right (passenger's) side	1–2–3
Firing order	1-4-2-5-3-6

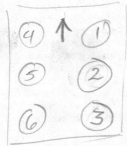

Camshaft

Valve stem-to-rocker arm clearance (collapsed tappet gap)	0.089 to 0.189 in
Lobe lift	
Intake	0.245 in
Exhaust	0.259 in
Allowable lobe lift loss	0.005 in
Theoretical valve lift @ zero lash	
Intake	0.424 in
Exhaust	0.447 in
Journal diameter (all)	2.0515 to 2.0505 in
Cam bearing inside diameter	2.0535 to 2.0525
Journal-to-bearing (oil) clearance	0.001 to 0.003 in
Journal runout limit	0.002 in (runout of no. 2 or 3 relative to 1 and 4)
Journal out-of-round limit	0.001 in
Oil pump	
Relief valve spring tension	17.1 to 15.2 lbs at 1.20 in
Relief valve-to-bore clearance	0.0017 to 0.0029 in
Gear backlash	0.008 to 0.0012 in
Gear radial clearance	0.002 to 0.0055 in
Gear height (beyond housing)	0.0005 to 0.0055 in

Torque Specifications

Ft-lbs (unless otherwise indicated)

Camshaft sprocket bolt	30 to 37
Crankshaft pulley-to-vibration damper bolts	20 to 28
Cylinder head bolts	
All models	
Step 1	37
Step 2	45
Step 3	52
Step 4	59
Step 5	Loosen all bolts 2 or 3 turns
Supercharged models only	
Step 6	48 to 55
Step 7	Rotate an additional 90 to 110-degrees
Non-supercharged models only	
Step 6 (all bolts)	11 to 18
Step 7	
Long bolts	Rotate an additional 85 to 105-degrees
Short bolts	Rotate an additional 65 to 85-degrees
Exhaust manifold bolts	15 to 22
Flywheel/driveplate mounting bolts	54 to 64
Intake manifold-to-cylinder head bolts	
Non-supercharged models	
Step 1	7
Step 2	15
Step 3	24
Supercharged models	
Step 1	8
Step 2	11
Oil pan mounting bolts	80 to 106 in-lbs
Oil pump cover bolts	18 to 22
Oil inlet tube-to-main bearing cap nut	30 to 40
Oil inlet tube-to-cylinder block nuts	15 to 22
Rocker arm fulcrum bolts	
Step 1	5 to 11
Step 2	18 to 26
Timing chain cover-to-block bolts	15 to 22
Valve cover bolts/studs	6 to 8.5
Vibration damper bolt	103 to 132

1   General information

This Part of Chapter 2 is devoted to in-vehicle repair procedures for the engine. All information concerning engine removal and installation and engine block and cylinder head overhaul can be found in Part B of this Chapter.

The following repair procedures are based on the assumption that the engine is installed in the vehicle. If the engine has been removed from the vehicle and mounted on a stand, many of the steps outlined in this Part of Chapter 2 will not apply.

The Specifications included in this Part of Chapter 2 apply only to the procedures contained in this Part. Part B of Chapter 2 contains the Specifications necessary for cylinder head and engine block rebuilding.

2   Repair operations possible with the engine in the vehicle

Many major repair operations can be accomplished without removing the engine from the vehicle.

Clean the engine compartment and the exterior of the engine with some type of pressure washer before any work is done. It will make the job easier and help keep dirt out of the internal areas of the engine.

It may help to remove the hood to improve access to the engine as repairs are performed (refer to Chapter 11 if necessary).

If vacuum, exhaust, oil or coolant leaks develop, indicating a need for gasket or seal replacement, the repairs can generally be made with the engine in the vehicle. The intake and exhaust manifold gaskets, timing cover gasket, oil pan gasket, crankshaft oil seals and cylinder head gaskets are all accessible with the engine in place.

Exterior engine components, such as the intake and exhaust manifolds, the oil pan (and the oil pump), the water pump, the starter motor, the alternator, the distributor (or synchronizer) and the fuel system components can be removed for repair with the engine in place.

Since the cylinder heads can be removed without pulling the engine, valve component servicing can also be accomplished with the engine in the vehicle. Replacement of the timing chain and sprockets is also possible with the engine in the vehicle.

In extreme cases caused by a lack of necessary equipment, repair or replacement of piston rings, pistons, connecting rods and rod bearings is possible with the engine in the vehicle. However, this practice is not recommended because of the cleaning and preparation work that must be done to the components involved.

3   Valve covers – removal and installation

Removal

Refer to illustrations 3.2, 3.4, 3.6a, 3.6b, 3.6c and 3.7

1   Disconnect the negative cable from the battery.

2   Note their locations, then detach the spark plug wire clips from the valve cover studs **(see illustration)**.

3   Refer to Chapter 1 and detach the spark plug wires from the plugs. Position the wires out of the way.

4   If the left (driver's) side valve cover is being removed, detach the oil fill cap and crankcase vent tube **(see illustration)**. Additionally, on supercharged models, remove the intercooler tubes and oil cooler inlet tube.

5   If the right (passenger's) side valve cover is being removed, position

3.2   Remove the spark plug wire clips (arrow)

3.4   Detach the crankcase vent tube

3.6a   Remove the five bolts and studs (arrows) from each valve cover

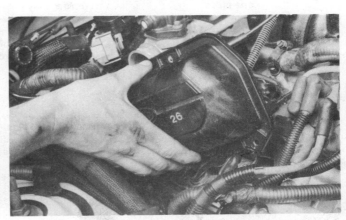

3.6b   Move the hoses aside and slip the cover out

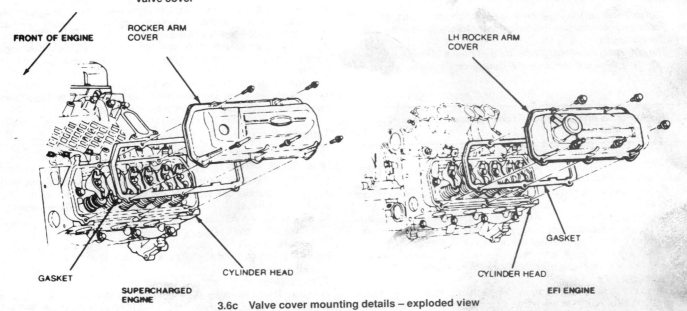

FRONT OF ENGINE

ROCKER ARM COVER

GASKET

SUPERCHARGED ENGINE

CYLINDER HEAD

LH ROCKER ARM COVER

GASKET

CYLINDER HEAD

EFI ENGINE

3.6c   Valve cover mounting details – exploded view

the air cleaner duct out of the way (see Chapter 4) and remove the PCV valve. Additionally, on supercharged models, remove the throttle body (see Chapter 4).

6   Remove the valve cover bolts/studs (**see illustrations**), then detach the cover from the head. **Note:** *If the cover is stuck to the head, bump one end with a block of wood and a hammer to jar it loose. If that doesn't work, try to slip a flexible putty knife between the head and cover to break the gasket seal. Don't pry at the cover-to-head joint or damage to the sealing surfaces may occur (leading to oil leaks in the future). Move the hoses aside and slip the cover from the engine compartment (**see illustration**).*

3.7   The gaskets may simply peel off in one piece

4.2   The rocker arm fulcrum bolts (arrow) may not have to be completely removed – loosen them several turns and see if the rocker arms can be pivoted out of the way to allow pushrod removal

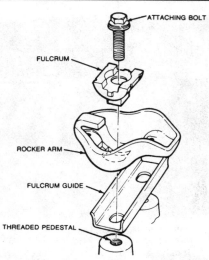

4.3   An exploded view of a rocker arm its and related components

Installation

7   The mating surfaces of each cylinder head and valve cover must be perfectly clean when the covers are installed. If necessary, use a gasket scraper to remove all traces of sealant and old gasket material **(see illustration)**, then clean the mating surfaces with lacquer thinner or acetone. If there's sealant or oil on the mating surfaces when the cover is installed, oil leaks may develop.

8   Clean the mounting bolt threads with a die to remove any corrosion and restore damaged threads. Make sure the threaded holes in the head are clean – run a tap into them to remove corrosion and restore damaged threads. Apply a small amount of light oil to the bolt threads.

9   The gaskets should be mated to the covers before the covers are installed. Make sure the tabs on the gaskets(s) engage in the slots in the cover(s).

10   Carefully position the cover on the head and install the bolts/nuts.

11   Tighten the bolts/studs in three steps to the torque listed in this Chapter's Specifications.

12   The remaining installation steps are the reverse of removal.

13   Start the engine and check carefully for oil leaks as the engine warms up.

---

4   Rocker arms and pushrods – removal, inspection and installation

Removal

Refer to illustrations 4.2, 4.3 and 4.4

1   Refer to Section 3 and detach the valve cover(s) from the cylinder head(s).

2   Beginning at the front of one cylinder head, remove the rocker arm fulcrum bolts **(see illustration)**. Store them separately in marked containers to ensure that they will be reinstalled in their original locations. **Note:** *If the pushrods are the only items being removed, loosen each bolt just enough to allow the rocker arms to be rotated to the side so the pushrods can be lifted out.*

3   Lift off the rocker arms, fulcrums and fulcrum guides – if used **(see illustration)**. Store them in the marked containers with the bolts (they must be reinstalled in their original locations).

4   Remove the pushrods and store them separately to make sure they don't get mixed up during installation **(see illustration)**.

Inspection

5   Check each rocker arm for wear, cracks and other damage, especially where the pushrods and valve stems contact the rocker arm faces.

6   Make sure the hole at the pushrod end of each rocker arm is open.

7   Check each rocker arm pivot area and fulcrum for wear, cracks and galling. If the rocker arms are worn or damaged, replace them with new ones and use new fulcrums as well.

8   Inspect the pushrods for cracks and excessive wear at the ends. Roll each pushrod across a piece of plate glass to see if it's bent (if it wobbles, it's bent).

Installation

Caution: *Make sure that both lifters for each cylinder are on the base circle of the cam lobe (both valves closed) before tightening the rocker arm bolts.*

9   Lubricate the lower end of each pushrod with clean engine oil or moly-base grease and install them in their original locations. Make sure each pushrod seats completely in the lifter.

10   Apply moly-base grease to the ends of the valve stems and the upper ends of the pushrods before positioning the rocker arms, fulcrums and guides.

11   Apply moly-base grease to the fulcrums to prevent damage to the mating surfaces before engine oil pressure builds up. Set the rocker arms and guides in place, then install the fulcrums and bolts.

Valve adjustment

Refer to illustrations 4.12 and 4.14

Note: *Adjustment is normally only needed when valve train components have been replaced or valves have been ground a considerable amount.*

12   Set the number one piston at Top Dead Center (TDC) on the compression stroke (see Section 9). This is position 1 **(see illustration)**.

13   In this position you can check the following valves:

   Intake – 1, 3 and 6
   Exhaust – 1, 2 and 4

Note: *The arrangement of intake and exhaust valves is as follows:*

   Left side – E-I-E-I-E-I
   Right side – I-E-I-E-I-E

14   Using Ford lifter bleed-down tool T70P-6513-A or equivalent **(see illustration)**, press on each rocker arm until the lifter leaks down completely. Check the clearance between the valve stem and rocker arm with a feeler gauge. Compare it to the Specifications in this Chapter and write it down. Repeat this procedure for each valve listed above.

15   Rotate the crankshaft to position 2 and check the following valves:

   Intake – no. 2, 4 and 5
   Exhaust – no. 3, 5 and 6

If the clearances are within specification, install the rocker arm covers.

4.4   A perforated cardboard box can be used to store the pushrods to ensure that they are reinstalled in their original locations – note the label indicating the front of the engine

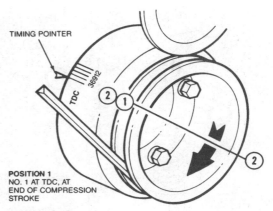

POSITION 1
NO. 1 AT TDC, AT
END OF COMPRESSION
STROKE

POSITION 2
ROTATE CRANKSHAFT
180 DEGREES (ONE-HALF
REVOLUTION) CLOCKWISE,
FROM POSITION 1
(ONE REVOLUTION — 360 DEGREES
ON 6 CYLINDER ENGINES)

4.12   Crankshaft position for checking and adjusting valve clearances

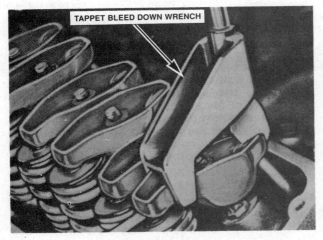

4.14   A special tool is required to bleed down the lifters when checking the valve stem-to-rocker arm clearance

5.8   Once the spring is compressed, the keepers can be removed with a small magnet or needle-nose pliers (a magnet is preferred to prevent dropping the keepers)

16   The clearance can be changed by using different length pushrods, available from your dealer. If there isn't enough clearance, use a shorter pushrod; too much clearance, use a longer one.

5   Valve springs, retainers and seals – replacement

Refer to illustrations 5.8, 5.9a, 5.9b and 5.14
Note: *Broken valve springs and defective valve stem seals can be replaced without removing the cylinder heads. Two special tools and a compressed air source are normally required to perform this operation, so read through this Section carefully and rent or buy the tools before beginning the job. If compressed air isn't available, a length of nylon rope can be used to keep the valves from falling into the cylinder during this procedure.*

1   Refer to Section 3 and remove the valve cover from the affected cylinder head. If all of the valve stem seals are being replaced, remove both valve covers.
2   Remove the spark plug from the cylinder which has the defective component. If all of the valve stem seals are being replaced, all of the spark plugs should be removed.
3   Turn the crankshaft until the piston in the affected cylinder is at top dead center on the compression stroke (refer to Section 9 for instructions). If you're replacing all of the valve stem seals, begin with cylinder number one and work on the valves for one cylinder at a time. Move from cylinder-to-cylinder following the firing order sequence 1-4-2-5-3-6.

4   Thread an adapter into the spark plug hole and connect an air hose from a compressed air source to it. Most auto parts stores can supply the air hose adapter. **Note:** *Many cylinder compression gauges utilize a screw-in fitting that may work with your air hose quick-disconnect fitting.*
5   Remove the bolt, fulcrum and rocker arm for the valve with the defective part and pull out the pushrod. If all of the valve stem seals are being replaced, all of the rocker arms and pushrods should be removed (refer to Section 4).
6   Apply compressed air to the cylinder. The valves should be held in place by the air pressure. If the valve faces or seats are in poor condition, leaks may prevent air pressure from retaining the valves – refer to the alternative procedure below.
7   If you don't have access to compressed air, an alternative method can be used. Position the piston at a point just before TDC on the compression stroke, then feed a long piece of nylon rope through the spark plug hole until it fills the combustion chamber. Be sure to leave the end of the rope hanging out of the engine so it can be removed easily. Use a large breaker bar and socket to rotate the crankshaft in the normal direction of rotation until slight resistance is felt.
8   Stuff shop rags into the cylinder head holes above and below the valves to prevent parts and tools from falling into the engine, then use a valve spring compressor to compress the spring/damper assembly. Remove the keepers with small needle-nose pliers or a magnet **(see illustration)**. **Note:** *A couple of different types of tools are available for compressing the valve springs with the head in place. One type, shown*

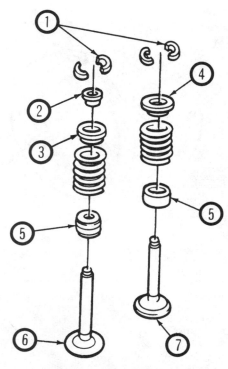

5.9a   Valves and related components – exploded view

1	Keepers	5	Valve stem seal
2	Sleeve (intake only)	6	Intake valve
3	Retainer	7	Exhaust valve
4	Exhaust valve rotator		

5.9b   The seal can be pulled off the guide with a pair of pliers

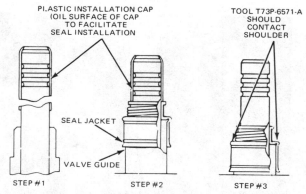

STEP #1 – WITH VALVES IN HEAD. PLACE PLASTIC INSTALLATION CAP OVER END OF VALVE STEM.
STEP #2 – START VALVE STEM SEAL CAREFULLY OVER CAP. PUSH SEAL DOWN UNTIL JACKET TOUCHES TOP OF GUIDE.
STEP #3 – REMOVE PLASTIC INSTALLATION CAP. USE INSTALLATION TOOL-T73P-6571-A OR SCREWDRIVERS TO BOTTOM SEAL ON VALVE GUIDE.

5.14   A special plastic cap is required to protect the new valve guide seals as they pass over the grooves in the valve stems

here, grips the lower spring coils and presses on the retainer as the knob is turned, while the other type utilizes the rocker arm bolt for leverage. Both types work very well, although the lever type is usually less expensive.

9   Remove the spring retainer or rotator, sleeve (used on some intake valves) and valve spring assembly, then remove the guide seal **(see illustrations)**. **Note:** *If air pressure fails to hold the valve in the closed position during this operation, the valve face and/or seat is probably damaged. If so, the cylinder head will have to be removed for additional repair operations.*

10   Wrap a rubber band or tape around the top of the valve stem so the valve won't fall into the combustion chamber, then release the air pressure. **Note:** *If a rope was used instead of air pressure, turn the crankshaft slightly in the direction opposite normal rotation.*

11   Inspect the valve stem for damage. Rotate the valve in the guide and check the end for eccentric movement, which would indicate that the valve is bent.

12   Move the valve up-and-down in the guide and make sure it doesn't bind. If the valve stem binds, either the valve is bent or the guide is damaged. In either case, the head will have to be removed for repair.

13   Reapply air pressure to the cylinder to retain the valve in the closed position, then remove the tape or rubber band from the valve stem. If a rope was used instead of air pressure, rotate the crankshaft in the normal direction of rotation until slight resistance is felt.

14   Lubricate the valve stem with engine oil and install a new seal **(see illustration)**.

15   Install the spring assembly in position over the valve.

16   Install the valve spring retainer or rotator. Some intake valves also have a sleeve that fits inside the retainer.

17   Compress the spring and position the keepers in the grooves. Apply a small dab of grease to the inside of each keeper to hold it in place if neces-

sary. Remove the pressure from the spring tool and make sure the keepers are seated.

18   Disconnect the air hose and remove the adapter from the spark plug hole. If a rope was used in place of air pressure, pull it out of the cylinder.

19   Refer to Section 4 and install the rocker arm(s) and pushrod(s).

20   Install the spark plug(s) and hook up the wire(s).

21   Refer to Section 3 and install the valve cover(s).

22   Start and run the engine, then check for oil leaks and unusual sounds coming from the valve cover area.

6   Intake manifold – removal and installation

Removal

Refer to illustrations 6.6, 6.8 and 6.13

1   Relieve the fuel pressure and remove the air duct assembly (see Chapter 4).

2   Disconnect the negative cable from the battery.

3   Drain the cooling system (see Chapter 1).

4   On supercharged models, refer to Chapter 4 and remove the supercharger and throttle body.

5   On non-supercharged models, remove the upper intake manifold and throttle body (see Chapter 4).

6.6   Cover the air intake with a cloth to prevent debris from falling into the engine

6.8   Label and disconnect the hoses and wiring

1   Sensor connector   *2   Vacuum line to fuel pressure regulator*

6.13   Pry against a casting protrusion to break the manifold loose

2A

6.14   After covering the lifter valley, use a gasket scraper to remove all traces of sealant and old gasket material from the head and manifold mating surfaces

6   Cover the air intake passages with a cloth (see illustration). Disconnect the upper radiator hose and heater hoses from the manifold fittings.

7   Detach any remaining brackets from the manifold.

8   Label and disconnect the vacuum and emissions hoses and wire harness connectors attached to the manifold (see illustration).

9   Disconnect the heater tube at the intake manifold. Remove the tube support bracket nut. **Note:** *The coolant bypass tube is pressed in and is not serviceable.*

10   On non-supercharged models with air conditioning, remove the compressor support bracket. **Warning:** *Do not disconnect any refrigerant lines!*

11   Remove the fuel injectors and fuel rail assembly (see Chapter 4).

12   Loosen the manifold mounting bolts in 1/4-turn increments until they can be removed by hand.

13   The manifold will probably be stuck to the cylinder heads and force may be required to break the gasket seal. A prybar can be positioned under the cast-in lug (see illustration) to pry up the front of the manifold, but make sure all bolts have been removed first! **Caution:** *Don't pry between the block and manifold or the heads and manifold or damage to the gasket sealing surfaces may occur, leading to vacuum and oil leaks.*

Installation

Refer to illustrations 6.14, 6.17, 6.20a and 6.20b

Note: *The mating surfaces of the cylinder heads, block and manifold must be perfectly clean when the manifold is installed. Gasket removal solvents in aerosol cans are available at most auto parts stores and may be helpful when removing old gasket material that's stuck to the heads and manifold*

(since the manifold and cylinder heads are made of aluminum, aggressive scraping can cause damage). Be sure to follow the directions printed on the container.

14   Use a gasket scraper to remove all traces of sealant and old gasket material, then clean the mating surfaces with lacquer thinner or acetone. If there's old sealant or oil on the mating surfaces when the manifold is installed, oil or vacuum leaks may develop. When working on the heads and block, cover the lifter valley with shop rags to keep debris out of the engine (see illustration). Use a vacuum cleaner to remove any gasket material that falls into the intake ports in the heads.

15   Use a tap of the correct size to chase the threads in the bolt holes, then use compressed air (if available) to remove the debris from the holes. **Warning:** *Wear safety glasses or a face shield to protect your eyes when using compressed air! Remove excessive carbon deposits and corrosion from the exhaust and coolant passages in the heads and manifold.*

16   Position the gaskets on the cylinder heads. The upper side of each gasket will have a TOP or THIS SIDE UP label stamped into it to ensure correct installation. **Note:** *Supercharged models use a special Graph-oil type intake gasket.*

17   Position the end seals on the block (see illustration), then apply a 1/8-inch wide bead of RTV sealant (Ford no. D7AZ-19B508-AA, or equivalent) to the four points where the end seals meet the heads.

18   Make sure all intake port openings, coolant passage holes and bolt holes are aligned correctly.

19   Carefully set the manifold in place while the sealant is still wet. **Caution:** *Don't disturb the gaskets and don't move the manifold fore-and-aft after it contacts the seals on the block. Make sure the end seals haven't been disturbed.*

20   Lightly oil the mounting bolts on non-supercharged models. On supercharged models, apply a light coating of pipe thread sealant with Teflon (Ford no. D8AZ-19554-A, or equivalent). Install the bolts and tighten them to the torque listed in this Chapter's Specifications, following the recommended sequence (see illustrations).

21   The remaining installation steps are the reverse of removal. Start the engine and check carefully for oil and coolant leaks at the intake manifold joints.

7   Exhaust manifolds – removal and installation

Warning: *Allow the engine to cool completely before beginning this procedure.*

Removal

Refer to illustrations 7.8, 7.10, 7.12a and 7.12b

1   Disconnect the negative battery cable from the battery.

2   Unplug the heated exhaust gas oxygen (HEGO) sensor wire, then label the spark plug wires and remove the spark plugs (see Chapter 1).

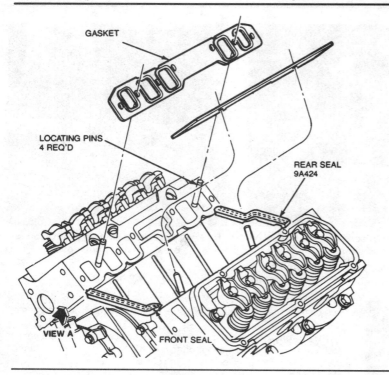

GASKET

LOCATING PINS
4 REQ'D

REAR SEAL
9A424

VIEW A

FRONT SEAL

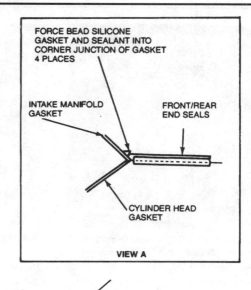

FORCE BEAD SILICONE
GASKET AND SEALANT INTO
CORNER JUNCTION OF GASKET
4 PLACES

INTAKE MANIFOLD
GASKET

FRONT/REAR
END SEALS

CYLINDER HEAD
GASKET

VIEW A

FRONT OF ENGINE

6.17 Gasket and end seal
details – exploded view

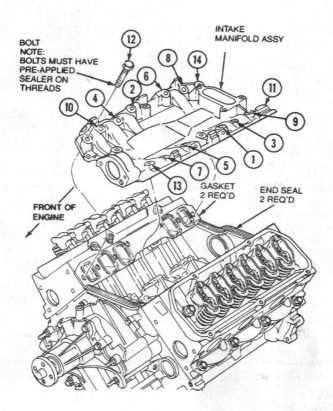

BOLT
NOTE:
BOLTS MUST HAVE
PRE-APPLIED
SEALER ON
THREADS

INTAKE
MANIFOLD ASSY

FRONT OF
ENGINE

GASKET
2 REQ'D

END SEAL
2 REQ'D

6.20a Supercharged engine intake manifold bolt
tightening sequence

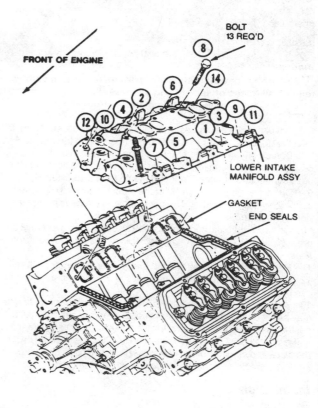

FRONT OF ENGINE

BOLT
13 REQ'D

LOWER INTAKE
MANIFOLD ASSY

GASKET

END SEALS

6.20b Non-supercharged engine intake manifold
bolt tightening sequence

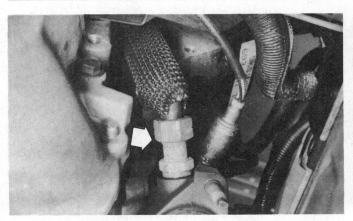

7.8 The EGR tube (arrow) connects to the lower end of the exhaust manifold

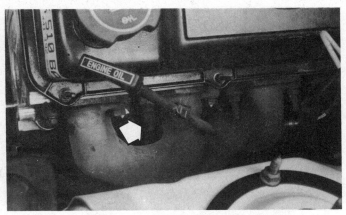

7.10 Detach the oil dipstick tube bracket (arrow)

3 Raise the vehicle and support it securely on jackstands.
4 Working under the vehicle, apply penetrating oil to the exhaust pipe-to-manifold studs and nuts (they're usually rusty).
5 Remove the nuts holding the exhaust crossover pipe to the manifold(s). In extreme cases you may have to heat them with a propane or acetylene torch in order to loosen them.

Passenger's (right) side manifold
6 Remove the air cleaner duct assembly (see Chapter 4).
7 On non-supercharged engines, disconnect the ignition secondary wire from the coil and distributor, then remove the outer heat shroud from the manifold, if equipped.
8 Disconnect the EGR tube **(see illustration)**.
9 Remove the automatic transmission dipstick tube (if equipped). Plug the hole to prevent the entry of dirt.

Driver's (left) side manifold
10 If it's in the way, remove the oil dipstick, tube and bracket **(see illustration)**.
11 On supercharged engines, remove the intercooler tubes (see Chapter 4) and oil cooler tube.

Both manifolds
12 Remove the mounting bolts, noting the locations of the stud bolts **(see illustrations)**. Separate the manifold from the head and lift it from the engine compartment.

Installation
13 Check the manifold for cracks and make sure the bolt threads are clean and undamaged. The manifold and cylinder head mating surfaces must be clean before the manifolds are reinstalled – use a gasket scraper to remove all carbon deposits and old gasket material.
14 If the manifold is being replaced, transfer the oxygen (HEGO) sensor to the new manifold (see Chapter 6).
15 Lightly oil the bolt threads. Position the manifold, gasket and inner heat shield (if equipped) on the head and install the mounting bolts. **Note:** *Exhaust manifold warpage is fairly common. Although some engines were built without gaskets, we recommend installing them. Install the pilot bolts first. On the left (driver's) side, this is the lower front bolt on the number five cylinder. On the right (passenger's) side, this is the lower rear bolt on the number two cylinder. Sometimes it's necessary to elongate the bolt holes in the manifolds to start the bolts – never file out the pilot bolt holes!*

2A

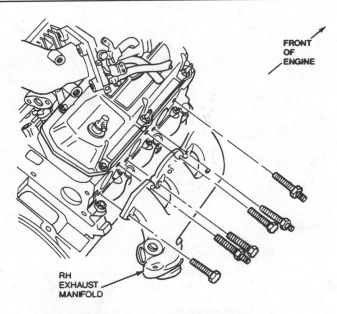

7.12a Exploded view of passenger's side exhaust manifold – typical

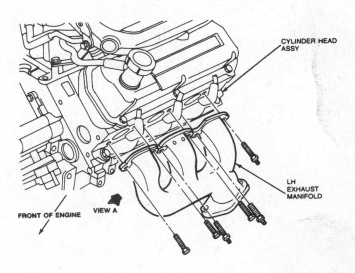

7.12b Exploded view of driver's side exhaust manifold – typical

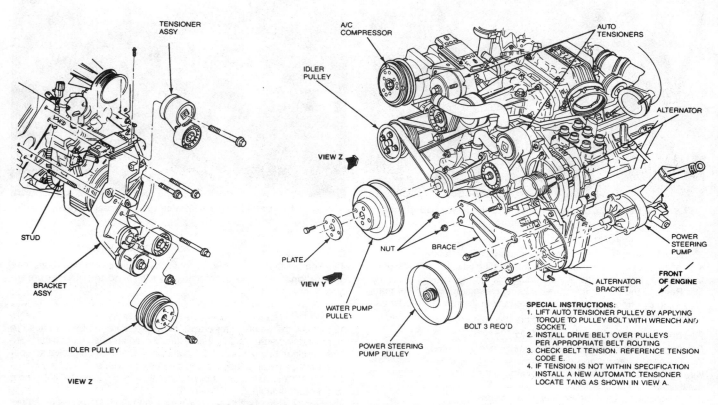

SPECIAL INSTRUCTIONS:
1. LIFT AUTO TENSIONER PULLEY BY APPLYING TORQUE TO PULLEY BOLT WITH WRENCH AND SOCKET.
2. INSTALL DRIVE BELT OVER PULLEYS PER APPROPRIATE BELT ROUTING
3. CHECK BELT TENSION. REFERENCE TENSION CODE E.
4. IF TENSION IS NOT WITHIN SPECIFICATION INSTALL A NEW AUTOMATIC TENSIONER LOCATE TANG AS SHOWN IN VIEW A.

8.8a Supercharged engine accessories – exploded view

3.8L EFI

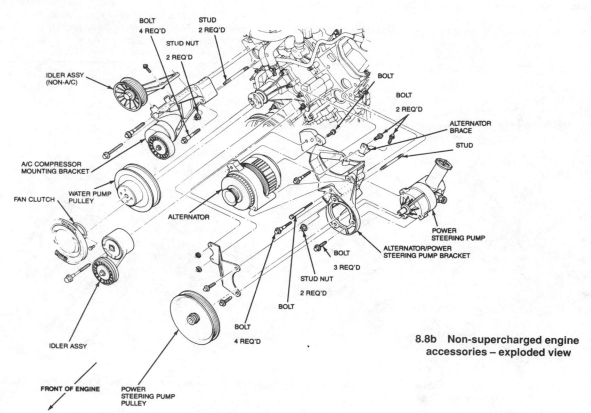

8.8b Non-supercharged engine accessories – exploded view

8.13   Using a casting protrusion, carefully lift the cylinder head to break the gasket seal

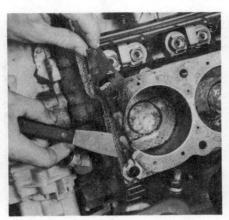

8.15   Scrape off every trace of old gasket material

8.17   Locating dowels (arrows) are used to position the gasket on the block – make sure the mark (circled) is correctly oriented

16   When tightening the mounting bolts, work from the center to the ends and be sure to use a torque wrench. Tighten the bolts in three equal steps until the torque listed in this Chapter's Specifications is reached.
17   The remaining installation steps are the reverse of removal.
18   Start the engine and check for exhaust leaks.

8   Cylinder heads – removal and installation

Caution: *The engine must be completely cool when the heads are removed. Failure to allow the engine to cool off could result in head warpage.*

Removal

Refer to illustration 8.8a, 8.8b and 8.13

1   Disconnect the negative cable from the battery. Remove the drivebelt and drain the cooling system (see Chapter 1).
2   Remove the valve cover(s) (see Section 3).
3   Remove the pushrods and rocker arms (see Section 4).
4   Remove the intake manifold (see Section 6).

Left (driver's side) cylinder head

5   Unbolt the power steering pump and tie it aside in an upright position. Leave the hoses connected (see Chapter 10).
6   Remove the exhaust manifold (see Section 7).
7   On supercharged models, remove the intercooler and intercooler tubes (see Chapter 4).
8   Disconnect the alternator wiring (see Chapter 5). Unbolt the alternator and power steering bracket from the engine **(see illustrations)**.
9   Proceed to Step 12.

Right (passenger's side) cylinder head

10   Unbolt the air conditioning compressor (if equipped) and position it out of the way (see Chapter 3). DO NOT disconnect the hoses!
11   Remove the exhaust manifold (see Section 7).

Both cylinder heads

12   Loosen the head bolts in 1/4-turn increments until they can be removed by hand. Work from bolt-to-bolt in a pattern that's the reverse of the tightening sequence. **Note:** *Head bolts should not be reused. Remove the bolts and discard them – NEW BOLTS MUST BE USED when installing the head(s).*
13   Lift the head(s) off the engine. If resistance is felt, DO NOT pry between the head and block as damage to the mating surfaces will result. To dislodge the head, place a prybar against a casting protrusion **(see illustration)**. Store the heads on blocks of wood to prevent damage to the gasket sealing surfaces.
14   Cylinder head disassembly and inspection procedures are covered in detail in Chapter 2, Part B.

8.20   Cylinder head bolt TIGHTENING sequence

Installation

Refer to illustrations 8.15, 8.17 and 8.20

15   The mating surfaces of the cylinder heads and block must be perfectly clean when the heads are installed. Use a gasket scraper to remove all traces of carbon and old gasket material **(see illustration)**, then clean the mating surfaces with lacquer thinner or acetone. If there's oil on the mating surfaces when the heads are installed, the gaskets may not seal correctly and leaks may develop. When working on the block, cover the lifter valley with shop rags to keep debris out of the engine. Use a vacuum cleaner to remove any debris that falls into the cylinders.
16   Check the block and head mating surfaces for nicks, deep scratches and other damage. If damage is slight, it can be removed with a file – if it's excessive, machining may be the only alternative.
17   Position the new gasket(s) over the dowel pins in the block. Make sure it's facing the right way **(see illustration)**.
18   Carefully position the head(s) on the block without disturbing the gasket(s).
19   Before installing the new head bolts, coat the threads of the four short bolts with pipe sealant (Ford part no. D8AZ-19554-A or equivalent). Lightly oil the threads of the remaining head bolts. **Caution:** *Head bolts are not interchangeable between supercharged and non-supercharged engines.*
20   Install the bolts and tighten them finger tight. Follow the recommended sequence **(see illustration)** and tighten the bolts in four steps to the torque listed in this Chapter's Specifications. After reaching the specified torque, loosen all of the head bolts two or three turns, then retighten

9.4   Make marks on the cap and housing (arrows)

9.6   Turn the crankshaft clockwise until the zero on the vibration damper scale is directly opposite the pointer

9.7   The rotor should be directly above the mark on the housing (arrows)

them (in two steps) in sequence to the specified final torque (and angle of rotation) listed in the Specifications.

21   The remaining installation steps are the reverse of removal.

22   Change the engine oil and filter and add coolant (see Chapter 1), then start the engine and check carefully for oil and coolant leaks.

Note: *When cylinder head bolts have been tightened using the above procedure, it isn't necessary to retighten them after extended operation, however, bolts may be checked for tightness if desired.*

---

9   Top Dead Center (TDC) for number one piston – locating

Refer to illustrations 9.4, 9.6 and 9.7

1   Top Dead Center (TDC) is the highest point in the cylinder that each piston reaches as it travels up-and-down when the crankshaft turns. Each piston reaches TDC on the compression stroke and again on the exhaust stroke, but TDC generally refers to piston position on the compression stroke. The timing marks on the vibration damper installed on the front of the crankshaft are referenced to the number one piston at TDC on the compression stroke.

2   Positioning the piston(s) at TDC is an essential part of many procedures such as rocker arm removal, valve adjustment, timing chain and sprocket replacement and distributor/synchronizer removal.

3   In order to bring any piston to TDC, the crankshaft must be turned using one of the methods outlined below. When looking at the front of the engine, normal crankshaft rotation is clockwise. **Warning:** *Before beginning this procedure, be sure to place the manual transmission in Neutral or the automatic in Park. On non-supercharged models, detach and ground the coil wire which goes to the center terminal of the distributor cap to disable the ignition system.*

  a) The preferred method is to turn the crankshaft with a large socket and breaker bar attached to the vibration damper bolt threaded into the front of the crankshaft.

  b) A remote starter switch, which may save some time, can also be used. Attach the switch leads to the S (switch) and B (battery) terminals on the starter motor. Once the piston is close to TDC, use a socket and breaker bar as described in the previous paragraph.

  c) If an assistant is available to turn the ignition switch to the Start position in short bursts, you can get the piston close to TDC without a remote starter switch. **Warning:** *Stay clear of the fan and drivebelt! Remove the ignition key before turning the crankshaft by hand. Use a socket and breaker bar as described in Paragraph a) to complete the procedure.*

Non-supercharged engines

4   Using a felt pen, make a mark on the distributor housing and cap directly below the number one spark plug wire terminal on the distributor cap **(see illustration)**. **Note:** *The terminal numbers may be marked on the spark plug wires near the distributor.*

5   Remove the hold-down screws and lift off the distributor cap, leaving the wires connected.

6   Turn the crankshaft (see Paragraph 3 above) until the zero mark on the vibration damper is aligned with the pointer **(see illustration)**. The pointer is located low on the front of the engine, near the pulley that turns the drivebelt.

7   The rotor should now be pointing directly at the mark on the distributor housing **(see illustration)**. If it is 180-degrees off, the piston is at TDC on the exhaust stroke.

8   If the rotor was 180-degrees off, turn the crankshaft one complete turn (360-degrees) clockwise. The rotor should now be pointing at the mark. When the rotor is pointing at the number one spark plug wire terminal in the distributor cap (which is indicated by the mark on the housing) and the ignition timing marks are aligned, the number one piston is at TDC on the compression stroke.

Supercharged engines

9   Have an assistant turn the crankshaft with a socket and ratchet as described in Step 3 above while you hold a finger over the number one spark plug hole.

10   When the piston approaches TDC, pressure will be felt at the spark plug hole. Have your assistant stop turning the crankshaft when the timing marks on the vibration damper are aligned **(see illustration 9.6)**.

11   If the timing marks are bypassed, turn the crankshaft two complete revolutions clockwise until the timing marks are properly aligned.

All engines

12   After the number one piston has been positioned at TDC on the compression stroke, TDC for any of the remaining cylinders can be located by turning the crankshaft clockwise in steps of 120-degrees and following the firing order (refer to the Specifications).

---

10   Timing chain cover – removal and installation

Removal

Refer to illustrations 10.4, 10.8a and 10.8b

1   Refer to Chapter 3 and remove the fan and water pump.

2   Drain the engine oil and remove the oil filter (see Chapter 1). On supercharged engines, remove the oil cooler.

3   Remove the crankshaft vibration damper (see Section 16).

4   Unbolt and remove all brackets attached to the timing chain cover **(see illustration)**. When unbolting the power steering pump, tie it aside with the hoses still connected. On air conditioned models, remove the compressor front support bracket, leaving the compressor in place.

5   Position the number one piston at TDC on the compression stroke (see Section 9), then remove the distributor or synchronizer and intermediate shaft as described in Chapter 5.

10.4 Remove the brackets (arrow)

10.8a Gently tap the timing cover loose with a soft-face hammer

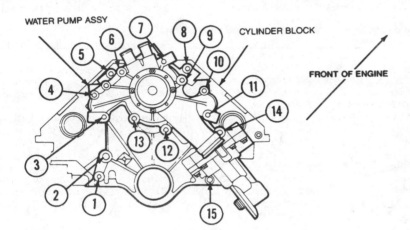

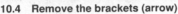

10.8b Timing chain cover and water pump fastener locations

FASTENER AND HOLE NO.	HOLE NO.		PART NAME
	WATER PUMP	FRONT COVER	
1.		4	STUD
2.		2	STUD
3.	2	9	STUD
4.	1	8	STUD
5.		10	BOLT
6.	9	15	BOLT
7.	8	16	BOLT
8.		11	BOLT
9.	7	17	STUD BOLT
10.	6	1	STUD BOLT
11.	5	7	STUD
12.*	4	13	BOLT
13.	3	14	BOLT
14.		6	BOLT
15.		5	CAP SCREW
3, 4, 10, 11	2, 1, 5	9, 8, 7	NUT

*EFI ENGINE IS A BOLT, SUPERCHARGED ENGINE IS A STUD

6　Remove the oil pan (see Section 14).

7　Unbolt the ignition timing indicator.

8　Remove all the fasteners **(see illustration)** and separate the timing chain cover from the block. If it's stuck, tap it gently with a soft-face hammer **(see illustration)**. **Caution:** *DO NOT use excessive force or you may crack the cover. If the cover is difficult to remove, double check to make sure all of the bolts are out. The bolt under the oil filter housing is easy to miss.*

Installation

Refer to illustration 10.16

9　Use a gasket scraper to remove all traces of old gasket material and sealant from the cover, oil pan and engine block, then clean them with lacquer thinner or acetone.

10　The oil pump is mounted in the timing chain cover. See Section 15 for oil pump information.

11　Lubricate the timing chain and crankshaft front oil seal lips with engine oil.

12　Apply a thin coat of RTV sealant to the block side of the new gasket, then position it on the engine. The dowel pins will hold it in place as the cover is installed.

13　Apply a thin coat of RTV sealant to the gasket surface of the cover and attach it to the engine. The dowel pins will position it correctly. Don't damage the seal and make sure the gasket remains in place.

14　Install the bolts finger tight. Tighten them to the torque listed in this Chapter's Specifications only after the water pump has been installed (some of the water pump bolts also hold the timing chain cover in place).

15　Install the oil pan (see Section 14).

16　Install the remaining parts in the reverse order of removal. On supercharged models, be sure to install the oil cooler as shown **(see illustration)**.

17　Add engine oil and coolant (see Chapter 1).

18　Run the engine, set the ignition timing (see Chapter 5) and check for leaks.

11　Timing chain and sprockets – inspection, removal and installation

Timing chain inspection

Refer to illustrations 11.4 and 11.8

Note: *The inspection procedure requires chain removal, therefore, if the chain has high mileage, it may be easier to replace it than to follow the factory inspection procedure.*

1　Disconnect the negative battery cable from the battery.

2　Refer to Section 9 and position the number one piston several degrees before TDC on the compression stroke.

3　Remove the right valve cover (see Section 3).

4　Remove the number three cylinder exhaust rocker arm bolt, rocker arm and fulcrum. It's the last one on the right (passenger's) side. Attach a dial indicator to the head with the plunger in-line with and resting on the pushrod **(see illustration)**.

5　Remove the timing chain cover (see Section 10).

6　Temporarily remove the timing chain and sprockets to remove the chain tensioner (see Removal and installation below).

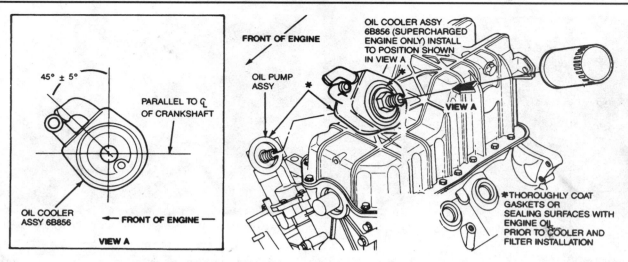

10.16   Install the oil cooler as shown (supercharged engine only)

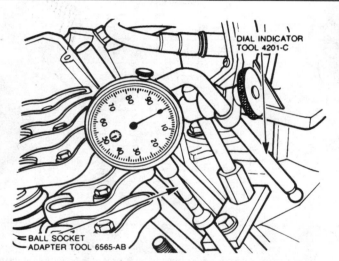

11.4   Dial indicator installed to measure timing chain deflection (a special cup-shaped adapter may be needed to keep the indicator plunger from sliding off the end of the pushrod)

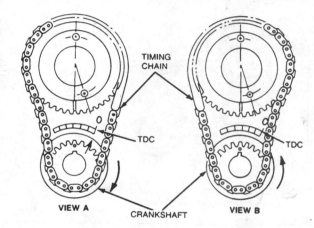

11.8   Timing chain deflection check

7   Temporarily reinstall the timing chain and sprockets without the tensioner and slip the timing chain cover and vibration damper in place to provide timing marks.

8   Turn the crankshaft clockwise until the number one piston is at TDC (see Section 9). This will take up the slack on the right side of the chain **(see illustration – view A).**

9   Zero the dial indicator.

10   Slowly turn the crankshaft counterclockwise until the slightest movement is seen on the dial indicator. Stop and note how far the number one piston has moved away from TDC by looking at the ignition timing marks (View B in illustration 11.8).

11   If the mark has moved more than 6-degrees, install a new timing chain and sprockets.

Removal and installation

Refer to illustrations 11.14, 11.16, 11.17, 11.18, 11.19, 11.21 and 11.25

Removal

12   Position the number one piston at TDC (see Section 9).

13   Remove the timing chain cover (see Section 10). Avoid turning the crankshaft during vibration damper removal.

14   Make sure the crankshaft and camshaft sprocket timing marks are aligned **(see illustration)**. If they aren't, install the vibration damper bolt and use it to turn the crankshaft with a wrench until the marks are aligned.

15   Remove the camshaft sprocket mounting bolt and distributor drive gear.

16   Pull the sprocket/chain off the camshaft **(see illustration)** and detach the chain from the crankshaft sprocket.

17   If you intend to remove the camshaft, slip the spacer off the camshaft **(see illustration)**.

18   Pry the chain tensioner back and insert a pin punch to cage the spring **(see illustration)**.

19   The crankshaft sprocket can be levered off with two large screwdrivers or a prybar **(see illustration)**.

Installation

20   Align the keyway in the crankshaft sprocket with the Woodruff key in the end of the crankshaft. Press the sprocket onto the crankshaft with the vibration damper bolt, a large socket and some washers or tap it gently into place until it's completely seated. **Caution:** *If resistance is encountered, DO NOT hammer the sprocket onto the shaft. It may eventually move into place, but it may be cracked in the process and fail later, causing extensive engine damage.*

21   Turn the crankshaft until the key is facing up (12 o'clock position) **(see illustration)**.

22   Reinstall the spacer on the camshaft, if removed.

23   Drape the chain over the camshaft sprocket and turn the sprocket until the timing mark faces down (six o'clock position). Mesh the chain with

11.14   Align the timing marks (arrows)

11.16   Pull the sprocket and chain off the camshaft

11.17   Slide the spacer off the camshaft, if you intend to remove the camshaft

2A

11.18   Push the spring in the chain tensioner back and insert a pin punch to hold it in place

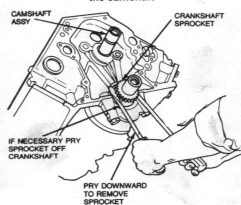

11.19   Pry the sprocket off the crankshaft

11.21   Position the crankshaft with the key facing UP (12 o'clock position)

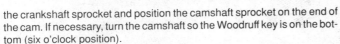

11.25   Align the keyway (arrow) on the distributor drive gear with the Woodruff key on the camshaft

12.3   Remove the retainer plate bolts (arrows)

the crankshaft sprocket and position the camshaft sprocket on the end of the cam. If necessary, turn the camshaft so the Woodruff key is on the bottom (six o'clock position).

24   When correctly installed, a straight vertical line should pass through the center of the camshaft, the camshaft timing mark (in the 6 o'clock position), the crankshaft timing mark (in the 12 o'clock position) and the center of the crankshaft **(see illustration 11.14)**. DO NOT proceed until the valve timing is correct!

25   Install the distributor drive gear **(see illustration)**

26   Apply Loc-Tite to the threads and install the camshaft sprocket bolt. Tighten the bolt to the torque listed in this Chapter's Specifications.

27   Remove the pin punch from the chain tensioner.

28   Reinstall the remaining parts in the reverse order of removal.

---

12   Valve lifters – removal, inspection and installation

Removal

Refer to illustrations 12.3, 12.4, 12.5a, 12.5b and 12.6

1   Remove the intake manifold (see Section 6).

2   Remove the rocker arms and pushrods (see Section 4).

3   Unbolt the retainer plates **(see illustration)**.

12.4   Remove the guide plates

12.5a   Stubborn lifters may be removed
with a special slide hammer puller

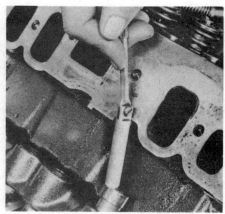

12.5b   You may be able to remove the
lifters with a magnet

4   Lift the guide plates off (see illustration).
5   There are several ways to extract the lifters from the bores. Special tools designed to grip and remove lifters (Ford tool no. T70L-6500-A or equivalent) are manufactured by many tool companies and are widely available (see illustration), but may not be needed in every case. On newer engines without a lot of varnish buildup, the lifters can often be removed with a small magnet (see illustration) or even with your fingers. A machinist's scribe with a bent end can be used to pull the lifters out by positioning the point under the retainer ring in the top of each lifter. Caution: Don't use pliers to remove the lifters unless you intend to replace them with new ones (along with the camshaft). The pliers may damage the precision machined and hardened lifters, rendering them useless. On engines with a lot of sludge and varnish, work the lifters up and down, using carburetor cleaner spray to loosen the deposits.
6   Before removing the lifters, arrange to store them in a clearly labelled box to ensure that they're reinstalled in their original locations. Remove the lifters and store them where they won't get dirty (see illustration).

Inspection

Refer to illustrations 12.8 and 12.9

7   Clean the lifters with solvent and dry them thoroughly without mixing them up.
8   Check each lifter wall and pushrod seat for scuffing, score marks and uneven wear. If the lifter walls are damaged or worn (which isn't very likely), inspect the lifter bores in the engine block as well. If the pushrod seats (see illustration) are worn, check the pushrod ends.
9   Check the rollers carefully for wear and damage and make sure they turn freely without excessive play (see illustration).
10   Used roller lifters can be reinstalled with a new camshaft and the original camshaft can be used if new lifters are installed.

Installation

11   The original lifters, if they're being reinstalled, must be returned to their original locations. Coat them with moly-base grease or engine assembly lube.
12   Install the lifters in the bores.
13   Install the guide plates and retainers.
14   Install the pushrods and rocker arms.
15   Install the intake manifold and valve covers.
16   If new lifters have been installed, check the valve clearances (see Section 4).

---

13   Camshaft and bearings – removal, inspection and installation

Camshaft lobe lift check

1   In order to determine the extent of cam lobe wear, the lobe lift should be checked prior to camshaft removal. Refer to Section 3 and remove the valve covers. The rocker arms must also be removed (see Section 4), but leave the pushrods in place.
2   Position the number one piston at TDC on the compression stroke (see Section 9).
3   Beginning with the number one cylinder, mount a dial indicator on the engine and position the plunger in-line with and resting on the first pushrod (see illustration 11.4).
4   Zero the dial indicator, then very slowly turn the crankshaft in the normal direction of rotation until the indicator needle stops and begins to move in the opposite direction. The point at which it stops indicates maximum cam lobe lift.

12.6   Store the lifters in a marked box
such as this to ensure they're reinstalled
in their original locations

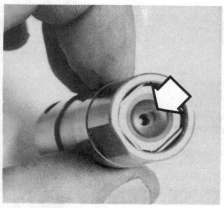

12.8   Check the pushrod seat (arrow) in
the top of each lifter for wear

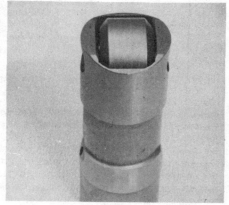

12.9   the roller must turn freely – check
for wear and excessive play as well

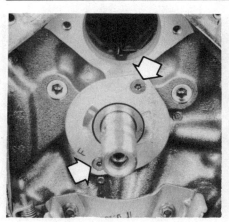

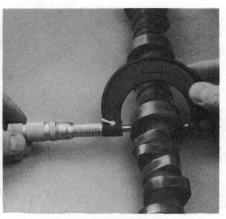

13.10   Remove the thrust plate bolts (arrows) with a Torx T-30 bit

13.12   Carefully guide the camshaft out of the block to avoid nicking the bearings with the lobes

13.14   The camshaft bearing journal diameters are checked to pinpoint excessive wear and out-of-round conditions

2A

Inspection

Refer to illustration 13.14

13   After the camshaft has been removed from the engine, cleaned with solvent and dried, inspect the bearing journals for uneven wear, pitting and evidence of seizure. If the journals are damaged, the bearing inserts in the block are probably damaged as well. Both the camshaft and bearings will have to be replaced. Replacement of the camshaft bearings requires special tools and techniques which place it beyond the scope of the home mechanic. The block will have to be removed from the vehicle and taken to an automotive machine shop for this procedure.

14   Measure the bearing journals with a micrometer to determine if they are excessively worn or out-of-round **(see illustration)**.

15   Check the camshaft lobes for heat discoloration, score marks, chipped areas, pitting and uneven wear. If the lobes are in good condition and if the lobe lift measurements are as specified, the camshaft can be reused.

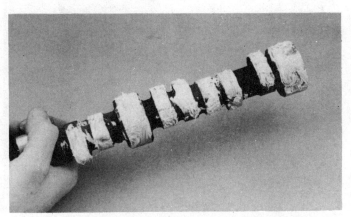

13.16   Apply moly-base grease or engine assembly lube to the camshaft lobes and journals prior to installation

Installation

Refer to illustration 13.16

16   Lubricate the camshaft bearing journals and cam lobes with moly-base grease or engine assembly lube **(see illustration)**.

17   Slide the camshaft into the engine. Support the cam near the block and be careful not to scrape or nick the bearings.

18   Turn the camshaft until the Woodruff key is in the six o'clock position.

19   Apply moly-base grease or engine assembly lube to both sides of the thrust plate, then position it on the block with the oil grooves facing in (against the block). Install the bolts and tighten them securely.

20   Refer to Section 11 and install the timing chain and sprockets.

21   Lubricate the lifters with clean engine oil and install them in the block. If the original lifters are being reinstalled, be sure to return them to their original locations.

22   The remaining installation steps are the reverse of removal. Refer to the appropriate Sections and install the lifters, pushrods, rocker arms, timing chain/sprocket, timing chain cover and valve covers.

23   Before starting and running the engine, change the oil and install a new oil filter (see Chapter 1).

5   Record this figure for future reference, then reposition the piston at TDC on the compression stroke.

6   Move the dial indicator to the remaining number one cylinder pushrod and repeat the check. Be sure to record the results for each valve.

7   Repeat the check for the remaining valves. Since each piston must be at TDC on the compression stroke for this procedure, work from cylinder-to-cylinder following the firing order sequence shown in this Chapter's Specifications.

8   After the check is complete, compare the results to this Chapter's Specifications. If camshaft lobe lift is less than that listed, cam lobe wear has occurred and a new camshaft should be installed.

Removal

Refer to illustrations 13.10 and 13.12

9   Refer to the appropriate Sections and remove the pushrods, the valve lifters and the timing chain and camshaft sprocket. The radiator should be removed as well (see Chapter 3). You also may have to remove the air conditioning condenser and the grille, but wait and see if the camshaft can be pulled out of the engine without these steps.

10   Remove the camshaft thrust plate bolts **(see illustration)**. A T-30 Torx bit is required for the bolts.

11   Check the camshaft thrust plate for visible wear. If it's grooved or otherwise worn, replace the thrust plate with a new one when the camshaft is reinstalled.

12   Partially install the cam sprocket bolt to use as a handle. Carefully pull the camshaft out. Support the cam so the lobes don't nick or gouge the bearings as it's withdrawn **(see illustration)**.

---

14   Oil pan – removal and installation

Removal

Refer to illustrations 14.9, 14.13, 14.14, 14.19 and 14.20

1   Disconnect the negative battery cable from the battery.

2   Remove the air cleaner duct assembly (see Chapter 4).

14.9   Unplug the oil level sensor (arrow)

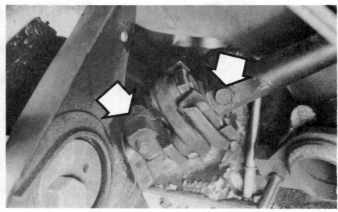

14.13   Remove the steering coupling bolts (arrows)

14.14   Remove the retaining strap (arrows)

14.19   Remove the oil pan bolts

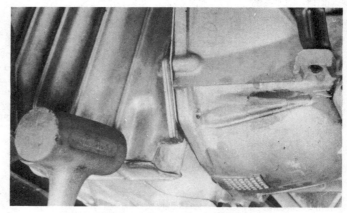

14.20   Use a mallet to break the oil pan loose

3   Remove the wiper arms and module (see Chapter 12).
4   Remove the weatherstrip and plastic covering from the cowl.
5   Remove the crankshaft position sensor shield, if equipped.
6   On supercharged models, remove the intercooler tubes (see Chapter 4).
7   Attach an engine support fixture (Ford no. D88L-6000-A or equivalent) to the engine lifting eyes adjacent to the exhaust manifolds. **Note:** *Many equipment rental yards have engine supports available.*
8   Raise the vehicle and support it securely on jackstands.
9   Remove the oil level dipstick and disconnect the oil level sensor on the side of the oil pan **(see illustration)**.
10   Drain the engine oil and remove the oil filter (see Chapter 1).
11   If you're working on a vehicle with an automatic transmission, disconnect the transmission cooler lines at the radiator (see Chapter 3).
12   Remove the starter motor (see Chapter 5), wire harness and ground strap.
13   Disconnect the steering flex coupling **(see illustration)**.
14   Remove the through bolts from the front engine mounts. Also remove the side mount retaining strap **(see illustration)**, if equipped.
15   Position a transmission jack or floor jack under the crossmember below the oil pan.
16   Remove the six bolts from the rear of the crossmember. Loosen the two bolts on the front of the crossmember.
17   Remove the shock absorber-to-control arm bolts and nuts (see Chapter 10).
18   Finish unbolting the crossmember and lower it.
19   Remove the oil pan mounting bolts **(see illustration)**, including the oil pan-to-bellhousing bolts.
20   Carefully separate the pan from the block. Don't pry between the block and pan or damage to the sealing surfaces may result and oil leaks

could develop. Instead, dislodge the pan with a large rubber mallet or a block of wood and a hammer **(see illustration)**.

Installation

Refer to illustration 14.23

21   Use a gasket scraper or putty knife to remove all traces of old gasket material and sealant from the pan and block. Be careful not to damage the delicate aluminum surfaces on the pan.
22   Clean the mating surfaces with lacquer thinner or acetone. Make sure the bolt holes in the block are clean.

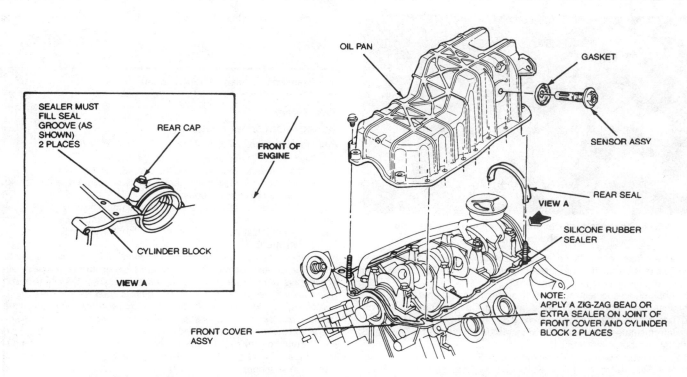

14.23 Apply sealant to the block inside of the bolt holes and in the grooves by the rear cap (View A)

15.3 After the filter is removed, the oil pump cover bolts are accessible (arrows)

15.7 The oil pressure relief valve plug is located inside the timing chain cover

23   Use RTV sealant to hold the new rear seal in place, then apply a bead of RTV sealant to the block (see illustration).

24   Carefully position the pan against the block and install the bolts finger tight. Make sure the gaskets haven't shifted, then tighten the bolts to the torque listed in this Chapter's Specifications. Start at the center of the pan and work out toward the ends in a spiral pattern.

25   The remaining steps are the reverse of removal. Caution: Don't forget to refill the engine with oil before starting it (see Chapter 1).

26   Start the engine and check carefully for oil leaks at the oil pan. Drive the vehicle and check again.

15   Oil pump – removal and installation

Refer to illustrations 15.3, 15.7 and 15.12

1   The oil pump is mounted externally on the timing chain cover.

2   Detach the oil filter (see Chapter 1). On supercharged models, re-move the oil cooler (see Section 10).

3   Remove the oil pump cover bolts (see illustration).

4   Detach the cover and gasket, then remove the gears from the cavity in the timing chain cover. Discard the gasket.

5   Clean and inspect the oil pump cavity. If the oil pump gear pocket in the timing chain cover is damaged or worn, replace the timing chain cover.

6   Remove all traces of gasket material from the oil pump cover, then check it for warpage with a straightedge and feeler gauges. If it's warped more than 0.0016-inch, replace it with a new one.

7   To remove the pressure relief valve, first detach the timing chain cover from the engine (see Section 10). Drill a hole in the plug (see illustration), then pry it out or remove it with a slide hammer and screw adapter. Re-move the spring and valve from the bore.

8   Remove all metal chips from the bore and the valve, then check them carefully for wear, score marks and galling. If the bore is worn or damaged, a new timing chain cover will be required. The valve should fit in the bore with no noticeable side play or binding.

15.12   To detach the pick-up tube, remove the nut and bolts (arrows)

9   If the spring appears to be fatigued or collapsed, replace it with a new one. The tension can be measured and compared to the Specifications in this Chapter to determine it's condition.

10   Apply clean engine oil to the valve and install it in the bore, small end first. Insert the spring, then install a new plug. Carefully tap it in until it's 0.010-inch below the machined surface of the cover.

11   Intermediate shaft removal and installation is covered in Chapter 5 with the distributor/synchronizer.

12   The oil pump pick-up is inside the oil pan. For access, remove the oil pan (see Section 14). Remove the pick-up tube nut and the two mounting bolts **(see illustration)**.

13   Installation is the reverse of removal. **Caution:** *Be sure to pack the oil pump with petroleum jelly before installing the cover. It must fill all voids between the gears, cavity and cover. If this isn't done, the pump may fail to prime when the engine is started.* Install a new cover gasket and tighten the bolts to the torque listed in this Chapter's Specifications in a criss-

cross pattern. Use a new pick-up tube gasket and tighten the mounting bolts securely.

16   Crankshaft oil seals – replacement

Front seal
Timing chain cover in place
Refer to illustrations 16.3, 16.4, 16.5, 16.6, 16.8 and 16.10

1   Disconnect the negative cable from the battery terminal.

2   Remove the fan assembly and the shroud (see Chapter 3).

3   Remove the drivebelt (see Chapter 1). Remove the upper and lower shields **(see illustration)**, if equipped.

4   Mark the crankshaft pulley and vibration damper so they can be reassembled in the same relative position. This is important, since the damper and pulley are initially balanced as a unit. Unbolt and remove the pulley **(see illustration)**.

5   Remove the bolt from the front of the crankshaft, then use a puller to detach the vibration damper **(see illustration)**. **Caution:** *Don't use a puller with jaws that grip the outer edge of the damper. The puller must be the type shown in the illustration that utilizes bolts to apply force to the damper hub only. Clean the crankshaft nose and the seal contact surface on the vibration damper with lacquer thinner or acetone. Leave the Woodruff key in place in the crankshaft keyway.*

6   Carefully pry the seal from the cover with a screwdriver or seal removal tool **(see illustration)**. Be careful not to damage the cover or scratch the wall of the seal bore.

7   Check the seal bore and crankshaft, as well as the seal contact surface on the vibration damper for nicks and burrs. **Note:** *If there's a groove worn in the balancer from contact with the seal, the new seal will probably leak also – a special sleeve can be installed over the balancer to cover this groove and prevent oil leaks.* Apply a small amount of oil to the lip of the new seal, then position it in the bore with the spring side of the seal facing

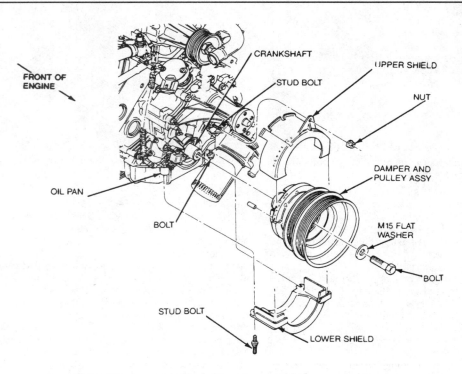

16.3   Crankshaft pulley/vibration damper components – exploded view

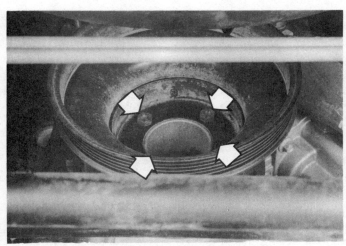

16.4   Mark the pulley and vibration damper before removing the four outer bolts (arrows) and detaching the pulley – the large center bolt is usually very tight, so use a six-point socket and breaker bar to loosen it

16.5   Use a bolt-type puller to remove the vibration damper – if a jaw-type puller is used, the damper will be damaged

IN. A small amount of oil applied to the outer edge of the new seal will make installation easier – don't overdo it!

8   Drive the seal into the bore with a large socket and hammer until it's completely seated **(see illustration)**. Select a socket that's the same outside diameter as the seal (a section of pipe can be used if a socket isn't available).

9   **Note:** *If a new vibration damper is being installed, balance pins must be located in the new damper in the same relative positions as the original. Also, the pulley must be attached to the damper with the same orientation to the pins as on the original. Apply moly-base grease or clean engine oil to the seal contact surface of the vibration damper and coat the keyway (groove) with a thin layer of RTV sealant.*

10   Install the damper on the end of the crankshaft. The keyway in the damper bore must be aligned with the Woodruff key in the crankshaft nose. If the damper can't be seated by hand, tap it into place with a soft-face hammer **(see illustration)** or slip a large washer over the bolt, install the bolt and tighten it to push the damper into place. Remove the large washer, then install the bolt and tighten it to the torque listed in this Chapter's Specifications.

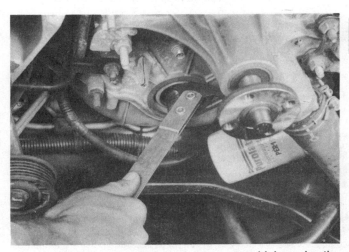

16.6   Carefully pry the seal from the cover – avoid damaging the cover or crankshaft

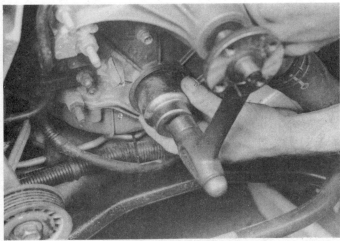

16.8   Clean the bore, apply a small amount of oil to the outer edge of the new seal and drive it squarely into the opening with a large socket and hammer – don't damage the seal in the process and make sure it's completely seated

16.10   A soft-face hammer can be used to tap the vibration damper onto the crankshaft – don't use a steel hammer!

16.17   If you're very careful not to damage the crankshaft or the seal bore, the rear seal can be pried out with a screwdriver – normally a special puller is used for this procedure

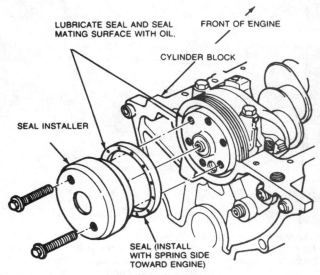

LUBRICATE SEAL AND SEAL MATING SURFACE WITH OIL.

FRONT OF ENGINE

CYLINDER BLOCK

SEAL INSTALLER

SEAL (INSTALL WITH SPRING SIDE TOWARD ENGINE)

NOTE: REAR FACE OF SEAL MUST BE WITHIN 0.127mm (0.005-INCH) OF THE REAR FACE OF THE BLOCK

16.19   Rear seal installation should be done with the special Ford tool to ensure that the seal isn't damaged

11   Install the remaining parts removed for access to the seal.
12   Start the engine and check for leaks at the seal-to-cover joint.

Timing chain cover removed

13   Use a punch or screwdriver and hammer to drive the seal out of the cover from the back side. Support the cover as close to the seal bore as possible. Be careful not to distort the cover or scratch the wall of the seal bore. If the engine has accumulated a lot of miles, apply penetrating oil to the seal-to-cover joint on each side and allow it to soak in before attempting to drive the seal out.
14   Clean the bore to remove any old seal material and corrosion. Support the cover on blocks of wood and position the new seal in the bore with the open end of the seal facing IN. A small amount of oil applied to the outer edge of the new seal will make installation easier – don't overdo it!
15   Drive the seal into the bore with a large socket and hammer until it's completely seated. Select a socket that's the same outside diameter as the seal (a section of pipe can be used if a socket isn't available).

Rear seal

Refer to illustrations 16.17 and 16.19
16   Refer to Chapter 7 and remove the transmission, then detach the flywheel/driveplate and the rear cover plate from the engine (see Section 17).
17   The old seal can be removed by prying it out with a screwdriver **(see illustration)**. Be sure to note how far it's recessed into the bore before removing it; the new seal will have to be recessed an equal amount. **Caution:** *Be very careful not to scratch or otherwise damage the crankshaft or the bore in the housing or oil leaks could develop!*
18   Clean the crankshaft and seal bore with lacquer thinner or acetone. Check the seal contact surface very carefully for scratches and nicks that could damage the new seal lip and cause oil leaks. If the crankshaft is damaged, the only alternative is a new or different crankshaft.
19   Make sure the bore is clean, then apply a thin coat of engine oil to the outer edge of the new seal. Apply moly-base grease to the seal lips. The seal must be pressed squarely into the bore, so hammering it into place is not recommended. If you don't have access to Ford tool no. T82L-6701-A **(see illustration)**, you may be able to tap the seal in with a large section of pipe and a hammer. If you must use this method, be very careful not to damage the seal or crankshaft, and carefully work the seal lip over the crankshaft with a blunt tool such as the rounded end of a socket extension.
20   Reinstall the engine rear cover plate, the flywheel/driveplate and the transmission.

17   Flywheel/driveplate – removal and installation

Refer to illustration 17.3
1   Refer to Chapter 7 and remove the transmission.
2   On manual transmission models, remove the pressure plate and clutch disc (see Chapter 8).
3   Remove the mounting bolts **(see illustration)**. On manual transmission models, jam a large screwdriver against the starter ring gear to keep the crankshaft from turning.
4   Pull straight back on the flywheel/driveplate to detach it from the crankshaft. Flywheels are fairly heavy, so be prepared to catch the weight. The rear cover plate can now be removed, if necessary.

17.3   On automatic transmission driveplates, insert a prybar through a hole to keep the crankshaft from turning when loosening/tightening the bolts

5   Inspect the rear oil seal and replace it if necessary (see Section 16).
6   Flywheels/driveplates must not be interchanged between super-charged and non-supercharged engines. If a driveplate with balance rivets must be replaced, install new balance pins/rivets in the same locations as the original.
7   Installation is the reverse of removal. The driveplate must be mounted with the torque converter pads facing the transmission. Note that the bolt holes are staggered so the driveplate can only fit one way and have the holes align. Use Ford sealant with Teflon (D8AZ-19554-A) or equivalent on the bolt threads and tighten them to the torque listed in this Chapter's Specifications in a criss-cross pattern.

18   Engine mounts – check and replacement

Refer to illustration 18.8

1   Engine mounts seldom require attention, but broken or deteriorated mounts should be replaced immediately or the added strain placed on the driveline components may cause damage.

Check

2   During the check, the engine must be raised slightly to remove the weight from the mounts. Disconnect the negative battery cable from the battery.
3   Raise the vehicle and support it securely on jackstands, then position the jack under the engine oil pan. Place a large block of wood between the jack head and the oil pan, then carefully raise the engine just enough to take the weight off the mounts.
4   Check the mounts to see if the rubber is cracked, hardened or separated from the metal plates. Sometimes the rubber will split right down the center. Rubber preservative may be applied to the mounts to slow deterioration.
5   Check for relative movement between the mount plates and the engine or frame (use a large screwdriver or prybar to attempt to move the mounts). If movement is noted, lower the engine and tighten the mount fasteners.

Replacement

6   On non-supercharged models, remove the fan shroud mounting screws and pull up on it, disengaging the shroud from the lower clips.
7   Detach the air cleaner duct.
8   Remove the engine mount through bolts **(see illustration)** and retaining strap bolt, when equipped.
9   Disconnect the shift linkage where it connects the transmission to the body (see Chapter 7).
10   Remove the accessories and oil cooler line retaining clips from the engine mount brackets.
11   Raise the engine high enough to clear the brackets. Do not force the engine up too high. If it touches anything before the mounts are free, remove the part for clearance. Temporarily place a block of wood between the oil pan and subframe as a safety precaution. **Note:** *Left (driver's) side engine mount removal may require lowering the crossmember (see Section 14).*

2A

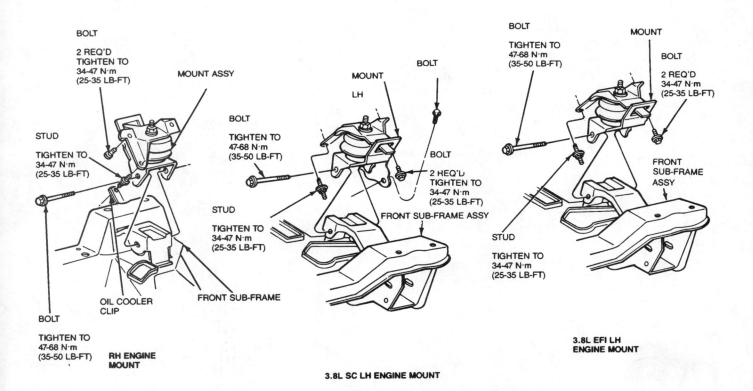

18.8   Engine mounts – exploded view

12   Unbolt the mounting bracket from the engine block and remove it from the vehicle. **Note:** *On vehicles equipped with self-locking nuts and bolts, replace them with new ones whenever they are disassembled. Prior to assembly, remove hardened residual adhesive from the engine block holes with an appropriate size bottoming tap.*

13   If a new mount is being installed, remove the nut and bracket from the mount and transfer them to the new mount. Remove the two bolts from the underside and transfer the bracket to the new mount.

14   Attach the new mount to the engine block and install the bolts and studs in the appropriate locations. Tighten the fasteners securely.

15   Lower the engine into place. Install the through bolts and tighten the nuts securely.

16   Complete the installation by reinstalling all parts removed to gain access to the mounts.

Chapter 2 Part B
General engine overhaul procedures

Contents

2B

Specifications

General

Displacement	3.8 liters (231 cu in)
Compression pressure	101 psi min (see accompanying chart)
Firing order	1-4-2-5-3-6
Bore	3.81 in. (96.8 mm)
Stroke	3.39 in. (86.0 mm)
Oil pressure (engine warm at 2500 rpm)	40 to 60 psi

Maximum PSI	Minimum PSI	Maximum PSI	Minimum PSI	Maximum PSI	Minimum PSI	Maximum PSI	Minimum PSI
134	101	164	123	194	145	224	168
136	102	166	124	196	147	226	169
138	104	168	126	198	148	228	171
140	105	170	127	200	150	230	172
142	107	172	129	202	151	232	174
144	108	174	131	204	153	234	175
146	110	176	132	206	154	236	177
148	111	178	133	208	156	238	178
150	113	180	135	210	157	240	180
152	114	182	136	212	158	242	181
154	115	184	138	214	160	244	183
156	117	186	140	216	162	246	184
158	118	188	141	218	163	248	186
160	120	190	142	220	165	250	187
162	121	192	144	222	166		

Cylinder compression variation chart – locate your maximum compression reading on the chart and look to the right to find the minimum acceptable compression (then compare it to your lowest reading)

Cylinder head and valve train

Head warpage limit	0.007 in
Minimum valve margin width	1/32 in
Intake valve	
Seat width	0.060 to 0.080 in
Seat angle	44.5-degrees
Seat runout limit	0.003 in (total indicator reading)
Stem diameter	0.3423 to 0.3415 in
Stem-to-guide clearance	0.001 to 0.0028 in
Valve face runout limit	0.002 in
Valve face angle	45.8-degrees
Exhaust valve	
Seat width	0.060 to 0.080 in
Seat runout limit	0.003 in (total indicator reading)
Seat angle	44.5-degrees
Stem diameter	0.3418 to 0.3410 in
Stem-to-guide clearance	0.0015 to 0.0033 in
Valve face runout limit	0.002 in
Valve face angle	45.8-degrees
Valve spring	
Pressure (not including damper)	
Valve open	220 lbs at 1.18 in
Valve closed	85 lbs at 1.65 in
Free length	Not available
Valve lifter	
Diameter (standard)	0.8740 to 0.8745 in
Lifter-to-bore clearance	
Standard	0.0007 to 0.0027 in
Service limit	0.005 in

Crankshaft and connecting rods

Connecting rod journal	
Diameter	2.3103 to 2.3111 in
Out-of-round limit	0.0003 in
Taper limit	0.0003 in per in
Bearing oil clearance	
Desired	0.001 to 0.0014 in
Allowable	0.00086 to 0.0027 in
Connecting rod side clearance (endplay)	
Standard	0.0047 to 0.0114 in
Service limit	0.014 in
Main journal	
Diameter*	
Non-supercharged engines (all journals)	2.5190 to 2.5198 in
1989 supercharged engines	
Journals 1, 2, and 3	2.5194 to 2.5186 in
Journal 4	2.5100 to 2.5092 in
1990 supercharged engines	
Journals 1, 2, and 3	2.5190 to 2.5198 in
Journal number 4	2.5104 to 2.5096 in
Out of round limit	0.0003 in
Taper limit	0.0003 in per in
Main bearing oil clearance	
Non-supercharged engines (all journals)	
Desired	0.001 to 0.0014 in
Allowable	0.0005 to 0.0023 in
1989 supercharged engines	
Journals 1, 2, and 3	0.0009 to 0.0026 in
Journal 4	0.0014 to 0.0032 in
1990 supercharged engines	
Journals 1, 2 and 3	0.0005 to 0.0023 in
Journal 4	0.0010 to 0.0028 in
Crankshaft endplay	0.004 to 0.008 in

*Note: *The crankshaft journals can't be machined more than 0.010 inch under the standard dimension. The rear journal on the crankshafts of super-charged engines can't be refinished at all, because it is already 0.010 inch undersize.*

Cylinder bore

Diameter	3.810 in
Out-of-round limit	0.001 in
Taper limit	0.002 in

Pistons and rings

Piston diameter

Coded red	3.8095 to 3.8101 in
Coded blue	3.8107 to 3.8113 in
Coded yellow	3.8119 to 3.8125 in

Piston-to-bore clearance limit

Non-supercharged engines	0.0014 to 0.0032 in
Supercharged engines	0.0040 to 0.0045 in

Piston ring end gap

Top compression ring	0.011 to 0.012 in
Bottom compression ring	0.009 to 0.020 in
Oil ring	0.015 to 0.0583 in
Piston ring side clearance	0.0016 to 0.0034 in

Torque specifications*

	Ft-lbs
Main bearing cap bolts	65 to 81
Connecting rod cap nuts	31 to 36

1 General information

Included in this portion of Chapter 2 are the general overhaul procedures for the cylinder heads and internal engine components.

The information ranges from advice concerning preparation for an overhaul and the purchase of replacement parts to detailed, step-by-step procedures covering removal and installation of internal engine components and the inspection of parts.

The following procedures have been written based on the assumption that the engine has been removed from the vehicle. For information concerning in-vehicle engine repair, as well as removal and installation of the external components necessary for the overhaul, see Part A of this Chapter and Section 7 of this Part.

The Specifications included here in Part B are only those necessary for the inspection and overhaul procedures which follow. Refer to Part A for additional Specifications.

2 Compression check

Refer to illustration 2.4

1 A compression check will tell you what mechanical condition the upper end (pistons, rings, valves, head gaskets) of your engine is in. Specifically, it can tell you if the compression is down due to leakage caused by worn piston rings, defective valves and seats or a blown head gasket. **Note:** *The engine must be at normal operating temperature and the battery must be fully charged for this check.*

2 Begin by cleaning the area around the spark plugs before you remove them (compressed air should be used, if available, otherwise a small brush or even a bicycle tire pump will work). The idea is to prevent dirt from getting into the cylinders as the compression check is being done. Remove all of the spark plugs from the engine (see Chapter 1).

3 Block the throttle wide open. On supercharged models, unplug the electrical connector from the ignition coil. On non-supercharged models, unplug the coil-to-distributor wire at the distributor and ground it.

4 With the compression gauge in the number one spark plug hole **(see illustration)**, depress the accelerator pedal all the way to the floor to open the throttle valve. Crank the engine over at least four compression strokes and watch the gauge. The compression should build up quickly in a healthy engine. Low compression on the first stroke, followed by gradually increasing pressure on successive strokes, indicates worn piston rings. A low compression reading on the first stroke, which doesn't build up during successive strokes, indicates leaking valves or a blown head gasket (a cracked head could also be the cause). Record the highest gauge reading obtained.

5 Repeat the procedure for the remaining cylinders and compare the results to this Chapter's Specifications.

2.4 A gauge with a threaded fitting for the spark plug hole is preferred over the type that requires hand pressure to maintain the seal during the compression check

6 If any of the reading are low, add some engine oil (about three squirts from a plunger-type oil can) to each cylinder, through the spark plug hole, and repeat the test.

7 If the compression increases after the oil is added, the piston rings are definitely worn. If the compression doesn't increase significantly, the leakage is occurring at the valves or head gasket. Leakage past the valves may be caused by burned valve seats and/or faces or warped, cracked or bent valves.

8 If two adjacent cylinders have equally low compression, there's a strong possibility that the head gasket between them is blown. The appearance of coolant in the combustion chambers or the crankcase would verify this condition.

9 If the compression is unusually high, the combustion chambers are probably coated with carbon deposits. If that's the case, the cylinder heads should be removed and decarbonized.

10 If compression is way down or varies greatly between cylinders, it would be a good idea to have a leak-down test performed by an automotive repair shop. This test will pinpoint exactly where the leakage is occurring and how severe it is.

3 Engine overhaul – general information

Refer to illustration 3.4

It's not always easy to determine when, or if, an engine should be completely overhauled, as a number of factors must be considered.

2B

3.4 Remove the oil pressure sender and install the oil pressure gauge (the sender is located near the alternator) – make sure the thread pitch is exactly the same on the tool fitting as the switch

High mileage is not necessarily an indication that an overhaul is needed, while low mileage doesn't preclude the need for an overhaul. Frequency of servicing is probably the most important consideration. An engine that's had regular and frequent oil and filter changes, as well as other required maintenance, will most likely give many thousands of miles of reliable service. Conversely, a neglected engine may require an overhaul very early in its life.

Excessive oil consumption is an indication that piston rings, valve seals and/or valve guides are in need of attention. Make sure that oil leaks aren't responsible before deciding that the rings and/or guides are bad. Have a cylinder compression or leakdown test performed by an experienced tune-up mechanic to determine the extent of the work required.

If the engine is making obvious knocking or rumbling noises, the connecting rod and/or main bearings may be at fault. Check the oil pressure with a gauge installed in place of the oil pressure sending unit or switch **(see illustration)** and compare it to this Chapter's Specifications. If it's extremely low, the bearings and/or oil pump are probably worn out.

Loss of power, rough running, excessive valve train noise and high fuel consumption rates may also point to the need for an overhaul, especially if they're all present at the same time. If a complete tune-up doesn't remedy the situation, major mechanical work is the only solution.

An engine overhaul involves restoring the internal parts to the specifications of a new engine. During an overhaul, the piston rings are replaced and the cylinder walls are reconditioned (rebored and/or honed). If a rebore is done, new pistons are required. The main bearings, connecting rod bearings and camshaft bearings are generally replaced with new ones and, if necessary, the crankshaft may be reground to restore the journals. Generally, the valves are serviced as well, since they're usually in less-than-perfect condition at this point. While the engine is being overhauled, other components, such as the distributor or synchronizer, starter and alternator, can be rebuilt as well. The end result should be like a new engine that will give many trouble free miles. **Note:** *Critical cooling system components such as the hoses, drivebelts, thermostat and water pump MUST be replaced with new parts when an engine is overhauled. The radiator should be checked carefully to ensure that it isn't clogged or leaking; if in doubt, replace it with a new one.*

Before beginning the engine overhaul, read through the entire procedure to familiarize yourself with the scope and requirements of the job. Overhauling an engine isn't difficult, but it is time consuming. Plan on the vehicle being tied up for a minimum of two weeks, especially if parts must be taken to an automotive machine shop for repair or reconditioning. Check on availability of parts and make sure that any necessary special tools and equipment are obtained in advance. Most work can be done with typical hand tools, although a number of precision measuring tools are required for inspecting parts to determine if they must be replaced. Often an automotive machine shop will handle the inspection of parts and offer ad-

vice concerning reconditioning and replacement. **Note:** *Always wait until the engine has been completely disassembled and all components, especially the engine block, have been inspected before deciding what service and repair operations must be performed by an automotive machine shop. Since the block's condition will be the major factor to consider when determining whether to overhaul the original engine or buy a rebuilt one, never purchase parts or have machine work done on other components until the block has been thoroughly inspected. As a general rule, time is the primary cost of an overhaul, so it doesn't pay to install worn or substandard parts.*

As a final note, to ensure maximum life and minimum trouble from a rebuilt engine, everything must be assembled with care in a spotlessly clean environment.

4   Engine rebuilding alternatives

The do-it-yourselfer is faced with a number of options when performing an engine overhaul. The decision to replace the engine block, piston/connecting rod assemblies and crankshaft depends on a number of factors, with the number one consideration being the condition of the block. Other considerations are cost, access to machine shop facilities, parts availability, time required to complete the project and the extent of prior mechanical experience on the part of the do-it-yourselfer.

Some of the rebuilding alternatives include:

Individual parts – If the inspection procedures reveal that the engine block and most engine components are in reusable condition, purchasing individual parts may be the most economical alternative. The block, crankshaft and piston/connecting rod assemblies should all be inspected carefully. Even if the block shows little wear, the cylinder bores should be surface honed.

Crankshaft kit – This rebuild package consists of a reground crankshaft and a matched set of pistons and connecting rods. The pistons will already be installed on the connecting rods. Piston rings and the necessary bearings will be included in the kit. These kits are commonly available for standard cylinder bores, as well as for engine blocks which have been bored to a regular oversize.

Short block – A short block consists of an engine block with a crankshaft and piston/connecting rod assemblies already installed. All new bearings are incorporated and all clearances will be correct. The existing camshaft, valve train components, cylinder head(s) and external parts can be bolted to the short block with little or no machine shop work necessary.

Long block – A long block consists of a short block plus an oil pump, oil pan, cylinder heads, valve covers, camshaft and valve train components, timing sprockets and chain and timing cover. All components are installed with new bearings, seals and gaskets incorporated throughout. The installation of manifolds and external parts is all that's necessary.

Give careful thought to which alternative is best for you and discuss the situation with local automotive machine shops, auto parts dealers and experienced rebuilders before ordering or purchasing replacement parts.

5   Engine removal – methods and precautions

If you've decided that the engine must be removed for overhaul or major repair work, several preliminary steps should be taken.

Locating a place to work is extremely important. Adequate work space, along with storage space for the vehicle, will be needed. If a shop or garage isn't available, at the very least a flat, level, clean work surface made of concrete or asphalt is required.

Cleaning the engine compartment and engine before beginning the removal procedure will help keep tools clean and organized.

An engine hoist or A-frame will also be necessary. Make sure the equipment is rated in excess of the combined weight of the engine and accessories. Safety is of primary importance, considering the potential hazards involved in lifting the engine out of the vehicle.

If the engine is being removed by a novice, a helper should be available. Advice and aid from someone more experienced would also be helpful. There are many instances when one person cannot simultaneously

6.21 Make sure the chain is securely attached to the engine and watch that it doesn't catch on any accessories when the engine is raised

6.22 Raise the engine and check for any wires or hoses that may still need to be disconnected

perform all of the operations required when lifting the engine out of the vehicle.

Plan the operation ahead of time. Arrange for or obtain all of the tools and equipment you'll need prior to beginning the job. Some of the equipment necessary to perform engine removal and installation safely and with relative ease are (in addition to an engine hoist) a heavy duty floor jack, complete sets of wrenches and sockets as described at the front of this manual, wood blocks and plenty of rags and cleaning solvent for mopping up spilled oil, coolant and gasoline. If the hoist must be rented, make sure you arrange for it in advance and perform all of the operations possible without it ahead of time. This will save you money and time.

Plan for the vehicle to be out of use for quite a while. A machine shop will be required to perform some of the work the do-it-yourselfer can't accomplish without special equipment. They often have a busy schedule, so it would be a good idea to consult them before removing the engine in order to accurately estimate the amount of time required to rebuild or repair components that may need work.

Always be extremely careful when removing and installing the engine. Serious injury can result from careless actions. Plan ahead, take your time and a job of this nature, although major, can be accomplished successfully.

6   Engine – removal and installation

Refer to illustrations 6.21, 6.22 and 6.24
Warning: *DO NOT place any part of your body under the engine when it's supported by a hoist or other lifting device. Hoist failure could result in severe injury or death! Sudden discharge of the air conditioning system can cause severe injuries, especially to the eyes. Have a service station or air conditioning shop discharge the system prior to disconnecting any A/C system components.*

Removal

1   Disconnect the negative battery cable from the battery.
2   Place fender covers over the fenders and cowl and remove the hood (see Chapter 11).
3   Remove the air cleaner and throttle body assembly (see Chapter 4).
4   Drain the cooling system and engine oil and remove the oil filter (see Chapter 1).
5   Relieve the fuel pressure from the fuel injection system and disconnect the fuel lines connecting the engine to the chassis (see Chapter 4). Plug or cap all open lines and fittings.

6   Disconnect all coolant hoses which connect the engine to the vehicle.
7   Remove the cooling fan, shroud and radiator (see Chapter 3). On models equipped with a supercharger, remove the intercooler and associated lines and the Supercharger (see Chapter 4).
8   Remove the drivebelts (see Chapter 1).
9   Label the vacuum lines, emission hoses, electrical connectors, ground straps and fuel lines to ensure correct reinstallation. Pieces of masking tape with numbers written on them work well.
10   Carefully disconnect the vacuum lines, emission hoses, fuel lines, ground straps and electrical connectors attached to the engine. Refer to Chapters 4, 5 and 6 as needed. **Note:** *Disconnect the ground wire assembly and coil wire assembly except on supercharged models. Disconnect the DIS module wiring on supercharged models.*
11   Disconnect the accelerator cable and TV linkage from the throttle body (see Chapter 4) and tie it out of the way.
12   On air conditioned equipped vehicles, unbolt the compressor from the bracket (see Chapter 3) and set it aside without disconnecting the hoses.
13   On power steering equipped vehicles, unbolt the power steering pump from the bracket and set it aside without disconnecting the hoses (except supercharged engines). Make sure it stays upright.
14   Remove the starter motor (see Chapter 5). On non-supercharged models, disconnect the alternator to voltage regulator wiring. On supercharged models remove the alternator (see Chapter 5).
15   Unbolt the exhaust system from the exhaust manifolds (see Chapter 4).
16   On automatic transmission equipped models, disconnect the cooler lines from the inlet and outlet tubes, then remove the converter housing inspection cover. Remove the torque converter-to-driveplate fasteners and push the converter back slightly toward the transmission, using only light pressure (don't use excessive force).
17   Remove the bellhousing-to-engine block bolts.
18   Remove the through bolts from the engine mounts (see Chapter 2A).
19   Recheck to be sure nothing is still connecting the engine to the vehicle. Disconnect anything still remaining.
20   Lower the vehicle and then support the transmission with a floor jack. Place a block of wood between them to prevent damage.
21   Attach an engine lifting sling or chain to the lifting brackets on the engine. Position a hoist and connect the sling or chain to it. Take up the slack until there's slight tension on the hoist **(see illustration)**.
22   Raise the engine slightly and carefully pull it away from the transmission. Slowly raise the engine out of the engine compartment. Avoid snagging or bending anything as you lift the engine out **(see illustration)**.
23   Place the engine on a strong workbench or remove the flywheel/driveplate and mount the engine on an engine stand.

6.24 Support the transmission after engine removal by slipping a pipe through the frame holes and threading two bolts into the transmission (arrows)

8.3   Use a valve spring compressor to compress the spring, then remove the keepers from the valve stem

24   Following engine removal, place a pipe across the frame and support the transmission with bolts **(see illustration)**.

Installation

25   Reposition the floor jack under the transmission and remove the support.
26   Carefully lower the engine into the engine compartment, ensuring that the exhaust system lines up.
27   On automatic transmission equipped models, guide the torque converter pilot into the crankshaft, following the procedure outlined in Chapter 7.
28   On manual transmission equipped models, use a clutch alignment tool to install the pressure plate (see Chapter 7), then guide the transmission shaft into the crankshaft pilot bearing until it slips in all the way (the bellhousing must be flush with the engine block).
29   Install the bellhousing bolts and tighten them securely. **Caution:** *DO NOT use the bolts to force the transmission and engine into alignment! You may crack or damage major components.*
30   Reinstall the remaining components and fasteners in the reverse order of removal. **Note:** *Refer to Chapter 4 when installing the supercharger, intercooler and associated components.*
31   Add coolant, oil, power steering and transmission fluids as needed.
32   Run the engine and check for proper operation and leaks. Correct as needed.

---

7   Engine overhaul – disassembly sequence

---

1   It's much easier to disassemble and work on the engine if it's mounted on a portable engine stand. A stand can often be rented quite cheaply from an equipment rental yard. Before the engine is mounted on a stand, the flywheel/driveplate should be removed from the crankshaft.
2   If a stand isn't available, it's possible to disassemble the engine with it blocked up on a sturdy workbench or on the floor. Be extra careful not to tip or drop the engine when working without a stand.
3   If you're going to buy a rebuilt engine, all external components must come off first, to be transferred to the replacement engine, just as they will if you're doing a complete engine overhaul yourself. They include:

Alternator and brackets
Air conditioning compressor and brackets
Power steering pump and brackets
Emissions control components
Distributor or synchronizer, spark plug wires and spark plugs
Thermostat and housing cover

Water pump
Supercharger (if equipped)
Intake/exhaust manifolds and related components
EFI components
Oil filter
Engine mounts
Clutch and flywheel or driveplate

Note: *When removing the external components from the engine, pay close attention to details that may be helpful or important during reassembly. Note the installed position of gaskets, seals, spacers, pins, washers, bolts and other small items.*

4   If you're installing a short block, which consists of the engine block, crankshaft, pistons and connecting rods all assembled, then the cylinder heads, oil pan and oil pump will have to be removed as well. See Engine rebuilding alternatives for additional information regarding the different possibilities to be considered.
5   If you're planning a complete overhaul, the engine must be disassembled and the internal components removed in the following general order:

Clutch and flywheel or driveplate
Valve covers
Intake and exhaust manifolds
Rocker arms and pushrods
Valve lifters
Cylinder heads
Timing chain cover and oil pump
Timing chain and sprockets
Camshaft
Oil pan
Piston/connecting rod assemblies
Crankshaft and main bearings

6   Critical cooling system components such as the hoses, drivebelts, thermostat and water pump MUST be replaced with new parts when an engine is overhauled.
7   Before beginning the disassembly and overhaul procedures, make sure the following items are available:

Common hand tools
Small cardboard boxes or plastic bags for storing parts
Gasket scraper
Ridge reamer
Vibration damper puller
Micrometers
Telescoping gauges

8.4 If the valve won't pull through the guide, deburr the edge of the stem end and the area around the top of the keeper groove with a file or whetstone

8.5 A small plastic bag, with an appropriate label, can be used to store the valve train components so they can be kept together and reinstalled in the original location

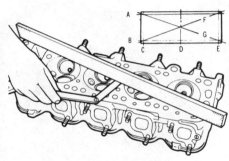

9.12 Check the cylinder head gasket surface for warpage by trying to slip a feeler gauge under the straightedge (see this Chapter's Specifications for the maximum warpage allowed and use a feeler gauge of that thickness)

Dial indicator set
Valve spring compressor
Cylinder surfacing hone
Piston ring groove cleaning tool
Electric drill motor
Tap and die set
Wire brushes
Oil gallery brushes
Cleaning solvent

8   Cylinder head – disassembly

Refer to illustrations 8.3, 8.4 and 8.5

Note: *New and rebuilt cylinder heads are commonly available for most engines at dealerships and auto parts stores. Due to the fact that some specialized tools are necessary for the disassembly and inspection procedures, and replacement parts may not be readily available, it may be more practical and economical for the home mechanic to purchase replacement heads rather than taking the time to disassemble, inspect and recondition the originals.*

1   Remove the rocker arms (see Part A).
2   Remove the deposits from the combustion chambers and valve heads with a scraper and a wire brush before removing the valves. **Caution:** *Be careful not to scratch the gasket surfaces.*
3   Compress the valve springs with a valve spring compressor. Remove the keepers and release the springs **(see illustration)**.
4   Remove the retainer (or rotator), spring assembly and seal from the valve. The valve can now be removed through the bottom of the head. If the valve binds in the guide (will not pull through), push it back into the head and deburr the area around the end of the stem with a fine file or whetstone **(see illustration)**.
5   Repeat the procedure for the remaining valves. Remember to keep all the parts for each valve together so they can be reinstalled in the same locations **(see illustration)**.
6   Once the valves have been removed and stored in an organized manner, the head should be thoroughly cleaned and inspected. If a complete engine overhaul is being done, finish the engine disassembly procedures before beginning the cylinder head cleaning and inspection process.

9   Cylinder head – cleaning and inspection

Refer to illustrations 9.12, 9.14, 9.20, 9.21a, 9.21b and 9.22

1   Thorough cleaning of the cylinder heads and related valve train com-

ponents, followed by a detailed inspection, will enable you to decide how much valve service work must be done during the engine overhaul.

Cleaning

2   Scrape all traces of old gasket material and sealing compound off the head gasket, intake manifold and exhaust manifold sealing surfaces.
3   Remove built-up scale from the coolant passages.
4   Run a stiff wire brush through the oil holes to remove any deposits that may have formed in them.
5   Run a tap into each of the threaded holes to remove corrosion and thread sealant that may be present. If compressed air is available, use it to clear the holes of debris produced by this operation. **Warning:** *Wear eye protection when using compressed air!*
6   Clean the rocker arm pivot bolt threads with a wire brush.
7   Clean the cylinder head with solvent and dry it thoroughly. Compressed air will speed the drying process and ensure that all holes and recessed areas are clean. **Note:** *Decarbonizing chemicals are available and may prove very useful when cleaning cylinder heads and valve train components. They are very caustic and should be used with caution. Be sure to follow the instructions on the container.*
8   Clean the rocker arms, fulcrums, bolts and pushrods with solvent and dry them thoroughly. Compressed air will speed the drying process and can be used to clean out the oil passages.
9   Clean all the valve springs, keepers, retainers, rotators, sleeves and shims with solvent and dry them thoroughly. Do the components from one valve at a time to avoid mixing up the parts.
10   Scrape off any heavy deposits that may have formed on the valves, then use a motorized wire brush to remove deposits from the valve heads and stems. Again, make sure the valves do not get mixed up.

Inspection

Cylinder head

11   Inspect the head very carefully for cracks, evidence of coolant leakage and other damage. If cracks are found, a new cylinder head should be obtained.
12   Using a straightedge and feeler gauge, check the head gasket mating surfaces for warpage **(see illustration)**. If the warpage exceeds specifications, the head can be resurfaced at an automotive machine shop. **Note:** *If the heads are resurfaced, the intake manifold flanges will also require machining.*
13   Examine the valve seats in each of the combustion chambers. If they're pitted, cracked or burned, the head will require valve service that's beyond the scope of the home mechanic.

9.14   A dial indicator can be used to determine the valve stem-to-guide clearance (move the valve stem as indicated by the arrows)

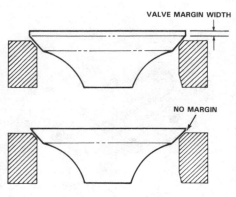

9.20   The margin width on each valve must be as specified (if no margin exists, the valve cannot be reused)

9.21a   Measure the free length of each valve spring with a dial or vernier caliper

9.21b   Check each valve spring for squareness

9.22   The exhaust valve rotators can be checked by turning the inner and outer sections in opposite directions – feel for smooth movement and excessive play

11.5   Apply a small dab of grease to each keeper as shown here before installation – it will hold them in place on the valve stem as the spring is released

14   Check the valve stem-to-valve guide clearance. Use a dial indicator to measure the lateral movement of each valve stem, parallel to the rocker arm, with the valve in the guide and approximately 1/16-inch off the seat **(see illustration)**. The valve stem-to-guide clearance is one-half the dial indicator reading. Compare the reading to the desired stem-to-guide clearance in this Chapter's Specifications. If, after this check, there is still some doubt as to the condition of the valve guides, the exact clearance and condition of the guides can be checked by an automotive machine shop, usually for a very small fee.

15   Clean all the parts thoroughly. Make sure that all oil passages are open.

Valve components

16   Check the rocker arm faces for pits, wear, galling and rough spots. Check the pivot contact areas as well as the fulcrums.

17   Inspect the pushrod ends for scuffing and excessive wear. Roll each pushrod on a flat surface, like a piece of plate glass, to determine if it's bent.

18   Any damaged or excessively worn parts must be replaced with new ones.

Valves

19   Carefully inspect each valve face for cracks, pits and burned spots. Check the valve stem and neck for cracks. Rotate each valve and check for any obvious indication that it's bent. Check the end of the stem for pits and excessive wear. The presence of any of these conditions indicates the

need for valve service by a machine shop.

20   Measure the width of the valve margin on each valve **(see illustration)** and compare it to the Specifications. Any valve with a margin narrower than listed in this Chapter's Specifications will have to be replaced with a new one.

Valve train components

21   Check each valve spring for wear on the ends and pits. Measure the free length **(see illustration)** and compare it to this Chapter's Specifications. Any springs that are shorter than specified have sagged and should not be reused. Check each valve spring for squareness **(see illustration)**.

22   Check the spring retainers and keepers for obvious wear and cracks. Make sure the rotators operate smoothly with no binding or excessive play **(see illustration)**. Any questionable parts should be replaced with new ones, as extensive damage will occur in the event of failure during engine operation.

23   If the inspection process indicates that the valve components are in generally poor condition and worn beyond the limits specified, which is usually the case in an engine that is being overhauled, reassemble the valves in the cylinder head and refer to Section 10 for valve servicing recommendations.

24   If the inspection turns up no excessively worn parts, and if the valve faces and seats are in good condition, the valve train components can be reinstalled in the cylinder head without major servicing. Refer to the appropriate Section for cylinder head reassembly procedures.

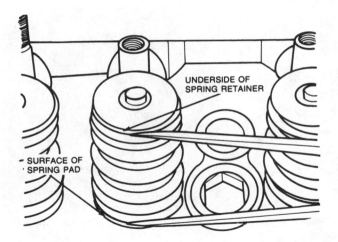

11.6 Be sure to check the valve spring installed height for each valve (the distance from the top of the seat/shims to the underside of the retainer)

---

10 Valves – servicing

1   Because of the complex nature of the job and the special tools and equipment needed, servicing of the valves, the valve seats and the valve guides, commonly known as a valve job, is best left to a shop.
2   The home mechanic can remove and disassemble the head, do the initial cleaning and inspection, then reassemble and deliver the head to a dealer service department or an automotive machine shop for the actual valve servicing.
3   The dealer service department, or automotive machine shop, will remove the valves and springs, recondition or replace the valves and valve seats, recondition the valve guides, check and replace the valve springs, spring retainers (or rotators) and keepers (as necessary), replace the valve seals with new ones, reassemble the valve components and make sure the installed spring height is correct. The cylinder head gasket surface will also be resurfaced if it is warped.
4   After the valve job has been performed by a shop the head will be in like new condition. When the head is returned, be sure to clean it again before installation on the engine to remove any metal particles and abrasive grit that may still be present from the valve service or head resurfacing operations. Use compressed air, if available, to blow out all the oil holes and passages.

11 Cylinder head – reassembly

Refer to illustrations 11.5 and 11.6
1   Regardless of whether or not the head was sent to an automotive repair shop for valve servicing, make sure it's clean before beginning reassembly.
2   If the head was sent out for valve servicing, the valves and related components will already be in place.
3   Lubricate and install the valves, then install new seals on each of the valve guides. Using a hammer and a deep socket, gently tap each seal into place until it's properly seated on the guide. Don't twist or cock the seals during installation or they will not seal properly on the valve stems. **Note:** *Because the intake and exhaust valves exhibit different leakage rates, the valve stem seals must NOT be interchanged.*
4   Install the valve spring shim(s) (if required) over the valve guide boss and set the valve spring, retainer (or rotator) and sleeve (used on some intake valves) in place.
5   Compress the spring and install the keepers. Release the compressor, making sure the keepers are seated properly in the valve stem grooves. If necessary, grease can be used to hold the keepers in place until the compressor is released **(see illustration)**.
6   Check the installed valve spring height **(see illustration)**. If it was correct before reassembly it should still be within the specified limits. If it isn't, install additional valve spring shims (available from a dealer) to bring the height to within the specified limit.
7   Install the rocker arms, fulcrums and bolts. Be sure to lubricate the fulcrums with moly base grease or engine assembly lube.

12 Piston/connecting rod assembly – removal

Refer to illustrations 12.1, 12.3 and 12.5
Note: *Prior to removing the piston/connecting rod assemblies, remove the cylinder heads, the oil pan and the oil pickup by referring to the appropriate Sections in Chapter 2, Part A.*
1   Completely remove the ridge at the top of each cylinder with a ridge reaming tool **(see illustration)**. Follow the manufacturer's instructions provided with the tool. Failure to remove the ridge before attempting to remove the piston/connecting rod assemblies may result in piston breakage.
2   After the cylinder ridges have been removed, turn the engine upside-down so the crankshaft is facing up.
3   Before the connecting rods are removed, check the endplay with feeler gauges. Slide them between each connecting rod and the crankshaft throw until the play is removed **(see illustration)**. The endplay is equal to

2B

12.1 A ridge reamer is required to remove the ridge from the top of each cylinder – do this before removing the pistons!

12.3 Check the connecting rod side clearance with a feeler gauge as shown

12.5   To prevent damage to the crankshaft journals and cylinder walls, slip sections of rubber or plastic hose over the rod bolts before removing the pistons

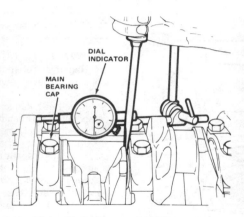

13.1   Checking crankshaft endplay with a dial indicator

13.3   Checking crankshaft endplay with a feeler gauge

the thickness of the feeler gauge(s). If the endplay exceeds the service limit, new connecting rods will be required. If new rods (or a new crankshaft) are installed, the endplay may fall under the specified minimum (if it does, the rods will have to be machined to restore it – consult an automotive machine shop for advice if necessary). Repeat the procedure for the remaining connecting rods.

4   Check the connecting rods and caps for identification marks. If they aren't plainly marked, use a small center punch to make the appropriate number of indentations on each rod and cap (1 – 6, depending on the cylinder they're associated with).

5   Loosen each of the connecting rod cap nuts 1/2-turn at a time until they can be removed by hand. Remove the number one connecting rod cap and bearing insert. Don't drop the bearing insert out of the cap. Slip a short length of plastic or rubber hose over each connecting rod cap bolt to protect the crankshaft journal and cylinder wall as the piston is removed **(see illustration)**. Push the connecting rod/piston assembly out through the top of the engine. Use a wooden hammer handle to push on the upper bearing insert in the connecting rod. If resistance is felt, double-check to make sure that all of the ridge was removed from the cylinder.

6   Repeat the procedure for the remaining cylinders. After removal, reassemble the connecting rod caps and bearing inserts in their respective connecting rods and install the cap nuts finger tight. Leaving the old

bearing inserts in place until reassembly will help prevent the connecting rod bearing surfaces from being accidentally nicked or gouged.

13   Crankshaft – removal

Refer to illustrations 13.1, 13.3, 13.4a and 13.4b

Note: *The crankshaft can be removed only after the engine has been removed from the vehicle. It's assumed that the flywheel or driveplate, vibration damper, timing chain, oil pan, oil pump and piston/connecting rod assemblies have already been removed.*

1   Before the crankshaft is removed, check the endplay. Mount a dial indicator with the stem in line with the crankshaft and just touching one of the crank throws **(see illustration)**.

2   Push the crankshaft all the way to the rear and zero the dial indicator. Next, pry the crankshaft to the front as far as possible and check the reading on the dial indicator. The distance that it moves is the endplay. If it's greater than specified, check the crankshaft thrust surfaces for wear. If no wear is evident, new main bearings should correct the endplay.

3   If a dial indicator isn't available, feeler gauges can be used. Gently pry or push the crankshaft all the way to the front of the engine. Slip feeler

13.4a   Use a center punch or number stamping dies to mark the main bearing caps to ensure installation in their original locations on the block (make the punch marks near one of the bolt heads)

13.4b   The arrow on the main bearing cap indicates the front of the engine

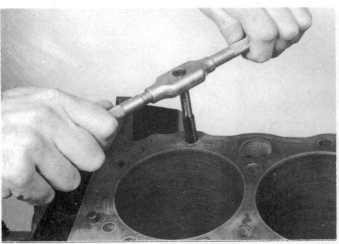

14.8   All bolt holes in the block – particularly the main bearing cap and head bolt holes – should be cleaned and restored with a tap (be sure to remove debris from the holes after this is done)

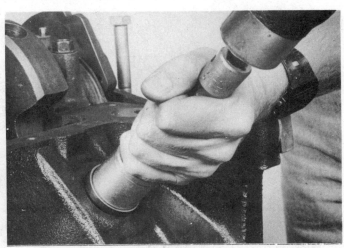

14.10   A large socket on an extension can be used to drive the new core plugs into the bores

gauges between the crankshaft and the front face of the thrust main bearing to determine the clearance (**see illustration**).

4   Check the main bearing caps to see if they're marked to indicate their locations. They should be numbered consecutively from the front of the engine to the rear. If they aren't, mark them with number stamping dies or a center punch (**see illustration**). Main bearing caps generally have a cast-in arrow, which points to the front of the engine (**see illustration**). Loosen each of the main bearing cap bolts 1/4-turn at a time each, until they can be removed by hand.

5   Gently tap the caps with a soft-face hammer, then separate them from the engine block. If necessary, use the bolts as levers to remove the caps. Try not to drop the bearing inserts if they come out with the caps.

6   Carefully lift the crankshaft out of the engine. It's a good idea to have an assistant available, since the crankshaft is quite heavy. With the bearing inserts in place in the engine block and main bearing caps, return the caps to their respective locations on the engine block and tighten the bolts finger tight. **Note:** *Do not refinish the crankshaft journals to more than 0.010 in. (0.25 mm). Further main journal refinishing may cause fatigue failure of the crankshaft. On Supercharged engines, do not refinish the crankshaft at all as the journals are already undersize 0.010 in.*

14   Engine block – cleaning

Refer to illustrations 14.8 and 14.10

1   Drill a small hole in the center of each core plug and pull them out with an auto body type dent puller. **Note:** *The core plugs (also known as freeze or soft plugs) may be difficult or impossible to retrieve if they're driven into the block coolant passages.*

2   Using a gasket scraper, remove all traces of gasket material from the engine block. Be very careful not to nick or gouge the gasket sealing surfaces.

3   Remove the main bearing caps and separate the bearing inserts from the caps and the engine block. Tag the bearings, indicating which cylinder they were removed from and whether they were in the cap or the block, then set them aside.

4   Remove all of the threaded oil gallery plugs from the rear of the block. The plugs are usually very tight – they may have to be drilled out and the holes retapped. Discard the plugs and use new ones when the engine is reassembled.

5   If the engine is extremely dirty it should be taken to an automotive machine shop to be steam cleaned or hot tanked.

6   After the block is returned, clean all oil holes and oil galleries one more time. Brushes specifically designed for this purpose are available at most

auto parts stores. Flush the passages with warm water until the water runs clear, dry the block thoroughly and wipe all machined surfaces with a light, rust preventative oil. If you have access to compressed air, use it to speed the drying process and to blow out all the oil holes and galleries. **Warning:** *Wear eye protection when using compressed air!*

7   If the block isn't extremely dirty or sludged up, you can do an adequate cleaning job with hot soapy water and a stiff brush. Take plenty of time and do a thorough job. Regardless of the cleaning method used, be sure to clean all oil holes and galleries very thoroughly, dry the block completely and coat all machined surfaces with light oil.

8   The threaded holes in the block must be clean to ensure accurate torque readings during reassembly. Run the proper size tap into each of the holes to remove any rust, corrosion, thread sealant or sludge and to restore any damaged threads (**see illustration**). If possible, use compressed air to clear the holes of debris produced by this operation. Now is a good time to clean the threads on the head bolts and the main bearing cap bolts as well.

9   Reinstall the main bearing caps and tighten the bolts finger tight.

10   After coating the sealing surfaces of the new core plugs with RTV sealant, install them in the engine block (**see illustration**). Make sure they're driven in straight and seated properly or leakage could result. Special tools are available for this purpose, but equally good results can be obtained using a large socket, with an outside diameter that will just slip into the core plug, a 1/2-inch drive extension and a hammer.

11   Apply non-hardening sealant (such as Permatex number 2 or Teflon tape) to the new oil gallery plugs and thread them into the holes at the rear of the block. Make sure they're tightened securely.

12   If the engine isn't going to be reassembled right away, cover it with a large plastic trash bag to keep it clean.

15   Engine block – inspection

Refer to illustrations 15.4a, 15.4b and 15.4c

1   Before the block is inspected, it should be cleaned as described in Section 14. Double-check to make sure the ridge at the top of each cylinder has been completely removed.

2   Visually check the block for cracks, rust and corrosion. Look for stripped threads in the threaded holes. It's also a good idea to have the block checked for hidden cracks by an automotive machine shop that has the special equipment to do this type of work. If defects are found, have the block repaired, if possible, or replaced.

3   Check the cylinder bores for scuffing and scoring.

2B

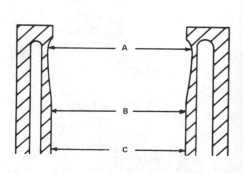

15.4a Measure the diameter of each cylinder just under the wear ridge (A), at the center (B) and at the bottom (C)

15.4b The ability to "feel" when the telescoping gauge is at the correct point will be developed over time, so work slowly and repeat the check until you're satisfied the bore measurement is accurate

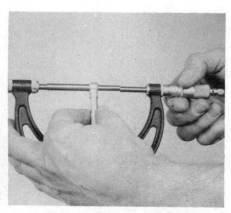

15.4c The gauge is then measured with a micrometer to determine the bore size

4   Measure the diameter of each cylinder at the top (just under the ridge area), center and bottom of the cylinder bore, parallel to the crankshaft axis (see illustrations). Next, measure each cylinder's diameter at the same three locations across the crankshaft axis. Compare the results to this Chapter's Specifications. If the cylinder walls are badly scuffed or scored, or if they're out-of-round or tapered beyond the limits given in the Specifications, have the engine block rebored and honed at an automotive machine shop. If a rebore is done, oversize pistons and rings will be required. **Note:** *Pistons are available for service in standard sizes and oversize. The standard size pistons are color-coded red, blue or yellow on the dome of the piston. Measure the cylinder bore diameter and select the piston to ensure the proper clearance. When the bore diameter is in the lower one-third of the specified range, a red piston should be used. When the bore diameter is in the middle one-third of the clearance range, a blue piston should be used. When the bore diameter is in the upper one-third, a yellow piston should be used.*

5   If the cylinders are in reasonably good condition and not worn to the outside of the limits, and if the piston-to-cylinder clearances can be maintained properly, then they don't have to be rebored. Honing is all that's necessary (see Section 16).

16.3a A "bottle brush" hone will produce better results if you've never honed cylinders before

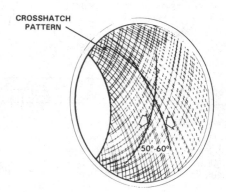

CROSSHATCH PATTERN

50°-60°

16.3b The cylinder hone should leave a smooth, crosshatch pattern with the lines intersecting at approximately a 60-degree angle

16 Cylinder honing

Refer to illustrations 16.3a and 16.3b

1   Prior to engine reassembly, the cylinder bores must be honed so the new piston rings will seat correctly and provide the best possible combustion chamber seal. **Note:** *If you don't have the tools or don't want to tackle the honing operation, most automotive machine shops will do it for a reasonable fee.*

2   Before honing the cylinders, install the main bearing caps and tighten the bolts to the torque listed in this Chapter's Specifications.

3   Two types of cylinder hones are commonly available – the flex hone or "bottle brush" type and the more traditional surfacing hone with spring-loaded stones. Both will do the job, but for the less experienced mechanic the "bottle brush" hone will probably be easier to use. You'll also need plenty of light oil or honing oil, some rags and an electric drill motor. Proceed as follows:

  a) Mount the hone in the drill motor, compress the stones and slip it into the first cylinder (see illustration). Be sure to wear safety goggles or a face shield!

  b) Lubricate the cylinder with plenty of oil, turn on the drill and move the hone up-and-down in the cylinder at a pace that will produce a fine crosshatch pattern on the cylinder walls. Ideally, the crosshatch lines should intersect at approximately a 60-degree angles (see illustration). Be sure to use plenty of lubricant and don't take off any more material than is absolutely necessary to produce the desired finish. **Note:** *Piston ring manufacturers may specify a smaller crosshatch angle than the traditional 60-degrees – read and follow any instructions included with the new rings.*

17.4a The piston ring grooves can be cleaned with a special tool, as shown here, . . .

17.4b . . . or a section of a broken ring

c) Don't withdraw the hone from the cylinder while it's running. Instead, shut off the drill and continue moving the hone up-and-down in the cylinder until it comes to a complete stop, then compress the stones and withdraw the hone. If you're using a "bottle brush" type hone, stop the drill motor, then turn the chuck in the normal direction of rotation while withdrawing the hone from the cylinder.

d) Wipe the oil out of the cylinder and repeat the procedure for the remaining cylinders.

4   After the honing job is complete, chamfer the top edges of the cylinder bores with a small file so the rings won't catch when the pistons are installed. Be very careful not to nick the cylinder walls with the end of the file!

5   The entire engine block must be washed again very thoroughly with warm, soapy water to remove all traces of the abrasive grit produced during the honing operation. **Note:** *The bores can be considered clean when a white cloth – dampened with clean engine oil – used to wipe them down doesn't pick up any more honing residue, which will show up as gray areas on the cloth. Be sure to run a brush through all oil holes and galleries and flush them with running water.*

6   After rinsing, dry the block and apply a coat of light rust preventive oil to all machined surfaces. Wrap the block in a plastic trash bag to keep it clean and set it aside until reassembly.

---

17   Piston/connecting rod assembly – inspection

Refer to illustrations 17.4a, 17.4b, 17.10 and 17.11

1   Before the inspection process can be carried out, the piston/connecting rod assemblies must be cleaned and the original piston rings removed from the pistons. **Note:** *Always use new piston rings when the engine is reassembled.*

2   Using a piston ring installation tool, carefully remove the rings from the pistons. Be careful not to nick or gouge the pistons in the process.

3   Scrape all traces of carbon from the top of the piston. A handheld wire brush or a piece of fine emery cloth can be used once the majority of the deposits have been scraped away. Do not, under any circumstances, use a wire brush mounted in a drill motor to remove deposits from the pistons. The piston material is soft and may be eroded away by the wire brush.

4   Use a piston ring groove cleaning tool to remove carbon deposits from the ring grooves. If a tool isn't available, a piece broken off the old ring will do the job. Be very careful to remove only the carbon deposits – don't remove any metal and don't nick or scratch the sides of the ring grooves **(see illustrations)**.

5   Once the deposits have been removed, clean the piston/rod assemblies with solvent and dry them with compressed air (if available). Make sure the oil return holes in the back sides of the ring grooves are clear.

6   If the pistons and cylinder walls aren't damaged or worn excessively,

and if the engine block is not rebored, new pistons won't be necessary. Normal piston wear appears as even vertical wear on the piston thrust surfaces and slight looseness of the top ring in its groove. New piston rings, on the other hand, should always be used when an engine is rebuilt.

7   Carefully inspect each piston for cracks around the skirt, at the pin bosses and at the ring lands.

8   Look for scoring and scuffing on the thrust faces of the skirt, holes in the piston crown and burned areas at the edge of the crown. If the skirt is scored or scuffed, the engine may have been suffering from overheating and/or abnormal combustion, which caused excessively high operating temperatures. The cooling and lubrication systems should be checked thoroughly. A hole in the piston crown is an indication that abnormal combustion (preignition) was occurring. Burned areas at the edge of the piston crown are usually evidence of spark knock (detonation). If any of the above problems exist, the causes must be corrected or the damage will occur again.

9   Corrosion of the piston, in the form of small pits, indicates that coolant is leaking into the combustion chamber and/or the crankcase. Again, the cause must be corrected or the problem may persist in the rebuilt engine.

10   Measure the piston ring side clearance by laying a new piston ring in each ring groove and slipping a feeler gauge in beside it **(see illustration)**. Check the clearance at three or four locations around each groove. Be sure to use the correct ring for each groove; they are different. If the side clearance is greater than specified, new pistons will have to be used.

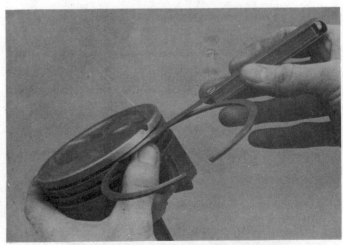

17.10 Check the ring side clearance with a feeler gauge at several points around the groove

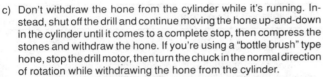

17.11   Measure the piston diameter at a 90-degree angle to the piston pin and in line with it

18.1   Use a wire or stiff plastic bristle brush to clean the oil passages in the crankshaft

18.3   Rubbing a penny lengthwise on each journal will reveal its condition – if copper rubs off and is embedded in the crankshaft, the journals should be reground

11   Check the piston-to-bore clearance by measuring the bore (see Section 15) and the piston diameter. Make sure the pistons and bores are correctly matched. Measure the piston at the piston skirt, at a 90-degree angle to and in line with the piston pin **(see illustration)**. Subtract the piston diameter from the bore diameter to obtain the clearance. If it's greater than specified, the block will have to be rebored and new pistons and rings installed.

12   Check the piston-to-rod clearance by twisting the piston and rod in opposite directions. Any noticeable play indicates excessive wear, which must be corrected. The piston/connecting rod assemblies should be taken to an automotive machine shop to have the pistons and rods rebored and new pins installed.

13   If the pistons must be removed from the connecting rods for any reason, they should be taken to an automotive machine shop. While they are there have the connecting rods checked for bend and twist, since automotive machine shops have special equipment for this purpose. **Note:** *Unless new pistons and/or connecting rods must be installed, do not disassemble the pistons and connecting rods.*

14   Check the connecting rods for cracks and other damage. Temporarily remove the rod caps, lift out the old bearing inserts, wipe the rod and cap bearing surfaces clean and inspect them for nicks, gouges and scratches. After checking the rods, replace the old bearings, slip the caps into place and tighten the nuts finger tight.

18   Crankshaft – inspection

Refer to illustrations 18.1, 18.3, 18.4, 18.6 and 18.8

1   Clean the crankshaft with solvent and dry it with compressed air (if available). **Warning:** *Wear eye protection when using compressed air.* Be sure to clean the oil holes with a stiff brush **(see illustration)** and flush them with solvent.

2   Check the main and connecting rod bearing journals for uneven wear, scoring, pits and cracks.

3   Rub a penny across each journal several times **(see illustration)**. If a journal picks up copper from the penny, it's too rough and must be reground.

4   Remove all burrs from the crankshaft oil holes with a stone, file or scraper **(see illustration)**.

5   Check the rest of the crankshaft for cracks and other damage. It should be magnafluxed to reveal hidden cracks – an automotive machine shop will handle the procedure.

6   Using a micrometer, measure the diameter of the main and connecting rod journals and compare the results to this Chapter's Specifications **(see illustration)**. By measuring the diameter at a number of points around each journal's circumference, you'll be able to determine whether or not the journal is out-of-round. Take the measurement at each end of the

18.4   The oil holes should be chamfered so sharp edges don't gouge or scratch the new bearings

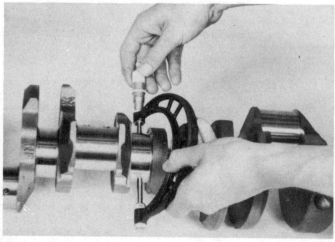

18.6   Measure the diameter of each crankshaft journal at several points to detect taper and out-of-round conditions

18.8 If the seals have worn grooves in the crankshaft journals, or if the seal contact surfaces are nicked or scratched, the new seals will leak

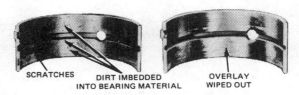

19.1 Typical bearing failures

2B

journal, near the crank throws, to determine if the journal is tapered.

7   If the crankshaft journals are damaged, tapered, out-of-round or worn beyond the limits given in the Specifications, have the crankshaft reground by an automotive machine shop. Be sure to use the correct size bearing inserts if the crankshaft is reconditioned. **Note:** *The crankshaft journals can't be machined more than 0.010 inch under the standard dimension. The rear journal on the crankshafts of supercharged engines can't be refinished at all, because it is already 0.010 inch undersize.*

8   Check the oil seal journals at each end of the crankshaft for wear and damage. If the seal has worn a groove in the journal, or if it's nicked or scratched (**see illustration**), the new seal may leak when the engine is reassembled. In some cases, an automotive machine shop may be able to repair the journal by pressing on a thin sleeve. If repair isn't feasible, a new or different crankshaft should be installed.

9   Refer to Section 19 and examine the main and rod bearing inserts.

19   Main and connecting rod bearings – inspection

Refer to illustration 19.1

1   Even though the main and connecting rod bearings should be replaced with new ones during the engine overhaul, the old bearings should be retained for close examination, as they may reveal valuable information about the condition of the engine (**see illustration**).

2   Bearing failure occurs because of lack of lubrication, the presence of dirt or other foreign particles, overloading the engine and corrosion. Regardless of the cause of bearing failure, it must be corrected before the engine is reassembled to prevent it from happening again.

3   When examining the bearings, remove them from the engine block, the main bearing caps, the connecting rods and the rod caps and lay them out on a clean surface in the same general position as their location in the engine. This will enable you to match any bearing problems with the corresponding crankshaft journal.

4   Dirt and other foreign particles get into the engine in a variety of ways. It may be left in the engine during assembly, or it may pass through filters or the PCV system. It may get into the oil, and from there into the bearings. Metal chips from machining operations and normal engine wear are often present. Abrasives are sometimes left in engine components after reconditioning, especially when parts are not thoroughly cleaned using the proper cleaning methods. Whatever the source, these foreign objects often end up embedded in the soft bearing material and are easily recognized. Large particles will not embed in the bearing and will score or gouge the bearing and journal. The best prevention for this cause of bearing failure is to clean all parts thoroughly and keep everything spotlessly clean during engine assembly. Frequent and regular engine oil and filter changes are also recommended.

5   Lack of lubrication (or lubrication breakdown) has a number of interrelated causes. Excessive heat (which thins the oil), overloading (which squeezes the oil from the bearing face) and oil leakage or throw off (from excessive bearing clearances, worn oil pump or high engine speeds) all contribute to lubrication breakdown. Blocked oil passages, which usually are the result of misaligned oil holes in a bearing shell, will also oil starve a bearing and destroy it. When lack of lubrication is the cause of bearing failure, the bearing material is wiped or extruded from the steel backing of the bearing. Temperatures may increase to the point where the steel backing turns blue from overheating.

6   Driving habits can have a definite effect on bearing life. Full throttle, low speed operation (lugging the engine) puts very high loads on bearings, which tends to squeeze out the oil film. These loads cause the bearings to flex, which produces fine cracks in the bearing face (fatigue failure). Eventually the bearing material will loosen in pieces and tear away from the steel backing. Short trip driving leads to corrosion of bearings because insufficient engine heat is produced to drive off the condensed water and corrosive gases. These products collect in the engine oil, forming acid and sludge. As the oil is carried to the engine bearings, the acid attacks and corrodes the bearing material.

7   Incorrect bearing installation during engine assembly will lead to bearing failure as well. Tight fitting bearings leave insufficient bearing oil clearance and will result in oil starvation. Dirt or foreign particles trapped behind a bearing insert result in high spots on the bearing which lead to failure.

20   Engine overhaul – reassembly sequence

1   Before beginning engine reassembly, make sure you have all the necessary new parts, gaskets and seals as well as the following items on hand:

Common hand tools
A 1/2-inch drive torque wrench
Piston ring installation tool

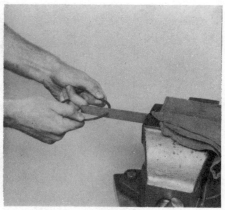

21.3   When checking piston ring end gap, the ring must be square in the cylinder bore (this is done by pushing the ring down with the top of a piston as shown)

21.4   With the ring square in the cylinder, measure the end gap with a feeler gauge

21.5   If the end gap is too small, clamp a file in a vise and file the ring ends (from the outside in only) to enlarge the gap slightly

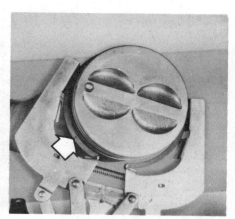

21.9a   Installing the spacer/expander in the oil control ring groove

21.9b   DO NOT use a piston ring installation tool when installing the oil ring side rails

21.12   Installing the compression rings with a ring expander – the mark (arrow) must face up

Piston ring compressor
Short lengths of rubber or plastic hose
to fit over connecting rod bolts
Plastigage
Feeler gauges
A fine-tooth file
New engine oil
Engine assembly lube or moly-base grease
RTV-type gasket sealant
Anaerobic-type gasket sealant
Thread locking compound

2   In order to save time and avoid problems, engine reassembly must be done in the following general order:
New camshaft/auxiliary shaft bearings (must be
done by automotive machine shop)
Piston rings
Crankshaft and main bearings
Piston/connecting rod assemblies
Camshaft and lifters
Cylinder heads, pushrods and rocker arms
Timing chain and sprockets
Timing chain cover/oil pump
Oil pan
Intake and exhaust manifolds
Valve covers
Flywheel/driveplate

21   Piston rings – installation

Refer to illustrations 21.3, 21.4, 21.5, 21.9a, 21.9b and 21.12

1   Before installing the new piston rings, the ring end gaps must be checked. It's assumed that the piston ring side clearance has been checked and verified correct (see Section 17).

2   Lay out the piston/connecting rod assemblies and the new ring sets so the ring sets will be matched with the same piston and cylinder during the end gap measurement and engine assembly.

3   Insert the top (number one) ring into the first cylinder and square it up with the cylinder walls by pushing it in with the top of the piston (see illustration). The ring should be near the bottom of the cylinder, at the lower limit of ring travel.

4   To measure the end gap, slip feeler gauges between the ends of the ring until a gauge equal to the gap width is found (see illustration). The feeler gauge should slide between the ring ends with a slight amount of drag. Compare the measurement to the Specifications. If the gap is larger or smaller than specified, double-check to make sure you have the correct rings before proceeding.

5   If the gap is too small, it must be enlarged or the ring ends may come in contact with each other during engine operation, which can cause serious damage to the engine. The end gap can be increased by filing the ring ends very carefully with a fine file. Mount the file in a vise equipped with soft jaws, slip the ring over the file with the ends contacting the file face and

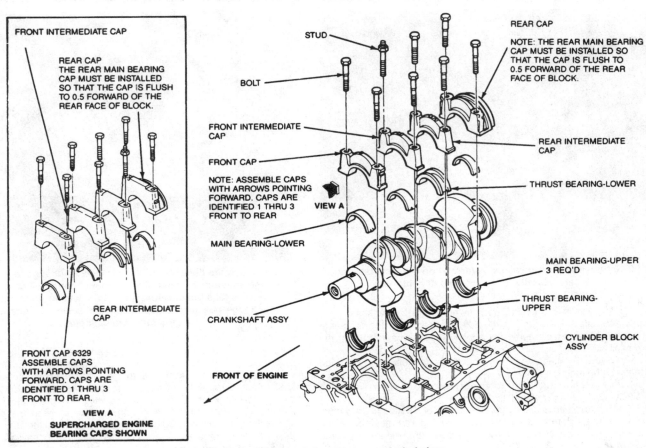

22.6   Crankshaft and main bearings – exploded view

slowly move the ring to remove material from the ends. When performing this operation, file only from the outside in **(see illustration)**.

6   Excess end gap isn't critical unless it's greater than 0.040-inch. Again, double-check to make sure you have the correct rings for your engine.

7   Repeat the procedure for each ring that will be installed in the first cylinder and for each ring in the remaining cylinders. Remember to keep rings, pistons and cylinders matched up.

8   Once the ring end gaps have been checked/corrected, the rings can be installed on the pistons.

9   The oil control ring (lowest one on the piston) is installed first. It's composed of three separate components. Slip the spacer/expander into the groove **(see illustration)**. If an anti-rotation tang is used, make sure it's inserted into the drilled hole in the ring groove. Next, install the lower side rail. Don't use a piston ring installation tool on the oil ring side rails, as they may be damaged. Instead, place one end of the side rail into the groove between the spacer/expander and the ring land, hold it firmly in place and slide a finger around the piston while pushing the rail into the groove **(see illustration)**. Next, install the upper side rail in the same manner.

10   After the three oil ring components have been installed, check to make sure that both the upper and lower side rails can be turned smoothly in the ring groove.

11   The number two (middle) ring is installed next. It's stamped with a mark which must face up; toward the top of the piston. **Note:** *Always follow the instructions printed on the ring package or box – different manufacturers may require different approaches. Do not mix up the top and middle rings, as they have different cross sections.*

12   Use a piston ring installation tool and make sure the identification mark is facing the top of the piston, then slip the ring into the middle groove on the piston **(see illustration)**. Don't expand the ring any more than is

necessary to slide it over the piston.

13   Install the number one (top) ring in the same manner. Make sure the mark is facing up. Be careful not to confuse the number one and number two rings.

14   Repeat the procedure for the remaining pistons and rings.

22   Crankshaft – installation and main bearing oil clearance check

Refer to illustrations 22.6, 22.10 and 22.14

1   Crankshaft installation is the first major step in engine reassembly. It's assumed at this point that the engine block and crankshaft have been cleaned, inspected and repaired or reconditioned.

2   Position the engine with the bottom facing up.

3   Remove the main bearing cap bolts and lift out the caps. Lay them out in the proper order to ensure correct installation.

4   If they're still in place, remove the old bearing inserts from the block and the main bearing caps. Wipe the main bearing surfaces of the block and caps with a clean, lint free cloth. They must be kept spotlessly clean.

5   Clean the back sides of the new main bearing inserts and lay one bearing half in each main bearing saddle in the block. Lay the other bearing half from each bearing set in the corresponding main bearing cap. Make sure the tab on the bearing insert fits into the recess in the block or cap. Also, the oil holes in the block must line up with the oil holes in the bearing insert. **Caution:** *Do not hammer the bearings into place and don't nick or gouge the bearing faces. No lubrication should be used at this time.*

6   The flanged thrust bearing must be installed in the third cap and saddle **(see illustration)**.

22.10   Lay the Plastigage strips (arrow) on the main bearing journals, parallel to the crankshaft centerline

22.14   Compare the width of the crushed Plastigage to the scale on the envelope to determine the main bearing oil clearance (always take the measurement at the widest point of the Plastigage); be sure to use the correct scale – standard and metric ones are included

7   Clean the faces of the bearings in the block and the crankshaft main bearing journals with a clean, lint free cloth. Check or clean the oil holes in the crankshaft, as any dirt here can go only one way – straight through the new bearings.

8   Once you're certain the crankshaft is clean, carefully lay it in position in the main bearings.

9   Before the crankshaft can be permanently installed, the main bearing oil clearance must be checked.

10   Trim several pieces of the appropriate size of Plastigage (they must be slightly shorter than the width of the main bearings) and place one piece on each crankshaft main bearing journal, parallel with the journal axis **(see illustration)**.

11   Clean the faces of the bearings in the caps and install the caps in their respective positions (don't mix them up) with the arrows pointing toward the front of the engine. Don't disturb the Plastigage.

12   Starting with the center main and working out toward the ends, tighten the main bearing cap bolts, in three steps, to the torque listed in this Chapter's Specifications. Don't rotate the crankshaft at any time during this operation.

13   Remove the bolts and carefully lift off the main bearing caps. Keep them in order. Don't disturb the Plastigage or rotate the crankshaft. If any of the main bearing caps are difficult to remove, tap them gently from side-to-side with a soft-face hammer to loosen them.

14   Compare the width of the crushed Plastigage on each journal to the scale printed on the Plastigage container to obtain the main bearing oil clearance **(see illustration)**. Check the Specifications to make sure it's correct.

15   If the clearance is not as specified, the bearing inserts may be the wrong size (which means different ones will be required). Before deciding that different inserts are needed, make sure that no dirt or oil was between the bearing inserts and the caps or block when the clearance was measured. If the Plastigage is noticeably wider at one end than the other, the journal may be tapered (see Section 18).

16   Carefully scrape all traces of the Plastigage material off the main bearing journals and/or the bearing faces. Don't nick or scratch the bearing faces.

17   Carefully lift the crankshaft out of the engine. Clean the bearing faces in the block, then apply a thin, uniform layer of clean moly-base grease or engine assembly lube to each of the bearing surfaces. Be sure to coat the thrust faces as well as the journal face of the third (thrust) bearing.

18   Make sure the crankshaft journals are clean, then lay the crankshaft back in place in the block. Clean the faces of the bearings in the caps, then apply lubricant to them. Install the caps in their respective positions with the arrows pointing toward the front of the engine. Install the bolts.

19   Tighten all except the third cap bolts (the one with the thrust bearing) to the torque listed in this Chapter's Specifications (work from the center

out and approach the final torque in three steps). Tighten the third cap bolts to 10-to-12 ft-lbs. Tap the ends of the crankshaft forward and backward with a lead or brass hammer to line up the main bearing and crankshaft thrust surfaces. Retighten all main bearing cap bolts to the torque listed in this Chapter's Specifications, starting with the center main and working out toward the ends. Note: Apply a 1/8 inch bead of silicone sealant to the rear main bearing cap-to-cylinder block mating line.

20   On manual transmission equipped models, install a new pilot bearing in the end of the crankshaft (see Chapter 8).

21   Rotate the crankshaft a number of times by hand to check for any obvious binding.

22   The final step is to check the crankshaft endplay with a feeler gauge or a dial indicator as described in Section 13. The endplay should be correct if the crankshaft thrust faces aren't worn or damaged and new bearings have been installed.

23   Install the rear main oil seal (see Section 23).

23   Rear main oil seal – installation

1   Make sure the engine block is clean to ensure a proper fit.

2   Apply a small amount of oil to the outer edge of the seal.

3   Coat the seal lip and crankshaft surface with engine oil.

4   Start the seal in the recess and install it with tool T82L-6701-A **(see illustration 16.19 in Part A)**. Alternatively, use a hammer and socket the same diameter as the seal to drive the seal into the bore.

5   Push the seal into position until it's completely seated.

24   Piston/connecting rod assembly – installation and rod bearing oil clearance check

Refer to illustrations 24.5, 24.8, 24.9, 24.11 and 24.13

1   Before installing the piston/connecting rod assemblies, the cylinder walls must be perfectly clean, the top edge of each cylinder must be chamfered, and the crankshaft must be in place.

2   Remove the connecting rod cap from the end of the number one connecting rod. Remove the old bearing inserts and wipe the bearing surfaces of the connecting rod and cap with a clean, lint free cloth. They must be kept spotlessly clean.

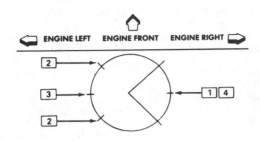

ENGINE LEFT   ENGINE FRONT   ENGINE RIGHT

24.5   Position the piston ring end gaps as shown here before installing the piston/connecting rod assemblies in the engine

1   Oil ring spacer gap (tang in hole or slot with arc)
2   Oil ring rail gaps
3   2nd compression ring gap
4   Top compression ring gap

24.8   The notch or the arrow in the top of each piston must face the FRONT of the engine as the pistons are installed

3   Clean the back side of the new upper bearing half, then lay it in place in the connecting rod. Make sure the tab on the bearing fits into the recess in the rod. Don't hammer the bearing insert into place and be very careful not to nick or gouge the bearing face. Don't lubricate the bearing at this time.

4   Clean the back side of the remaining bearing insert and install it in the rod cap. Again, make sure the tab on the bearing fits into the recess in the cap, and don't apply any lubricant. It's critically important that the mating surfaces of the bearing and connecting rod are perfectly clean and oil free when they're assembled.

5   Position the piston ring gaps at intervals around the piston **(see illustration)**, then slip a section of plastic or rubber hose over each connecting rod cap bolt.

6   Lubricate the piston and rings with clean engine oil and attach a piston ring compressor to the piston. Leave the skirt protruding about 1/4-inch to guide the piston into the cylinder. The rings must be compressed until they're flush with the piston.

7   Rotate the crankshaft until the number one connecting rod journal is at BDC (bottom dead center) and apply a coat of engine oil to the cylinder walls.

8   With the notch or arrow on top of the piston **(see illustration)** facing the front of the engine, gently insert the piston/connecting rod assembly into the number one cylinder bore and rest the bottom edge of the ring

compressor on the engine block. Tap the top edge of the ring compressor to make sure it's contacting the block around its entire circumference.

9   Carefully tap on the top of the piston with the end of a wooden hammer handle **(see illustration)** while guiding the end of the connecting rod into place on the crankshaft journal. The piston rings may try to pop out of the ring compressor just before entering the cylinder bore, so keep some downward pressure on the ring compressor. Work slowly, and if any resistance is felt as the piston enters the cylinder, stop immediately. Find out what's hanging up and fix it before proceeding. Do not, for any reason, force the piston into the cylinder, as you might break a ring and/or the piston!

10   Once the piston/connecting rod assembly is installed, the connecting rod bearing oil clearance must be checked before the rod cap is permanently bolted in place.

11   Cut a piece of the appropriate size Plastigage slightly shorter than the width of the connecting rod bearing and lay it in place on the number one connecting rod journal, parallel with the journal axis **(see illustration)**.

12   Clean the connecting rod cap bearing face, remove the protective hoses from the connecting rod bolts and install the rod cap. Make sure the mating mark on the cap is on the same side as the mark on the connecting rod. Install the nuts and tighten them to the torque listed in this Chapter's Specifications, working up to it in three steps. **Note:** *Use a thin-wall socket to avoid erroneous torque readings that can result if the socket is wedged*

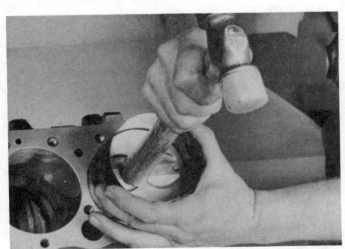

24.9   Drive the piston gently into the cylinder bore with the end of a wooden or plastic hammer handle

24.11   Lay the Plastigage strips on each rod bearing journal, parallel to the crankshaft centerline

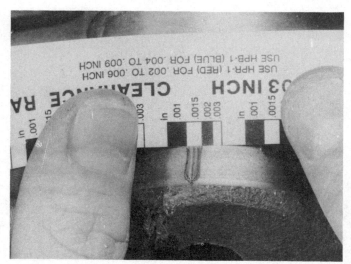

24.13 Measuring the width of the crushed Plastigage to determine the rod bearing oil clearance (be sure to use the correct scale – standard and metric ones are included)

between the rod cap and nut. Do not rotate the crankshaft at any time during this operation!

13   Remove the rod cap, being very careful not to disturb the Plastigage. Compare the width of the crushed Plastigage to the scale printed on the Plastigage container to obtain the oil clearance **(see illustration)**. Compare it to the Specifications to make sure the clearance is correct. If the clearance is not as specified, the bearing inserts may be the wrong size (which means different ones will be required). Before deciding that different inserts are needed, make sure that no dirt or oil was between the bearing inserts and the connecting rod or cap when the clearance was measured. Also, recheck the journal diameter. If the Plastigage was wider at one end than the other, the journal may be tapered (refer to Section 18).

14   Carefully scrape all traces of the Plastigage material off the rod journal and/or bearing face. Be very careful not to scratch the bearing – use your fingernail or a credit card. Make sure the bearing faces are perfectly clean, then apply a uniform layer of clean moly-base grease or engine assembly lube to both of them. You'll have to push the piston into the cylinder to expose the face of the bearing insert in the connecting rod – be sure to slip the protective hoses over the rod bolts first.

15   Slide the connecting rod back into place on the journal, remove the protective hoses from the rod cap
bolts, install the rod cap and tighten the nuts to the torque listed in this Chapter's Specifications. Again, work up to the torque in three steps.

16   Repeat the entire procedure for the remaining piston/connecting rod assemblies. Keep the back sides of the bearing inserts and the inside of the connecting rod and cap perfectly clean when assembling them. Make sure you have the correct piston for the cylinder and that the notch on the piston faces to the front of the engine when the piston is installed. Remember, use plenty of oil to lubricate the piston before installing the ring compressor. Also, when installing the rod caps for the final time, be sure to lubricate the bearing faces adequately.

17   After all the piston/connecting rod assemblies have been properly installed, rotate the crankshaft a number of times by hand to check for any obvious binding.

18   As a final step, the connecting rod endplay must be checked. Refer to Section 12 for this procedure. Compare the measured endplay to the Specifications to make sure it's correct. If it was correct before disassembly and the original crankshaft and rods were reinstalled, it should still be right. If new rods or a new crankshaft were installed, the endplay may be too small. If so, the rods will have to be removed and taken to an automotive machine shop for resizing.

25   Initial start-up and break-in after overhaul

1   Once the engine has been installed in the vehicle, double-check the engine oil and coolant levels.

2   With the spark plugs out of the engine and the ignition system disabled (see Section 2), crank the engine until oil pressure registers on the gauge.

3   Install the spark plugs, hook up the plug wires and restore the ignition system functions (see Section 2).

4   Start the engine. It may take a few moments for the gasoline to reach the injectors, but the engine should start without a great deal of effort.

5   After the engine starts, it should be allowed to warm up to normal operating temperature. While the engine is warming up, make a thorough check for oil and coolant leaks.

6   Shut the engine off and recheck the engine oil and coolant levels.

7   Drive the vehicle to an area with minimum traffic, accelerate at full throttle from 30 to 50 mph, then allow the vehicle to slow to 30 mph with the throttle closed. Repeat the procedure 10 or 12 times. This will load the piston rings and cause them to seat properly against the cylinder walls. Check again for oil and coolant leaks.

8   Drive the vehicle gently for the first 500 miles (no sustained high speeds) and keep a constant check on the oil level. It is not unusual for an engine to use oil during the break-in period.

9   At approximately 500 to 600 miles, change the oil and filter.

10   For the next few hundred miles, drive the vehicle normally. Do not pamper it or abuse it.

11   After 2000 miles, change the oil and filter again and consider the engine fully broken in.

Chapter 3   Cooling, heating and air conditioning systems

Contents

Specifications

General

Coolant capacity	See Chapter 1
Radiator cap pressure rating	16 psi
Thermostat rating (starts to open)	193 to 200-degrees F

Torque specifications

	Ft-lbs (unless otherwise indicated)
Thermostat housing bolts	72 to 96 in-lbs
Water pump-to-block bolts	15 to 22
Fan-to-fan clutch bolts	12 to 18
Fan clutch-to-water pump	15 to 22

1   General information

Engine cooling system

All vehicles covered by this manual employ a pressurized engine cooling system with thermostatically controlled coolant circulation. An impeller type water pump mounted on the front of the block pumps coolant through the engine. The coolant flows around each cylinder and toward the rear of the engine. Cast-in coolant passages direct coolant around the intake and exhaust ports, near the spark plug areas and in close proximity to the exhaust valve guide inserts.

A wax pellet type thermostat is located near the front of the intake manifold. During warm up, the closed thermostat prevents coolant from circulating through the radiator. When the engine reaches normal operating temperature, the thermostat opens and allows hot coolant to travel through the radiator, where it is cooled before returning to the engine.

Supercharged models utilize a copper/brass downflow radiator. On non-supercharged models, an aluminum cross-flow radiator with plastic end tanks is used. On models with automatic transmissions, a heat exchanger is mounted in the radiator to transfer heat from the automatic transmission fluid to the coolant.

The cooling system is sealed by a pressure type radiator cap. This raises the boiling point of the coolant and the higher boiling point of the coolant increases the cooling efficiency of the radiator. If the system pressure exceeds the cap pressure relief value, the excess pressure in the system forces the spring-loaded valve inside the cap off its seat and allows the coolant to escape through the overflow tube into a coolant reservoir. When the system cools the excess coolant is automatically drawn from the reservoir back into the radiator.

The coolant reservoir does double duty as both the point at which fresh coolant is added to the cooling system to maintain the proper fluid level and as a holding tank for overheated coolant.

This type of cooling system is known as a closed design because coolant that escapes past the pressure cap is saved and reused.

Heater

The heater consists of a blower fan and heater core located under the dashboard, the inlet and outlet hoses connecting the heater core to the engine cooling system and the heater/air conditioning control head on the dashboard. Hot engine coolant is circulated through the heater core at all times. When the heater mode is activated, a flap door opens to expose the heater box to the passenger compartment. A fan switch on the control head activates the blower motor, which forces air through the core, heating the air.

Air conditioning system

The air conditioning system consists basically of a condenser mounted in front of the radiator, an evaporator mounted under the dash, a compressor mounted on the engine, a filter-drier (accumulator) which contains a high pressure relief valve and the plumbing connecting all of the above.

A blower fan forces the warmer air of the passenger compartment through the evaporator core (sort of a radiator-in-reverse), transferring the heat from the air to the refrigerant. The liquid refrigerant boils off into low pressure vapor, taking the heat with it when it leaves the evaporator.

2   Antifreeze – general information

Warning: *Do not allow antifreeze to come in contact with your skin or painted surfaces of the vehicle. Rinse off spills immediately with plenty of water. Antifreeze is highly toxic if ingested. Never leave antifreeze lying around in an open container or in puddles on the floor; children and pets are attracted by it's sweet smell and may drink it. Check with local authorities about disposing of used antifreeze. Many communities have collection centers which will see that antifreeze is disposed of safely.*

The cooling system should be filled with a water/ethylene glycol based antifreeze solution, which will prevent freezing down to at least -20-degrees F, or lower if local climate requires it. It also provides protection against corrosion and increases the coolant boiling point.

The cooling system should be drained, flushed and refilled at least every other year (see Chapter 1). The use of antifreeze solutions for periods of longer than two years is likely to cause damage and encourage the formation of rust and scale in the system. If your tap water is "hard", use distilled water with the antifreeze.

Before adding antifreeze to the system, check all hose connections, because antifreeze tends to search out and leak through very minute openings. Engines do not normally consume coolant. Therefore, if the level goes down find the cause and correct it.

The exact mixture of antifreeze-to-water which you should use depends on the relative weather conditions. The mixture should contain at least 50-percent antifreeze, but should never contain more than 70-percent antifreeze. Consult the mixture ratio chart on the antifreeze container before adding coolant. Hydrometers are available at most auto parts stores to test the ratio of antifreeze to water. Use antifreeze which meets Specification ESE-M97B44-A (part no. E2FZ-19549-AA) or equivalent.

3   Thermostat – check and replacement

Warning: *Do not allow antifreeze to come in contact with your skin or painted surfaces of the vehicle. Rinse off spills immediately with plenty of water. Antifreeze is highly toxic if ingested. Never leave antifreeze lying around in an open container or in puddles on the floor; children and pets are attracted by it's sweet smell and may drink it. Check with local authorities about disposing of used antifreeze. Many communities have collection centers which will see that antifreeze is disposed of safely. Do not attempt to remove the radiator cap, coolant or thermostat until the engine has cooled completely.*

Caution: *Do not drive the vehicle without a thermostat. The computer may stay in open loop and emissions and fuel economy will suffer.*

Check

1   Before assuming the thermostat is to blame for a cooling system problem, check coolant level, drivebelt tension (see Chapter 1) and temperature gauge (or light) operation.
2   If the engine takes a long time to warm up, the thermostat is probably stuck in the open position. Replace the thermostat with a new one.
3   If the engine runs hot, use your hand to check the temperature of the upper radiator hose. If the hose is not hot, but the engine is, the thermostat is probably stuck in the closed position, preventing the coolant inside the engine from escaping to the radiator. Replace the thermostat.
4   If the upper radiator hose is hot, it means that the coolant is flowing and the thermostat is open. Consult the Troubleshooting Section at the front of this manual for further diagnosis.

Replacement

Refer to illustrations 3.9, 3.11, 3.13 and 3.14
5   Disconnect the negative cable from the battery.
6   Drain the coolant from the radiator (see Chapter 1).
7   On some models it may be necessary to remove the engine air ducts to access the upper radiator hose.
8   Remove the upper radiator hose from the thermostat housing.
9   Remove the two bolts from the thermostat housing and detach the housing **(see illustration)**. Be prepared for some coolant to spill as the gasket seal is broken.
10   Note the position of the thermostat prior to removal. Remove the thermostat by turning it counterclockwise to release it from the housing.
11   Remove all traces of gasket material from the sealing surfaces **(see illustration)**.
12   Apply gasket sealant to both sides of a new gasket and position it on the engine.
13   Place the thermostat into position and twist it clockwise until secure **(see illustration)**. **Note:** *Some thermostats have round bleeder valves. When installing these, locate the bleeder at the 12 o'clock position as viewed from the front of the engine.*
14   Two types of gaskets are available; an adhesive-backed gasket and a plain one. Coat both sides of the plain gasket with RTV sealant just before installation. Peel the paper off the adhesive-backed gasket and use the adhesive to hold the gasket in place **(see illustration)**.

3.9   Remove the mounting bolts (arrows)

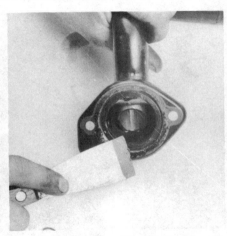

3.11   Remove all traces of old gasket material

3.13   Insert the thermostat with the spring facing out, engage the locking recess and twist the thermostat clockwise

3.14   Position the new gasket over the thermostat (adhesive-backed gasket shown)

4.2   Squeeze the spring-type clamps together with a plier and slip them back over the hoses

3

15   Install the thermostat housing and bolts. Tighten the bolts to the torque listed in this Chapter's Specifications.

16   Install the upper radiator hose, then reinstall the air inlet and outlet tubes, if necessary.

17   Refill the cooling system (see Chapter 1).

4   Radiator – removal and installation

Refer to illustrations 4.2, 4.4, 4.5 and 4.6

Warning: *Do not allow antifreeze to come in contact with your skin or painted surfaces of the vehicle. Rinse off spills immediately with plenty of water. Antifreeze is highly toxic if ingested. Never leave antifreeze lying around in an open container or in puddles on the floor; children and pets are attracted by it's sweet smell and may drink it. Check with local authorities about disposing of used antifreeze. Many communities have collection centers which will see that antifreeze is disposed of safely.*

Removal

1   Drain the cooling system (see Chapter 1).

2   Disconnect the upper and lower radiator hoses and overflow hose from the radiator **(see illustration)**.

3   On supercharged models, remove the intercooler (see Chapter 4) and electric cooling fan (see Section 5).

4.4   Remove the upper fan shroud bolts (arrows) and lift the shroud out of the lower retaining clips, then lay the shroud back over the fan

4   On non-supercharged models, remove the upper fan shroud mounting bolts at the radiator support **(see illustration)**. Lift the shroud sufficiently to disengage the lower retaining clips and lay the shroud back over the fan.

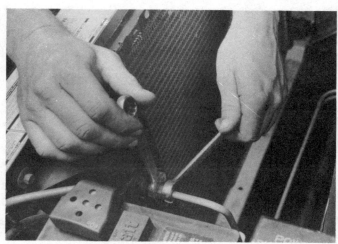

4.5   Hold the inner fitting with a back-up wrench and unscrew the coupling nut with a flare-nut wrench

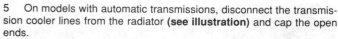

4.6   Remove the radiator mounting bolts (driver's side shown)

5   On models with automatic transmissions, disconnect the transmission cooler lines from the radiator **(see illustration)** and cap the open ends.

6   Remove the mounting bolts **(see illustration)** and lift the radiator out of the vehicle.

Installation

7   Installation is the reverse of removal.

8   Refill the cooling system and, on automatic transmission models, check the transmission fluid level (see Chapter 1).

---

5   Engine cooling fan and clutch – check, removal and installation

---

Warning: *To avoid possible injury or damage, DO NOT operate the engine with a damaged fan. Do not attempt to repair fan blades – replace any fan which is damaged.*

Note: *The supercharged engine has an electric fan. Other models have a conventional engine-mounted fan and viscous clutch.*

Check

Supercharged engines

Refer to illustration 5.3

1   The supercharged engine has an electric cooling fan system with two speeds that is regulated by the integrated relay control assembly and EEC-IV module. The ignition switch must be on for the fan to work. The fan

low speed should come on at a coolant temperature of about 222-degrees F or whenever the air conditioning is on and vehicle speed is below 43 mph. The high speed should come on at a coolant temperature of about 230-degrees F.

2   To test the fan, unplug the electrical connector at the motor and use fused jumper wires to connect the fan directly to the battery. If the fan still does not work, replace the motor.

3   If the motor tested OK, the fault lies in the coolant temperature switch, the integrated relay control assembly, the EEC-IV system (see Chapter 6) or the wiring which connects these components. Carefully check all wiring and connections **(see illustration)**. If no obvious problems are found, further diagnosis should be done by a Ford or Lincoln-Mercury dealer service department or repair shop.

Non-supercharged engines

Refer to illustration 5.4

4   Disconnect the negative battery cable and rock the fan back and forth by hand to check for excessive bearing play **(see illustration)**. Visually inspect for fluid leakage from the clutch assembly. Either problem calls for replacement of the clutch assembly.

5   With the engine completely warmed up, shut off the engine and disconnect the negative battery cable. Turn the fan by hand. Some drag should be evident. If the fan turns very easily or is locked solid, replace the fan clutch.

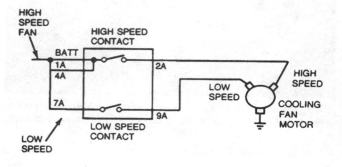

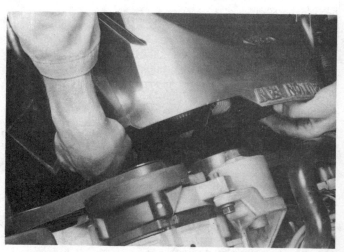

5.3   Electric cooling fan circuit

5.4   Rock the blades back and forth to check for excessive bearing play

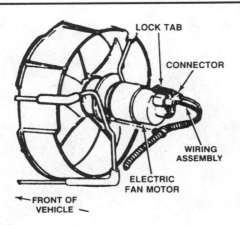

5.7   Unplug the fan electrical connector

Removal and installation

Supercharged engines

Refer to illustrations 5.7 and 5.8

6   Disconnect the negative battery cable.

7   Insert a small screwdriver into the plug to lift the lock tab and unplug the fan electrical connector **(see illustration)**. Unclip the wiring harness.

8   Detach the overflow hose and unbolt the fan bracket and shroud assembly **(see illustration)**. Lift it out of the engine compartment.

9   Installation is the reverse of removal. Be sure to reconnect the wiring and check the operation of the fan.

Non-supercharged engines

Refer to illustrations 5.11, 5.12, 5.13 and 5.15

10   Disconnect the negative cable from the battery.

11   Remove the bolts attaching the fan/clutch assembly to the water pump hub **(see illustration)**

12   Remove the fan shroud attaching bolts **(see illustration)** and lift the shroud out of the lower locating clips.

3

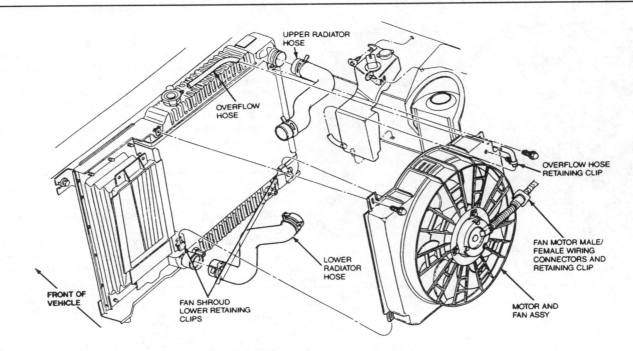

5.8   Electric cooling fan mounting details – exploded view

5.11   Remove the fan clutch-to-water pump bolts (arrows)

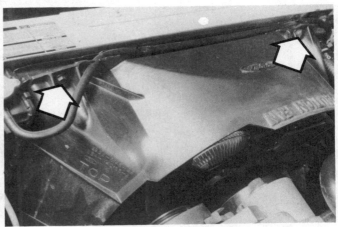

5.12   Remove the fan shroud bolts (arrows)

5.13   Lift the fan shroud out of the engine compartment

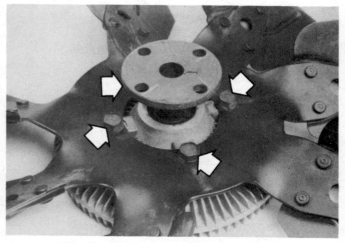

5.15   Remove the fan-to-clutch bolts (arrows)

6.9a   Coolant temperature sending unit location (arrow) –
non-supercharged engine

13   Lift the fan/clutch assembly and shroud out of the engine compartment at the same time **(see illustration)**.
14   Carefully inspect the fan blades for damage and defects. Replace if necessary.
15   At this point, the fan may be unbolted from the clutch, if desired **(see illustration)**. If the fan clutch is stored, place it with the radiator side facing down.
16   Installation is the reverse of removal. Tighten the bolts to the torque listed in this Chapter's Specifications.

---

6   Coolant temperature sending unit – check and replacement

Warning: *The engine must be completely cool before removing the sending unit.*

Note: *The following procedure applies only to the standard analog instruments. The diagnosis procedure for the optional digital panel requires special equipment the home mechanic is not likely to have.*

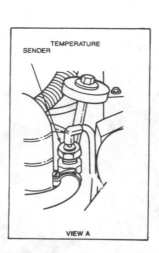

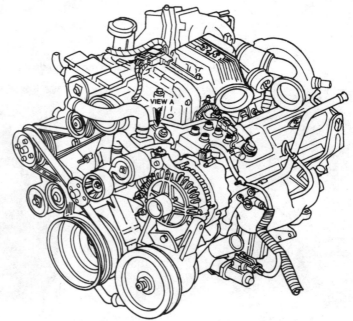

6.9b   Coolant temperature sending unit
location – supercharged engine

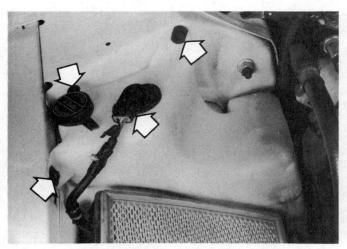

7.2   Unplug the electrical connector and remove the screws (arrows)

8.3   If coolant runs out of this hole (arrow), replace the pump (pump removed for clarity)

Check

1   If the coolant temperature gauge or light is inoperative, check the fuses first (see Chapter 12).
2   If the temperature indicator shows excessive temperature after running a while, see the Troubleshooting Section in the front of the manual.
3   If the temperature gauge or light indicates "Hot" shortly after the engine is started cold, disconnect the wire at the coolant temperature sensor. If the gauge reading drops or the light goes out, replace the sending unit. If the reading remains high, the wire to the gauge or light may be shorted to ground or the gauge is faulty.
4   If the coolant temperature gauge fails to indicate after the engine has been warmed up (approx. 10 minutes) and the fuses checked out OK, shut off the engine. Disconnect the wire at the sending unit and using a jumper wire, connect it to a clean ground on the engine. Turn on the ignition without starting the engine. If the gauge now indicates "Hot", replace the sending unit.
5   If the gauge still does not work, the circuit may be open or the gauge may be faulty. See Chapter 12 for additional information.

Replacement

Refer to illustrations 6.9a and 6.9b
6   With the engine completely cool, remove the cap from the radiator to release any pressure, then replace the cap. This reduces coolant loss during sender replacement.
7   Disconnect the electrical connector from the sending unit.
8   Prepare the new sending unit for installation by wrapping Teflon tape around the threads.
9   Unscrew the sending unit from the engine (**see illustrations**) and quickly install the new one to prevent coolant loss.
10   Tighten the sending unit securely and connect the wiring harness.
11   Refill the cooling system (see Chapter 1) and run the engine. Check for leaks and proper light or gauge operation.

7   Coolant reservoir – removal and installation

Refer to illustration 7.2
Warning: *Do not allow antifreeze to come in contact with your skin or painted surfaces of the vehicle. Rinse off spills immediately with plenty of water. Antifreeze is highly toxic if ingested. Never leave antifreeze lying around in an open container or in puddles on the floor; children and pets are attracted by it's sweet smell and may drink it. Check with local authorities about disposing of used antifreeze. Many communities have collection centers which will see that antifreeze is disposed of safely.*
1   Disconnect the coolant overflow hose at the radiator neck.
2   Unplug the electrical connector from the top of the reservoir (**see illustration**).

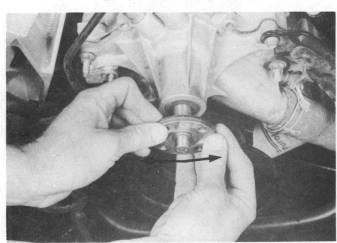

8.4   Rock the shaft up and down to check for play

3   Remove the screws attaching the reservoir to the inner fender.
4   Installation is the reverse of removal.

8   Water pump – check

Refer to illustrations 8.3 and 8.4
1   A failure in the water pump can cause overheating and serious engine damage because a defective pump will not circulate coolant through the engine.
2   There are two ways to check the operation of the water pump while it's in place on the engine. If either check indicates that the pump is defective, replace it with a new or rebuilt unit.
3   The water pump body has a "weep" hole in the underside (**see illustration**). If the pump seal fails, coolant will leak out of the hole. You'll need to get underneath the water pump to see the hole, so raise the vehicle and place it on jackstands. Use a flashlight to help determine if coolant is leaking from the pump.
4   If the water pump shaft bearing fails it will usually make a squealing sound (don't confuse drivebelt slippage, which makes a similar sound, with water pump bearing failure). Even before the bearing actually fails, shaft wear can be detected by grasping the pulley or flange firmly and moving it up-and-down (**see illustration**). If excessive play is noted, the shaft and/or bearing are worn and the pump should be replaced. **Note:** *In and out play is normal.*

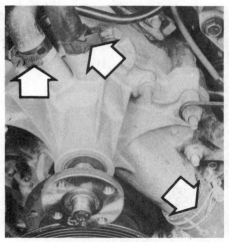

9.6   Detach the coolant hoses (arrows) – non-supercharged engine shown

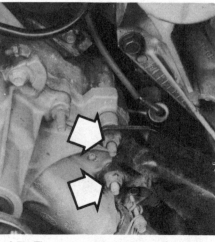

9.7   The power steering pump bracket fits over the water pump mounting studs (arrows)

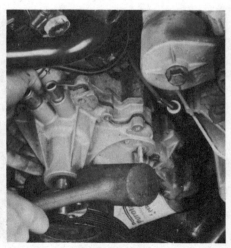

9.8   Use a soft-face mallet to break the gasket seal

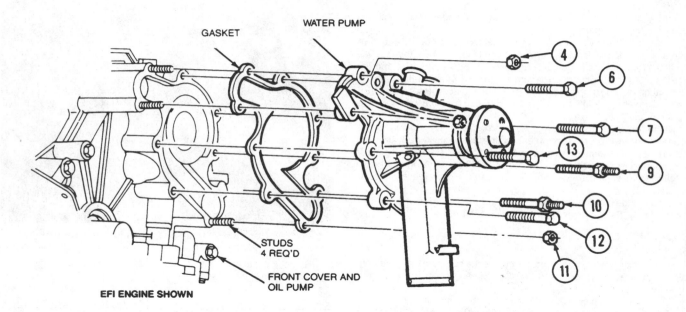

9.9   Water pump mounting details – exploded view (non-supercharged engine shown, supercharged engine similar)

9   Water pump – replacement

Refer to illustrations 9.6, 9.7, 9.8, 9.9, 9.10 and 9.12

Warning: *Do not allow antifreeze to come in contact with your skin or painted surfaces of the vehicle. Rinse off spills immediately with plenty of water. Antifreeze is highly toxic if ingested. Never leave antifreeze lying around in an open container or in puddles on the floor; children and pets are attracted by it's sweet smell and may drink it. Check with local authorities about disposing of used antifreeze. Many communities have collection centers which will see that antifreeze is disposed of safely.*

1   Disconnect the negative battery cable.
2   Drain the cooling system (see Chapter 1).
3   Remove the air cleaner assembly and air intake duct, if necessary (see Chapter 4).
4   Remove the cooling fan and shroud (see Section 5).

5   Remove the drivebelts, idler pulley bracket (see Chapter 1) and the pulley at the end of the water pump shaft.
6   Disconnect the coolant hoses from the water pump **(see illustration)**.
7   Remove all accessory drive brackets from the water pump **(see illustration)**. If you have the special tools for power steering pump pulley removal and installation, detach the pulley and remove the bracket (see Chapter 10). If you don't have the special tools, remove the alternator (see Chapter 5) and power steering pump and bracket assembly (see Chapter 10). **Note:** *If you remove the power steering pump and air conditioning compressor, do not disconnect the hoses, but rather tie the units aside with the hoses attached.*
8   Unbolt and remove the water pump **(see illustration)**.
9   Note the length and types of bolts as they are removed to ensure correct installation **(see illustration)**.
10   Thoroughly clean all gasket surfaces **(see illustration)**.

9.10   Remove all traces of old gasket material

9.12   Apply sealant to the threads of the bolt in this location (arrow)

11   Apply a thin film of RTV sealant to the new gasket and position it on the engine.

12   Prior to installation, coat only one bolt **(see illustration)** with Teflon tape (Ford D8AZ-19554-A or equivalent). Lightly oil the remaining bolts.

13   Install the pump and tighten the bolts to the torque listed in this Chapter's Specifications.

14   Reinstall all parts removed in the reverse order of removal.

15   Refill the cooling system and check belt tension (see Chapter 1), run the engine and check for coolant leaks.

10   Heater and air conditioning blower motor – removal and installation

Refer to illustrations 10.2, 10.3, 10.4 and 10.5

1   Disconnect the negative battery cable.

2   Lower the glove compartment door by squeezing the sides together and disengaging the tabs **(see illustration)**.

3   Working through the glove compartment opening, unplug the blower motor by depressing the locking tabs and pulling the connector off. Unscrew the blower motor from the housing **(see illustration)**.

4   Pull the motor and mounting plate out as a unit **(see illustration)**.

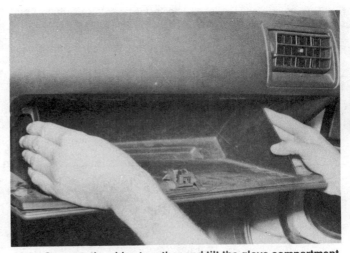

10.2   Squeeze the sides together and tilt the glove compartment door down

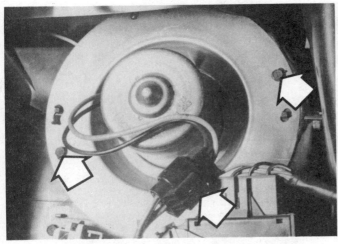

10.3   Unplug the connector and remove the mounting screws (arrows)

10.4   Slip the blower assembly out of the housing

3

10.5   Remove the retaining clip (arrow)

5   If the motor is being replaced, transfer the fan to the new motor by removing the clip **(see illustration)** and pulling the fan off the shaft.
6   Installation is the reverse of removal. Reconnect the battery cable, check operation of the blower and then reset the glove compartment door.

11   Heater core – removal and installation

Refer to illustrations 11.8 and 11.13
Warning: *The air conditioning system is under high pressure. DO NOT disassemble any part of the system (hoses, compressor, line fittings, etc.)*

until after the system has been depressurized by a dealer service department or service station.

Removal

1   If the vehicle you are working on has air conditioning, take it to a dealer or service station to have the refrigerant gas discharged.
2   Disconnect the negative battery cable.
3   Drain the cooling system (see Chapter 1).
4   Remove the instrument panel (see Chapter 12).
5   On air conditioned models, disconnect the refrigerant lines which go through the firewall. Use a backup wrench to prevent twisting the tubing. Cap all open ends.
6   Disconnect the heater hoses which go through the firewall. Cap all open ends.
7   Disconnect the black vacuum supply hose from the inline vacuum check valve in the engine compartment.
8   Disconnect the blower motor wiring and remove the ducts **(see illustration)**.
9   Working under the hood, remove the two nuts retaining the heater/evaporator case to the dash panel.
10   In the passenger compartment, remove the screw attaching the heater/evaporator case support bracket to the cowl top panel.
11   Remove the nut retaining the bracket below the heater/evaporator case to the dash panel.
12   Carefully pull the heater/evaporator case away from the dash panel and remove the case assembly from the vehicle.
13   Remove the four heater core access cover screws and detach the access cover **(see illustration)**.
14   Remove the tube seal from the heater core tubes. Lift the heater core and seals from the case.

Installation

15   Install the heater core into the case with the tube seal on the outside of the case.

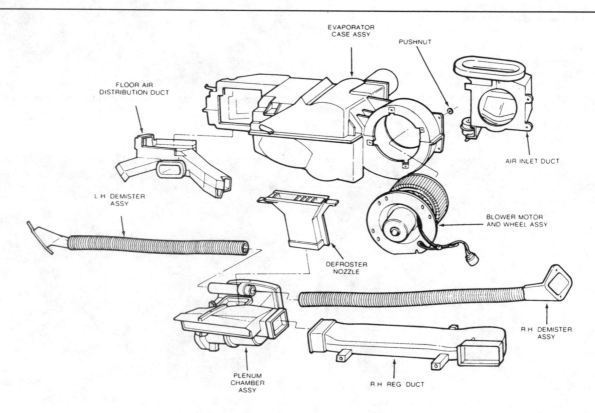

11.8   Heater/evaporator components – exploded view

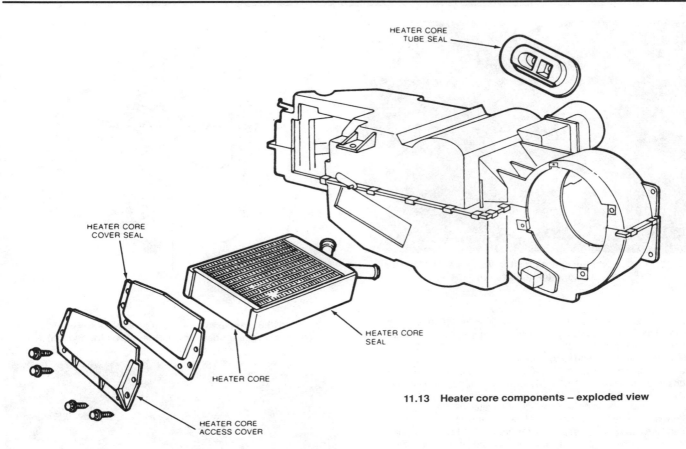

11.13   Heater core components – exploded view

3

16   Position the heater core access cover on the case. Install the four attaching screws.
17   Install the heater/evaporator case assembly in the vehicle in the reverse order of removal.
18   Refill the cooling system and check for leaks.
19   Return the vehicle to the shop which discharged the air conditioning for evacuating, recharging and leak testing the system. Ford recommends that the air conditioner accumulator be replaced before recharging the system – consult your dealer.

12   Air conditioning system – check and maintenance

Refer to illustration 12.14
Warning: *The air conditioning system is under high pressure. DO NOT disassemble any part of the system (hoses, compressor, line fittings, etc.) until after the system has been depressurized by a dealer service department or service station.*

1   Regularly inspect the condenser fins (located ahead of the radiator) and brush away leaves and bugs.
2   Clean out the evaporator drain tube by slipping a wire into the opening.
3   Check the condition of the refrigerant hoses. If there is any sign of deterioration or hardening, have them replaced by a dealer or air conditioning shop.
4   At the recommended intervals, check the compressor drivebelt as described in Chapter 1.
5   The air conditioning compressor should be run for at least 10 minutes a month. This is especially important during the winter months because

long term non-use can cause hardening of the seals. Use of the defroster activates the compressor.
6   Because of the complexity of the air conditioning system and the special equipment required to service it, in depth troubleshooting and repairs are beyond the scope of this manual. However, simple checks and component replacement procedures are provided in this Chapter.
7   The most common cause of poor cooling is simply a low refrigerant charge. If a noticeable drop in cooling ability occurs, the following quick checks will help you determine whether the refrigerant level is low.
8   Warm up the engine to its normal operating temperature.
9   Switch on the air conditioning to its coldest setting and put the blower on high speed. Open the windows so the air conditioning doesn't cycle off as it cools the interior.
10   With the compressor engaged – the clutch will make an audible click and the center of the clutch will rotate – feel the evaporator inlet pipe between the orifice tube and the accumulator with one hand while placing your other hand on the surface of the accumulator housing.
11   If both surfaces feel about the same temperature and if both feel a little cooler than the surrounding air, the refrigerant charge is probably okay. Further inspection of the system is beyond the scope of this manual and should be left to a professional.
12   If the inlet pipe has frost accumulation or feels cooler than the accumulator surface, the refrigerant charge is low. Add refrigerant as described below.

Adding refrigerant

13   Buy an automotive charging kit at an automotive parts store. A charging kit typically includes a 14-ounce can of refrigerant, a tap valve and a short section of hose which can be used to connect the tap valve to the system low side service port. Because one can may not be sufficient to bring the system charge up to its proper level, it's a good idea to buy a few

12.14 Connect the charging kit to the low-side of the air conditioning system

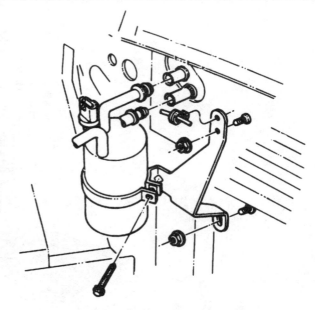

13.3 Accumulator details – exploded view (supercharged model shown, non-supercharged similar)

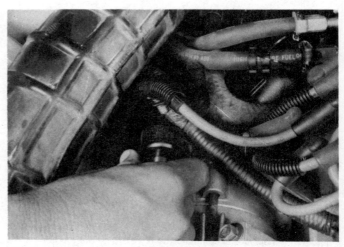

13.5 Use the spring lock tool to disconnect the refrigerant line behind the compressor

additional cans. Make sure the first can contains red refrigerant dye. If the system leaks, the dye will leak out with the refrigerant and help you pinpoint the location of the leak. Never add more than three cans.

14 Connect the charging kit by following the manufacturer's instructions **(see illustration)**. **Warning:** *DO NOT connect the charging kit hose to the high pressure side of the system. The high side has smaller diameter tubing than the low side.*

15 Warm up the engine and operate the system.

16 Add refrigerant to the low side of the system until both the accumulator and the evaporator inlet pipe (at the firewall) feel about the same temperature. Allow stabilization time between each refrigerant addition.

17 Once the accumulator surface and the evaporator inlet pipe feel about the same temperature, add the contents remaining in the can.

13 Air conditioning system accumulator – removal and installation

Refer to illustrations 13.3 and 13.5

Warning: *The air conditioning system is under high pressure. DO NOT disassemble any part of the system (hose, compressor, line fittings, etc.) until after the system has been depressurized by a dealer service department or service station.*

Removal

1 Have the air conditioning system discharged by a dealer or service station.

2 Disconnect the negative battery cable.

3 Unplug the electrical connector from the pressure switch on top of the accumulator **(see illustration)**.

4 Using a spring lock tool, disconnect the refrigerant line from the accumulator at the firewall.

5 Using a spring lock tool, disconnect the other refrigerant line from the accumulator. On supercharged models, the connection is at the accumulator. On non-supercharged models, follow the refrigerant line from the accumulator to the rear of the air conditioning compressor. The connection is just behind the compressor **(see illustration)**.

6 Plug any open fittings to prevent entry of dirt and moisture.

7 Loosen the pinch bolt on the mounting bracket and lift the accumulator out.

8 If a new accumulator is being installed, remove the pressure switch and Schrader valve and pour the oil out into a measuring cup, noting the amount. Add fresh refrigerant oil to the new accumulator equal to the amount removed from the old unit.

Installation

9 Installation is the reverse of removal. Replace O-rings at connections with new ones designed for air conditioning systems and lubricated with refrigerant oil.

10 Take the vehicle back to the shop that discharged it. Have the air conditioning system evacuated, charged and leak tested.

14 Air conditioning system compressor – removal and installation

Refer to illustrations 14.6a and 14.6b

Warning: *The air conditioning system is under high pressure. DO NOT disassemble any part of the system (hoses, compressor, line fittings, etc.) until after the system has been depressurized by a dealer service department or service station.*

Note: *Ford recommends that the orifice tube and the accumulator (see Section 13) be replaced whenever the compressor is replaced. Have the orifice tube replaced by a dealer service department or repair shop.*

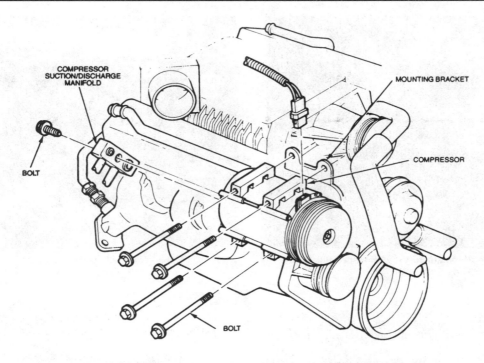

14.6a   Compressor mounting details – supercharged models

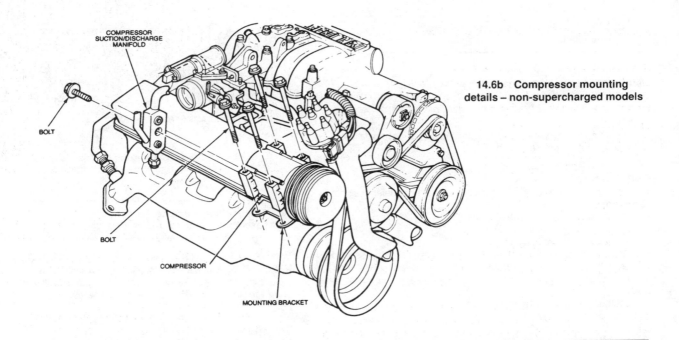

14.6b   Compressor mounting details – non-supercharged models

Removal

1   Have the air conditioning system discharged by a dealer or air conditioning shop.
2   Disconnect the negative cable from the battery.
3   Disconnect the compressor clutch wiring harness.
4   Remove the drivebelt (see Chapter 1).

5   Disconnect the refrigerant lines from the rear of the compressor. On vehicles having "spring lock" type couplings, slip the special tool of the proper size over the fitting, push the tool into the spring lock and pull the tubing out of the fitting. Some lines bolt to the rear of the compressor. Plug the open fittings to prevent entry of dirt and moisture.
6   Unbolt the compressor from the mounting brackets **(see illustrations)** and lift it out of the vehicle.

15.5   Disconnect the fittings (arrows) with a spring lock tool

15.6a   Remove the mounting bolts (arrows)

Installation

7   If a new compressor is being installed, follow the directions which come with the compressor regarding the draining of excess oil prior to installation.

8   Installation is the reverse of removal. Replace any O-rings with new ones specifically made for the purpose and lubricate them with refrigerant oil.

9   Have the system evacuated, recharged and leak tested by the shop that discharged it.

---

15   Air conditioning system condenser – removal and installation

Refer to illustrations 15.5, 15.6a and 15.6b

Warning: *The air conditioning system is under high pressure. DO NOT disassemble any part of the system (hoses, compressor, line fittings, etc.) until after the system has been depressurized by a dealer service department or service station.*

Note: *Ford recommends that the accumulator be replaced whenever the condenser is replaced (see Section 13).*

Removal

1   Have the air conditioning system discharged by a dealer or air conditioning shop.

2   Disconnect and remove the battery.

3   Drain the cooling system (see Chapter 1).

4   Remove the radiator (see Chapter 3).

5   Disconnect the refrigerant lines from the upper right (passenger's) corner of the condenser **(see illustration)** using a "spring lock" tool.

6   Remove the mounting bolts from the condenser brackets **(see illustrations)**.

7   Lift the condenser out of the vehicle and plug the lines to prevent dirt and moisture from entering.

Installation

8   If the same condenser will be reinstalled, store it with the line fittings on top to prevent oil from draining out.

9   If a new condenser is being installed, pour one ounce of refrigerant oil into the new condenser prior to installation.

10   Reinstall the components in the reverse order of removal. Be sure the rubber pads are in place under the condenser.

11   Have the system evacuated, recharged and leak tested by the shop that discharged it.

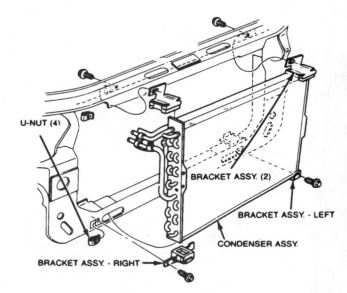

15.6b   Condenser mounting details – exploded view

---

16   Air conditioner and heater control assembly – removal and installation

Refer to illustrations 16.2, 16.3a, 16.3b, 16.3c, 16.4, 16.5, 16.6 and 16.9

Note: *This Section applies to the manually controlled system. The optional automatic temperature control system requires tools and expertise beyond the scope of the average home mechanic and is therefore not covered in this manual.*

Removal

1   Disconnect the negative battery cable.

2   Obtain two control removal tools (Ford T87P-19061-A, or equivalent). If these are unavailable, fabricate two "U" shaped tools from coat hanger wire and push them into the four holes in the faceplate **(see illustration)**.

3   Apply a side load to the control to disengage the clips. Pull the control assembly out from the dash sufficiently to unplug the electrical connectors **(see illustrations)**.

4   Disconnect the vacuum connector by removing the push nut and pulling off the plug **(see illustration)**.

16.2   Insert a U-shaped wire into the holes in the faceplate

16.3a   Pull the control out of the dash . . .

16.3b   . . . and release the connector clips with a small screwdriver

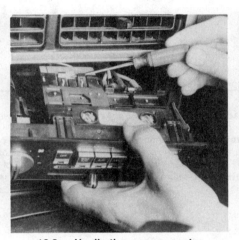

16.3c   Unclip the rear connector

16.4   Detach the vacuum connector

3

16.5   Unclip the temperature control cable

16.6   To replace a bulb, twist the socket

5   Remove the temperature control cable retaining clip and slip the cable from the lever **(see illustration)**.

6   To replace the light bulbs, twist the socket counterclockwise and pull the socket and bulb out **(see illustration)**. Insert the new bulb in the socket and twist it into place clockwise.

Installation

7   Reconnect the electrical connectors.

8   Reconnect the vacuum connector and push on the retaining nuts. **Caution:** *Do Not attempt to screw the nuts on, as the posts will crack.*

9   Check to ensure the self-adjusting clip is at least 3/4 inch from the end

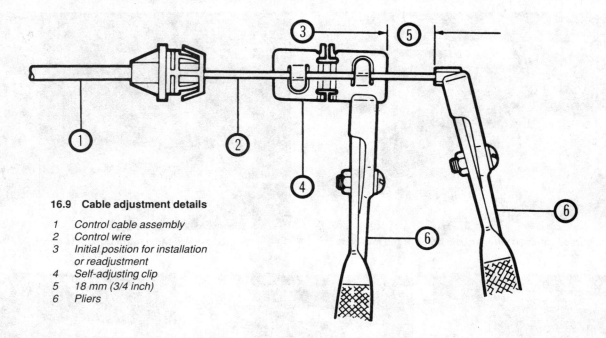

16.9   Cable adjustment details

1   Control cable assembly
2   Control wire
3   Initial position for installation
    or readjustment
4   Self-adjusting clip
5   18 mm (3/4 inch)
6   Pliers

loop of the control cable. If necessary, slide the self-adjusting clip down the control wire (away from the end) approximately 3/4 inch **(see illustration)**.

10   Snap the cable housing into place in the control assembly. Connect the loop end of the control cable to the temperature lever arm on the control assembly.

11   Install a pushnut to retain the cable end loop on the temperature lever arm.

12   Push the control assembly into the instrument panel until it snaps into place.

13   The temperature control cable is self-adjusting with the movement of the temperature selector lever to the right. Move the temperature selector lever to the right end of the slot (WARM) in the bezel face of the control assembly to position the self-adjusting clip.

14   Check for proper control operation.

Chapter 4 Fuel and exhaust systems

Contents

4

Specifications

Fuel pressure

Engine running
  Non-supercharged .... 30-45 psi
  Supercharged .... 30-40 psi
Key on, engine off
  Non-supercharged .... 35-45 psi
  Supercharged .... 35-40 psi

Torque specifications

Ft-lbs (unless otherwise indicated)

Air bypass-to-throttle body bolts	87 in-lbs
Fuel pressure regulator-to-fuel rail screws	34 in-lbs
Fuel rail-to-intake manifold bolts	87 in-lbs
Intake elbow bolts	90 in-lbs
Intercooler-to-tube(s) retaining nuts	14 to 22
Intercooler-to-radiator support retaining screws	36 to 60 in-lbs
Outlet tube-to-bracket bolt or stud	30 to 40
Outlet tube-to-bracket nut	30 to 40
Supercharger adapter collar nut	148
Supercharger outlet retaining bolts	15 to 22
Supercharger retaining bolts	
8 mm	14 to 22
12 mm	52 to 70
Throttle body retaining bolts	19
Upper-to-lower intake manifold bolts	24

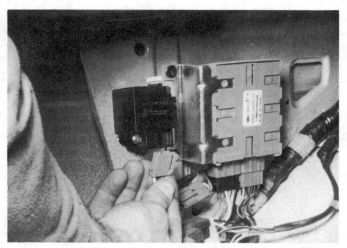

2.2   To relieve the fuel pressure, disconnect the inertia switch and run the engine until it stops

1   General information

Fuel system

The fuel system consists of the fuel tank, the fuel pump, an air cleaner assembly, a fuel injection system (with a supercharger on SC engines) and the various steel, plastic and/or nylon lines and fittings connecting everything together. The fuel pump is electric and is mounted inside the fuel tank.

Exhaust system

All vehicles are equipped with a pair of manifolds, a pair of catalytic converters (below each exhaust manifold), an exhaust pipe, a resonator and a muffler.

2   Fuel pressure relief procedure

Refer to illustration 2.2

1   The inertia switch, which shuts off fuel to the engine in the event of a collision, affords a simple and convenient means by which fuel pressure can be relieved before servicing fuel injection components.

2   Open the trunk lid, peel back the carpet from the left side of the trunk and locate the inertia switch **(see illustration)**.

3   Unplug the electrical connector from the inertia switch. Start the engine and allow it to run until it stops.

4   The fuel system pressure is now relieved. Before beginning work on the fuel system, disconnect the cable from the negative terminal of the battery.

5   Even though the system is now depressurized, always place a rag over any fuel fitting that is being disconnected.

6   When finished working on the fuel system, simply plug the electrical connector back into the switch. Reconnect the cable to the negative terminal of the battery.

3   Fuel lines and fittings – replacement

Warning: *Gasoline is extremely flammable, so take extra precautions when you work on any part of the fuel system. Don't smoke or allow open flames or bare light bulbs near the work area, and don't work in a garage*

where a natural gas-type appliance (such as a water heater or clothes dryer) with a pilot light is present. If you spill any fuel on your skin, rinse it off immediately with soap and water. When you perform any kind of work on the fuel system, wear safety glasses and have a Class B type fire extinguisher on hand.

Spring lock couplings – disassembly and reassembly

Refer to illustrations 3.1, 3.5, 3.6 and 3.7

1   The fuel supply and return lines utilize spring lock couplings. The male end of the spring lock coupling, which is girded by two O-rings, is inserted into a female flared fitting. The coupling is secured by a garter spring which prevents disengagement by gripping the flared end of the female fitting **(see illustration)**.

2   The fuel feed and return line fittings are not the same diameter. To disconnect the 1/2-inch feed line coupling, you will need to obtain a spring lock coupling tool D87L-9280-B or its equivalent; for the 3/8-inch return fitting, get tool D87L-9280-A or its equivalent (Ford dealers may not have these tools on hand, but they are readily available from tool manufacturers like Kent-Moore, Snap-on and Mac, and may be available at some auto parts stores).

Disconnecting the coupling

3   Before detaching the spring lock couplings, relieve the system fuel pressure (see Section 2).

4   Detach the cable from the negative terminal of the battery.

5   Pry the safety clip from each fitting with a small screwdriver **(see illustration)**.

6   Place the appropriately sized spring lock coupling tool in position **(see illustration)**.

7   Close the tool and push it into the open side of the cage to expand the garter spring and release the female fitting **(see illustration)**. **Note:** *The garter spring may not release if the tool is cocked while pushing it into the cage opening.*

8   Once the garter spring is expanded, pull the fittings apart.

9   Remove the tool.

Connecting the coupling

10   Make sure the garter spring is in the cage of the male fitting. If it's missing, install a new spring by pushing it into the cage opening. If the garter spring is damaged, remove it from the cage with a small wire hook (do not use a screwdriver) and install a new spring **(see illustration 3.1** for garter spring sizes).

11   Clean all dirt or foreign material from both pieces of the coupling. **Warning:** *Use only the specified O-rings – they are made of a special material and the use of any other O-ring may allow the connection to leak during vehicle operation.*

12   Lubricate the male fitting and O-rings and the inside of the the female fitting with clean engine oil.

13   Install the plastic indicator ring into the cage opening if the indicator ring is to be used.

14   Fit the female fitting onto the male fitting and push them together until the garter spring snaps over the flared end of the female fitting. **Note:** *If the fitting is equipped with a plastic indicator ring, the ring will snap out of the cage opening when the coupling is connected to indicate engagement. If no indicator ring is used, make sure that the coupling is engaged by visual verification that the garter spring is over the flared end of the female fitting* **(see illustration)**.

4   Fuel pump – check

Warning: *Gasoline is extremely flammable, so take extra precautions when you work on any part of the fuel system. Don't smoke or allow open flames or bare light bulbs near the work area, and don't work in a garage where a natural gas-type appliance (such as a water heater or clothes dry-*

Connection and Disconnection Procedures

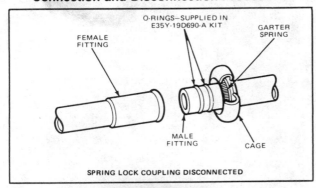

FEMALE FITTING

O-RINGS—SUPPLIED IN E35Y-19D690-A KIT

GARTER SPRING

MALE FITTING

CAGE

SPRING LOCK COUPLING DISCONNECTED

TO DISCONNECT COUPLING

CAUTION—DISCHARGE SYSTEM BEFORE DISCONNECTING COUPLING

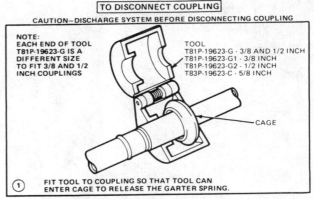

NOTE: EACH END OF TOOL T81P-19623-G IS A DIFFERENT SIZE TO FIT 3/8 AND 1/2 INCH COUPLINGS

TOOL
T81P-19623-G - 3/8 AND 1/2 INCH
T81P-19623-G1 - 3/8 INCH
T81P-19623-G2 - 1/2 INCH
T83P-19623-C - 5/8 INCH

CAGE

① FIT TOOL TO COUPLING SO THAT TOOL CAN ENTER CAGE TO RELEASE THE GARTER SPRING.

TO CONNECT COUPLING

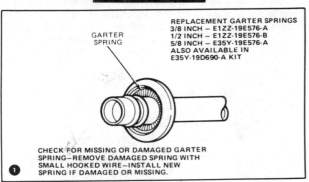

GARTER SPRING

REPLACEMENT GARTER SPRINGS
3/8 INCH — E1ZZ-19E576-A
1/2 INCH — E1ZZ-19E576-B
5/8 INCH — E35Y-19E576-A
ALSO AVAILABLE IN E35Y-19D690-A KIT

CHECK FOR MISSING OR DAMAGED GARTER SPRING—REMOVE DAMAGED SPRING WITH SMALL HOOKED WIRE—INSTALL NEW SPRING IF DAMAGED OR MISSING.

①

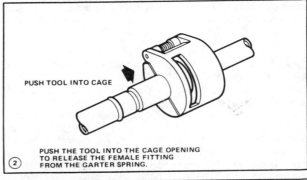

PUSH TOOL INTO CAGE

② PUSH THE TOOL INTO THE CAGE OPENING TO RELEASE THE FEMALE FITTING FROM THE GARTER SPRING.

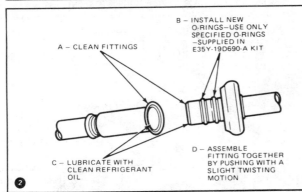

A – CLEAN FITTINGS

B – INSTALL NEW O-RINGS—USE ONLY SPECIFIED O-RINGS —SUPPLIED IN E35Y-19D690-A KIT

C – LUBRICATE WITH CLEAN REFRIGERANT OIL

D – ASSEMBLE FITTING TOGETHER BY PUSHING WITH A SLIGHT TWISTING MOTION

②

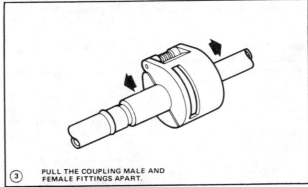

③ PULL THE COUPLING MALE AND FEMALE FITTINGS APART.

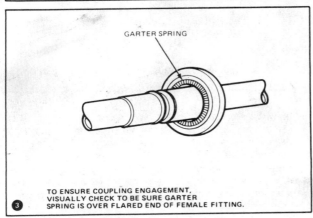

GARTER SPRING

TO ENSURE COUPLING ENGAGEMENT, VISUALLY CHECK TO BE SURE GARTER SPRING IS OVER FLARED END OF FEMALE FITTING.

③

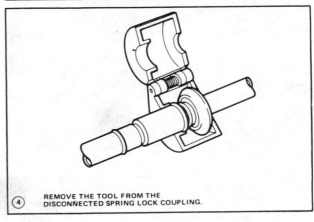

④ REMOVE THE TOOL FROM THE DISCONNECTED SPRING LOCK COUPLING.

3.1   When disconnecting and connecting spring lock couplings, refer to this illustration for the proper garter spring, O-ring and spring lock coupling tool part numbers

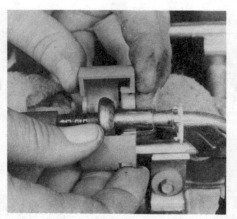

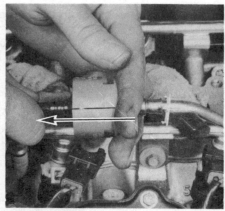

3.5   If the spring lock couplings are equipped with safety clips, pry them off with a small screwdriver

3.6   Open the spring-loaded halves of the spring lock coupling tool and place it in position around the coupling, then close it

3.7   To Disconnect the coupling, push the tool into the cage opening to release the female fitting from the garter spring, then pull the male and female fittings apart

er) with a pilot light is present. If you spill any fuel on your skin, rinse it off immediately with soap and water. When you perform any kind of work on the fuel system, wear safety glasses and have a Class B type fire extinguisher on hand.

Note: *The electric fuel pump and circuit are an integral part of the EEC-IV system, so a complete diagnosis must determine whether the pump and the circuit are operating properly. Such a procedure is beyond the scope of the average home mechanic. However, a loss of fuel flow and/or pressure, usually indicated by a reduction in performance, is often a sign that the fuel pump has malfunctioned. Therefore, perform the following check of the pump if the above symptoms occur. Further investigation of the fuel pump circuit, however, should be left to a dealer service department or other well-equipped repair shop.*

1   Always verify that there is fuel in the tank and none of the lines and fittings are leaking fuel before starting this procedure.
2   The easiest way to determine whether the electric in-tank fuel pump is working is to have an assistant turn the ignition key to Start while you put your ear to the filler neck and listen for the telltale whirring sound that indicates the pump is operating. If the pump is silent, proceed to the next Step.
3   Locate the inertia switch (see Section 2) and, using a self-powered test light or ohmmeter, make sure there is continuity between the switch terminals. If the switch has opened, reset it.
4   If the switch has not opened, check the power and ground circuits to the pump (refer to the Wiring Diagrams at the end of this book).
5   If the power and ground circuits are okay, use a self-powered test light or ohmmeter to check the continuity between the pump positive and ground terminals (you must lower the fuel tank to do this – see Section 5).
6   If there is no continuity, the pump is defective. Replace it (see Section 7).
7   If there is continuity, bypass the pump circuit and, using a fused jumper wire, apply battery voltage to the positive terminal of the pump while grounding the negative terminal of the pump with another jumper wire.
8   If the pump operates, there is an open or short-circuit condition somewhere in the power circuit.
9   If the pump doesn't operate, replace it (see Section 7).
10   Any further testing of the electric fuel pump, its relay or the circuit should be conducted by a dealer service department or other repair shop.

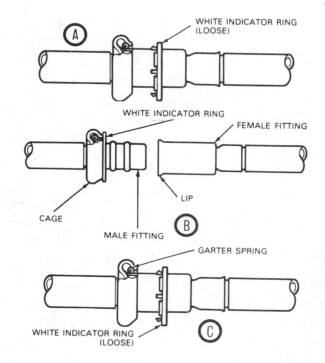

3.14   Spring lock coupling reconnection

---

5   Fuel tank – removal and installation

Refer to illustrations 5.7, 5.9 and 5.10
Warning: *Gasoline is extremely flammable, so take extra precautions when you work on any part of the fuel system. Don't smoke or allow open flames or bare light bulbs near the work area, and don't work in a garage where a natural gas-type appliance (such as a water heater or clothes dry-*

er) with a pilot light is present. If you spill any fuel on your skin, rinse it off immediately with soap and water. When you perform any kind of work on the fuel system, wear safety glasses and have a Class B type fire extinguisher on hand.

Note: *Don't begin this procedure until the fuel gauge indicates the tank is empty or nearly empty. If the tank must be removed when it's full (for example, if the fuel pump malfunctions), siphon any remaining fuel from the tank prior to removal.*

1   Relieve the fuel system pressure (see Section 2).
2   Disconnect the cable from the negative terminal of the battery.
3   Raise the vehicle and support it securely on jackstands.
4   Unless the vehicle has been driven far enough to completely empty the tank, it's a good idea to siphon the residual fuel out before removing the

5.7   Location of the fuel vapor cross-over tube (arrow)

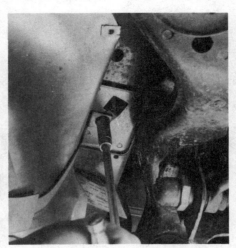

5.9   Support the tank before loosening the retaining strap bolts

5.10   Lower the tank enough to gain access to the electrical connectors and hoses

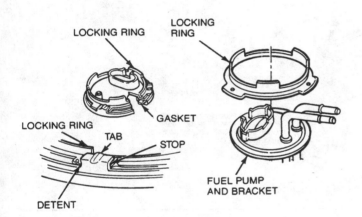

7.4   To remove the fuel pump locking ring, you must turn it counterclockwise

tank from the vehicle. **Warning:** *DO NOT start the siphoning action by mouth! Use a siphoning kit, available at most auto parts stores.*

5   Remove the exhaust pipe and exhaust shield.

6   Loosen the hose clamps securing the fuel filler neck hose and the breather hose to the fuel tank, then detach both hoses.

7   Detach the end of the vapor cross-over hose near the rear of the drive-shaft **(see illustration).**

8   Place a transmission jack or floor jack under the tank and position a block of wood between the jack pad and the tank. Raise the jack until it's supporting the tank. Be careful not to deform the fuel tank, fuel tank support or straps.

9   Remove the bolts from the fuel tank retaining straps **(see illustration).**

10   Lower the tank enough to disconnect the fuel lines and electrical connectors from the tank **(see illustration).**

11   Remove the fuel tank from the vehicle.

12   Installation is the reverse of removal.

6   Fuel tank cleaning and repair – general information

1   Repairs to the fuel tank or filler neck should be performed by a professional with the proper training to carry out this critical and potentially dan-

gerous work. Even after cleaning and flushing, explosive fumes can remain and could explode during repair of the tank.

2   If the fuel tank is removed from the vehicle, it should not be placed in an area where sparks or open flames could ignite the fumes coming out of the tank. Be especially careful inside garages where a natural gas appliance is located because the pilot light could cause an explosion.

7   Fuel pump – removal and installation

Refer to illustration 7.4

Warning: *Gasoline is extremely flammable, so take extra precautions when you work on any part of the fuel system. Don't smoke or allow open flames or bare light bulbs near the work area, and don't work in a garage where a natural gas-type appliance (such as a water heater or clothes dryer) with a pilot light is present. If you spill any fuel on your skin, rinse it off immediately with soap and water. When you perform any kind of work on the fuel system, wear safety glasses and have a Class B type fire extinguisher on hand.*

1   Relieve the fuel system pressure (see Section 2).

2   Remove the fuel tank (see Section 5).

3   Remove any dirt that has accumulated around the fuel pump attaching flange so that it won't fall into the tank when the fuel pump/sending unit is pulled out.

4   Using a brass punch, tap the locking ring counterclockwise until it's loose **(see illustration).** Pull the the fuel pump/sending unit assembly from the tank, being careful not to bend the sending unit arm.

5   Remove the old locking ring gasket and discard it.

6   If you're planning to reinstall the original fuel pump/sending unit, remove the strainer, wash it in clean solvent, then push it back onto the metal pipe on the end of the pump. If you're installing a new pump/sending unit, the assembly will include a new strainer.

7   Clean the fuel pump mounting flange, the tank mounting surface and the seal ring groove.

8   Installation is the reverse of removal. Apply a thin coat of heavy grease to the new locking ring gasket to hold it in place during assembly. When installing the locking ring, make sure the detents on the ring fully engage with the tabs on the tank.

8   Air cleaner housing – removal and installation

Refer to illustrations 8.1 and 8.7

1   Loosen the clamps on the air cleaner air outlet tube and remove the tube **(see illustration).**

4

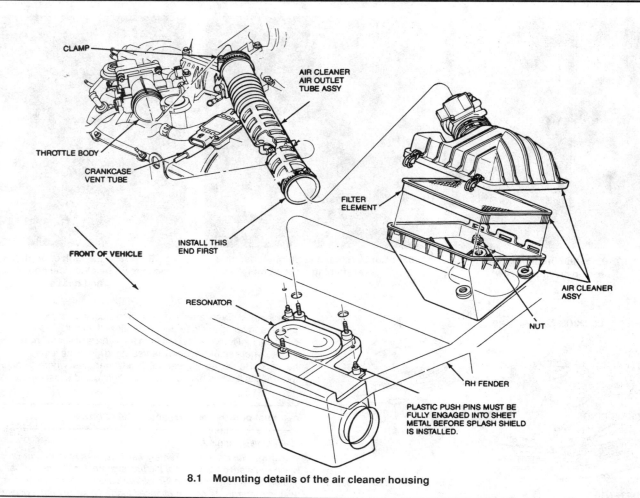

CLAMP

AIR CLEANER
AIR OUTLET
TUBE ASSY

THROTTLE BODY

CRANKCASE
VENT TUBE

FILTER
ELEMENT

FRONT OF VEHICLE

INSTALL THIS
END FIRST

AIR CLEANER
ASSY

RESONATOR

NUT

RH FENDER

PLASTIC PUSH PINS MUST BE
FULLY ENGAGED INTO SHEET
METAL BEFORE SPLASH SHIELD
IS INSTALLED.

8.1 Mounting details of the air cleaner housing

2   By unsnapping the elbow from the PCV retainer clip, disconnect the PCV hose at the air cleaner.
3   Slide off the hoses from the PCV filter adapter.
4   Remove the air cleaner cover and filter element.
5   Remove the PCV filter retaining clip and remove the retainer from the air cleaner tray.
6   Remove the filter pack from the retainer.
7   Remove the nuts retaining the air cleaner assembly to the resonator **(see illustration)**.
8   Remove the air cleaner and/or resonator.
9   When installing the resonator be sure the plastic push pins are fully engaged into the sheet metal. The remainder of installation is the reverse of removal.

---

9   Accelerator cable – removal and installation

Refer to illustration 9.3
1   Push the accelerator cable nylon bushing out of the arm of the accelerator pedal.
2   Remove the cruise control cable (if equipped).
3   Using a screwdriver, detach the accelerator cable at the throttle body **(see illustration)**.
4   Remove the screw retaining the cable housing-to-engine mounting bracket.
5   Remove the cable from the retainer on the upper intake manifold brace.
6   From inside the passenger compartment, remove the cable housing from the dash panel by depressing the two vertical snap tabs in and push-

ing out.
7   Installation is the reverse of removal.
8   After installation, make sure the throttle closes and opens fully, without binding.

---

10   Fuel injection system – general information

The Electronic Fuel Injection (EFI) system used is known as a multi-point, pulse time, speed density control design. Fuel is metered into the intake air stream in accordance with engine demand through six injectors mounted on a tuned intake manifold. The injectors are energized in sequence to follow the engine firing order. Each injector is activated once every other crankshaft revolution.

An on-board Electronic Engine Control (EEC-IV) computer accepts inputs from various engine sensors to compute the required fuel flow rate necessary to maintain a prescribed air/fuel ratio throughout the entire engine operational range. The computer then outputs a command to the fuel injectors to meter the approximate quantity of fuel.

The period of time that the injectors are energized (known as "on time" or "pulse width") is controlled by the EEC computer. Air entering the engine is sensed by speed, pressure and temperature sensors. The information from these sensors are processed by the EEC-IV computer. The computer determines the needed injector pulse width and outputs a command to the injector to meter the exact quantity of fuel.

The EEC-IV engine control system also compensates for changes in altitude.

An electric in-tank fuel pump forces pressurized fuel through a series of metal and plastic lines and an inline fuel filter/reservoir to the fuel rail.

8.7 After removing the air filter, remove the air cleaner assembly retaining nuts

9.3 Use a screwdriver to pry the cable from the throttle shaft

11.3 Connect the fuel pressure gauge to the Schrader valve on the fuel rail, start the engine and note the fuel pressure

12.7 Remove the six bolts securing the upper intake manifold to the lower intake manifold (arrows)

The rail assembly incorporates electrically actuated fuel injectors directly above each intake port. When energized, the injectors spray a metered quantity of fuel into the intake air stream.

A constant fuel pressure is maintained in the fuel rail by a pressure regulator. The regulator is positioned downstream from the fuel injectors. Excess fuel passes through the regulator and returns to the fuel tank through a fuel return line.

11 Fuel injection system – pressure check

Refer to illustration 11.3

Warning: *Gasoline is extremely flammable, so take extra precautions when you work on any part of the fuel system. Don't smoke or allow open flames or bare light bulbs near the work area, and don't work in a garage where a natural gas-type appliance (such as a water heater or clothes dryer) with a pilot light is present. If you spill any fuel on your skin, rinse it off immediately with soap and water. When you perform any kind of work on the fuel system, wear safety glasses and have a Class B type fire extinguisher on hand.*

1 With a Ford T80L-9974-B fuel pressure gauge (or equivalent) and adapter T85L-9974-A (or equivalent), the fuel pressure can be measured easily and quickly. The fuel rails on these vehicles are equipped with

Schrader valves, so it is not necessary to detach any fuel lines to read the fuel pressure.

2 The special Ford fuel pressure gauge/adapter assembly specified above is designed to relieve fuel pressure, as well as measure it, through the Schrader valve. If you have this gauge, you can use this method as an alternative to the fuel pressure relief procedure outlined in Section 2. **Warning:** *Never, however, attempt to relieve fuel pressure through the Schrader valve without this special setup.*

3 To attach the gauge, simply remove the valve cap, screw on the adapter and attach the gauge to the adapter (**see illustration**).

4 Start the engine and allow it to reach a steady idle. Note the indicated fuel pressure reading and compare it to the value listed in this Chapter's Specifications.

5 If the indicated fuel pressure is lower than specified, the problem is probably either a leaking fuel line (possibly inside the fuel tank at the pump hose), a malfunctioning fuel pump, faulty fuel pressure regulator or a leaking injector. Carefully pinch the fuel return line (the one that doesn't connect to the Schrader valve side of the fuel rail) with a pair of pliers (place a folded rag over the line first to prevent damage) and watch the pressure gauge. If the pressure now increases, the pressure regulator is defective.

6 If the indicated pressure is higher than specified, the cause could be a blocked fuel return line or a stuck fuel pressure regulator. Try tapping on the pressure regulator – if the needle on the gauge drops, replace the regulator.

12 Fuel injection system – component removal and installation

Upper intake manifold and throttle body assembly (non-supercharged models)

Refer to illustrations 12.7 and 12.8

Removal

1 Detach the cable from the negative terminal of the battery.

2 Remove the air cleaner housing outlet tube (see Section 8).

3 Unplug the electrical connectors from the air bypass valve, throttle position sensor and EGR transducer.

4 Disconnect the throttle cable, cruise control cable (if equipped) and the downshift cable from the throttle shaft (see Section 9).

5 Clearly label, then detach, the vacuum lines from the vacuum tree, the EGR valve, the fuel pressure regulator and the canister purge lines from the fittings on the throttle body.

6 Detach the PCV hose from the fitting on the rear of the upper manifold.

7 Remove the six upper intake manifold retaining bolts (**see illustration**).

12.8   Exploded view of intake manifold assembly (non-super charged engine)

1   Cap-Schrader valve
2   Schrader valve
3   Fuel rail
4   Fuel pressure regulator
5   Fuel injector
6   Retainer
7   Thermostat
8   Gasket
9   Housing
10 Bolt
11 Throttle body
12 Gasket
13 Gasket
14 Throttle air bypass valve
15 EGR valve assembly
16 Gasket
17 Bolt/stud
18 Upper intake manifold
19 Gasket
20 Lower intake manifold
21 Stud/bolt
22 Fuel rail assembly
23 Bolt

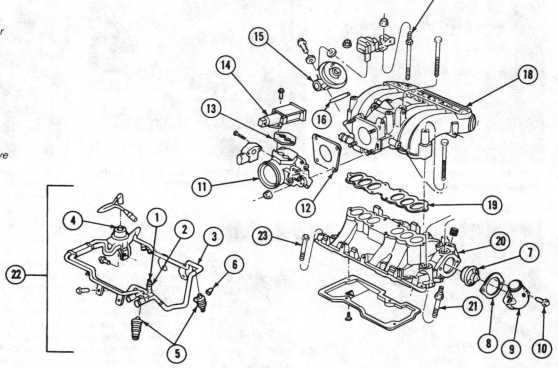

8   Remove the upper intake manifold and throttle body as an assembly from the lower intake manifold **(see illustration)**.
9   Remove the old gasket and discard it.

Installation

10   Clean and inspect the gasket surfaces of the upper and lower intake manifolds. If it's necessary to scrape away any old gasket material, be extremely careful not to damage either gasket mating surface.
11   Position the new gasket on the mounting face of the lower intake manifold. The use of alignment studs may be helpful.
12   Using the alignment studs to keep the gasket in position, place the upper intake manifold and throttle body assembly in position on the lower manifold. **Note:** *If the manifold is not equipped with alignment studs, make sure that the gasket remains in place when positioning the upper intake manifold and throttle body.*
13   Install the six upper intake manifold retaining bolts and tighten them to the torque listed in this Chapter's Specifications.
14   The remainder of installation is the reverse of removal.

Throttle body

Refer to illustration 12.19

Removal

15   Detach the cable from the negative terminal of the battery.
16   Remove the air cleaner housing outlet tube (see Section 8).
17   Unplug the electrical connectors from the throttle position sensor and throttle air bypass valve.
18   Detach the throttle body coolant hose (if equipped). Detach the throttle cable, cruise control cable (if equipped) and transmission downshift cable (see Section 9).
19   Remove the four throttle body mounting nuts and the throttle body (see accompanying illustration and illustration 12.8).

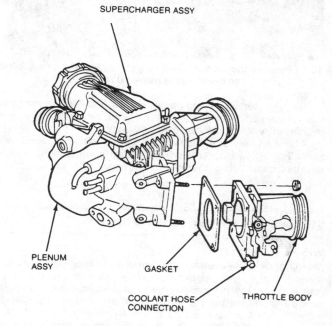

12.19   Throttle body mounting details (supercharged engine)

20   Remove and discard the gasket between the throttle body and its mounting surface.

12.25a Use a screwdriver to disconnect the electrical connector for the throttle air bypass valve

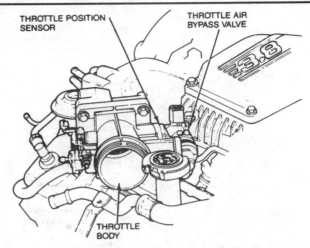

12.25b Locations of the throttle position sensor and throttle air bypass valve on the supercharged engine

Installation

21 Clean the gasket mating surfaces. If scraping is necessary, be extremely careful not to damage either gasket surface or allow material to drop into the manifold or plenum.
22 Install the throttle body gasket over the mounting studs, then install the throttle body.
23 Tighten the nuts to the torque listed in this Chapters Specifications.
24 The remainder of installation is the reverse of removal.

Throttle air bypass valve

Refer to illustrations 12.25a, 12.25b and 12.26

Removal

25 Unplug the electrical connector from the air bypass valve assembly **(see illustrations)**.
26 Remove both mounting bolts from the air bypass valve **(see illustration)**.
27 Remove the air bypass valve and gasket.

Installation

28 Clean the gasket mating surfaces. **Note:** *If scraping is necessary, be extremely careful not to damage the air bypass valve or the throttle body gasket surfaces or drop material into the throttle body.*
29 The remainder of installation is the reverse of removal. Be sure to tighten the mounting bolts securely.

Throttle Position (TP) sensor

Refer to illustration 12.32

Removal

30 Unplug the electrical connector from the TP sensor.
31 Scribe a reference mark across the edge of the sensor and to the throttle body to ensure that the TP sensor is positioned correctly during installation.
32 Remove the two retaining screws from the throttle position sensor (see accompanying illustration and illustration 12.25b).
33 Remove the TP sensor.

Installation

34 Installation is the reverse of the removal procedure.

Fuel rail assembly

Refer to illustrations 12.39, 12.41, and 12.42

Removal

35 Remove the fuel tank filler cap to release fuel tank pressure.
36 Relieve the fuel system pressure (see Section 2).
37 Detach the cable from the negative terminal of the battery.
38 Remove the upper intake manifold and throttle body assembly (see Step 1).
39 Unplug the electrical connectors from the fuel injectors **(see illustration)**.

12.26 Remove the throttle air bypass mounting bolts

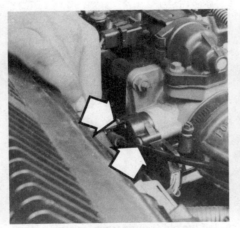

12.32 You'll have to use a stubby screwdriver to remove the screws mounting the throttle position sensor – non-supercharged engine shown

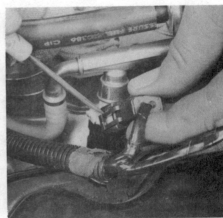

12.39 Use a small screwdriver to loosen the locking tangs on the electrical connectors for the injectors

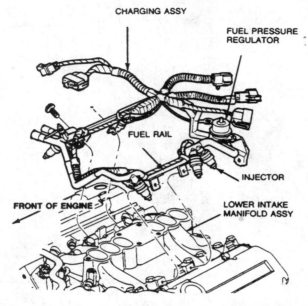

CHARGING ASSY

FUEL PRESSURE
REGULATOR

FUEL RAIL

INJECTOR

FRONT OF ENGINE

LOWER INTAKE
MANIFOLD ASSY

12.41 Mounting details of the fuel rail assembly

40 Using a special spring lock coupling tool, disconnect the crossover fuel hose from the fuel rail assembly (see Section 3).
41 Remove the four (two per side) fuel rail assembly retaining bolts **(see illustration)**.
42 Carefully disengage the fuel rail from the fuel injectors and remove it. **Note:** *If it's easier, simply detach the fuel rail from the lower intake manifold with the fuel injectors still attached* **(see illustration)**, *then detach the fuel injectors from the fuel rail (see below).*

Installation

43 There are two ways to install the fuel rail:
   a) Install each of the injectors into the lower intake manifold first (see below), then place the fuel rail assembly over the injectors and push it onto them until it's firmly seated.
   b) Install the injectors into the fuel rail assembly first, place the fuel rail assembly and injectors in position on the lower intake manifold and carefully push and wiggle the injectors into their respective bores in the lower intake manifold.
44 Secure the fuel rail assembly to the lower intake manifold with the four

retaining bolts and tighten them securely.
45 The remainder of installation is the reverse of removal.

Fuel injectors

Refer to illustrations 12.48 and 12.49
Removal
46 Remove the fuel rail assembly (see Step 35).
47 Grasp each injector body and pull on it while gently rocking it from side-to-side (from the fuel rail or manifold).
48 After noting the positions of the O-rings on the injectors, remove and discard them **(see illustration)**.
49 Inspect the washer and the plastic "hat" covering the pintle on the end of each injector **(see illustration)** for signs of deterioration. Replace them if necessary. **Note:** *If the hat is missing, look for it in the intake manifold.*

Installation
50 Lubricate the new O-rings with light grade oil (ESE-M2C39-F or equivalent) and install them on the ends of each injector. **Note:** *Do not use silicone grease – it will clog the injectors.*
51 Using a light twisting, pushing motion, install the injectors into either the lower intake manifold or the fuel rail assembly (use whichever method is easier for you).
52 Install the fuel rail assembly as outlined previously.
53 The remainder of installation is the reverse of removal.

Fuel pressure regulator

Refer to illustration 12.58
Removal
54 Remove the fuel tank filler cap to relieve pressure in the fuel tank.
55 Relieve the fuel system pressure (see Section 2).
56 Detach the ground cable from the battery.
57 Remove the fuel rail (see Step 35).
58 Remove the three Allen screws from the underside of the pressure regulator mounting plate **(see illustration)**.
59 Remove the pressure regulator assembly, gasket and O-ring. Discard the old gasket and O-ring.

Installation
60 Make sure that the gasket surfaces of the fuel pressure regulator and fuel rail assembly are clean. If scraping is necessary, be careful not to damage the fuel pressure regulator or fuel supply line gasket surfaces.
61 Lubricate the pressure regulator O-ring with clean engine oil.
62 Install the new O-ring and gasket on the regulator.
63 Install the fuel pressure regulator on the fuel rail assembly and tighten the three retaining screws to the torque listed in this Chapter's Specifications.

12.42 Use a gentle rocking motion to remove the fuel rail

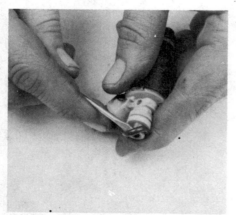

12.48 Use a small screwdriver to peel off the old O-rings from the ends of the injectors – be extremely careful not to damage the sealing areas or the sensitive fuel metering orifices

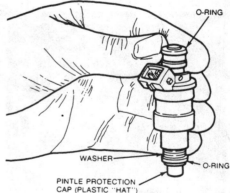

O-RING

O-RING

WASHER

PINTLE PROTECTION
CAP (PLASTIC "HAT")

12.49 In addition to replacing the two O-rings on the injectors, always inspect the washer and the plastic "hat" that protects the pintle – if either shows evidence of deterioration, replace it

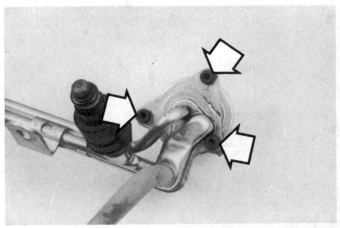

12.58   Remove the three Allen screws (arrows) to detach the fuel pressure regulator from the fuel rail

13.1   Detaching the exhaust from an exhaust hanger

13   Exhaust system servicing – general information

Refer to illustration 13.1

Warning: *Inspection and repair of exhaust system components should be done only after enough time has elapsed after driving the vehicle to allow the system components to cool completely. Also, when working under the vehicle, make sure it is securely supported on jackstands.*

1   The exhaust system consists of the exhaust manifolds, the catalytic converters, the muffler, the tailpipe and all connecting pipes, brackets, hangers and clamps. The exhaust system is attached to the body with mounting brackets and rubber hangers **(see illustration)**. If any of the parts are improperly installed, excessive noise and vibration will be transmitted to the body.

2   Conduct regular inspections of the exhaust system to keep it safe and quiet. Look for any damaged or bent parts, open seams, holes, loose connections, excessive corrosion or other defects which could allow exhaust fumes to enter the vehicle. Deteriorated exhaust system components should not be repaired; they should be replaced with new parts.

3   If the exhaust system components are extremely corroded or rusted together, welding equipment will probably be required to remove them. The convenient way to accomplish this is to have a muffler repair shop remove the corroded sections with a cutting torch. If, however, you want to save money by doing it yourself (and you don't have a welding outfit with a cutting torch), simply cut off the old components with a hacksaw. If you have compressed air, special pneumatic cutting chisels can also be used. If you do decide to tackle the job at home, be sure to wear safety goggles to protect your eyes from metal chips and work gloves to protect your hands.

4   Here are some simple guidelines to follow when repairing the exhaust system:

  a) Work from the back to the front when removing exhaust system components.
  b) Apply penetrating oil to the exhaust system component fasteners to make them easier to remove.
  c) Use new gaskets, hangers and clamps when installing exhaust systems components.
  d) Apply anti-seize compound to the threads of all exhaust system fasteners during reassembly.
  e) Be sure to allow sufficient clearance between newly installed parts and all points on the underbody to avoid overheating the floor pan and possibly damaging the interior carpet and insulation. Pay particularly close attention to the catalytic converter and heat shield.

14   Supercharger – general information

Refer to illustration 14.1

The supercharger is not a bolt-on option. It is part of an integrated engine system. The supercharger is a blow-through type system with port fuel injection. The supercharger is belt driven off the crankshaft and, if damaged, is replaced as a unit (it is not serviceable). The throttle body controls the amount of intake air to the supercharger through the inlet plenum. The pressurized air from the supercharger is routed through the intercooler, which cools and condenses the air/fuel charge, and then to the intake manifold **(see illustration)**.

A vacuum controlled bypass valve is installed at the supercharger outlet. The bypass valve controls the amount of pressurized air back into the supercharger. At low throttle, the engine runs under normal engine vacuum. As the throttle opening is increased, the bypass valve actuator closes the bypass valve, which directs all the air from the supercharger to the intake manifold.

15   Supercharger – diagnosis

Due to the need for special tools and expertise, diagnosis of the supercharger is beyond the scope of the home mechanic and should be left to a dealer service department or other qualified repair shop.

However, other systems which affect the operation of the supercharger can be inspected, which may help to isolate the problem. Check the following:

Ducts between the air inlet adapter and the intercooler or between the supercharger an the intercooler – check for leaks

Check the supercharger drivebelt – make sure the supercharger turns and the belt doesn't slip

Tap on the air bypass actuator – if it's sticky, it may resume functioning normally when tapped

Check the exhaust system for an obstruction

Check all vacuum hoses for leaks

Check the fuel pressure

Check for leaky seals, which will be characterized by a film of oil around the front of the supercharger, and may also be accompanied by noise

16   Supercharger and related components – removal and installation

Air bypass actuator

Refer to illustration 16.3

1   Detach the actuator vacuum hose.
2   Remove the inlet plenum assembly (see Step 70).

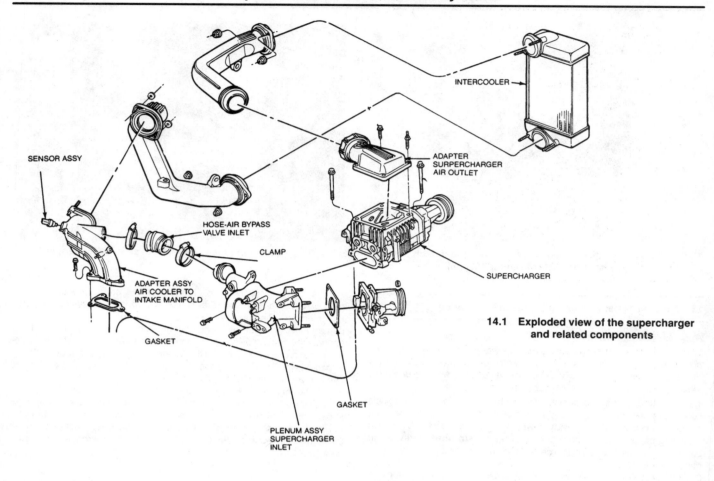

14.1   Exploded view of the supercharger and related components

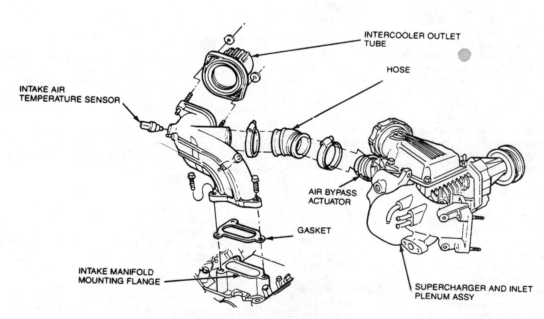

16.3   View of the air bypass actuator location

3   Remove the bolt retaining the actuator to the supercharger **(see illustration)**.

4   Remove the two self-tapping screws.

5   Rotate the actuator to allow the rod to pass through the keyed slot in the bypass lever and remove the actuator.

6   Installation is the reverse of removal.

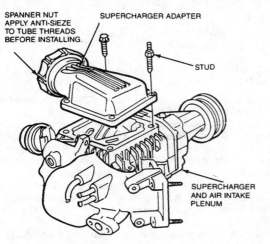

16.7   Air outlet adapter-to-supercharger mounting details

Inlet tube

Refer to illustrations 16.7 and 16.8

Removal

7   Using spanner nut wrench (T89P-6634-A) or equivalent, detach the inlet tube from the supercharger adapter **(see illustration)**.

8   Remove four nuts retaining the inlet and the outlet tubes-to-intercooler **(see illustration)**. **Caution:** *Carefully disconnect the outlet tube from the intercooler so the sealing surfaces and retaining studs are not damaged while removing the inlet tube.*

9   Remove the nut and push-on nut retaining the inlet tube-to-alternator/steering pump bracket.

10   Remove the stud from the alternator/steering pump bracket.

11   Remove the inlet tube. **Caution:** *Be very careful during removal and installation of the intercooler tubes so you don't scratch, nick or contaminate the sealing surfaces.*

Installation

12   Whenever the intercooler outlet is disconnected, the outlet tube-to-intercooler sealing surface must be resealed.

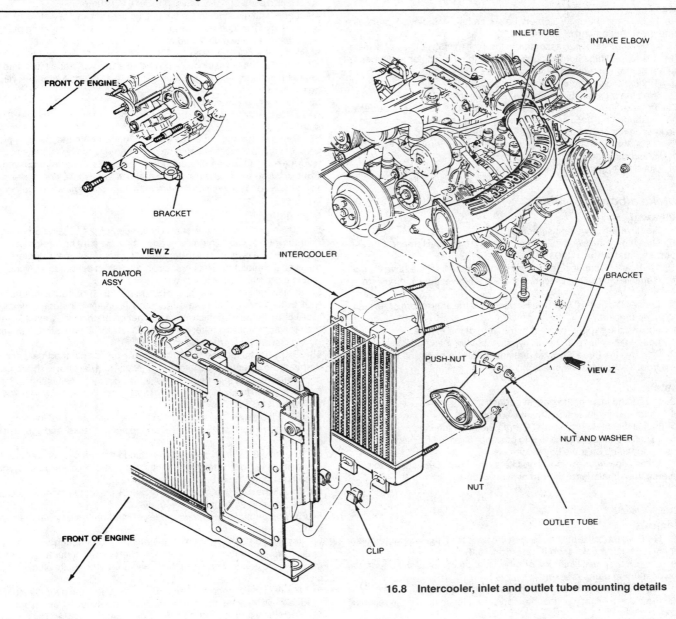

16.8   Intercooler, inlet and outlet tube mounting details

13   Clean and inspect the sealing surfaces of the supercharger outlet adapter, intake elbow, intercooler and tubes. Be sure there is no foreign material on the sealing surfaces. It is important that the intercooler tubes seal completely. Any air leak will cause poor operation and performance.

14   Install gasket sealant tape (ESE-M4G168-B) from Kit (E9PE-6F091-AA), or equivalent, to the seat surfaces of the intercooler tubes (four places). Install the tape approximately 1/8-inch from the inner diameter of the tubes. Overlap the tape ends approximately 1/4-inch. Do not stretch the tape. **Note:** *During proper installation, a slight wrinkling will occur on the tape edge at the inner diameter.*

15   Apply regular grade anti-seize and lubricating compound (ESE-M12A4-A) or equivalent from kit (E9PE-6F091-AA) to the inner backside seat and thread to the collar of the supercharger outlet adapter. **Caution:** *The system must be tightened in the correct sequence (explained below) for proper sealing of the intercooler tubes.*

16   Position the inlet tube, then install the upper stud into the alternator/power steering pump bracket.

17   Install the push-on nut onto the stud, tight it enough to retain the tube against alternator/steering bracket surface but free enough to allow tube movement to ensure seating on the inlet tube to supercharger outlet adapter.

18   Using hand pressure, tighten the supercharger outlet adapter collar onto the threaded end of the inlet tube.

19   Install the intercooler assembly to the inlet and the outlet tubes. Install the nuts to the studs tight enough to retain the intercooler and tubes together but free enough to allow movement on the seats.

20   Tighten the supercharger adapter securely.

21   Wait ten minutes minimum and retighten the collar.

22   Tighten the inlet and outlet tube-to-intercooler nuts to the torque listed in this Chapter's Specifications. The clamping connectors should be installed so they are parallel to the studs of the intercooler.

23   Install the nut that retains the inlet tube to the alternator/power steering pump bracket and tighten it securely.

24   Start the engine and check for vacuum leaks.

Intake elbow assembly
Removal
25   Remove the cowl vent screens.

26   Disconnect the electrical connector at the intake air temperature sensor **(see illustration 16.103).**

27   Mark and disconnect the vacuum lines at the intake elbow.

28   Remove the two nuts securing the outlet tube of the intercooler to the elbow.

29   Loosen the outlet tube of the intercooler at the alternator/power steering pump bracket.

30   Loosen the support bracket at the front of the engine.

31   Loosen the clamp at the air bypass actuator inlet hose.

32   Remove the three elbow to manifold retaining bolts and slide the elbow from the hose to remove it.

Installation
33   Clean and inspect the gasket surfaces.

34   Install a new gasket on the intake manifold.

35   Install the intake elbow and tighten the retaining bolts.

36   Install the air bypass hose into position (align the paint stripe on the hose with the rib on the elbow assembly).

37   While allowing the support bracket at the front of the engine to pivot, reverse the remainder of the removal procedure.

Intercooler
Removal
38   Remove the four nuts connecting the upper and the lower intercooler tubes to the intercooler **(see illustration 16.8).**

39   Loosen the upper intercooler tube (inlet tube) nut at the alternator/power steering pump bracket.

40   Remove the intercooler retaining screws and washers.

41   Push down slightly on the intercooler to release it from the retaining clips.

Installation
42   Use teflon tape on the tube sealing surfaces of the intercooler and reverse the removal procedure.

Outlet tube
Removal
43   Remove the two nuts retaining the outlet tube to the intake elbow assembly **(see illustration 16.8).**

44   Raise and securely support the front of the vehicle on jackstands.

45   Remove the bolt retaining the outlet tube to the upper support bracket located at the front of the engine. Loosen the support bracket at the front of the engine. **Note:** *The bracket must remain close enough to the front of the engine to allow it to pivot during outlet tube reinstallation.*

46   Remove the nut and push-on nut retaining the bracket for the outlet tube-to-alternator/steering pump. **Note:** *If you are just reselling the tube, it does not have to be removed from the vehicle. Proceed to the outlet tube installation procedure.*

47   Remove the intercooler tube upper stud from the alternator/steering pump bracket.

48   Remove the belt that drives the steering pump.

49   Label and disconnect the spark plug wires from the coil.

50   Remove the stud nuts for the bracket brace of the steering pump.

51   Remove the two bolts and one stud nut retaining the steering pump bracket to the cylinder head.

52   Install a bolt 6-1/2 inches long, with the proper thread pitch, into the top hole in the steering pump bracket. Thread the bolt into the cylinder head about five turns.

53   Remove the steering pump filler cap.

54   Slide the steering pump bracket assembly forward on the 6-1/2 inch long bolt.

55   Remove the outlet tube by pulling it underneath the steering pump bracket and up through the engine compartment. It may be necessary to pivot the outlet tube clamping connector to gain clearance during removal. **Caution:** *Use extreme care during removal and installation of the intercooler tubes to prevent scratching, nicking or contaminating the sealing surface.*

Installation
56   Clean and inspect the sealing surfaces of the supercharger outlet adapter, intake elbow, intercooler and tubes. Be sure no foreign particles are on the sealing surfaces of the tubes. It is important that the intercooler tubes seal completely. The engine control system demands a sealed system to calculate proper fuel flow.

57   Install gasket sealant tape (ESE-M4G168-B) or equivalent from kit (E9PE-6F091-AA) to the seal surfaces of the intercooler tubes. Install tape approximately 1/8-inch from the inner diameter of the tubes. Overlap the tape ends approximately 1/4-inch. **Caution:** *Do not stretch the tape during installation or the seal may leak.*

58   Guide the outlet tube down through the engine compartment and underneath the steering pump bracket. Use extreme care not to scratch, nick or contaminate the sealing surfaces. **Note:** *It may be necessary to rotate the lower outlet tube clamping connector to gain clearance while installing the outlet tube.*

59   Slide the power steering pump bracket assembly into position.

60   Install the nut that retains the steering pump bracket and tighten it securely.

61   Remove 6-1/2 inch bolt installed during the removal procedure.

62   Install the bolts retaining the steering pump bracket to the cylinder head and tighten it securely.

63   Install the nuts that retain the bracket brace for the steering pump to the water pump and tighten it securely.

64   Install the outlet tube over the lower stud on the alternator/steering pump bracket.

65   Install the push-on nut onto the stud, tight it enough to retain tube against the alternator/steering pump bracket but free enough to allow tube movement to ensure seating of the outlet tube to the intake elbow assembly.

66   Position the clamping connector for the outlet tube over the studs on the intake elbow assembly and secure it using two nuts. Tighten both nuts to the torque listed in this Chapter's Specifications. **Note:** *The clamping*

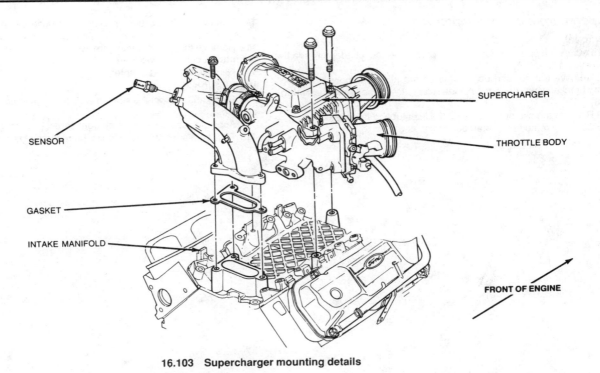

16.103 Supercharger mounting details

SENSOR

GASKET

INTAKE MANIFOLD

SUPERCHARGER

THROTTLE BODY

FRONT OF ENGINE

connector should be installed so it is parallel to the stud mounting face of the intake elbow assembly.

67   Install the proper nut to the stud on alternator/steering pump bracket and tighten it securely.

68   Install the proper bolt to secure the outlet tube to the engine support bracket and tighten it to the torque listed in this Chapter's Specifications.

69   Tighten the nut and bolt retaining the support bracket to the front of the engine..

Plenum assembly

Removal

70   Partially drain the cooling system.

71   Remove the cowl vent screens, intake elbow assembly (see procedure beginning with Step 25) and the intake air tube for the throttle valve.

72   Disconnect the accelerator cable (see Section 9).

73   Disconnect the coolant hoses at the throttle body.

74   Remove the accelerator cable bracket retaining bolts and position the bracket out of the work area.

75   Disconnect the PCV tube.

76   Mark and disconnect the vacuum lines from the plenum assembly and the EGR transducer.

77   Disconnect the electrical connections at the throttle position sensor, the throttle air bypass valve **(see illustration 12.25b)** and the EGR transducer.

78   Remove the two bolts retaining the EGR valve and pull the EGR valve away from the plenum (if equipped).

79   Remove the screw mounting the EGR transducer bracket and remove the transducer.

80   Remove the four bolts retaining the plenum assembly.

81   Loosen the bypass hose clamp and remove the plenum.

Installation

82   Use new gaskets on the plenum mating joints.

83   Installation is the reverse of removal procedure.

Supercharger

Refer to illustration 16.103

Note: *The supercharger can't be rebuilt or overhauled. If the supercharger malfunctions, it will be necessary to replace the supercharger as a unit.*

Removal

84   Clean the area around the supercharger.

85   Disconnect the negative battery cable.

86   Remove the air inlet tube from the throttle body **(see illustration 16.8).**

87   Remove the vent screens for the cowl.

88   Drain the cooling system (see Chapter 1).

89   Mark and disconnect the right side spark plug wires at the coil assembly and position them out of the work area.

90   Disconnect the electrical connectors at the air bypass valve, the throttle position sensor and the intake air temperature sensors **(see illustration 16.3).**

91   Mark and disconnect the vacuum lines from the inlet plenum assembly.

92   Disconnect the vacuum line from the EGR transducer and remove the transducer from the bracket.

93   Disconnect the tube from the PCV valve.

94   Disconnect the accelerator cable at the throttle housing (see Section 9).

95   Remove the linkage bracket attaching bolts and position the bracket aside.

96   Disconnect the cruise control cable (if equipped).

97   Remove the two EGR valve attaching bolts and move the EGR valve away from intake assembly (if equipped).

98   Disconnect the coolant hoses from the throttle body.

99   Remove the supercharger drive belt.

100 Remove the intercooler inlet and outlet tubes (see procedure in this section).

101 Remove the three bolts mounting the intake elbow.

102 Remove the three bolts mounting the supercharger.

103 Lift the supercharger and the intake assembly from the vehicle as an assembly **(see illustration). Note:** *To prevent entry of foreign material, all engine openings should be covered with clean rags after the unit is removed.*

Installation

104 Clean and inspect the gasket surfaces.

105 Apply RTV sealant to the intake plenum mating surfaces.

106 Installation is the reverse of the removal procedure.

4

Supercharger outlet adapter

Removal

107 Loosen the spanner nut on the supercharger outlet adapter **(see illustration 16.7)**.

108 Remove the nut and upper stud on the alternator/power steering pump bracket which supports the intercooler inlet tube **(see illustration 16.8)**.

109 Remove the two nuts mounting the inlet tube to the intercooler.

110 Carefully remove the intercooler inlet tube.

111 Remove the three bolts retaining the outlet adapter to the supercharger.

112 Remove the stud mounting the wiring harness bracket and position the bracket out of the work area.

113 Remove the outlet adapter.

Installation

114 Clean and inspect the sealing surfaces of the supercharger sealing surface.

115 Apply sealant to the supercharger sealing surfaces.

116 The remainder of installation is the reverse of removal.

Chapter 5   Engine electrical systems

Contents

Specifications

General

Coil-to-cap wire resistance	7k ohms per ft. max
Drivebelt deflection	See Chapter 1
Battery voltage	
Engine off	12 volts
Engine running (charging voltage)	14-to-15 volts

Torque specifications

	Ft-lbs (unless otherwise indicated)
Crankshaft sensor mounting bolts	22 to 31 in-lbs
Camshaft sensor/synchronizer clamp bolt	15 to 22

1   General information

The engine electrical systems include all ignition, charging and starting components. Because of their engine-related functions, these components are considered separately from chassis electrical devices such as the lights, instruments, etc.

Be very careful when working on the engine electrical components. They are easily damaged if checked, connected or handled improperly. The alternator is driven by an engine drivebelt which could cause serious injury if your hands, hair or clothes become entangled in it with the engine running. Both the starter and alternator are connected directly to the battery and could arc or even cause a fire if mishandled, overloaded or shorted out.

Never leave the ignition switch on for long periods of time with the engine off. Don't disconnect the battery cables while the engine is running. Correct polarity must be maintained when connecting battery cables from another source, such as another vehicle, during jump starting. Always disconnect the negative cable first and hook it up last or the battery may be shorted by the tool being used to loosen the cable clamps.

Additional safety related information on the engine electrical systems can be found in Safety first near the front of this manual. It should be referred to before beginning any operation included in this Chapter.

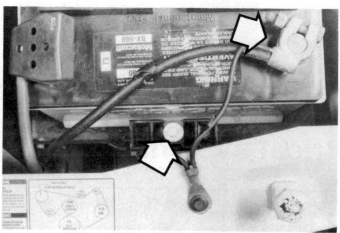

2.2   When removing the battery, remove the cable from the negative terminal first – the mounting bolt for the battery hold-down clamp is shown (arrows)

2   Battery – removal and installation

Refer to illustration 2.2

1   Disconnect both cables from the battery terminals. **Caution:** *Always disconnect the negative cable first and hook it up last or the battery may be shorted by the tool being used to loosen the cable clamps.*
2   Locate the battery hold-down clamp between the battery and the radiator support **(see illustration)**. Remove the bolt and the hold-down clamp.
3   Lift out the battery. Special straps that attach to the battery posts are available – lifting and moving the battery is much easier if you use one.
4   Installation is the reverse of removal.

3   Battery – emergency jump starting

Refer to the *Booster battery (jump) starting* procedure in the front part of this manual.

4   Battery cables – check and replacement

1   Periodically inspect the entire length of each battery cable for damage, cracked or burned insulation and corrosion. Poor battery cable connections can cause starting problems and decreased engine performance.
2   Check the cable-to-terminal connections at the ends of the cables for cracks, loose wire strands and corrosion. The presence of white, fluffy deposits under the insulation at the cable terminal connection is a sign that the cable is corroded and should be replaced. Check the terminals for distortion, missing mounting bolts and corrosion.
3   When replacing the cables, *always disconnect the negative cable first and hook it up last, or the battery may be shorted by the tool used to loosen the cable clamps.* Even if only the positive cable is being replaced, be sure to disconnect the negative cable from the battery first.
4   Disconnect and remove the cable. Make sure the replacement cable is the same length and diameter as the cable being replaced.
5   Clean the threads of the relay or ground connection with a wire brush to remove rust and corrosion. Apply a light coat of petroleum jelly to the threads to help prevent future corrosion.
6   Attach the cable to the relay or ground connection and tighten the mounting nut/bolt securely.
7   Before connecting the new cable to the battery, make sure that it reaches the battery post without having to be stretched.
8   Connect the positive cable first, followed by the negative cable.

5   Ignition system – general information

Non-supercharged models

The ignition system on these models is a solid state electronic design consisting of an ignition module, coil, distributor, spark plug wires and the spark plugs. Mechanically, the system is similar to a breaker point system, except that the distributor cam and ignition points are replaced by a "Hall Effect" vane stator switch assembly. The coil primary circuit is controlled by an amplifier module, the "Hall Effect" vane stator switch and the ECA.

When the ignition is switched on, the ignition primary circuit is energized. When the beginning edge of the window of the rotary vane cup (located in the distributor) passes between the distributor hall effect device and the permanent magnet assembly, a signal is produced which is used by the amplifier module and the ECA to turn off the coil primary current.

When the primary circuit is on, current flows from the battery through the ignition switch, the coil primary winding, the amplifier module and then to ground. When the current is interrupted, the magnetic field in the ignition coil collapses, inducing a high voltage in the coil secondary windings. The voltage is conducted to the distributor where the rotor directs it to the appropriate spark plug. This process is repeated continuously.

Supercharged models

These models use a Distributorless Ignition System (DIS). The following components are used in the system:

  a) Electronic Control Assembly (ECA)
  b) Camshaft sensor
  c) Coil pack
  d) Crankshaft sensor
  e) Ignition module
  f) Related wiring
  g) Spark plugs

This system is very complex and requires special tools and training to diagnose, therefore we shall limit information on this system to removal and installation of components.

6   Ignition system – check

Warning: *Because of the very high voltage generated by the ignition system, extreme care should be taken when this check is performed.*

6.1   To use a calibrated ignition tester (available at most auto parts stores), simply disconnect a spark plug wire, attach the wire to the tester and clip the tester to a good ground – if there is enough power to fire the plug, sparks will be clearly visible between the electrode tip and the tester body as the engine is turned over

Non-supercharged models

Refer to illustration 6.1

1   If the engine turns over but won't start, disconnect the spark plug wire from any spark plug and attach it to a calibrated ignition tester (available at most auto parts stores). Connect the clip on the tester to a bolt or metal bracket on the engine **(see illustration)**. Make sure the tester is designed for Ford ignition systems if a universal tester isn't available. If you're unable to obtain a calibrated ignition tester, remove the wire from one of the spark plugs and, using an insulated tool, hold the end of the wire about 1/4-inch from a good ground.

2   Crank the engine and watch the end of the tester or spark plug wire to see if bright blue, well-defined sparks occur. If you're not using a calibrated tester, have an assistant crank the engine for you.

3   If sparks occur, sufficient voltage is reaching the plug to fire it (repeat the check at the remaining plug wires to verify that the distributor cap and rotor are OK). However, the plugs themselves may be fouled, so remove and check them as described in Chapter 1.

4   If no sparks or intermittent sparks occur, remove the distributor cap and check the cap and rotor as described in Chapter 1. If moisture is pres-

ent, dry out the cap and rotor, then reinstall the cap and repeat the spark test.

5   If there's still no spark, detach the coil secondary wire from the distributor cap and hook it up to the tester (reattach the plug wire to the spark plug), then repeat the spark check. Again, if you don't have a tester, hold the end of the wire about 1/4-inch from a good ground.

6   If sparks now occur, the distributor cap, rotor or plug wire(s) may be defective.

7   If no sparks occur, check the primary wire connections at the coil to make sure they're clean and tight. Check for voltage to the coil. Make any necessary repairs, then repeat the check again.

8   If there's still no spark, the coil-to-cap wire may be bad (check the resistance with an ohmmeter and compare it to the Specifications). If a known good wire doesn't make any difference in the test results, the ignition module may be defective.

Supercharged models

9   These models use a Distributorless Ignition System (DIS). This system is very complex and requires special tools and training to diagnose, therefore we shall limit information on this system to removal and installation of components. Take the vehicle to a dealer service department or other qualified shop for diagnosis.

---

7   Ignition coil and coil pack – removal and installation

Coil (non-supercharged models)

Refer to illustration 7.2

1   Detach the cable from the negative terminal of the battery.

2   Detach the electrical connectors from the coil, located near the air cleaner assembly **(see illustration)**.

3   Remove the bolts mounting the coil bracket-to-fender.

4   Remove the coil and the bracket.

5   Remove the coil-to-bracket mounting bolts.

6   Installation is the reverse of removal.

Coil pack (supercharged models)

Refer to illustrations 7.9 and 7.10

7   Detach the cable from the negative terminal of the battery.

8   Disconnect the electrical connector from the coil pack.

9   Remove the spark plug wires by squeezing the locking tabs to release the boot retainers **(see illustration)**.

10   Remove the screws mounting the coil pack and remove the pack **(see illustration)**.

11   Installation is the reverse of removal.

5

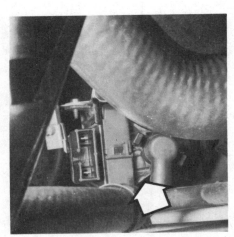

7.2   The ignition coil (arrow) is near the air cleaner housing

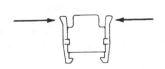

SQUEEZE
LOCKING TABS
TO REMOVE

7.9   Squeeze the locking tabs to release the spark plug wire boots

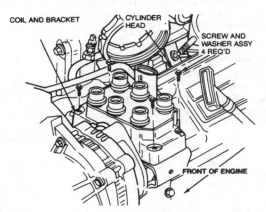

7.10   Coil pack mounting details

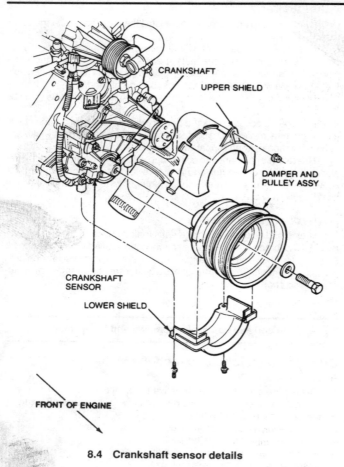

8.4   Crankshaft sensor details

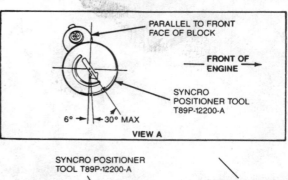

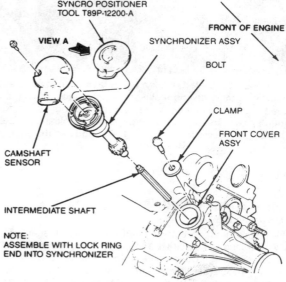

9.4   Camshaft sensor and synchronizer assembly
installation details

8   Crankshaft sensor – removal and installation

Removal

Refer to illustration 8.4

1   Detach the cable from the negative side of the battery.
2   Detach the sensor electrical connector.
3   Raise the vehicle and support it securely using jack stands.
4   Remove the vibration damper shields **(see illustration)**.
5   Rotate the crankshaft by hand to position the metal vane of the shutter (attached to the rear of the damper) outside of the sensor air gap.
6   Remove the sensor mounting screws and the sensor.

Installation

7   Position the sensor on the bracket.
8   Install the two sensor retaining screws but do not tighten them.
9   Install the Crankshaft Sensor Gauge (T89-6316-AH) to the outside surface of one vane of the shutter. This will set the gap between the shutter and the sensor. **Note:** *The gauge is magnetic and will conform to the vane of the shutter. If this tool is not available, slip the cover of a matchbook between the sensor and the shutter to set the gap.*
10   Rotate the crankshaft by hand to position the gauge into the sensor air gap.
11   Push the sensor housing inward to contact the gauge.
12   Tighten the screws that retain the sensor to the torque listed in this Chapter's Specifications. **Caution:** *This is a critical torque.*
13   Rotate the crankshaft by hand and remove the gauge.
14   Install the damper shields.
15   Lower the vehicle.

9   Camshaft sensor and synchronizer assembly – removal and installation

Refer to illustration 9.4

Removal

1   Prior to starting this procedure, set cylinder no. One to 26-degrees After Top Dead Center (ATDC) of the compression stroke.
2   Reference mark the position of the camshaft sensor electrical connector to the engine. The installation procedure requires that the connector be located in the same position.
3   Detach the cable from the negative terminal of the battery.
4   Detach the electrical connector from the sensor **(see illustration)**.
5   Remove the two camshaft sensor mounting screws and the sensor assembly.
6   Reference mark the synchronizer vane to the synchronizer housing.
7   Remove the synchronizer hold-down clamp.
8   Remove the synchronizer from the front of the engine cover assembly.

Installation

9   Set cylinder no. One to 26-degrees After Top Dead Center (ATDC) of the compression stroke, if you haven't done so already.
10   Align the reference marks made during removal and reverse removal procedure.
11   If reference marks are not available, the use of a synchro positioner tool (T89P-12200-A or equivalent) must be obtained prior to installation of the synchronizer.
12   Attach the synchro positioner as follows:
   a)   Position the synchronizer vane into the radial slot of the tool.

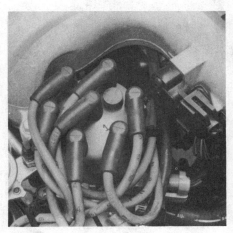

10.2   Look for the raised "1" on the top of the distributor cap next to the terminal for the number 1 spark plug wire – this is where the rotor should be pointing before you remove the distributor

10.6   Mark the position of the rotor by painting or scribing an alignment mark on the edge of the distributor base directly under the tip of the rotor (arrow) to ensure proper reinstallation

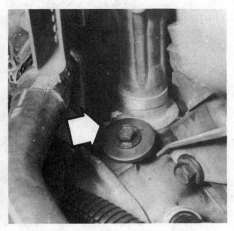

10.7 After marking the position of the distributor in relation to the intake manifold (arrow), remove the hold-down bolt and clamp

b) Rotate the tool on the synchronizer base until the tool boss engages the base notch (the tool should be square and in contact with entire tip of the synchronizer base).

13   Install the intermediate shaft so the ring faces the synchronizer.

14   With the no. One cylinder at 26-degrees ATDC, install the synchronizer assembly so that the gear engagement occurs when the arrow on the locater tool is pointing approximately 30-degrees counterclockwise from the front face of the engine block.

15   Install the synchronizer clamp bolt and tighten it to the torque listed in this Chapter's Specifications.

16   Remove the positioner tool. **Caution:** *If the camshaft sensor electrical connector is not positioned properly (contacting the air conditioning bracket or forward of the supercharger drive belt), do not reposition the connector by rotating the synchronizer base. Remove the synchronizer and repeat the installation procedure.*

17   Connect the negative battery cable.

10   Distributor – removal and installation

Refer to illustrations 10.2, 10.6 and 10.7

Removal

1   Unplug the primary electrical connector from the distributor.

2   Note the raised "1" on the distributor cap **(see illustration)**, which marks the terminal for the plug wire leading to the number 1 cylinder.

3   Remove the distributor cap (see Chapter 1).

4   If you have a remote starter:
a) Remove the spark plug from the number 1 cylinder (see Chapter 1).
b) Hook up the remote starter to the starter relay and the battery positive terminal in accordance with the manufacturer's instructions.
c) Turn the engine over carefully by turning and releasing the ignition key, or by quickly pushing and releasing the remote control starter switch button until the rotor is pointing toward the terminal for the number 1 cylinder.
d) Detach the cable from the negative terminal of the battery.
e) Proceed to Step 6.

5   If you don't have a remote starter:
a) Detach the cable from the negative terminal of the battery.
b) Locate the large bolt in the front of the crankshaft. Attach a ratchet and socket to the bolt.

c) Rotate the crankshaft until the rotor is pointing toward the number 1 plug wire terminal.

6   Make a mark on the edge of the distributor base directly below the rotor tip and in line with it (if the rotor has more than one tip, use the center one for reference) **(see illustration)**. Also, mark the distributor base and the engine block to ensure that the distributor is installed correctly.

7   Remove the distributor hold down-bolt and clamp **(see illustration)**, then pull the distributor straight up to remove it. Be careful not to disturb the intermediate driveshaft. **Caution:** *Do not turn the crankshaft while the distributor is removed, or the alignment marks will be useless.*

Installation

8   Insert the distributor into the engine in exactly the same relationship to the block that it was in when removed.

9   To mesh the helical gears on the camshaft and the distributor, it may be necessary to turn the rotor slightly. If the distributor doesn't seat completely, the hex shaped recess in the lower end of the distributor shaft is not mating properly with the oil pump shaft. Recheck the alignment marks between the distributor base and the block to verify that the distributor is in the same position it was in before removal. Also check the rotor to see if it's aligned with the mark you made on the edge of the distributor base. Then, using a socket and ratchet on the crankshaft pulley bolt, turn the crankshaft in the normal direction of rotation (clockwise, viewed from the front). Because the gear on the distributor shaft is engaged with the gear on the camshaft, their relationship to one another will not change as long as the distributor is not lifted from the engine. Therefore, the rotor will turn but the oil pump shaft will not, because the two shafts are not yet engaged. When the hex shaped recess in the end of the distributor shaft and the oil pump shaft are aligned, the distributor will drop down over the pump shaft and the distributor housing will seat against the block.

Note: *If the crankshaft has been moved while the distributor is out, locate Top Dead Center (TDC) for the number one piston by removing the spark plug from the number 1 cylinder and, using a remote starter (or a socket and ratchet on the crankshaft pulley), rotate the crankshaft until the TDC mark on the crankshaft pulley (see Chapter 2) is aligned with the stationary pointer on the timing chain/belt cover. To verify that the number 1 piston is at TDC (and not beginning the intake stroke), place your thumb or finger tightly against the spark plug hole and try to prevent any air from escaping. If it is on TDC, the air pressure will force its way past your finger.*

10   With the base of the distributor seated against the block, turn the distributor to align the marks made on the distributor base and the block.

11   With the distributor marks aligned, the rotor should be pointing at the mark on the distributor housing.

5

11.3   Before checking the ignition timing, unplug the SPOUT connector (if you don't, the EEC-IV system will still be controlling the base ignition timing)

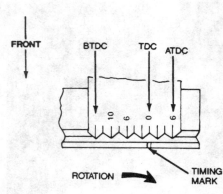

11.5   Ignition timing marks

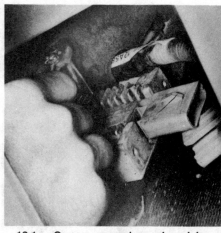

12.1a   On non-supercharged models, the module is located on the right front of the radiator support (viewed from below)

12   Place the hold-down clamp in position and loosely install the bolt.
13   Install the distributor cap and tighten the cap screws securely.
14   Plug in the module electrical connector.
15   Reattach the spark plug wires to the plugs.
16   Connect the cable to the negative terminal of the battery.
17   Check the ignition timing (refer to Section 11) and tighten the distributor hold-down bolt securely.

11   Ignition timing – check and adjustment

Non-supercharged models

Refer to illustrations 11.3 and 11.5

1   Apply the parking brake and block the wheels. Place the transmission in Park (automatic) or Neutral (manual). Turn off all accessories (heater, air conditioner, etc.).
2   Start the engine and warm it up. Once it has reached operating temperature, turn it off.
3   Unplug the in-line SPOUT connector located in the right rear corner of the engine compartment **(see illustration)**.
4   Connect an inductive timing light and a tachometer in accordance with the manufacturer's instructions. **Caution:** *Make sure that the timing light and tachometer wires don't hang anywhere near the electric cooling fan or they may become entangled in the fan blades when it comes on.*
5   Locate the timing mark on the crankshaft vibration damper **(see illustration)**. **Note:** *You may have to clean the degree scale on the timing chain cover with a wire brush and solvent.*
6   Start the engine again.
7   Point the timing light at the timing mark on the vibration damper and note whether it is aligned with the proper numbered degree mark (see the VECI label) on the timing chain cover.
8   If the proper marks are not aligned, loosen the distributor hold-down bolt. Turn the distributor until the correct timing marks are aligned. Tighten the distributor hold-down bolt securely when the timing is correct and re-check it to make sure it didn't change position when the bolt was tightened.
9   Turn off the engine.
10   Plug in the spout connector.
11   Restart the engine and check the idle speed. Because the engine is equipped with automatic idle speed control, idle rpm is not adjustable. If the idle rpm is not within the specified range (see the VECI label), take the vehicle to a dealer service department or repair shop. Adjustment requires specialized test equipment and procedures that are beyond the scope of the home mechanic.
12   Turn off the engine.
13   Remove the timing light and tachometer.

Supercharged models

Note: *Ignition timing is not adjustable on these models.*

12   Ignition module – replacement

Refer to illustrations 12.1a and 12.1b

1   Remove the screws or bolts retaining the heatsink assembly to the radiator support bracket on non-supercharged models **(see illustration)**, or the belt pulley bracket on supercharged models **(see illustration)**.

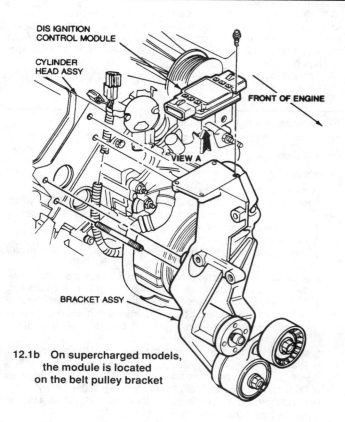

12.1b   On supercharged models, the module is located on the belt pulley bracket

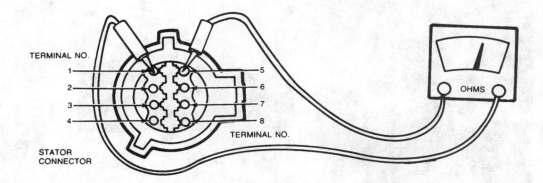

13.3   Terminal identification of the stator connector

2   On non-supercharged models, remove the two screws retaining the module to the heatsink.
3   On all models, disconnect the electrical connector from the module.
4   Before installation, use silicone dielectric compound WA-10, D7AZ-19A331-A or equivalent to uniformly coat the metal baseplate of the module.
5   Installation is the reverse of the removal procedure.

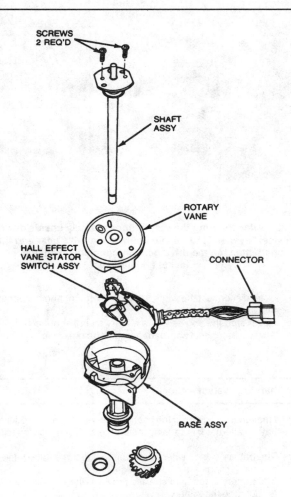

13.11   Exploded view of the distributor

13   Distributor stator – check and replacement

Check

Refer to illustration 13.3
1   Disconnect the electrical connector from the distributor.
2   Inspect the terminals for dirt, corrosion and damage.
3   Measure the resistance between stator connector terminals 1 and 5 **(see illustration)**.
4   If the resistance measures five ohms or more, replace the stator.
5   If the resistance measures less than five ohms, check the resistance between terminal no. 2 and the distributor base.
6   Measure the resistance between terminal no. 6 and the distributor base.
7   If the resistance was more than one ohm in Steps 5 or 6, inspect the retaining screws to the stator in the distributor bowl. If they are okay, replace the stator.
8   Further testing requires the use of special tools and therefore is beyond the scope of the home mechanic.

Replacement

Refer to illustrations 13.11, 13.13, 13.14, 13.15, 13.20 and 13.22
9   Remove the distributor (see Section 10).
10   Remove the rotor.
11   While holding the distributor gear, remove the two screws holding the rotary vane assembly and remove the vane **(see illustration)**.
12   To ease reassembly, reference mark the distributor shaft to the driven gear.
13   Using a drift and a hammer, remove and discard the roll pin in the gear **(see illustration)**.

13.13   With the distributor mounted securely in a vise lined with several shop rags to prevent damage to the housing, drive out the roll pin with the proper size drift

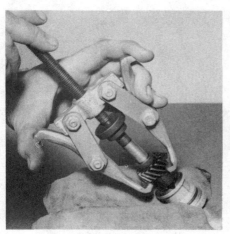

13.14   With the distributor shaft pointing up like this, use a small puller to separate the drive gear from the shaft

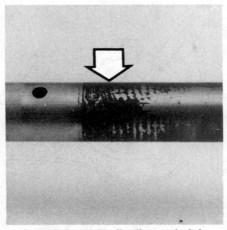

13.15   Inspect the distributor shaft for burrs and residue build-up like this in the vicinity of the hole for the drive gear roll pin – remove it with emery cloth to prevent damage to the distributor shaft bushing when removing and installing the shaft

13.20   If the O-ring at the base of the distributor is worn or damaged, replace it with a new one

14   Use a puller to remove the gear (**see illustration**).

15   Deburr and polish the shaft with emery cloth so the shaft will slide out from the distributor base (**see illustration**).

16   Remove the shaft assembly.

17   Remove the two stator assembly screws.

18   Remove the stator assembly from the top of the distributor bowl.

19   Inspect the bowl bushing for wear and signs of excessive heat concentration (bluing). Replace the complete distributor assembly if damaged.

20   Inspect the base O-ring for cuts or damage and replace the O-ring if necessary (**see illustration**).

21   Inspect the distributor base for cracks and wear. Replace the complete distributor assembly if damaged.

22   Reassembly is the reverse of disassembly (**see illustration**).

13.22   After securing the distributor assembly upside down in a vise, "eyeball" the roll pin holes in the drive gear and the shaft, then tap the drive gear onto the shaft with a deep socket and hammer

14   Charging system – general information and precautions

The charging system includes the alternator, an internal voltage regulator, a charge indicator or warning light, the battery, a fusible link and the wiring between all the components. The charging system supplies electrical power for the ignition system, the lights, the radio, etc. The alternator is driven by a drivebelt at the front of the engine.

The purpose of the voltage regulator is to limit the alternator's voltage to a preset value. This prevents power surges, circuit overloads, etc., during peak voltage output.

The fusible link is a short length of insulated wire integral with the engine compartment wiring harness. The link is four wire gauges smaller in diameter than the circuit it protects. Production fusible links and their identification flags are identified by the flag color. Refer to Chapter 12 for detailed information regarding the identification colors of both production and service fusible links.

The charging system doesn't ordinarily require periodic maintenance. However, the drivebelt, battery and wires and connections should be inspected at the intervals outlined in Chapter 1.

Be very careful when making electrical circuit connections to a vehicle equipped with an alternator and note the following:

a) When reconnecting wires to the alternator from the battery, be sure to note the polarity.

b) Before using arc welding equipment to repair any part of the vehicle, disconnect the wires from the alternator and the battery terminals.

c) Never start the engine with a battery charger connected.

d) Always disconnect both battery cables before using a battery charger.

15   Charging system – check

1   If a malfunction occurs in the charging circuit, do not immediately assume that the alternator is causing the problem. First check the following items:

a) The battery cables where they connect to the battery. Make sure the connections are clean and tight.

b) The battery electrolyte specific gravity (where applicable). If it is low, charge the battery.

c) Check the external alternator wiring and connections.

d) Check the drivebelt condition and tension (see Chapter 1).

16.2   Disconnect the electrical connectors from the alternator

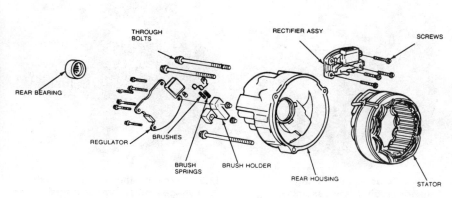

16.3   Remove the bolts retaining the alternator to the bracket

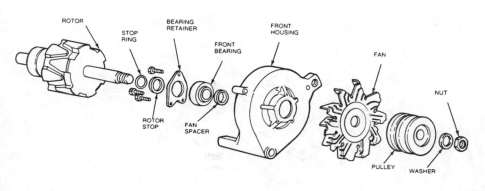

17.3a   Exploded view of the external fan type alternator

5

e) Check the alternator mounting bolts for tightness.
f) Run the engine and check the alternator for abnormal noise.

2   Using a voltmeter, check the battery voltage with the engine off. It should be approximately 12 volts.

3   Start the engine and check the battery voltage again. It should now be approximately 14 to 15 volts.

4   If the indicated voltage reading is less or more than the specified charging voltage, replace the voltage regulator. If replacing the regulator fails to restore the voltage to the specified range, the problem may be within the alternator.

5   Due to the special equipment necessary to test or service the alternator, is recommended that if a fault is suspected the vehicle be taken to a dealer or a shop with the proper equipment. Because of this the home mechanic should limit maintenance to checking connections and the inspection and replacement of the brushes.

6   The ammeter (ALT) gauge or alternator warning light on the instrument panel indicates charge or discharge – current passing into or out of the battery. With the electrical equipment switched on and the engine idling, the gauge needle may show a discharge condition. At fast idle or at normal driving speeds the needle should stay on the charge side of the gauge, with the charged state of the battery determining just how far over.

7   If the gauge does not show a change or the alternator light (if equipped) remains on, there is a problem in the system. Before inspecting the brushes or replacing the alternator, the battery condition, belt tension and electrical cable connections should be checked.

16   Alternator – removal and installation

Refer to illustrations 16.2 and 16.3

1   Detach the cable from the negative terminal of the battery.

2   Detach the electrical connectors from the alternator **(see illustration)**.

3   Loosen the alternator adjustment and pivot bolts and detach the drivebelt **(see illustration)**.

4   Remove the adjustment and pivot bolts and detach the alternator from the engine.

5   Installation is the reverse of removal.

6   After the alternator is installed, adjust the drivebelt tension (see Chapter 1).

17   Voltage regulator/alternator brushes – replacement

External fan type alternator

Refer to illustrations 17.3a, 17.3b, 17.5 and 17.9

1   Remove the alternator (refer to Section 16).

2   Set the alternator on a clean workbench.

3   Remove the four voltage regulator mounting screws **(see illustrations)**.

17.3b   To detach the voltage regulator/brush holder assembly, remove the four screws (arrows)

17.5   To remove the brushes from the voltage regulator/brush holder assembly, remove the two brush lead wire screws (arrows)

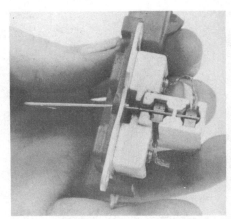

17.9   Before installing the voltage regulator/brush holder assembly, insert a paper clip, as shown, to hold the brushes in place during installation – after installation simply pull the paper clip out

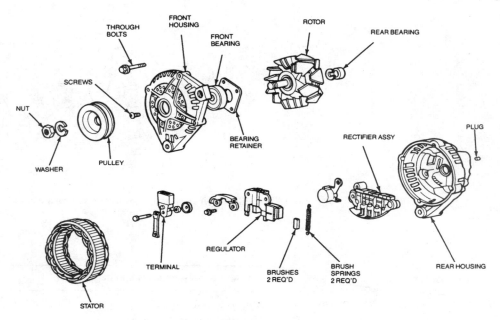

17.14   Exploded view of the internal fan type alternator

4   Detach the voltage regulator.

5   Detach the plastic cover over one of the two brush retaining screws. Remove the brush lead retaining screws and nuts to separate the brush leads from the holder **(see illustration)**. Note that the screws have Torx heads and require a special screwdriver.

6   After noting the relationship of the brushes to the brush holder assembly, remove both brushes. Don't lose the springs.

7   If you're installing a new voltage regulator, insert the old brushes into the brush holder of the new regulator. If you're installing new brushes, insert them into the brush holder of the old regulator. Make sure the springs are properly compressed and the brushes are properly inserted into the recesses in the brush holder.

8   Install the brush lead retaining screws and nuts. Cover the head of the "A" terminal screw with a piece of electrical tape.

9   Insert a thin wire, such as a straightened-out paper clip **(see illustration)** to hold the brushes in the retracted position during regulator installation.

10   Carefully install the regulator. Make sure the brushes don't hang up on the rotor and the bush leads are looped toward the brush end of the brush holder.

11   Install the voltage regulator screws and tighten them securely.

12   Remove the paper clip.

13   Install the alternator (refer to Section 16).

Internal fan type alternator

Refer to illustrations 17.14, 17.15, 17.16, 17.17, 17.18, 17.19 and 17.20

14   With the alternator removed, remove the four through bolts retaining the alternator case together **(see illustration)**.

15   Place a 200 watt soldering iron on the bearing portion of the rear case for three or four minutes **(see illustration)**.

16   With the rear case still warm, carefully insert a flat-bladed screwdriver between the stator core and the mounting flange **(see illustration)**. Remove the rear cover.

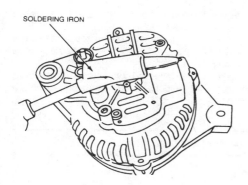

17.15 When installing or removing the rear case, you must heat the rear bearing area

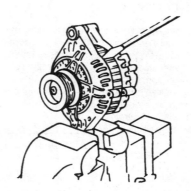

17.16 After heating the rear bearing area pry the cases apart

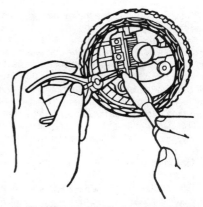

17.17 When unsoldering or soldering components, do not leave the heat on any one area longer than about five seconds

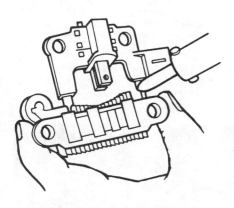

17.18 Unsoldering the regulator/brush holder assembly from the rectifier

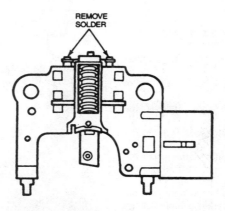

17.19 The brush pigtails should be cleaned of solder

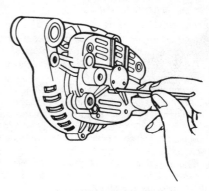

17.20 When installing the rear cover, retain the brushes in the retracted position with a paper clip – after installation simply pull the paper clip out

5

17   Use a soldering iron to remove the solder from the rectifier and stator lead **(see illustration)**. **Caution:** *To avoid damage to components touch the soldering iron no more than about five seconds on any one spot.*
18   Use a soldering iron to unsolder the regulator/brush holder assembly from the rectifier **(see illustration)**.
19   Remove the solder from the brush pigtails **(see illustration)**.
20   To install, reverse the removal procedure. **Note:** *When you're ready to install the rear cover, push the brushes into the holder and install a paper clip into the back of the case to retain them in this position* **(see illustration)**. *Be sure to use the soldering iron to heat the rear case bearing area before installing the rear case* **(see illustration 17.15)**. *Remove the paper clip after the rear case has been installed.*

18   Starting system – general information

The function of the starting system is to crank the engine to start it. The system is composed of the starter motor, starter relay, battery, switch and connecting wires.
Turning the ignition key to the Start position actuates the starter relay through the starter control circuit. The starter relay then connects the battery to the starter. The battery supplies the electrical energy to the starter motor, which does the actual work of cranking the engine.
Vehicles equipped with an automatic transmission have a Neutral start switch in the starter control circuit, which prevents operation of the starter unless the shift lever is in Neutral or Park. The circuit on vehicles with a

manual transmission prevents operation of the starter motor unless the clutch pedal is depressed.
Never operate the starter motor for more than 15 seconds at a time without pausing to allow it to cool for at least two minutes. Excessive cranking can cause overheating, which can seriously damage the starter.

19   Starter motor and circuit – in-vehicle check

Note: *Before diagnosing starter problems, make sure the battery is fully charged.*

General check

1   If the starter motor doesn't turn at all when the switch is operated, make sure the shift lever is in Neutral or Park (automatic transmission) or the clutch pedal is depressed (manual transmission).
2   Make sure the battery is charged and that all cables at the battery and starter relay terminals are secure.
3   If the starter motor spins but the engine doesn't turn over, then the drive assembly in the starter motor is slipping and the starter motor must be replaced (see Section 20).
4   If, when the switch is actuated, the starter motor doesn't operate at all but the starter relay operates (clicks), then the problem lies with either the battery, the starter relay contacts, the starter motor connections or the motor itself.
5   If the starter relay doesn't click when the ignition switch is actuated, either the starter relay circuit is open or the relay itself is defective. Check

the starter relay circuit (see the wiring diagrams at the end of this book) or replace the relay (see Section 21).

6   To check the starter relay circuit, remove the push-on connector from the relay wire. Make sure that the connection is clean and secure and the relay bracket is grounded. If the connections are good, check the operation of the relay with a jumper wire. To do this, place the transmission in Park (automatic) or Neutral (manual). Remove the push-on connector from the relay. Connect a jumper wire between the battery positive terminal and the exposed terminal on the relay. If the starter motor now operates, the starter relay is okay. The problem is in the ignition switch, Neutral start switch or in the starting circuit wiring (look for open or loose connections).

7   If the starter motor still doesn't operate, replace the starter relay (see Section 21).

8   If the starter motor cranks the engine at an abnormally slow speed, first make sure the battery is fully charged and all terminal connections are clean and tight. Also check the connections at the starter relay and battery ground. Eyelet terminals should not be easily rotated by hand. Also check for a short to ground. If the engine is partially seized, or has the wrong viscosity oil in it, it will crank slowly.

Starter cranking circuit test

Refer to illustration 19.12
Note: *To determine the location of excessive resistance in the starter circuit, perform the following simple series of tests.*

9   Disconnect the ignition coil wire from the distributor cap and ground it on the engine.

10   Connect a remote control starter switch from the battery terminal of the starter relay to the S terminal of the relay.

11   Connect a voltmeter positive lead to the starter motor terminal of the starter relay, then connect the negative lead to ground.

12   Make the test connections as shown **(see illustration)**. Refer to this illustration as you perform the following four tests.

13   Operate the ignition switch and take the voltmeter readings as soon as a steady figure is indicated. Don't allow the starter motor to turn for more than 15 seconds at a time.

14   The voltage drop in the circuit will be indicated by the voltmeter (put the voltmeter on the 0 to 2-volt range). The maximum allowable voltage drop should be:

a) 0.5-volt with the voltmeter negative lead connected to the starter battery terminal and the positive lead connected to the battery positive terminal (Connection 1 in illustration 19.12).

b) 0.1-volt with the voltmeter negative lead connected to the starter relay (battery side) and the positive lead connected to the positive terminal of the battery (Connection 2).

c) 0.3-volt with the voltmeter negative lead connected to the starter relay (starter side) and the positive lead connected to the positive terminal of the battery (Connection 3).

d) 0.3-volt with the voltmeter negative lead connected to the negative terminal of the battery and the positive lead connected to the engine ground (Connection 4).

---

20   Starter motor – removal and installation

Refer to illustration 20.4
1   Disconnect the negative cable from the battery.
2   Raise the vehicle.
3   Disconnect the battery cable from the starter motor.
4   Remove the bolts mounting the starter **(see illustration)**.
5   Installation is the reverse of removal.

---

21   Starter relay – removal and installation

Refer to illustration 21.2
1   Detach the cable from the negative terminal of the battery.
2   Label and disconnect the wires from the relay **(see illustration)**.
3   Remove the mounting bolts and detach the relay.
4   Installation is the reverse of removal.

20.4   Mounting bolt locations for the starter motor (arrows)

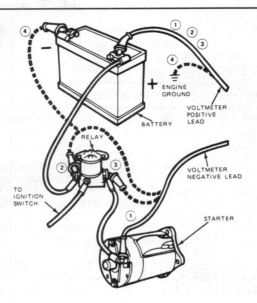

19.12   The four test lead connections for the starter cranking circuit test

21.2   To avoid confusion, label the wires before disconnecting them from the starter relay

Chapter 6   Emissions control systems

Contents

1   General information

Refer to illustration 1.7

To prevent pollution of the atmosphere from incompletely burned and evaporating gases, and to maintain good driveability and fuel economy, a number of emission control systems are incorporated. They include the:

Electronic Engine Control (EEC-IV) system
Exhaust Gas Recirculation (EGR) system
Fuel evaporative emissions control system
Positive Crankcase Ventilation (PCV) system
Catalytic converter

All of these systems are linked, directly or indirectly, to the EEC-IV system.

The Sections in this Chapter include general descriptions, checking procedures within the scope of the home mechanic and component replacement procedures (when possible) for each of the systems listed above.

Before assuming that an emissions control system is malfunctioning, check the fuel and ignition systems carefully. The diagnosis of some emission control devices requires specialized tools, equipment and training. If checking and servicing become too difficult or if a procedure is beyond your ability, consult a dealer service department.

This doesn't mean, however, that emission control systems are in general particularly difficult to maintain and repair. You can quickly and easily perform many checks and do most (if not all) of the regular maintenance at home with common tune-up and hand tools. **Note:** *The most frequent cause of emissions problems is simply a loose or broken vacuum hose or wire, so always check the hose and wiring connections first.*

Pay close attention to any special precautions outlined in this Chapter. It should be noted that the illustrations of the various systems may not ex-actly match the system installed on your vehicle because of changes made by the manufacturer during production or from year to year.

A Vehicle Emissions Control Information label is located in the engine compartment **(see illustration)**. This label contains important emissions specifications and adjustment information, as well as a vacuum hose schematic with emissions components identified. When servicing the engine or emissions systems, the VECI label in your particular vehicle should always be checked for up-to-date information.

6

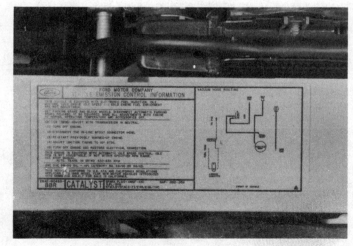

1.7   The Vehicle Emissions Control Information (VECI) label is located on the radiator support

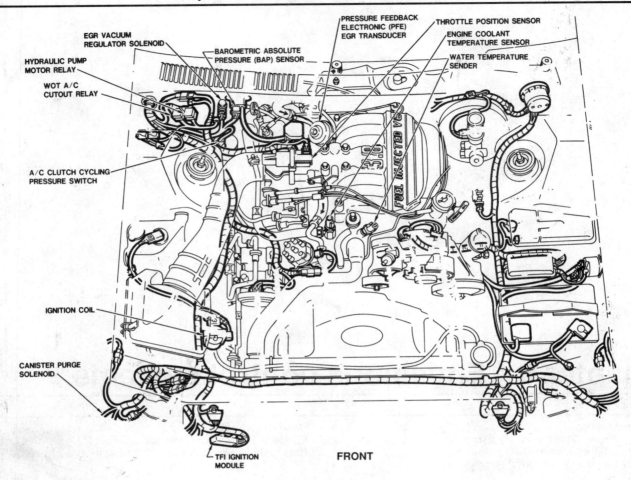

2.1a   EEC-IV system components – non-supercharged engine

2   Electronic Engine Control (EEC-IV) system

General description

Refer to illustrations 2.1a and 2.1b

1   The Electronic Engine Control (EEC-IV) system consists of an on-board computer, known as the Electronic Control Assembly (ECA), and the information sensors, which monitor various functions of the engine and send data to the ECA **(see illustrations)**. Based on the data and the information programmed into the computer's memory, the ECA generates output signals to control various engine functions.

2   The ECA, located inside the dashboard (behind the glove box), is the "brain" of the EEC-IV system. It receives data from a number of sensors and other electronic components (switches, relays, etc.). Based on the information it receives, the ECA generates output signals to control various relays, solenoids and other actuators (see below). The ECA is specifically calibrated to optimize the emissions, fuel economy and driveability of your vehicle. **Note:** *Because of a Federally-mandated extended warranty which covers the ECA, the information sensors and all components under its control, and because any damage to the ECA, the sensors and/or the control devices may void the warranty, it isn't a good idea to attempt diagnosis or replacement of the ECA at home. Take your vehicle to a dealer service department if the ECA or a system component malfunctions while the vehicle is still covered by this warranty.*

Inputs

Air Charge Temperature (ACT) sensor

Refer to illustration 2.3

3   This sensor is threaded into a runner of the intake manifold **(see accompanying illustration and 2.1b)**, provides the ECA with fuel/air mixture temperature information. The ECA uses this information to correct fuel flow and control fuel flow during cold enrichment (cold starts).

Air Conditioner (A/C) on signal

4   When battery voltage is applied to the air conditioner compressor clutch, a signal is sent to the ECA, which interprets the signal as an added load created by the compressor and increases engine idle speed accordingly to compensate.

Barometric Absolute Pressure (BAP) sensor (supercharged models)

5   This sensor is mounted on the firewall **(see illustration 2.1b)**. During key on engine off or wide open throttle, this sensor measures the barometric (outside air) pressure. Signals sent to the ECA from this sensor are used to adjust EGR flow, ignition timing or fuel flow.

Engine Coolant Temperature (ECT) sensor

6   This sensor is located near the water outlet connection **(see illustration 2.1a)**. It monitors engine coolant temperature. The ECT sends the ECA a constantly varying voltage signal which influences ECA control of the fuel mixture, ignition timing and EGR operation.

Knock sensor (supercharged models)

Refer to illustration 2.7

7   This sensor is located on the right side of the engine **(see illustration)**. It signals the ECA when the engine "knocks," causing the ECA to retard the ignition timing.

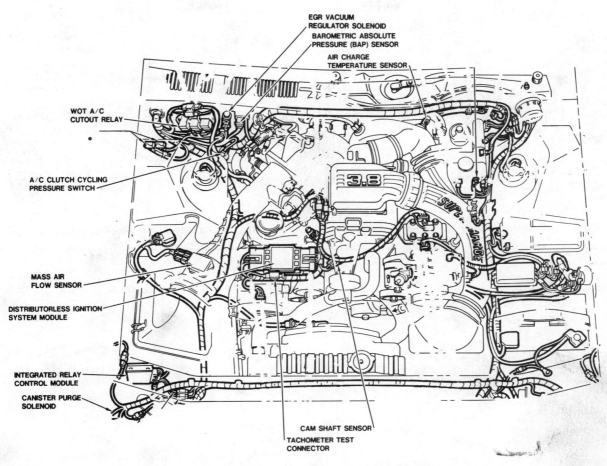

2.1b   EEC-IV system components – supercharged engine

The diagram is labeled with:
- EGR VACUUM REGULATOR SOLENOID
- BAROMETRIC ABSOLUTE PRESSURE (BAP) SENSOR
- AIR CHARGE TEMPERATURE SENSOR
- WOT A/C CUTOUT RELAY
- A/C CLUTCH CYCLING PRESSURE SWITCH
- MASS AIR FLOW SENSOR
- DISTRIBUTORLESS IGNITION SYSTEM MODULE
- INTEGRATED RELAY CONTROL MODULE
- CANISTER PURGE SOLENOID
- CAM SHAFT SENSOR
- TACHOMETER TEST CONNECTOR

6

2.3   On non-supercharged models, to replace the Air Charge Temperature sensor (arrow) you must first remove the upper intake manifold

2.7   The knock sensor (arrow), is located on the right side of the engine block

2.8   The MAP sensor is secured to the firewall with two screws

Manifold Absolute Pressure (MAP) (non-supercharged models)

Refer to illustration 2.8

8   This sensor is mounted on the firewall (see illustration). The MAP sensor has two functions:

a) Measures the vacuum of the intake manifold.

b) During key on engine off or wide open throttle, this sensor measures the barometric (outside air) pressure.

Signals sent to the ECA from this sensor are used to adjust the EGR flow, the ignition timing or the fuel flow.

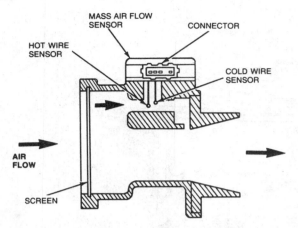

2.9   Details of the mass airflow sensor (supercharged models)

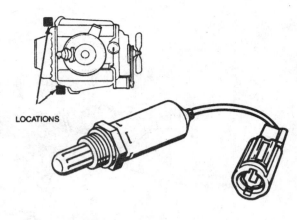

2.10   Two oxygen sensors are used on these engines

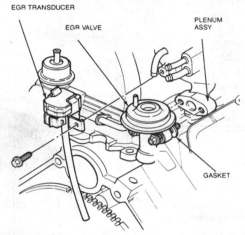

2.11   EGR valve and transducer mounting details

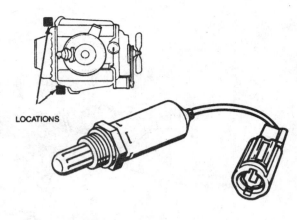

2.14   The canister purge valve should not allow air to pass when it is not energized

Mass airflow sensor (supercharged models)

Refer to illustration 2.9

9   This sensor is located between the air cleaner and the air cleaner outlet tube **(see illustration 2.1b**), it measures the air flowing into the engine. This sensor uses a hot and cold wire for measurement **(see illustration)**. This sensor helps determine how long to hold the injectors open.

Oxygen sensor

Refer to illustration 2.10

10   One of these sensors is threaded into each exhaust manifold **(see illustration)**. They constantly monitor the oxygen content of the exhaust gases. A voltage signal which varies in accordance with the difference between the oxygen content of the exhaust gases and the surrounding atmosphere is sent to the ECA. The ECA translates this exhaust gas oxygen content signal to fuel/air ratio, then alters it to the ideal ratio for current engine operating conditions.

Pressure Feedback Electronic (PFE) EGR transducer

Refer to illustration 2.11

11   This sensor converts a varying exhaust pressure signal into a proportional analog voltage which is digitized by the ECA **(see accompanying illustration and 2.1a)**. The ECA uses the signal from the PFE transducer to compute the optimum EGR flow. See Section 3 for more information.

Throttle Position Sensor (TPS)

12   This sensor is mounted on the side of the throttle body and connected directly to the throttle shaft. It senses throttle movement and position, then transmits an electrical signal to the ECA. This signal enables the ECA to determine when the throttle is closed, in its normal cruise condition or wide open. For more information, see Chapter 4.

Wide Open Throttle (WOT) signal

13   The air conditioning compressor circuit is de-energized by the ECA when a WOT condition is detected. During WOT, the ECA cuts power to the air conditioning compressor clutch until sometime after partial throttle operation resumes (see Air Conditioning Cutout Relay under Outputs in this section).

Outputs

Canister purge solenoid (CANP)

Refer to illustration 2.14

14   Located in front of the radiator support and behind the right headlight **(see illustration)**, this solenoid switches manifold vacuum to operate the canister purge valve when a signal is received from the ECA. Vacuum opens the purge valve when the solenoid is energized. For further information see Section 4.

EGR control solenoid

15   This solenoid, located on the right side of the engine firewall **(see illustration 2.1a and 2.1b)**, switches manifold vacuum to operate the EGR valve on command from the ECA. Vacuum opens the EGR valve when the solenoid is energized.

Fuel injectors

16   Six injectors are located in the intake ports. The ECA controls the length of time each injector is open. The open or "On time" of the injector determines the amount of fuel delivered. For further information, see Chapter 4.

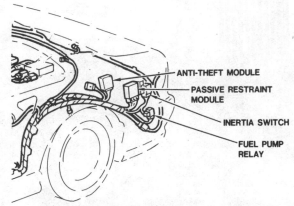

2.17   The fuel pump relay is located in the trunk under the inertia switch

- ANTI-THEFT MODULE
- PASSIVE RESTRAINT MODULE
- INERTIA SWITCH
- FUEL PUMP RELAY

2.41   Use a screwdriver to pry apart the clips that retain the electrical connector to the coolant temperature sensor

Fuel pump relay
Refer to illustration 2.17

17   Located in the trunk on the left rear quarter panel **(see illustration)**, the relay is activated by the ECA when the ignition switch is in the On and Start positions. When the ignition switch is turned to the On position, the relay is activated for one second to supply initial line pressure to the system. The relay is also activated when the ignition "Hall Effect" switch outputs a Profile Ignition Pickup (PIP) signal to the ECA. For information regarding fuel pump check and replacement, see Chapter 4.

Idle Speed Control (ISC) motor
18   This motor changes idle speed in accordance with signals from the ECA. For more information, see Chapter 4.

Wide Open Throttle (WOT) air conditioning cutout relay
19   This relay is located on the right side of the firewall (see illustrations 2.1a and 2.1b). When a WOT condition is detected (by the throttle position sensor), the air conditioning compressor circuit is de-energized by this relay (via the ECA).

Checking
20   Because of the specialized test equipment needed to check the input and output devices, diagnosis of the components described above is well beyond the scope of the home mechanic. If engine driveability deteriorates, take the vehicle to a dealer service department to have the EEC-IV system checked.

Component replacement
Note: *Because of the Federally-mandated extended warranty which covers the ECA, the information sensors and the devices it controls, there's no point in replacing any of the following components yourself unless the warranty has expired. However, once the warranty has expired, you may wish to perform some of the following component replacement procedures yourself after having the problem diagnosed by a dealer service department or repair shop.*

Air Charge Temperature (ACT) sensor
21   Detach the cable from the negative terminal of the battery.
22   On non-supercharged models, remove the upper intake manifold (see Chapter 4).
23   On all models, locate the ACT sensor on the intake manifold **(see illustration 2.1b or 2.3)**.
24   Unplug the electrical connector from the sensor.
25   Remove the sensor with a wrench.
26   Wrap the threads of the new sensor with Teflon tape to prevent air leaks.
27   Installation is the reverse of removal.

Barometric Absolute Pressure (BAP) sensor (supercharged models).
28   Detach the cable from the negative terminal of the battery.

29   Locate the BAP sensor on the firewall **(see illustration 2.1b)**.
30   Unplug the electrical connector from the sensor.
31   Detach the vacuum line from the sensor.
32   Remove the two mounting bolts and detach the sensor.
33   Installation is the reverse of removal.

Canister purge solenoid
34   Detach the cable from the negative terminal of the battery.
35   Locate the canister purge solenoid between the radiator support and the right headlight **(see illustration 2.14)**.
36   Unplug the electrical connector from the solenoid.
37   Label the vacuum hoses and ports, then detach the hoses.
38   Remove the solenoid.
39   Installation is the reverse of removal.

Engine Coolant Temperature (ECT) sensor
Refer to illustration 2.41

40   Detach the cable from the negative terminal of the battery.
41   Locate the ECT sensor near the water outlet connection **(see accompanying illustration and 2.1a)**.
42   Unplug the electrical connector from the sensor.
43   Remove the sensor with a wrench.
44   Wrap the threads of the new sensor with Teflon tape to prevent coolant leakage.
45   Installation is the reverse of removal.

Oxygen sensor(s)
46   Detach the cable from the negative terminal of the battery.
47   Raise the vehicle and support it securely on jackstands. Locate the sensor(s) on the exhaust manifold(s) **(see illustration 2.10)**.
48   Unplug the electrical connector from the sensor(s).
49   Remove the sensor(s) with a wrench.
50   Coat the threads of the new sensor(s) with anti-seize compound to prevent the threads from welding themselves to the manifold.
51   Installation is the reverse of removal.

Knock sensor
52   Locate the sensor on the lower right side of the block **(see illustration 2.7)**.
53   Disconnect the electrical connector.
54   Using a wrench remove the sensor.
55   Installation is the reverse of removal

Manifold Absolute Pressure (MAP) (non-supercharged models)
56   Detach the cable from the negative terminal of the battery.
57   Locate the MAP sensor on the firewall **(see illustration 2.8)**.
58   Unplug the electrical connector from the sensor.
59   Detach the vacuum line from the sensor.

6

3.13   Be sure to let the engine cool before disconnecting the exhaust tube from the EGR valve

3.16   Pry the clips away from the transducer to remove it

60   Remove the two mounting screws and detach the sensor.
61   Installation is the reverse of removal.

Throttle Position Sensor (TPS) switch

62   Don't attempt to replace the TPS switch before studying the replacement procedure for the switch on your vehicle (see Chapter 4).

---

3   Exhaust Gas Recirculation (EGR) system

Refer to illustrations 3.13 and 3.16

General description

1   The EGR system is designed to reintroduce small amounts of exhaust gas into the combustion cycle, thus reducing the generation of oxides of nitrogen (NOx) emissions. The amount of exhaust gas reintroduced and the timing of the cycle is controlled by various factors such as engine speed, altitude, manifold vacuum, exhaust system backpressure, coolant temperature and throttle angle. The EGR valve is vacuum actuated and the vacuum diagram for your particular vehicle is shown on the Emissions Control Information label in the engine compartment **(see illustration 1.7)**. A Pressure Feedback Electronic (PFE) valve is used.
2   The PFE valve is a conventional ported EGR valve with a back pressure sensing tube attached to it. The valve is used in conjunction with a pressure transducer which supplies pressure feedback to the EEC-IV processor. The EGR flow rate is proportional to the pressure drop across a remotely mounted, sharp-edged orifice.
3   Make sure that all vacuum hoses are correctly routed and securely attached. Replace cracked, crimped or broken hoses.
4   Make sure that there is no vacuum to the EGR valve at idle with the engine at normal operating temperature.
5   Install a tachometer in accordance with the manufacturer's instructions.
6   Unplug the Idle Air Bypass valve electrical connector.
7   Place the transmission in Neutral, start the engine, warm it up and allow it to idle. **Note:** *The engine's idle speed should not be altered. If the idle speed is high or low, have it adjusted by a dealer service department before proceeding with this test.*
8   Disconnect the vacuum line from the EGR valve and plug the line.
9   Attach a hand vacuum pump to the EGR valve vacuum nipple and slowly apply five to ten inches of mercury vacuum.
10   If any of the following conditions occur when vacuum is applied to the EGR valve, replace the valve:
   a) The idle speed does not drop more than 100 rpm or the engine does not stall.
   b) The idle speed does not return to normal ($\pm$ 25 rpm) after the vacuum pump is detached.
11   Unplug the vacuum pump and reattach the EGR vacuum supply line and the idle air bypass valve.

Component replacement

EGR valve

12   Detach the cable from the negative terminal of the battery.
13   Using a wrench, unscrew the threaded fitting that attaches the EGR pipe to the EGR valve **(see illustration)**.
14   Remove the EGR valve mounting bolts **(see illustration 2.11)** and detach the valve and gasket from the intake manifold. Discard the old gasket.
15   Installation is the reverse of removal. Make sure the gasket mating surfaces are clean and be sure to use a new EGR valve gasket. **Note:** *It's a good idea to use anti-seize compound on the threads of the EGR pipe to prevent them from welding to the EGR valve.*

EGR transducer

16   Use a screwdriver to pull the retaining clip away from the transducer body **(see illustration)**.
17   Detach the hose and the electrical connector and remove the transducer.
18   Installation is the reverse of removal.

---

4   Fuel evaporative emissions control system

General description

Refer to illustration 4.3

1   This system is designed to prevent hydrocarbons from being released into the atmosphere, by trapping and storing fuel vapor from the fuel tank.
2   The serviceable parts of the system include a charcoal filled canister, purge control solenoid, the connecting lines, fuel tank filler cap and the fuel injection system.
3   Vapor trapped in the gas tank is vented through a valve in the top of the tank. The vapor leaves the valve through a single line and is routed to a charcoal canister located between the right front wheel well and the front bumper, where it's stored until the next time the engine is started **(see illustration)**.
4   The canister outlet is connected to an electrically actuated canister purge solenoid (also see Section 2) which is connected to the intake system. The canister purge solenoid valve is normally closed. When the engine is started, the solenoid is energized by a signal from the ECA and allows intake vacuum to open the line between the canister and the air cleaner housing, which draws vapor stored in the canister.

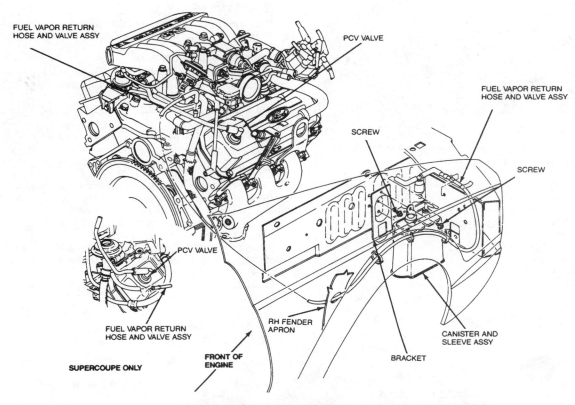

4.3   Charcoal canister mounting and hose routing details

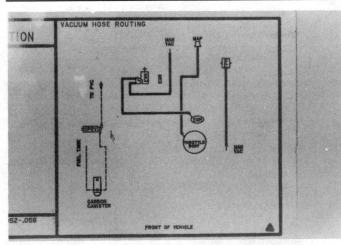

**4.13   Typical hose routing on the VECI label
(located on the radiator support)**

Checking

Charcoal canister

5   There are no moving parts and nothing to wear in the canister. Check for loose, missing, cracked or broken fittings and inspect the canister for cracks and other damage. If the canister is damaged, replace it (see Step 9).

Canister purge solenoid valve

6   Remove the valve (see Step 13).

7   With the valve de-energized, apply five in-Hg to the vacuum source port **(see illustration 2.14)**. The valve should not pass air. If it does, replace the valve.

8   Using jumper wires, apply battery voltage to the terminals on the end of the valve. The valve should open and pass air. If it doesn't, replace the valve.

Component replacement

Refer to illustration 4.13

Charcoal canister

9   Locate the canister between the radiator support and the right headlight.

10   Reach up above the canister and remove the single mounting bolt **(see illustration 4.3)**.

11   Lower the canister, detach the hose from the purge solenoid valve and remove the canister.

12   Installation is the reverse of removal.

All other components

13   Referring to the vacuum hose routing schematic on the VECI label of your vehicle, locate the component to be replaced **(see illustration)**.

14   Label the hoses and fittings, then detach the hoses and remove the component.

15   Installation is the reverse of removal.

---

5   Positive Crankcase Ventilation (PCV) system

General description

Refer to illustration 5.1

1   The Positive Crankcase Ventilation (PCV) system **(see illustration)** cycles crankcase vapors back through the engine, where they are burned. The valve regulates the amount of ventilating air and blow-by gas to the intake manifold and prevents backfire from traveling into the crankcase.

2   The PCV system consists of a replaceable PCV valve, a crankcase ventilation filter and the connecting hoses.

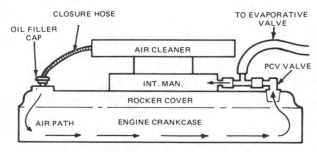

5.1   A typical Positive Crankcase Ventilation (PCV) system

3   The air source for the crankcase ventilation system is in the air cleaner. Air passes through a hose connected to the air cleaner housing and to the oil filler cap. From the oil filler cap, the air flows into the valve cover and the crankcase, from which it circulates up into another section of the valve cover and finally enters a spring loaded regulator valve (PCV valve) that controls the amount of flow as operating conditions vary. The vapors are routed to the intake manifold through the crankcase vent hose tube and fittings. This process goes on continuously while the engine is running.

Checking

4   Checking procedures for the PCV system components are included in Chapter 1.

Component replacement

5   Component replacement involves simply installing a new valve or hose in place of the one removed during the checking procedure.

---

6   Catalytic converter

Refer to illustrations 6.1 and 6.2

General description

1   The catalytic converters **(see illustration)** are designed to reduce hydrocarbon, carbon monoxide and oxides of nitrogen pollutants in the exhaust. The converters "oxidize" these components (speeds up the heat producing chemical reaction between the exhaust gas constituents) and converts them to water and carbon dioxide.

2   The converters, which closely resemble mufflers, are located in the exhaust system immediately below the exhaust manifolds **(see illustration)**.

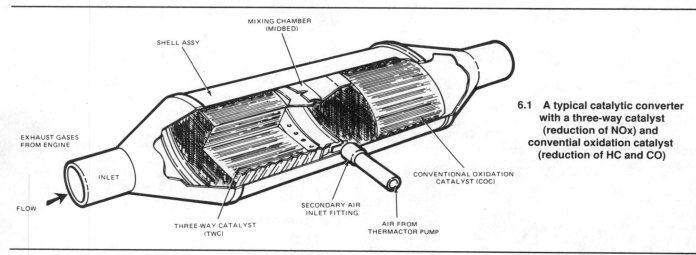

6.1   A typical catalytic converter with a three-way catalyst (reduction of NOx) and convential oxidation catalyst (reduction of HC and CO)

3   **Warning:** *If large amounts of unburned gasoline enter the converters, it may overheat and cause a fire. Always observe the following precautions:*

Use only unleaded gasoline
Avoid prolonged idling
Do not run the engine with a nearly empty fuel tank

Checking

Note: *An infrared sensor is required to check the actual operation of the catalytic converter. Such a device is prohibitively expensive. Take the vehicle to a dealer service department or a service station for this procedure. However, there are a few things you should check whenever the vehicle is raised for any reason.*

4   Check the bolts at the flange between the converter pipes and the manifolds. Check the flange bolts at the tail pipe.

5   Check the converters for dents (maximum 3/4-inch deep) and other damage which could affect performance.

6   Inspect the heat insulator plates above and below the catalytic converter for damage and loose fasteners.

Component replacement

Warning: *Don't attempt to work on the exhaust system until the system is cool.*

7   Raise the vehicle and place it securely on jackstands. Apply penetrating oil to the flange nuts at the manifolds and the tailpipe.

8   Remove the flange nuts from both ends of the catalytic converter pipe.

9   Remove the catalytic converter pipe.

10   Installation is the reverse of removal. Be sure to use new flange gaskets.

11   Start the engine and check for leaks.

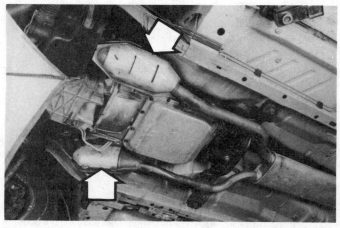

6.2   This system incorporates two catalytic converters (arrows)

Chapter 7 Part A Manual transmission

Contents

Specifications

General

Transmission type .... M5R2 5-speed synchromesh
Lubricant type .... See Chapter 1

Torque specifications

	Ft-lbs
Shift lever-to-case bolt	18 to 24
Transmission bellhousing-to-engine bolts	30 to 50
Drive shaft flange bolts	70 to 95
Transmission mount-to-crossmember nut	65 to 85
Transmission mount-to-extension housing bolts	50 to 75
Transmission crossmember-to-body bracket bolts	35 to 50

---

1 General information

All vehicles covered in this manual come equipped with either a 5-speed manual transmission or an automatic transmission. All information on the manual transmission is included in this Part of Chapter 7. Information on the automatic transmission can be found in Part B of this Chapter.

The manual transmission used in these models is a 5-speed unit with the 5th gear being an overdrive.

Due to the complexity, unavailability of replacement parts and the special tools necessary, internal repair by the home mechanic is not recommended. The information in this Chapter is limited to general information and removal and installation of the transmission.

Depending on the expense involved in having a faulty transmission overhauled, it may be a good idea to replace the unit with either a new or rebuilt one. Your local dealer or transmission shop should be able to supply you with information concerning cost, availability and exchange policy. Regardless of how you decide to remedy a transmission problem, you can still save a lot of money by removing and installing the unit yourself.

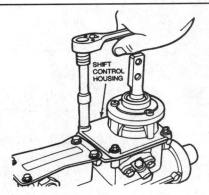

2.3   Use a socket and extension to remove the four bolts, then separate the housing from the transmission by prying gently with a screwdriver

---

2   Shift lever – removal and installation

Refer to illustration 2.3

Removal

1   Remove the center console (Chapter 11).
2   Remove the shift boot.
3   Remove the four mounting bolts and detach the lever assembly from the transmission (**see illustration**). Pry carefully on the shift control housing to detach it, then lift the housing and lever assembly up and out of the transmission case.

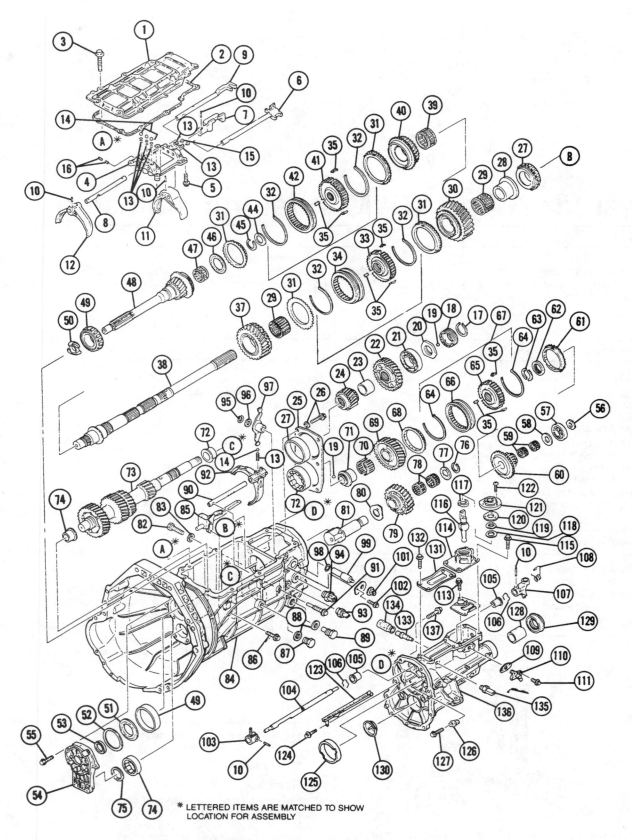

* LETTERED ITEMS ARE MATCHED TO SHOW
  LOCATION FOR ASSEMBLY

4.4   M5R2 5-speed transmission – exploded view

1	Top cover	69	5th gear
2	Gasket	70	5th gear split bearing assembly
3	Bolt	71	5th gear bearing sleeve
4	Shift control frame	72	Countershaft center bearing assembly
5	Bolt	73	Countershaft
6	5th/reverse shift rod	74	Countershaft front bearing assembly
7	3rd/4th shift gate	75	Countershaft bearing shim
8	3rd/4th shift rod	76	Reverse idler retaining snap-ring
9	1st/2nd shift rod	77	Reverse idler thrust spacer
10	Roll-pin	78	Reverse idler gear bearing assembly
11	1st/2nd shift fork	79	Reverse gear
12	3rd/4th shift fork	80	Reverse idler thrust washer
13	Detent spring	81	Reverse idler shaft
14	Shift detent ball	82	Reverse idler shaft bolt
15	Shift rod damper seat	83	Reverse idler shaft bolt washer
16	Interlock pin	84	Transmission case
17	Speedometer gear snap ring	85	Front bearing oil trough
18	Speedometer drive gear	86	Oil trough retaining bolt
19	Ball	87	Fill plug
20	Output shaft locknut	88	Fill/drain plug gasket
21	Output shaft rear bearing assembly	89	Magnetic drain plug
22	Reverse drive gear	90	5th/Reverse shift fork rod
23	Output shaft 5th/Reverse sleeve	91	5th/Reverse shift fork bolt
24	5th drive gear	92	5th/Reverse shift fork
25	Center bearing cover	93	5th gear position switch
26	Center bearing cover bolt and	94	Back-up light switch
	washer assembly	95	Snap-ring
27	Output shaft center bearing assembly	96	Washer
28	1st gear bearing sleeve	97	5th/Reverse counter lever
29	1st/2nd gear bearing assembly	98	Counter lever pin O-ring
30	1st gear	99	Counter lever pivot pin
31	Synchro blocking (1st, 2nd, 3rd, 4th) ring	100	Counter lever pin retaining plate
32	Synchro 1st/2nd/3rd/4th spring	101	Counter lever pin locking nut
33	1st/2nd synchro clutch hub	102	Counter lever retaining plate bolt
34	1st/2nd synchro sleeve	103	Shift rail selector finger
35	Synchro insert key	104	Extension shift rail
36	1st/2nd synchro assembly	105	Shift rail bushing
37	2nd gear	106	Shift rail bushing snap-ring
38	Output shaft	107	Shift rail offset lever
39	3rd gear bearing assembly	108	Control selector spring
40	3rd gear	109	Gasket
41	3rd/4th synchro clutch hub	110	5th/Reverse inhibitor assembly
42	3rd/4th synchro sleeve	111	Bolt
43	3rd/4th synchro assembly	112	Gearshift lever guide
44	3rd/4th synchro hub spacer	113	Gearshift lever guide bolt
45	3rd/4th synchro retaining snap ring	114	Shift control housing
46	Output shaft thrust bearing assembly	115	Shift control housing bolt
47	Output shaft pilot bearing assembly	116	Shift lever
48	Input shaft	117	Shift lever bushing
49	Input shaft bearing assembly	118	Shift lever bushing shim
50	Input shaft oil scoop ring	119	Shift lever bushing wave washer
51	Input shaft bearing oil baffle	120	Shift lever retaining plate
52	Input shaft bearing shim	121	Dust boot assembly
53	Input shaft seal	122	Dust boot assembly bolt
54	Front bearing cover	123	Rear oil trough
55	Front bearing cover bolt	124	Rear oil trough bolt
56	Countershaft locknut	125	Output shaft rear bearing sleeve
57	Countershaft rear bearing assembly	126	Rear bearing sleeve plate
58	Reverse gear thrust washer	127	Rear bearing sleeve plate bolt
59	Reverse drive bearing assembly	128	Extension housing output shaft bushing
60	Reverse drive gear	129	Extension housing oil seal
61	Synchro blocking (Reverse) ring	130	Countershaft oil funnel
62	5th/Reverse synchro thrust washer	131	Extension housing blind cover
63	5th/Reverse synchro split washer	132	Extension housing blind cover bolt
64	Synchro 5th/Reverse spring	133	Breather assembly
65	5th/Reverse synchro clutch hub	134	Breather assembly cover
66	5th/Reverse synchro sleeve	135	Neutral sensing switch
67	5th/Reverse synchro assembly	136	Extension housing
68	Synchro blocking (5th) ring	137	Extension housing bolt

Installation

4   Place the shift lever housing in position and install the bolts. Tighten the bolts securely.
5   Install the shift boot and console.

---

3   Manual transmission – removal and installation

Removal

1   Disconnect the negative cable from the battery.
2   Working inside the vehicle, remove the shift lever (Section 2).
3   Raise the vehicle and support it securely on jackstands.
4   Disconnect the speedometer cable and wire harness connectors from the transmission.
5   Remove the driveshaft (Chapter 8). Use a plastic bag to cover the end of the transmission to prevent fluid loss and contamination.
6   Remove the exhaust system components as necessary for clearance (Chapter 4).
7   Support the engine. This can be done from above with an engine hoist, or by placing a jack (with a block of wood as an insulator) under the engine oil pan. The engine should remain supported at all times while the transmission is out of the vehicle.
8   Support the transmission with a jack – preferably a special jack made for this purpose. Safety chains will help steady the transmission on the jack.
9   Remove the two mount-to-transmission extension housing bolts. Raise the transmission enough to allow removal, remove the crossmember-to-frame bolts, then lower the crossmember.
10   Raise the transmission slightly, remove the crossmember bolts, then lower the crossmember.
11   Remove the bolts securing the transmission bellhousing to the engine.
12   Make a final check that all wires and hoses have been disconnected from the transmission and then move the transmission and jack toward the rear of the vehicle until the transmission input shaft is clear of the clutch housing. Keep the transmission level as this is done.
13   Once the input shaft is clear, lower the transmission and remove it from under the vehicle. **Caution:** *Do not depress the clutch pedal while the transmission is out of the vehicle.*
14   The clutch components can now be inspected (Chapter 8). In most cases, new clutch components should be routinely installed if the transmission is removed.

Installation

15   If removed, install the clutch components (Chapter 8).
16   With the transmission secured to the jack as on removal, raise the transmission into position behind the engine and then carefully slide it forward, engaging the input shaft with the clutch plate hub. Do not use excessive force to install the transmission – if the input shaft does not slide into place, readjust the angle of the transmission so it is level and/or turn the input shaft so the splines engage properly with the clutch.
17   Install the transmission bellhousing-to-engine bolts. Tighten the bolts to the specified torque.
18   Install the transmission mount and crossmember through-bolts. Tighten the bolts and nuts securely.
19   Remove the jacks supporting the transmission and the engine.
20   Install the various items removed previously, referring to Chapter 8 for the installation of the driveshaft and Chapter 4 for information regarding the exhaust system components.
21   Make a final check that all wires, hoses and the speedometer cable have been connected and that the transmission has been filled with lubricant to the proper level (Chapter 1). Lower the vehicle.
22   Working inside the vehicle, install the shift lever (see Section 2).
23   Connect the negative battery cable. Road test the vehicle for proper operation and check for leakage.

---

4   Manual transmission overhaul – general information

Refer to illustration 4.4

Overhauling a manual transmission is a difficult job for the do-it-yourselfer. It involves the disassembly and reassembly of many small parts. Numerous clearances must be precisely measured and, if necessary, changed with select fit spacers and snap-rings. As a result, if transmission problems arise, it can be removed and installed by a competent do-it-yourselfer, but overhaul should be left to a transmission repair shop. Rebuilt transmissions may be available – check with your dealer parts department and auto parts stores. At any rate, the time and money involved in an overhaul is almost sure to exceed the cost of a rebuilt unit.

Nevertheless, it's not impossible for an inexperienced mechanic to rebuild a transmission if the special tools are available and the job is done in a deliberate step-by-step manner so nothing is overlooked.

The tools necessary for an overhaul include internal and external snap-ring pliers, a bearing puller, a slide hammer, a set of pin punches, a dial indicator and possibly a hydraulic press. In addition, a large, sturdy workbench and a vise or transmission stand will be required.

During disassembly of the transmission, make careful notes of how each piece comes off, where it fits in relation to other pieces and what holds it in place. An exploded view is included **(see illustration)** to show where the parts go – but actually noting how they are installed when you remove the parts will make it much easier to get the transmission back together.

Before taking the transmission apart for repair, it will help if you have some idea what area of the transmission is malfunctioning.

Certain problems can be closely tied to specific areas in the transmission, which can make component examination and replacement easier. Refer to the *Troubleshooting* section at the front of this manual for information regarding possible sources of trouble.

Chapter 7 Part B Automatic transmission

Contents

Specifications

General

Transmission type . . . . AOD 4-speed automatic
Lubricant type . . . . See Chapter 1

Torque specifications

	Ft-lbs
Transmission-to-engine bolts	30 to 50
Transmission mount-to-crossmember nut	65 to 85
Transmission mount-to-extension housing bolts	50 to 75
Transmission crossmember-to-body bracket bolts	35 to 50
Drive shaft flange bolts	70 to 95
Neutral start switch	8 to 11
Torque converter-to-driveplate nuts	20 to 34
Torque converter drain plug	8 to 28

---

1 General information

All vehicles covered in this manual come equipped with either a 5-speed manual transmission or an automatic transmission. All information on the automatic transmission is included in this Part of Chapter 7. Information on the manual transmission can be found in Part A of this Chapter.

Due to the complexity of the automatic transmissions covered in this manual and the need for specialized equipment to perform most service operations, this Chapter contains only general diagnosis, routine maintenance, adjustment and removal and installation procedures.

If the transmission requires major repair work, it should be left to a dealer service department or an automotive or transmission repair shop. You can, however, remove and install the transmission yourself and save the expense, even if the repair work is done by a transmission shop.

2 Diagnosis – general

Note: *Automatic transmission malfunctions may be caused by five general conditions: poor engine performance, improper adjustments, hydraulic malfunctions, mechanical malfunctions or malfunctions in the computer or its signal network. Diagnosis of these problems should always begin with a check of the easily repaired items: fluid level and condition (Chapter 1), shift linkage adjustment and throttle linkage adjustment. Next, perform a road test to determine if the problem has been corrected or if more diagnosis is necessary. If the problem persists after the preliminary tests and cor-*

rections are completed, additional diagnosis should be done by a dealer service department or transmission repair shop. Refer to the troubleshooting Section at the front of this manual for information on symptoms of transmission problems.

Preliminary checks

1   Drive the vehicle to warm the transmission to normal operating temperature.
2   Check the fluid level as described in Chapter 1:
   a) If the fluid level is unusually low, add enough fluid to bring the level within the designated area of the dipstick, then check for external leaks (see below).
   b) If the fluid level is abnormally high, drain off the excess, then check the drained fluid for contamination by coolant. The presence of engine coolant in the automatic transmission fluid indicates that a failure has occurred in the internal radiator walls that separate the coolant from the transmission fluid (see Chapter 3).
   c) If the fluid is foaming, drain it and refill the transmission, then check for coolant in the fluid or a high fluid level.
3   Check the engine idle speed. **Note:** *If the engine is malfunctioning, do not proceed with the preliminary checks until it has been repaired and runs normally.*
4   Check the throttle valve cable for freedom of movement. Adjust it if necessary (Section 5). **Note:** *The throttle cable may function properly when the engine is shut off and cold, but it may malfunction once the engine is hot. Check it cold and at normal engine operating temperature.*
5   Inspect the shift control linkage (Section 3). Make sure that it's properly adjusted and that the linkage operates smoothly.

Fluid leak diagnosis

6   Most fluid leaks are easy to locate visually. Repair usually consists of replacing a seal or gasket. If a leak is difficult to find, the following procedure may help.

7   Identify the fluid. Make sure it's transmission fluid and not engine oil or brake fluid (automatic transmission fluid is a deep red color).

8   Try to pinpoint the source of the leak. Drive the vehicle several miles, then park it over a large sheet of cardboard. After a minute or two, you should be able to locate the leak by determining the source of the fluid dripping onto the cardboard.

9   Make a careful visual inspection of the suspected component and the area immediately around it. Pay particular attention to gasket mating surfaces. A mirror is often helpful for finding leaks in areas that are hard to see.

10   If the leak still cannot be found, clean the suspected area thoroughly with a degreaser or solvent, then dry it.

11   Drive the vehicle for several miles at normal operating temperature and varying speeds. After driving the vehicle, visually inspect the suspected component again.

12   Once the leak has been located, the cause must be determined before it can be properly repaired. If a gasket is replaced but the sealing flange is bent, the new gasket will not stop the leak. The bent flange must be straightened.

13   Before attempting to repair a leak, check to make sure that the following conditions are corrected or they may cause another leak.

Note: *Some of the following conditions cannot be fixed without highly specialized tools and expertise. Such problems must be referred to a transmission repair shop or a dealer service department.*

Gasket leaks

14   Check the pan periodically. Make sure the bolts are tight, no bolts are missing, the gasket is in good condition and the pan is flat (dents in the pan may indicate damage to the valve body inside).

15   If the pan gasket is leaking, the fluid level or the fluid pressure may be too high, the vent may be plugged, the pan bolts may be too tight, the pan sealing flange may be warped, the sealing surface of the transmission housing may be damaged, the gasket may be damaged or the transmission casting may be cracked or porous. If sealant instead of gasket material has been used to form a seal between the pan and the transmission housing, it may be the wrong sealant.

Seal leaks

16   If a transmission seal is leaking, the fluid level or pressure may be too high, the vent may be plugged, the seal bore may be damaged, the seal itself may be damaged or improperly installed, the surface of the shaft protruding through the seal may be damaged or a loose bearing may be causing excessive shaft movement.

17   Make sure the dipstick tube seal is in good condition and the tube is properly seated. Periodically check the area around the speedometer gear or sensor for leakage. If transmission fluid is evident, check the O-ring for damage.

Case leaks

18   If the case itself appears to be leaking, the casting is porous and will have to be repaired or replaced.

19   Make sure the oil cooler hose fittings are tight and in good condition.

Fluid comes out vent pipe or fill tube

20   If this condition occurs, the transmission is overfilled, there is coolant in the fluid, the case is porous, the dipstick is incorrect, the vent is plugged or the drain back holes are plugged.

---

3   Shift linkage – check and adjustment

Check

1   Try to start the engine in each shift lever position; the starter should operate Park and Neutral only. If the starter does not operate in Park or Neutral or operates in any position other than Park and Neutral, the shift linkage is need of adjustment or the Neutral start switch is defective (see Section 5).

Adjustment

Refer to illustration 3.6

2   Place the selector lever in Overdrive. The lever must be held against the rear Overdrive stop during the adjustment procedure.

3   Raise the vehicle and support it securely on jackstands.

4   Loosen the shift cable bracket retaining nut.

5   Move the transmission lever to the Overdrive position, which is the third detent from the full counterclockwise position.

6   With both the selector and transmission levers now in the same positions, tighten the retaining nut securely **(see illustration)**.

7   After adjustment, check the shift selector for proper operation.

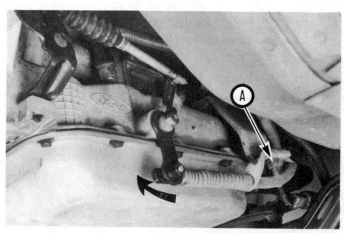

3.6   With the shift lever held in the Overdrive position (3rd detent from the full counterclockwise position), tighten the cable bracket retaining nut (A)

---

4   Throttle valve (TV) cable – adjustment

Refer to illustrations 4.4, 4.5, 4.6 and 4.7

1   The throttle valve (TV) cable and linkage controls transmission line pressure, shift points, shift feel, part throttle downshifts and detent downshifts. If the TV linkage is broken, sticky or misadjusted, the vehicle will experience a number of problems such as early and/or soft upshifts and no downshift or a harsh downshift function.

2   The engine should not be running and the shift lever must be in Neutral during this adjustment.

3   Remove the air cleaner assembly and inlet tube for access to the TV cable at the throttle lever.

4   Pry the grooved pin on the cable assembly out of the grommet on the throttle body lever with a wide bladed screwdriver **(see illustration)**.

5   Push the white locking tab out with a small screwdriver **(see illustration)**.

6   Make sure the plastic block with the pin and tab slides freely on the notched rod **(see illustration)**. If it doesn't, the white tab may not be pushed out far enough.

7   Hold the throttle lever firmly against the idle stop and push the grooved pin into the grommet on the throttle lever as far as it will go **(see illustration)**. Make sure not to move the throttle lever away from the idle stop during this procedure.

8   Install the air cleaner assembly.

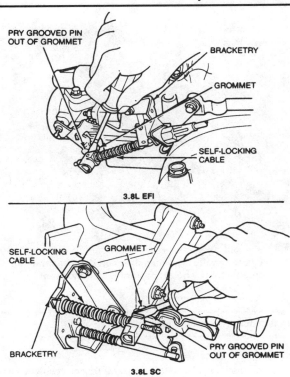

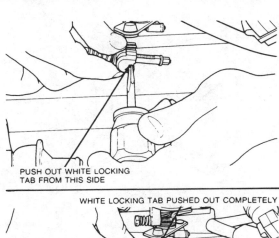

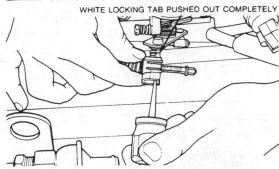

4.4   Pry the grooved pin out of the grommet with a wide bladed screwdriver

4.5   Push the white locking tab out (non-supercharged (EFI) models top, supercharged (SC) models, bottom)

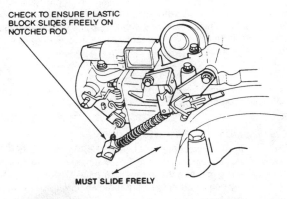

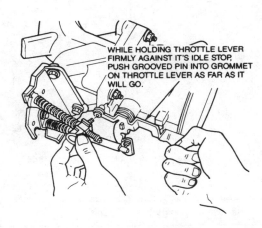

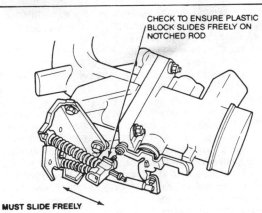

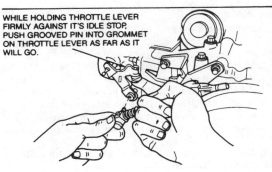

4.6   The plastic block must slide freely, with no binding

4.7   Make sure the grooved pin is securely installed

7B

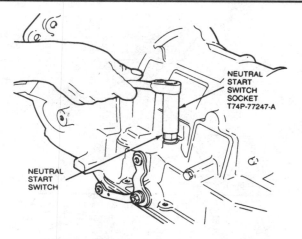

5.5   The Neutral start switch can be unscrewed after unplugging it – the switch is very fragile, so a special socket is recommended for installation

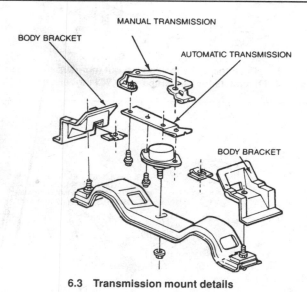

6.3   Transmission mount details

6.2   Pry between the crossmember and the transmission mount – there should be very little movement

5   Neutral start switch – replacement

Refer to illustration 5.5

1   Place the shift lever in Low.
2   Raise the vehicle and support it securely on jackstands.
3   Disconnect the negative cable at the battery.
4   Disconnect the electrical connector from the neutral start switch.
5   Carefully remove the switch and O-ring using Ford socket tool T74P-77247-A **(see illustration)**, if possible.
6   Install the switch and new O-ring and tighten to the specified torque using the Ford tool. This tool is designed to remove and install the switch without damaging it. **Caution:** *It is easy to crush or puncture the walls of the switch.*
7   Install the electrical connector. If the tool is not available, be very careful not to overtighten the switch.
8   Connect the negative battery cable.
9   Check that the engine starts only when the selector is in the Neutral and Park positions.

6   Transmission mount – check and replacement

Refer to illustrations 6.2 and 6.3

1   Insert a large screwdriver or pry bar into the space between the transmission extension housing and the crossmember and try to pry the transmission up slightly.
2   The transmission should not move away from the mount much at all **(see illustration)**.
3   To replace the mount, remove the nut attaching the mount to the crossmember, then remove the bolts attaching the mount to the transmission extension housing **(see illustration)**.
4   Raise the transmission slightly with a jack and remove the mount.
5   Installation is the reverse of the removal procedure. Be sure to tighten the nuts/bolts securely.

7   Oil seal replacement

Refer to illustrations 7.3, 7.5 and 7.8

1   Oil leaks frequently occur due to wear of the extension housing oil seal and bushing (if equipped), and/or the speedometer drive gear oil seal and O-ring. Replacement of these seals is relatively easy, since the repairs can usually be performed without removing the transmission from the vehicle.
2   The extension housing oil seal is located at the extreme rear of the transmission, where the driveshaft is attached. If leakage at the seal is suspected, raise the vehicle and support it securely on jackstands. If the seal is leaking, transmission lubricant will be built up on the front of the driveshaft and may be dripping from the rear of the transmission.
3   Using a screwdriver or pry bar, carefully pry the oil seal out of the rear of the transmission **(see illustration)**. Do not damage the splines on the transmission output shaft.
4   If the oil seal cannot be removed with a screwdriver or pry bar, a special oil seal removal tool (available at auto parts stores) will be required.
5   Using a large section of pipe or a very large deep socket as a drift, install the new oil seal. Drive it into the bore squarely and make sure it's completely seated **(see illustration)**.
6   Lubricate the splines of the transmission output shaft and the outside of the driveshaft sleeve yoke with lightweight grease, then install the driveshaft. Be careful not to damage the lip of the new seal.
7   The speedometer cable and driven gear housing is located on the side of the extension housing. Look for transmission oil around the cable housing to determine if the seal and O-ring are leaking.

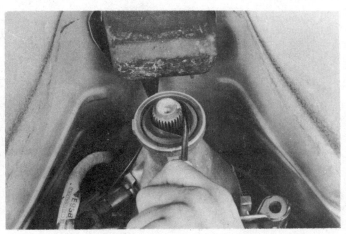

7.3 Use a large screwdriver (shown) or a seal removal to pry the seal out of the transmission extension housing

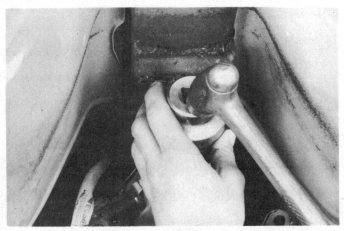

7.5 A large socket and hammer can be used to tap the new seal evenly into the bore

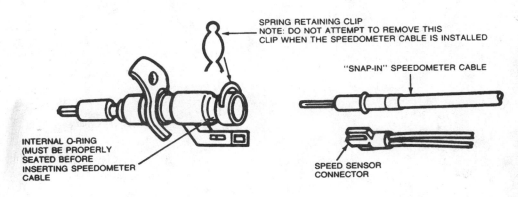

SPRING RETAINING CLIP
NOTE: DO NOT ATTEMPT TO REMOVE THIS
CLIP WHEN THE SPEEDOMETER CABLE IS INSTALLED

"SNAP-IN" SPEEDOMETER CABLE

INTERNAL O-RING
(MUST BE PROPERLY
SEATED BEFORE
INSERTING SPEEDOMETER
CABLE

SPEED SENSOR
CONNECTOR

7.8 Speedometer driven gear details

8   Disconnect the speedometer cable or electrical connector **(see illustration)**.
9   Using a hook, remove the seal.
10   Install a new O-ring in the driven gear housing and reinstall the driven gear housing and cable assembly on the extension housing.

8   Automatic transmission – removal and installation

Removal

1   Disconnect the negative cable for the battery.
2   Raise the vehicle and support it securely on jackstands.
3   Drain the transmission fluid (Chapter 1), then reinstall the pan.
4   Remove the torque converter cover.
5   Mark the torque converter and one of the studs with white paint so they can be installed in the same position **(see illustration)**.
6   Remove the torque converter-to-driveplate nuts. Turn the crankshaft for access to each nut. Turn the crankshaft in a clockwise direction only (as viewed from the front).
7   Rotate the torque converter until the drain plug is at it's lowest point. Place the pan under the torque converter, remove the drain plug an allow the fluid to drain. Install the drain plug and tighten it securely.
8   Remove the starter motor (Chapter 5).
9   Remove the driveshaft (Chapter 8).
10   Disconnect the speedometer cable or speed sensor electrical connector.
11   Detach the wire harness connectors from the transmission.

12   Remove any exhaust components which will interfere with transmission removal (Chapter 4).
13   Disconnect the TV cable.
14   Disconnect the shift linkage.
15   Support the engine with a jack. Use a block of wood under the oil pan to spread the load.
16   Support the transmission with a jack – preferably a jack made for this purpose. Safety chains will help steady the transmission on the jack.
17   Remove the two mount-to-transmission extension housing bolts.
18   Raise the transmission enough to allow removal, remove the crossmember-to-frame bolts, then lower the crossmember.
19   Remove the bolts securing the transmission to the engine.
20   Lower the transmission slightly and disconnect and plug the transmission fluid cooler lines.
21   Remove the transmission dipstick tube.
22   Move the transmission to the rear to disengage it from the engine block dowel pins and make sure the torque converter is detached from the driveplate. Secure the torque converter to the transmission so it won't fall out during removal.

Installation

23   Prior to installation, make sure the torque converter hub is securely engaged in the pump.
24   With the transmission secured to the jack, raise it into position. Be sure to keep it level so the torque converter does not slide forward. Connect the transmission fluid cooler lines.
25   Turn the torque converter to line up the studs with the holes in the driveplate. The white paint mark on the torque converter and the stud made

7B

in Step 5 must line up.

26   Move the transmission forward carefully until the dowel pins and the torque converter are engaged.

27   Install the transmission housing-to-engine bolts. Tighten them securely.

28   Install the torque converter-to-driveplate nuts. Tighten the nuts to the specified torque.

29   Install the transmission mount and crossmember through-bolts. Tighten the bolts and nuts securely.

30   Remove the jacks supporting the transmission and the engine.

31   Install the dipstick tube.

32   Install the starter motor (Chapter 5).

33   Connect the vacuum hose(s) (if equipped).

34   Connect the shift and TV linkage.

35   Plug in the transmission wire harness connectors.

36   Install the torque converter cover.

37   Install the driveshaft.

38   Connect the speedometer cable or speed sensor connector.

39   Adjust the shift linkage.

40   Install any exhaust system components that were removed or disconnected.

41   Lower the vehicle.

42   Fill the transmission with the specified fluid (Chapter 1), run the engine and check for fluid leaks.

Chapter 8   Clutch and driveline

Contents

8

Specifications

General

Fluid type	See Chapter 1
Halfshaft length	28 7/8 in

Torque specifications

	Ft-lbs
Bellhousing-to-engine bolts	40 to 50
Differential carrier mounting bolts	80 to 100
Driveshaft-to-companion flange bolts	70 to 95
Pressure plate-to-flywheel bolts	15 to 25
Slave cylinder-to-transmission bolts	15 to 20

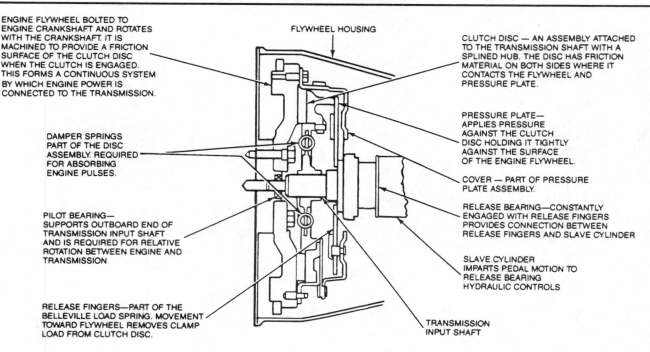

ENGINE FLYWHEEL BOLTED TO ENGINE CRANKSHAFT AND ROTATES WITH THE CRANKSHAFT. IT IS MACHINED TO PROVIDE A FRICTION SURFACE OF THE CLUTCH DISC WHEN THE CLUTCH IS ENGAGED. THIS FORMS A CONTINUOUS SYSTEM BY WHICH ENGINE POWER IS CONNECTED TO THE TRANSMISSION.

FLYWHEEL HOUSING

CLUTCH DISC — AN ASSEMBLY ATTACHED TO THE TRANSMISSION SHAFT WITH A SPLINED HUB. THE DISC HAS FRICTION MATERIAL ON BOTH SIDES WHERE IT CONTACTS THE FLYWHEEL AND PRESSURE PLATE.

DAMPER SPRINGS PART OF THE DISC ASSEMBLY. REQUIRED FOR ABSORBING ENGINE PULSES.

PRESSURE PLATE— APPLIES PRESSURE AGAINST THE CLUTCH DISC HOLDING IT TIGHTLY AGAINST THE SURFACE OF THE ENGINE FLYWHEEL.

COVER — PART OF PRESSURE PLATE ASSEMBLY.

PILOT BEARING— SUPPORTS OUTBOARD END OF TRANSMISSION INPUT SHAFT AND IS REQUIRED FOR RELATIVE ROTATION BETWEEN ENGINE AND TRANSMISSION

RELEASE BEARING—CONSTANTLY ENGAGED WITH RELEASE FINGERS PROVIDES CONNECTION BETWEEN RELEASE FINGERS AND SLAVE CYLINDER

SLAVE CYLINDER IMPARTS PEDAL MOTION TO RELEASE BEARING HYDRAULIC CONTROLS

RELEASE FINGERS—PART OF THE BELLEVILLE LOAD SPRING. MOVEMENT TOWARD FLYWHEEL REMOVES CLAMP LOAD FROM CLUTCH DISC.

TRANSMISSION INPUT SHAFT

2.1   Cutaway view of the clutch components

1   General information

The information in this Chapter deals with the components from the rear of the engine to the rear wheels, except for the transmission, which is dealt with in the previous Chapter.

For the purposes of this Chapter, these components are grouped into three categories: clutch, driveshaft and rear axle assembly. Separate Sections within this Chapter offer general descriptions and checking procedures for components in each of the three groups.

Since nearly all the procedures covered in this Chapter involve working under the vehicle, make sure it's securely supported on sturdy jackstands or on a hoist where the vehicle can be easily raised and lowered.

2   Clutch – description and check

Refer to illustration 2.1

1   All models equipped with a manual transmission use a single dry plate, diaphragm spring type clutch **(see illustration)**. The clutch disc has a splined hub which allows it to slide along the splines of the transmission input shaft. The clutch and pressure plate are held in contact by spring pressure exerted by the diaphragm in the pressure plate.

2   The clutch release system is operated by hydraulic pressure. The hydraulic release system consists of the clutch pedal, a master cylinder and fluid reservoir, the hydraulic line, and a release (or slave) cylinder which actuates clutch release (or throwout) bearing.

3   When pressure is applied to the clutch pedal to release the clutch, hydraulic pressure is exerted against the release bearing. The bearing pushes against the fingers of the diaphragm spring of the pressure plate assembly, which in turn releases the clutch plate.

4   Terminology can be a problem when discussing the clutch components because common names are in some cases different from those used by the manufacturer. For example, the driven plate is also called the clutch plate or disc, the clutch release bearing is sometimes called a throwout bearing, the release cylinder is sometimes called the operating or slave cylinder.

5   Other than to replace components with obvious damage, some preliminary checks should be performed to diagnose clutch problems.

   a) The first check should be of the fluid level in the clutch master cylinder. If the fluid level is low, add fluid as necessary and inspect the hydraulic system for leaks. If the master cylinder reservoir has run dry, bleed the system as described in Section 8 and retest the clutch operation.

   b) To check "clutch spin down time," run the engine at normal idle speed with the transmission in Neutral (clutch pedal up – engaged). Disengage the clutch (pedal down), wait several seconds and shift the transmission into Reverse. No grinding noise should be heard. A grinding noise would most likely indicate a problem in the pressure plate or the clutch disc.

   c) To check for complete clutch release, run the engine (with the parking brake applied to prevent movement) and hold the clutch pedal approximately 1/2-inch from the floor. Shift the transmission between 1st gear and Reverse several times. If the shift is hard or the transmission grinds, component failure is indicated. Check the fluid level in the clutch master cylinder and bleed the system (see Section 8).

   d) Visually inspect the pivot bushing at the top of the clutch pedal to make sure there is no binding or excessive play.

3   Clutch components – removal, inspection and installation

Warning: *Dust produced by clutch wear and deposited on clutch components may contain asbestos, which is hazardous to your health. DO NOT blow it out with compressed air and DO NOT inhale it. DO NOT use gasoline or petroleum-based solvents to remove the dust. Brake system cleaner should be used to flush the dust into a drain pan. After the clutch components are wiped clean with a rag, dispose of the contaminated rags and cleaner in a covered, marked container.*

Removal

Refer to illustration 3.6

1   Access to the clutch components is normally accomplished by removing the transmission, leaving the engine in the vehicle. If, of course, the engine is being removed for major overhaul, then check the clutch for

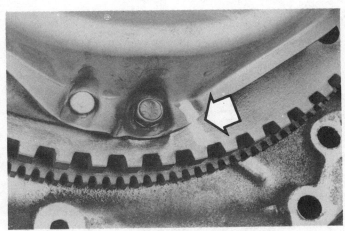

3.6   If you're going to re-use the same pressure plate, mark it's relationship to the flywheel (arrow)

3.11   Check the clutch plate lining, springs and splines (arrows) for wear

wear and replace worn components as necessary. However, the relatively low cost of the clutch components compared to the time and trouble spent gaining access to them warrants their replacement anytime the engine or transmission is removed, unless they are new or in near perfect condition. The following procedures are based on the assumption the engine will stay in place.

2   Referring to Chapter 7 Part A, remove the transmission from the vehicle. Support the engine while the transmission is out. Preferably, an engine hoist should be used to support it from above. However, if a jack is used underneath the engine, make sure a piece of wood is positioned between the jack and oil pan to spread the load. **Caution:** *The pickup for the oil pump is very close to the bottom of the oil pan. If the pan is bent or distorted in any way, engine oil starvation could occur.*

3   Remove the bellhousing-to-engine bolts and then detach the housing. It may have to be gently pried off the alignment dowels with a screwdriver or pry bar.

4   The release (slave) cylinder and release bearing can remain attached to the housing for the time being.

5   To support the clutch disc during removal, install a clutch alignment tool through the clutch disc hub.

6   Carefully inspect the flywheel and pressure plate for indexing marks. The marks are usually an X, an O or a white letter. If they cannot be found, scribe marks yourself so the pressure plate and the flywheel will be in the same alignment during installation **(see illustration)**.

7   Turning each bolt only a little at a time, loosen the pressure plate-to-flywheel bolts. Work in a criss-cross pattern until all spring pressure is relieved. Then hold the pressure plate securely and completely remove the bolts, followed by the pressure plate and clutch disc.

Inspection

Refer to illustrations 3.11 and 3.13

8   Ordinarily, when a problem occurs in the clutch, it can be attributed to wear of the clutch driven plate assembly (clutch disc). However, all components should be inspected at this time.

9   Inspect the flywheel for cracks, heat checking, grooves and other obvious defects. If the imperfections are slight, a machine shop can machine the surface flat and smooth, which is highly recommended regardless of the surface appearance. Refer to Chapter 2 Part B for the flywheel removal and installation procedure.

10   Inspect the pilot bearing (see Section 4).

11   Inspect the lining on the clutch disc. There should be at least 1/16-inch of lining above the rivet heads. Check for loose rivets, distortion, cracks, broken springs and other obvious damage **(see illustration)**. As mentioned above, ordinarily the clutch disc is routinely replaced, so if in doubt about the condition, replace it with a new one.

12   The release bearing should also be replaced along with the clutch disc.

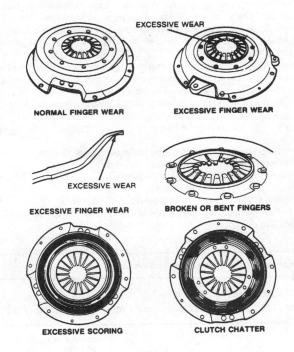

3.13   Replace the pressure plate if excessive wear is noted

13   Check the machined surfaces and the diaphragm spring fingers of the pressure plate **(see illustration)**. If the surface is grooved or otherwise damaged, replace the pressure plate. Also check for obvious damage, distortion, cracking, etc. Light glazing can be removed with medium grit emery cloth. If a new pressure plate is required, new and factory-rebuilt units are available.

Installation

Refer to illustrations 3.15a and 3.15b

14   Before installation, clean the flywheel and pressure plate machined surfaces with brake cleaner, lacquer thinner or acetone. It's important that no oil or grease is on these surfaces or the lining of the clutch disc. Handle the parts only with clean hands.

8

3.15a   Use a clutch alignment tool to center the clutch disc, then tighten the pressure plate bolts

3.15b   Make sure the clutch disc is installed with the marked face against the flywheel

15   Position the clutch disc and pressure plate against the flywheel with the clutch held in place with an alignment tool **(see illustration)**. Make sure it's installed properly. Most replacement clutch plates will be marked "flywheel side" or something similar – if not marked, install the clutch disc with the damper springs toward the transmission **(see illustration)**.
16   Tighten the pressure plate-to-flywheel bolts only finger tight, working around the pressure plate.
17   Center the clutch disc by ensuring the alignment tool extends through the splined hub and into the pilot bearing in the crankshaft. Wiggle the tool up, down or side-to-side as needed to bottom the tool in the pilot bearing. Tighten the pressure plate-to-flywheel bolts a little at a time, working in a criss-cross pattern to prevent distorting the cover. After all of the bolts are snug, tighten them to the torque listed in this Chapter's Specifications. Remove the alignment tool.
18   Install the slave cylinder as described in Section 6. Tighten all fasteners to the proper torque specifications.
19   Using high-temperature grease, lubricate the inner surface of the release bearing.
20   Install the release bearing as described in Section 5.
21   Install the bellhousing and tighten the bolts to the torque listed in this Chapter's Specifications.

pressed into the rear of the crankshaft **(see illustration)**. It is greased at the factory and does not require additional lubrication. Its primary purpose is to support the front of the transmission input shaft. The pilot bearing should be inspected whenever the clutch components are removed from the engine. Due to its inaccessibility, if you are in doubt as to its condition, replace it with a new one. **Note:** *If the engine has been removed from the vehicle, disregard the following steps which do not apply.*
2   Remove the transmission (see Chapter 7 Part A).
3   Remove the clutch components (see Section 3).
4   Inspect for any excessive wear, scoring, lack of grease, dryness or obvious damage. If any of these conditions are noted, the bearing should be replaced. A flashlight will be helpful to direct light into the recess.
5   Removal can be accomplished with a special puller and slide hammer **(see illustration)**, but an alternative method also works very well.
6   Find a solid steel bar which is slightly smaller in diameter than the bearing. Alternatives to a solid bar would be a wood dowel or a socket with a bolt fixed in place to make it solid.
7   Check the bar for fit – it should just slip into the bearing with very little clearance.
8   Pack the bearing and the area behind it (in the crankshaft recess) with heavy grease. Pack it tightly to eliminate as much air as possible.

4   Pilot bearing – inspection and replacement

Refer to illustrations 4.1, 4.5 and 4.9
1   The clutch pilot bearing is a needle roller type bearing which is

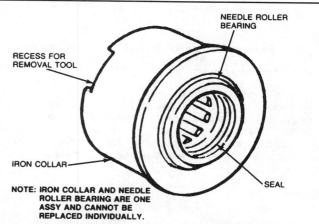

NEEDLE ROLLER BEARING

RECESS FOR REMOVAL TOOL

IRON COLLAR

SEAL

NOTE: IRON COLLAR AND NEEDLE ROLLER BEARING ARE ONE ASSY AND CANNOT BE REPLACED INDIVIDUALLY.

4.1   The pilot bearing incorporates an O-ring seal which can't be replaced separately – if there is any evidence that the seal has been leaking, or if the bearing is dry, replace it

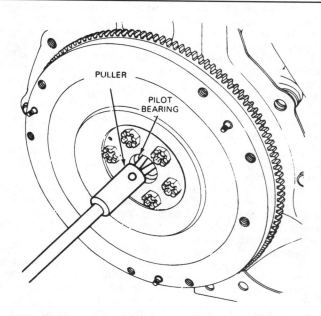

PULLER

PILOT BEARING

4.5   One method of removing the pilot bearing requires a puller connected to a slide hammer

4.9 Pack the cavity behind the pilot bearing with heavy grease and force it out hydraulically with a rod slightly smaller than the bore in the bearing – when the hammer strikes the rod, the bearing will pop out of the crankshaft

9   Insert the bar into the bearing bore and strike the bar sharply with a hammer which will force the grease to the back side of the bearing and push it out **(see illustration)**. Remove the bearing and clean all grease from the crankshaft recess.

10   To install the new bearing, lightly lubricate the outside surface with lithium-based grease, then drive it into the recess with a soft-face hammer. The seal must face out **(see illustration 4.1)**.

11   Install the clutch components, transmission and all other components removed previously, tightening all fasteners properly.

---

5   Clutch release bearing – removal, inspection and installation

Refer to illustration 5.2

Warning: *Dust produced by clutch wear and deposited on clutch components may contain asbestos, which is hazardous to your health. DO NOT blow it out with compressed air and DO NOT inhale any of it. DO NOT use gasoline or petroleum-based solvents to remove the dust. Brake system cleaner should be used to flush the dust into a drain pan. After the clutch components are wiped clean with a rag, dispose of the contaminated rags and cleaner in a covered container.*

Removal

1   Remove the transmission following the procedure described in Chapter 7 Part A.

2   Turn the bearing/carrier assembly until resistance is felt, then turn it slightly further which will disengage the carrier from the slave cylinder **(see illustration)**.

Inspection

3   Inspect the bearing for cracks, wear and other damage. Hold the center of the bearing and turn the outer race while applying pressure to it. If the bearing doesn't turn smoothly or if it is noisy, replace it with a new one. It is a good idea to replace the bearing whenever a clutch job is performed, to decrease the possibility of bearing failure in the future, although Ford states that this is not absolutely necessary.

4   If it is decided to re-use the old release bearing, clean the external surfaces and inside diameter with a solvent-moistened rag. Do not immerse the bearing in solvent, as it is packed with grease from the factory (sealed for life) and to do so would ruin it.

Installation

5   Fill the groove in the inside diameter of the bearing with lithium-based grease. Also apply a thin coat of this grease to the entire inner diameter.

6   Properly position the bearing on the shaft and push it on **(see illustration 5.2)**.

7   The remainder of the assembly procedure is the reverse of removal. Be sure to bleed the clutch hydraulic system as described in Section 8.

---

6   Clutch slave cylinder – removal and installation

Refer to illustrations 6.3 and 6.5

Warning: *Dust produced by clutch wear and deposited on clutch components may contain asbestos, which is hazardous to your health. DO NOT blow it out with compressed air and DO NOT inhale any of it. DO NOT use gasoline or petroleum-based solvents to remove the dust. Brake system cleaner should be used to flush the dust into a drain pan. After the clutch components are wiped clean with a rag, dispose of the contaminated rags and cleaner in a covered container.*

Removal

1   Disconnect the cable from the negative battery terminal.

2   Raise the vehicle and support it securely on jackstands.

8

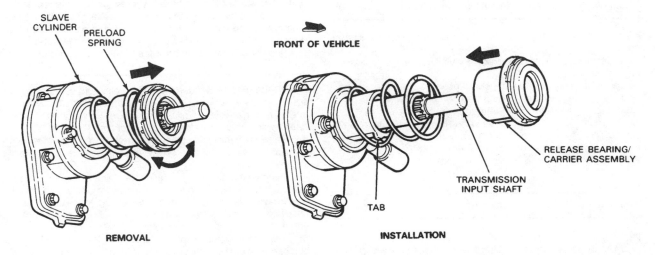

5.2 To remove the release bearing/carrier, twist the bearing until it unlocks – to install it, just push it on until the tab on the slave cylinder engages with the carrier

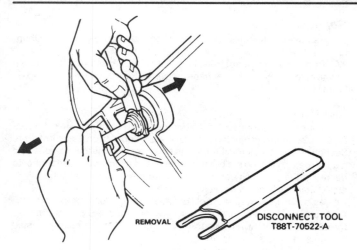

6.3   To disconnect the hydraulic line from the slave cylinder or master cylinder, use the tool shown (or an equivalent substitute) to push the white plastic sleeve back while pulling on the line

3   Disconnect the hydraulic line at the slave cylinder. Slide the white plastic sleeve toward the slave cylinder while lightly pulling on the hydraulic line **(see illustration)**. Have a small can or some rags handy to catch the spilling fluid.
4   Remove the transmission as described in Chapter 7 Part A.
5   Remove the two slave cylinder bolts and pull the cylinder off the transmission input shaft **(see illustration)**.
6   Separate the release bearing from the slave cylinder as described in Section 5.

Installation

7   Install the release bearing to the slave cylinder (see Section 5).
8   Slide the cylinder over the transmission input shaft and install the two bolts, tightening them to the torque listed in this Chapter's Specifications.
9   Install the transmission.
10   Connect the hydraulic line to the slave cylinder, fill the fluid reservoir with brake fluid conforming to DOT 3 specifications and bleed the clutch system as outlined in Section 8.
11   Reconnect the negative battery cable.

7   Clutch master cylinder – removal and installation

1   Detach the hydraulic line from the clutch master cylinder **(see illustration 6.3)**.
2   Remove the two push pins retaining the clutch master cylinder reservoir to the left shock tower.
3   Disconnect the pushrod from the clutch pedal.
4   Rotate the master cylinder 45-degrees counterclockwise.
5   Carefully pull the master cylinder through the firewall.
6   Note the routing of the hydraulic line to the slave cylinder and remove the master cylinder from the engine compartment.
7   Installation is the reverse of removal.
8   Bleed the clutch hydraulic system (see Section 8).

8   Clutch hydraulic system – bleeding

Refer to illustration 8.4

1   The hydraulic system should be bled of all air whenever any part of the system has been removed or if the fluid level has been allowed to fall so low that air has been drawn into the master cylinder. The procedure is very similar to bleeding a brake system.

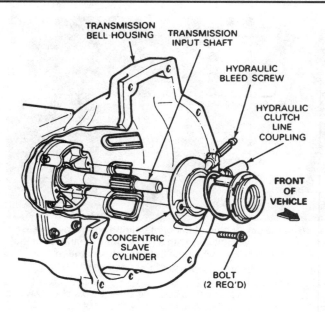

6.5   Slave cylinder mounting details

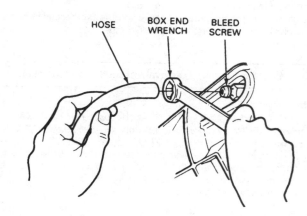

8.4   The slave cylinder bleeder screw opening is located on the left side of the transmission – connect a hose to the bleeder screw, place the other end of the hose in a container of clean brake fluid and have an assistant depress the clutch pedal – any air will show up as bubbles in the tube and container

2   Fill the master cylinder with new brake fluid conforming to DOT 3 specifications. **Caution:** *Do not re-use any of the fluid coming from the system during the bleeding operation or use fluid which has been inside an open container for an extended period of time.*
3   Raise the vehicle and place it securely on jackstands to gain access to the slave cylinder bleeder screw, which is located next to the hydraulic line inlet connection.
4   Remove the dust cap (if equipped) which fits over the bleed screw. Place a box end wrench over the bleed screw and then push a length of plastic hose over the screw **(see illustration)**. Place the other end of the hose into a clear container with about two inches of brake fluid. The hose end must be in the fluid at the bottom of the container.
5   Have an assistant depress the clutch pedal and hold it. Open the bleeder valve on the slave cylinder, allowing fluid to flow through the hose. Close the bleeder valve when your assistant signals that the clutch pedal is at the bottom of its travel. Once closed, have your assistant release the pedal.

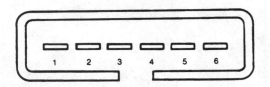

9.2   Terminal identification for the clutch/starter interlock switch

6   Continue this process until all air is evacuated from the system, indicated by a full, solid stream of fluid being ejected from the bleeder valve each time and no air bubbles in the hose or container. Keep a close watch on the fluid level inside the master cylinder; if the level drops too low, air will be sucked back into the system and the process will have to be started all over again.

9   Clutch/starter interlock switch – check and replacement

Check

Refer to illustration 9.2

1   Detach the electrical connector from the switch.
2   Using an ohmmeter, probe the switch terminals for the correct switch function as follows:
   a) Probe terminals 5 and 6 with an ohmmeter (**see illustration**). With the clutch pedal at rest, the meter should indicate infinity (open), but should indicate continuity when the pedal is depressed about two inches.
   b) When the meter leads are connected to terminals 3 and 4 the meter should indicate continuity, but should read infinity when the pedal is depressed about two inches.
   c) Probe terminals 1 and 2 with the ohmmeter leads. The meter should indicate infinity, but should indicate continuity when the clutch pedal is depressed to about one inch from full travel. If the switch fails any of these tests, replace it.

Replacement

Refer to illustration 9.4

3   Detach the electrical connector from the switch.
4   Pull down on the orientation clip and separate if from the tab on the switch (**see illustration**).
5   Rotate the switch half a turn to expose the plastic retainer.
6   Push the tabs together, slide the retainer rearward and separate it from the switch.
7   Remove the switch from the pushrod.
8   Installation is the reverse of removal.

10   Driveshaft – inspection

1   Raise the rear of the vehicle and support it securely on jackstands.
2   Crawl under the vehicle and visually inspect the driveshaft. Look for any dents or cracks in the tubing. If any are found, the driveshaft must be replaced.
3   Check for any oil leakage at the front and rear of the driveshaft. Leakage where the driveshaft enters the transmission indicates a defective transmission rear seal. Leakage where the driveshaft enters the differential indicates a defective pinion seal.
4   While under the vehicle, have an assistant turn the rear wheel so the driveshaft will rotate. As it does, make sure the universal joints are operating properly without binding, noise or looseness.
5   The universal joints can also be checked with the driveshaft motionless, by gripping your hands on either side of the joint and attempting to twist the joint. Any movement at all in the joint is a sign of considerable

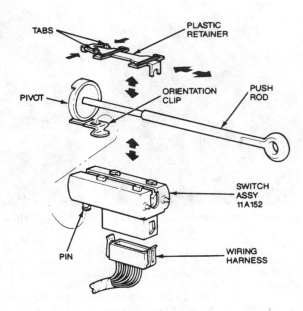

9.4   Mounting details for the clutch/starter interlock switch

11.3   Removing the mounting bolts for the cross brace in front of the fuel tank

wear. Lifting up on the shaft will also indicate movement in the universal joints.
6   Finally, check the driveshaft mounting bolts at the ends to make sure they are tight.

11   Driveshaft – removal and installation

Refer to illustrations 11.3, 11.9, 11.15 and 11.16

1   If the fuel tank is not empty (or near empty), siphon the fuel into an approved fuel container. Use a siphoning kit, available at most auto parts stores. DO NOT start the siphoning action by mouth!
2   Raise the rear of the vehicle an support it securely on jackstands.
3   Remove the cross brace in front of the fuel tank (**see illustration**).
4   Detach the exhaust pipe from the left hanger (see Chapter 4).
5   Detach the exhaust pipe from the rear hanger.
6   Detach the tailpipe at the muffler.
7   Lower the exhaust pipe and support it with wire or rope.
8   Remove the heat shield for the fuel tank.

8

11.9   The driveshaft hoop is secured by two bolts (arrows)

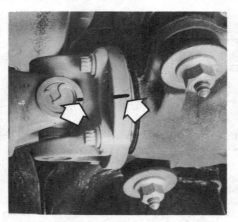

11.15   Before detaching the driveshaft, always reference mark the driveshaft to the companion flange

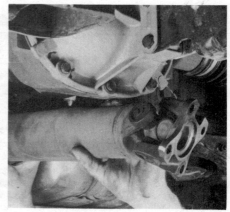

11.16   Lower the driveshaft and pull it to the rear

9   Remove the driveshaft hoop located to the rear of the fuel tank (see illustration).
10   Remove the bolt retaining the fuel tank filler tube to the right frame rail.
11   Place a floor jack or transmission jack under the fuel tank. If a floor jack is used, place a wood block on the jack head to act as a cushion.
12   Remove the support on the forward side of the fuel tank.
13   Detach the fuel tank support straps (see Chapter 4 if necessary).
14   Lower the fuel tank about six inches.
15   Reference mark the driveshaft to the differential companion flange (see illustration).
16   Remove the bolts and separate the driveshaft from the differential companion flange (a 12-point socket or box end wrench will be necessary). Pull the driveshaft toward the rear to remove it (see illustration).
17   Wrap a plastic bag tightly around the extension housing of the transmission to prevent fluid loss.
18   Installation is the reverse of removal. Be sure to align the reference marks made during removal.

12   Universal joints – replacement

Refer to illustrations 12.2a, 12.2b, 12.4 and 12.9
Note: *A press or large vise will be required for this procedure. It may be advisable to take the driveshaft to a local dealer service department, ser-*

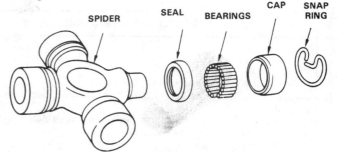

12.2a   Exploded view of the universal joint components

vice station or machine shop where the universal joints can be replaced for you, normally at a reasonable charge.
1   Remove the driveshaft as outlined in the previous Section.
2   Using a small pair of pliers, remove the snap-rings from the spider (see illustrations).
3   Supporting the driveshaft, place it in position on a workbench equipped with a vise.
4   Place a piece of pipe or a large socket with the same inside diameter over one of the bearing caps. Position a socket which is of slightly smaller diameter than the cap on the opposite bearing cap (see illustration) and use the vise or press to force the cap out (inside the pipe or large socket),

12.2b   A pair of needle-nose pliers can be used to remove the universal joint snap-rings

12.4   To press the universal joint out of the driveshaft yoke, set it up in a vise with the small socket pushing the joint and bearing cap into the large socket

12.9   If the snap-ring will not seat in the groove, strike the yoke with a brass hammer – this will relieve the tension that has set up in the yoke, and slightly spring the yoke ears (this should also be done if the joint feels tight when assembled)

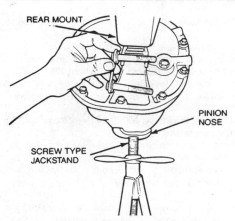

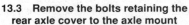

13.3   Remove the bolts retaining the rear axle cover to the axle mount

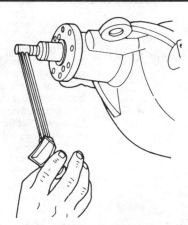

13.10   Using an inch-pound torque wrench, measure the amount of torque required to turn the pinion (pinion preload)

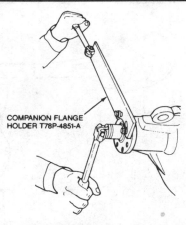

13.12   Hold the companion flange while removing the pinion nut

stopping just before it comes completely out of the yoke. Use the vise or large pliers to work the cap the rest of the way out.

5   Transfer the sockets to the other side and press the opposite bearing cap out in the same manner.

6   Pack the new universal joint bearings with grease. Ordinarily, specific instructions for lubrication will be included with the universal joint servicing kit and should be followed carefully.

7   Position the spider in the yoke and partially install one bearing cap in the yoke.

8   Start the spider into the bearing cap and then partially install the other cap. Align the spider and press the bearing caps into position, being careful not to damage the dust seals.

9   Install the snap-rings. If difficulty is encountered in seating the snap-rings, strike the driveshaft yoke sharply with a hammer. This will spring the yoke ears slightly and allow the snap-rings to seat in the groove **(see illustration)**.

10   Install the grease fitting and fill the joint with grease. Be careful not to overfill the joint, as this could blow out the grease seals.

11   Install the driveshaft, tightening the companion flange bolts to the torque listed in this Chapter's Specifications.

13   Differential pinion seal – replacement

Removal

Refer to illustrations 13.3, 13.10, 13.12, 13.14 and 13.17

1   Raise the vehicle and support it using jack stands.

2   Place a screw type jackstand (or a floor jack) under the pinion nose.

3   Remove the bolts and nuts retaining the rear axle cover to the axle mount **(see illustration)**.

4   Install the bolt for the rear mount in the lower bolt hole and allow the axle to pivot forward.

5   Reference mark the driveshaft to the companion flange **(see illustration 11.15).**

6   Remove the driveshaft-to-companion flange bolts.

7   Slide the driveshaft forward and allow it to rest on the driveshaft hoop.

8   Remove the nuts retaining the carrier to the front mount.

9   To gain access to the companion flange, slowly lower the carrier.

10   Using an inch-pound torque wrench and proper socket on the pinion nut **(see illustration)**, measure the torque required to maintain rotation of the pinion through several revolutions. Write down this measurement for later use.

11   Reference mark the companion flange to the pinion shaft so the companion flange can be reinstalled in the same position.

12   Using holding tool (T78P-4851-A) or equivalent, and a breaker bar and socket, remove the pinion nut **(see illustration)**. If this tool isn't available, install two bolts into two adjacent holes in the companion flange and brace a large prybar across them to prevent the pinion from turning.

13   Remove the companion flange.

14   Wedge a screwdriver blade between the metal flange of the pinion seal and the housing **(see illustration)**.

15   Pry up on the metal flange of the pinion seal.

16   Using locking pliers, grab the edge of the seal.

17   Hit the pliers with a hammer until the pinion seal is removed **(see illustration).**

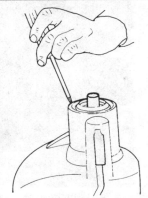

13.14   Pry between the metal flange of the pinion seal and the housing

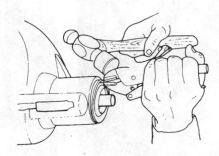

13.17   Grab the edge of the seal and use a hammer to remove it

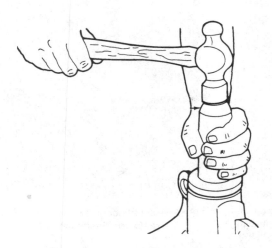

13.18   Install the seal squarely or it will leak

Installation

Refer to illustration 13.18

18   Using seal installer (T79P-4676-A) or a section of pipe with an outside diameter slightly smaller than that of the seal, drive the seal into place **(see illustration)**. **Note:** *Be sure not to cock the seal in the housing or you will destroy the seal.*

19   Inspect the companion flange and pinion mating surfaces for burrs. Remove any found using emery cloth.

20   Using the reference marks made during removal, install the companion flange on the pinion shaft.

21   Install a new companion flange retaining nut. Tighten the companion flange retaining nut in small increments. Rotate the companion flange frequently to seat the bearing. Without exceeding the value recorded during removal, be sure that the same turning torque for the pinion preload is reached. **Note:** *If you exceed the specified preload a new collapsible spacer and pinion nut must be installed, a job that should be performed by a dealer service department or other repair shop, due to the special tools necessary. The pinion nut must not be backed off to obtain proper preload.*

14   Halfshafts, Constant Velocity (CV) joints and boots – check

1   The halfshafts, CV joints and boots should be inspected periodically and whenever the vehicle is raised for any reason. The most common symptom of halfshaft or CV joint failure is knocking or clicking noises when turning.

2   Raise the vehicle and support it securely on jackstands.

3   Inspect the CV joint boots for cracks, leaks and broken retaining bands. If lubricant leaks out through a hole or crack in the boot, the CV joint will wear prematurely and require replacement. Replace any damaged boots immediately (see Section 16). It's a good idea to disassemble, clean, inspect and repack the CV joint whenever replacing a CV joint boot, to ensure that the joint is not contaminated with moisture or dirt, which would cause premature CV joint failure.

4   Check the entire length of each halfshaft to make sure they aren't cracked, dented, twisted or bent.

5   Grasp each halfshaft and rotate it in both directions while holding the CV joint housings to check for excessive movement, indicating worn splines or loose CV joints.

6   If a boot is damaged or loose, remove the halfshaft as described in Section 15. Disassemble and inspect the CV joint as outlined in Section 16. **Note:** *Some auto parts stores carry "split" type replacement boots, which can be installed without removing the halfshaft from the vehicle. This is a convenient alternative; however, it's recommended that the halfshaft be removed and the CV joint disassembled and cleaned to ensure that the joint is free from contaminants such as moisture and dirt, which will accelerate CV joint wear.*

15   Halfshaft – removal and installation

Removal

Refer to illustrations 15.4, 15.5, 15.7a, 15.7b, 15.8a, 15.8b and 15.9

1   Loosen the rear wheel lug nuts, raise the rear of the vehicle and support it securely on jackstands.

2   Remove the wheel.

3   On models equipped with rear disc brakes, remove the rear caliper and disc (see Chapter 9).

4   On all models, remove the rear hub nut **(see illustration)**.

5   Remove the upper control arm nut and bolt **(see illustration)**.

6   Use wire or rope to support the upper control arm.

7   With the lower arm in the relaxed position, reference mark the position of the lower control arm to the knuckle **(see illustration)**. **Caution:** *Failure to mark this position will cause bushing "wind-up" on assembly and the wrong ride height.* Remove the nut and bolt retaining the lower control arm-to-knuckle **(see illustration)**.

8   With the hub nut removed, use a two-jaw puller to push the halfshaft out of the hub **(see illustration)**. Allow the halfshaft to rest on the lower control arm. Support the knuckle assembly with rope or wire **(see illustration)**.

15.4   Brace a pry bar across two studs to prevent the hub from turning as the nut is loosened

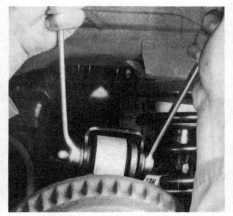

15.5   Removing the upper control arm nut

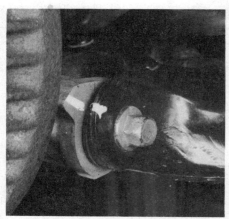

15.7a   With the lower arm in the relaxed position, mark the position of the lower control arm to the knuckle

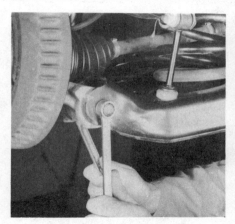

15.7b   Remove the nut and bolt retaining the lower control arm to the knuckle

15.8a   Use a puller to push the halfshaft from the hub – on models with drum brakes a special attachment that fits over the studs will be necessary, or this method may be used if the drum is removed first

15.8b   Support the knuckle assembly with wire or rope

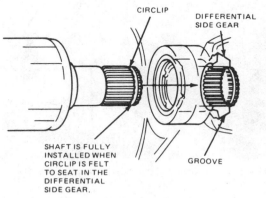

15.9   Pry the halfshaft loose from the differential housing

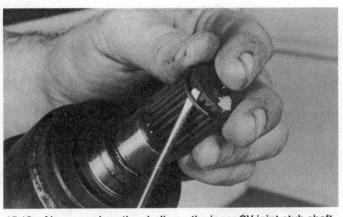

15.12   Always replace the circlip on the inner CV joint stub shaft before reinstalling the halfshaft

15.15   The halfshaft is completely seated when the circlip on the shaft snaps into the groove in the differential side gear

9   Pry the halfshaft loose from the differential **(see illustration)**. Caution: *Care must be taken not to damage the differential oil seal, the housing, the CV joint boots or the anti-lock brake sensor ring (if equipped).*
10   It's a good idea to replace the differential oil seal whenever the halfshaft is removed (see Section 17).
11   Insert a plug or "balled-up" rag into the differential housing to prevent lubricant loss.

Installation
Refer to illustrations 15.12 and 15.15
12   Install a new circlip on the inner end of the halfshaft **(see illustration)**. Do not bend or twist the circlip.
13   Remove the plug from the differential housing.
14   Lightly lubricate the halfshaft splines and carefully align the splines of the inner stub shaft with the splines in the differential.
15   Push the halfshaft into the differential until you feel the circlip engage with the groove in the differential side gear **(see illustration)**.
16   With the exception of using new hub nuts, the remainder of installation is the reverse of removal. Be sure to align the previously made matchmarks before tightening the lower control arm-to-knuckle bolts. Also, tighten the knuckle-to-control arm bolts to the torque listed in the Chapter 10 Specifications.

8

16   Constant Velocity (CV) joint – boot replacement and overhaul

Inner CV joint and boot
Disassembly
Refer to illustrations 16.2 and 16.3
1   With the half shaft removed (see Section 15), cut off the boot clamps and slide the boot towards the center of the halfshaft. Mark the tri-pot housing and the shaft so it can be returned to its original position, then slide the housing off of the spider assembly.

16.2   Snap-ring pliers should be used to remove both the inner and outer retaining rings

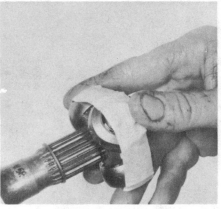

16.3   If you wrap tape around the spider bearing assembly, it will make the job much easier

16.8   Before installing the CV joint boot, wrap the axle splines with tape to prevent damage to the boot

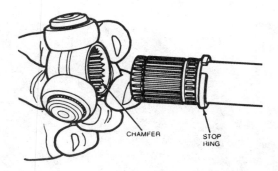

16.9   When reinstalling the spider bearing assembly, the chamfered inner diameter must face in (towards the stop-ring)

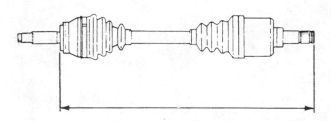

16.12   Be sure the halfshaft is the proper length before installation

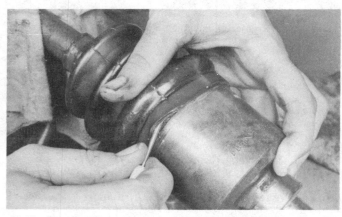

16.13   Equalize the pressure inside the boot by inserting a small screwdriver between the boot and the outer race

16.14   Securing the boot clamp with special pliers (available at auto parts stores)

2   Mark the spider assembly to the shaft. Remove the spider assembly from the shaft by first removing the inner retaining ring **(see illustration)** and sliding the spider assembly back to expose the outer retaining ring. Remove the outer retaining ring and slide the joint off the shaft.

3   Use tape or a cloth wrapped around the spider bearing assembly to retain the bearings during removal and installation **(see illustration)**.

4   Remove the spider assembly from the shaft.

5   Slide the boot off the shaft.

Inspection

6   Clean the old grease from the housing and spider assembly. Carefully disassemble each section of the spider assembly, one at a time, and clean the needle bearings with solvent. Inspect the rollers, spider cross, bearings and housing for scoring, pitting or other signs of abnormal wear, which will warrant the replacement of the inner CV joint.

Reassembly

Refer to illustrations 16.8, 16.9, 16.12, 16.13, and 16.14

7   Apply a coat of CV joint grease to the inner bearing surfaces to hold the needle bearings in place when reassembling the spider assembly. Pack the housing with half of the grease furnished with the new boot and place the remainder in the boot (total amount of grease used should be 9 ounces for vehicles without anti-lock brakes and 10 1/2 ounces for vehicles with anti-lock brakes).

16.18   After the old grease has been rinsed away and the solvent has been blown out with compressed air, rotate the outer joint through its full range of motion and inspect the bearing surfaces for wear and damage – if any of the ball bearings, the race or the cage are damaged, replace the halfshaft and outer joint assembly

8   Wrap the halfshaft splines with tape to avoid damaging the boot, then slide the boot onto the shaft **(see illustration)**.
9   Install the inner stop-ring onto the shaft. Install the spider assembly with the chamfer facing the stop-ring **(see illustration)**.
10   Install a new circlip on the end of the shaft, slide the spider bearing against the circlip and seat the stop-ring in the groove.
11   Install the tri-pot housing.
12   Position the boot on the housing and the shaft so the halfshaft length listed in this Chapter's Specifications is obtained **(see illustration)**.
13   With the halfshaft set to the proper length, release any air pressure in the boot by inserting a blunt screwdriver between the boot and the housing **(see illustration)**. Don't damage the boot with the tool.
14   Install the boot clamps. A pair of special clamp-crimping pliers are used to tighten the clamp. The pliers are available at most auto parts stores **(see illustration)**.
15   Work the CV joint through its full range of travel. The joint should flex, extend and compress smoothly.
16   Install the halfshaft (see Section 15). Be sure to install a new circlip on the inner CV joint stub shaft.

Outer CV joint and boot
Refer to illustration 16.18

17   The outer CV joint is permanently retained to the connecting shaft and can't be disassembled. Outer CV joints are serviced as assemblies only.
18   If boot replacement is necessary, check the CV joint condition. If the joint is reusable, clean it thoroughly and repack it with grease **(see illustration)**.
19   To replace the boot, you must disassemble the inner joint and slide the boot off and on the inner end of the shaft.
20   Position the boot so the proper halfshaft length is obtained **(see illustration 16.12)**.
21   With the halfshaft set to the proper length, release any air pressure in the boot by inserting a blunt screwdriver between the boot and the housing **(see illustration 16.13)**. Don't damage the boot with the tool.
22   Install the boot clamps. A pair of special clamp-crimping pliers are used to tighten the clamp. The pliers are available at most auto parts stores **(see illustration 16.14)**.

---

17   Differential side oil seal – replacement

Removal
Refer to illustration 17.3

1   Remove the halfshaft assembly (see Section 15).

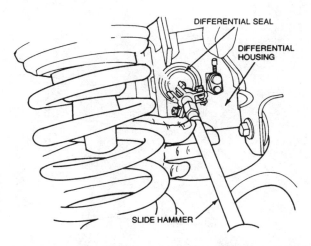

17.3   Removing the differential carrier halfshaft seal using a seal puller and slide hammer

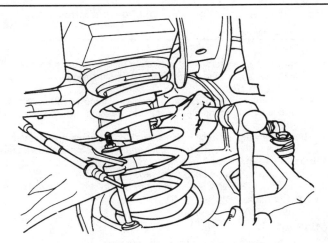

17.6   Drive the seal squarely into place

---

2   Insert seal puller into the differential halfshaft bore (so the tangs on the tool firmly grab the inside of the oil seal). If this tool is not available, a large prybar can be used to pry the seals out.
3   Connect a slide hammer to the seal puller and remove the seal **(see illustration)**.

Installation
Refer to illustration 17.6

4   Lubricate the lip of the seal with multi-purpose grease.
5   Carefully align the seal with the housing bore.
6   Using the proper driver or a socket, extension and a hammer, install the oil seal **(see illustration)**. **Caution:** *If the seal becomes cocked in the bore during installation, remove it and install a new one.*
7   Install the halfshaft assembly (see Section 15).

---

18   Differential carrier – removal and installation

Removal
Refer to illustrations 18.6 and 18.7

1   Remove the right halfshaft (see Section 15)
2   Reference mark the driveshaft in relation to the companion flange **(see illustration 11.15)**.
3   Remove the driveshaft retaining bolts.

8

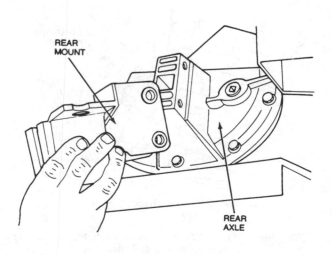

18.6   Remove the rear mount from the carrier cover

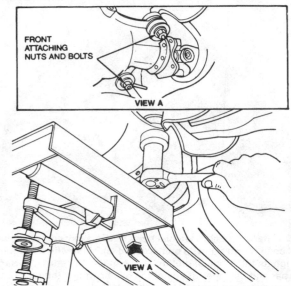

18.7   Remove the front mounting bolts, nuts, bushings and washers

4   Slide the driveshaft forward and rest it on the driveshaft hoop.
5   With a jack supporting the differential housing, remove the bolts retaining the rear mount.
6   Remove the rear mount from the carrier cover **(see illustration)**.
7   Remove the front mounting bolts, nuts, bushings and washers **(see illustration)**.
8   Partially lower the housing. While lowering the housing, move it to the right and use a prybar to detach the left halfshaft from the housing **(see illustration 15.9)**. **Note:** *The differential side seals should be replaced whenever a halfshaft has been removed.*
9   Install plug (T89P-4850-B) or equivalent in the left side of the housing and lower the assembly.

Installation

Refer to illustration 18.15

10   Replace the side oil seals.
11   Install a new circlip on the left halfshaft. **Note:** *Do not bend or twist the circlip.*
12   Lubricate the left halfshaft splines.
13   Position the carrier on a jack and partially raise it to align the left halfshaft into the differential side gear. **Note:** *Be careful not to damage the differential pilot bearing and oil seal.*
14   Connect the carrier to the front mounting bolts and engage the left halfshaft until the circlip seats in the differential side gear.
15   Properly install the bushings **(see illustration)**, washers and nuts on the front mount and tighten them to the torque listed in this Chapter's

Specifications.
16   Install the rear mount to the housing cover.
17   Install the bolts and nuts retaining the rear mount-to-crossmember.
18   Align the reference marks on the driveshaft and companion flange. Install the retaining bolts and tighten them to the torque listed in this Chapter's Specifications.
19   Install the right halfshaft (see Section 15).

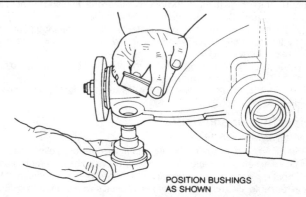

18.15   Install the front bushings as shown

Chapter 9   Brakes

Contents

Specifications

Brake fluid type . . . . See Chapter 1

Disc brakes

Front brake disc
   Standard thickness . . . . 1.024 in
   Minimum thickness* . . . . 0.935 in
   Front disc runout limit . . . . 0.003 in
Front disc thickness variation (parallelism) . . . . 0.0005 in
Rear brake disc
   Standard thickness . . . . 0.945 in
   Minimum thickness* . . . . 0.900 in
   Rear disc runout limit . . . . 0.003 in
   Rear disc thickness variation (parallelism) . . . . 0.0005 in
   Minimum brake pad thickness . . . . See Chapter 1
* Refer to marks stamped on the disc (they supercede information printed here)

Drum brakes

Drum diameter
   Standard . . . . 9.800 in
   Maximum* . . . . 9.900 in
* Refer to marks cast into the drum (they supercede information printed here)

Torque specifications

	Ft-lbs
Front brake caliper locating pins	19 to 25
Rear brake caliper slider pin pinch bolt	23 to 26
Anchor plate retaining bolts	45 to 65
Master cylinder-to-booster nuts	13 to 25
Power brake booster nuts	13 to 25
Wheel cylinder bolts	9 to 13
Brake hose to caliper banjo bolt	30 to 40
Rear backing plate to knuckle bolts	45 to 60
Wheel lug nuts	See Chapter 1

9

1 General information

Refer to illustration 1.3

General

All vehicles covered by this manual are equipped with hydraulically operated power assisted brake systems. All front brake systems are disc type, while the rear brakes are either disc or drum type. Some models are equipped with an Anti-lock Brake System (ABS), which is described in Section 2.

All brakes are self-adjusting. The front and rear disc brakes automatically compensate for pad wear, while the rear drum brakes incorporate an adjustment mechanism which is activated as the brakes are applied when the vehicle is driven in forward or reverse, not when the parking brake is applied.

The hydraulic system is a split design, meaning there are separate circuits for the front and rear brakes **(see illustration)**. If one circuit fails, the other circuit will remain functional and a warning indicator will light up on the dashboard, showing that a failure has occurred.

Master cylinder

The master cylinder is located under the hood, mounted to the power brake booster, and is best recognized by the large fluid reservoir on top. The removable plastic reservoir is partitioned to prevent total fluid loss in the event of a front or rear brake hydraulic system failure.

The master cylinder is designed for the "split system" mentioned earlier and has separate primary and secondary piston assemblies, the piston nearest the firewall being the primary piston, which applies hydraulic pressure to the front brakes.

Brake control valve

The brake control valve is located in the master cylinder between the brake lines and the master cylinder body on base production models. The control valve assembly contains a proportioning valve in an aluminum body. It also contains a pressure switch.

The proportioning valve regulates the hydraulic pressure in the rear brake system. It is located between the rear brake system's inlet and outlet ports in the control valve. When the brake pedal is applied, the rear brake fluid pressure passes through the proportioning valve to the rear brake system until the valve's split point is reached. Above its split point, the proportioning valve begins to reduce the hydraulic pressure to the rear brakes thereby balancing the braking condition between the front and rear brakes. This condition will prevent the rear wheel from locking up and the vehicle from skidding out of control.

The brake control valve is not serviceable – if a problem develops with the valve, it must be replaced as an assembly.

Parking brake

The parking brake mechanically operates the rear brakes only.

On drum brake models the parking brake cables pull on a lever attached to the brake shoe assembly, causing the shoes to expand against the drum. On models with rear disc brakes, the cables pull on levers that are attached to screw-type actuators in the caliper housings, which apply force to the caliper pistons, clamping the brake pads against the brake disc.

Precautions

There are some general cautions and warnings involving the brake system on this vehicle:

a) Use only brake fluid conforming to DOT 3 specifications.

b) The brake pads and linings may contain asbestos fibers which are hazardous to your health if inhaled. Whenever you work on brake system components, clean all parts with brake system cleaner or denatured alcohol. Do not allow the fine dust to become airborne.

c) Safety should be paramount whenever any servicing of the brake components is performed. Do not use parts or fasteners which are not in perfect condition, and be sure that all clearances and torque specifications are adhered to. If you are at all unsure about a certain procedure, seek professional advice. Upon completion of any brake system work, test the brakes carefully in a controlled area before putting the vehicle into normal service.

If a problem is suspected in the brake system, don't drive the vehicle until it's fixed.

2 Anti-lock brake system (ABS) – general information

Refer to illustrations 2.2, 2.3 and 2.5

The optional anti-lock brake system is designed to maintain vehicle steerability, directional stability and optimum deceleration under severe braking conditions and on most road surfaces. It does so by monitoring the rotational speed of each wheel and controlling the brake line pressure to each wheel during braking. This prevents the wheel from locking-up and provides maximum vehicle controllability.

Components

Actuation assembly

The actuation assembly consists of the master cylinder, an electric hydraulic pump and accumulator assembly, a solenoid valve body assembly and a fluid reservoir **(see illustration)**.

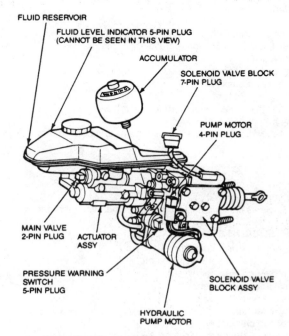

2.2 Details of ABS actuation assembly

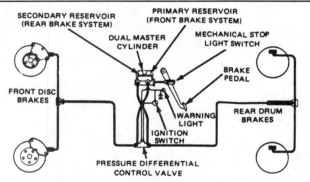

1.3 Typical dual master cylinder brake system

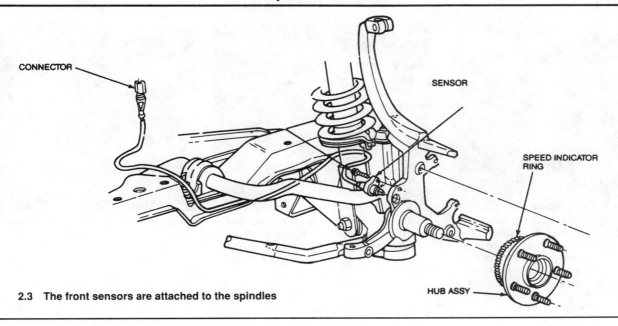

2.3 The front sensors are attached to the spindles

a) The electric pump provides hydraulic pressure to charge the accumulator, which supplies pressure to the braking system. The pump and accumulator are mounted to the actuation assembly.

b) The solenoid valve body assembly mounts to the side of the actuation assembly and modulates brake line pressure during ABS operation. The valve body contains three pairs of valves – one pair for each front wheel and a pair for the both of the rear wheels combined.

Wheel sensors

These sensors are located at each wheel and generate small electrical pulsations when the toothed sensor rings are turning, sending a signal to the electronic controller indicating wheel rotational speed (**see illustration**).

The front wheel sensors are mounted to the front spindles in close relationship to the toothed sensor rings, which are pressed into the inside of the rotors.

The rear wheel sensors bolt to the rear disc brake axle adapters (**see illustration**). The sensor rings are pressed onto the axle shafts.

Electronic controller

The electronic controller is mounted on a package tray in the luggage compartment and is the "brain" for the ABS system. The function of the control module – consisting primarily of two microprocessors and the related circuits needed for their operation – is to accept and process information received from the wheel speed sensors to control the hydraulic line pressure, avoiding wheel lock-up. The controller also constantly monitors the system, even under normal driving conditions, to find faults within the system.

If a problem develops within the system, an amber "Check Anti-lock Brakes" and/or the "Brake" light will glow on the dashboard. A diagnostic code will also be stored in the controller, which, when retrieved by a service technician, will indicate the problem area or component.

Diagnosis and repair

If a dashboard warning light comes on and stays on while the vehicle is in operation, the ABS system requires attention.

Although a special electronic ABS diagnostic tester is necessary to properly diagnose the system, the home mechanic can perform a few preliminary checks before taking the vehicle to a dealer who is equipped with this tester.

a) Check the brake fluid level in the reservoir.

b) Open the trunk lid and remove the lower right side module panel. Check that the controller electrical connector is securely connected.

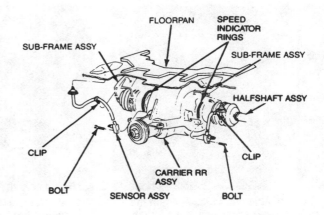

REAR SENSORS

2.5 The rear sensors are attached to the axle housing

c) Check the electrical connectors at the actuation assembly.

d) Check the fuses.

e) Follow the wiring harness to each wheel and check that all connections are secure and that the wiring is not damaged.

If the above preliminary checks do not rectify the problem, the vehicle should be diagnosed by a dealer service department. Due to the rather complex nature of this system, all actual repair work must be done by a dealer.

9

---

3   Front brake pads – replacement

Refer to illustrations 3.5 and 3.6a through 3.6h

Warning: *Disc brake pads must be replaced on both front wheels at the same time – never replace the pads on only one wheel. Also, the dust created by the brake system may contains asbestos, which is harmful to your health. Never blow it out with compressed air and don't inhale any of it. An approved filtering mask should be worn when working on the brakes. Do not, under any circumstances, use petroleum-based solvents to clean brake parts. Use brake cleaner or denatured alcohol only!*

Note: *When servicing the disc brakes, use only high quality, nationally recognized brand name pads.*

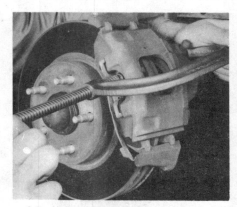

3.5   Using a large C-clamp, push the piston back into the caliper bore just enough to allow the caliper to slide off the brake disc easily – note that one end of the clamp is on the flat area on the inner side of the caliper and the other end (screw end) is pressing on the outer pad

3.6a   Remove the two caliper locating pins (arrows) that hold the caliper to the spindle (this will require a T-40 Torx socket), then lift the caliper from the spindle

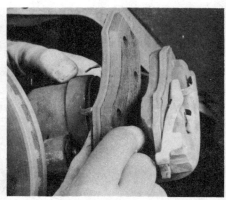

3.6b   Pull the inner brake pad out of the caliper piston

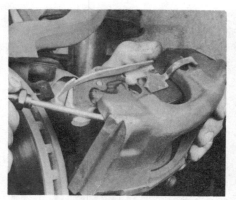

3.6c   Pry the outer brake pad off the caliper frame – note how it fits into the frame as this is done

3.6d   Using a C-clamp and a block of wood, bottom the piston in the caliper bore

3.6e   The brake pads are marked for left and right sides – be sure they are installed in the correct positions

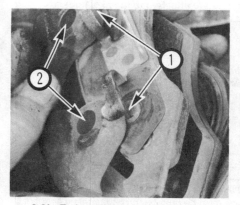

3.6f   To install the new pads in the caliper, carefully push the inner pad retaining clips straight into the piston until the backing plate rests on the piston face – slide the outer pad into the caliper as shown (be sure the locating lugs on the pad [1] seat in the holes in the caliper frame [2], if equipped)

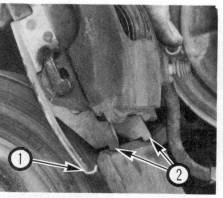

3.6g   Position the anti-rattle spring on the outer pad (1) under the arm of the spindle, with the notches in the edges of the pads engaging with the arm of the spindle (2), then rotate the caliper assembly over the disc

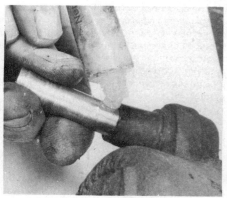

3.6h   Apply silicone grease to the caliper locating pins and install the pins, tightening them to the torque listed in this Chapter's Specifications

4.5   With the caliper padded to catch the piston, use compressed air to force the piston out of its bore – make sure your hands or fingers are not between the piston and caliper!

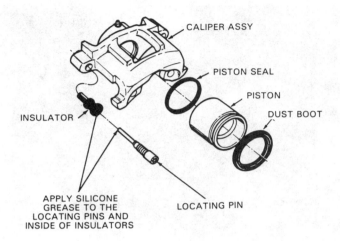

4.6a   Exploded view of the front brake caliper components

1   Remove the cover from the brake fluid reservoir.
2   Loosen the wheel lug nuts, raise the front of the vehicle and support it securely on jackstands.
3   Remove the front wheels. Work on one brake assembly at a time, using the assembled brake for reference if necessary.
4   Inspect the brake disc carefully as outlined in Section 5. If machining is necessary, follow the information in that Section to remove the disc, at which time the pads can be removed from the caliper as well.
5   Push the piston back into its bore using a large C-clamp (see illustration). As the piston is depressed to the bottom of the caliper bore, the fluid in the master cylinder will rise. Make sure that it doesn't overflow. If necessary, siphon off some of the fluid.
6   Follow the accompanying photos, beginning with illustration 3.6a, for the actual pad replacement procedure. Be sure to stay in order and read the caption under each illustration.
7   When reinstalling the caliper, be sure to tighten the locating pins to the torque listed in this Chapter's Specifications. After the job has been completed, firmly depress the brake pedal a few times to bring the pads into contact with the disc.

---

4   Front brake caliper – removal, overhaul and installation

Warning: Dust created by the brake system contains asbestos, which is harmful to your health. Never blow it out with compressed air and don't inhale any of it. An approved filtering mask should be worn when working on the brakes. Do not, under any circumstances, use petroleum-based solvents to clean brake parts. Use brake cleaner or denatured alcohol only!

Note: If an overhaul is indicated (usually because of fluid leakage) explore all options before beginning the job. New and factory-rebuilt calipers are available on an exchange basis, which makes this job quite easy. If it is decided to rebuild the calipers, make sure that a rebuild kit is available before proceeding. Always rebuild the calipers in pairs - never rebuild just one of them.

Removal

1   Apply the parking brake and block the rear wheels. Loosen the wheel lug nuts, raise the front of the vehicle and support it securely on jackstands. Remove the wheel.
2   Unscrew the brake hose banjo bolt and detach the hose from the caliper. Wrap a plastic bag around the end of the hose to prevent fluid loss and

4.6b   Remove the dust boot from the caliper bore groove

contamination. **Note:** If the caliper will not be completely removed from the vehicle – as for pad inspection or disc removal – leave the hose connected and suspend the caliper with a length of wire. This will save the trouble of bleeding the brake system.
3   Refer to the first few steps in Section 3 to separate the caliper from the spindle – it's part of the brake pad replacement procedure.

Overhaul

Refer to illustrations 4.5, 4.6a, 4.6b, 4.7, 4.12, 4.14, 4.17, 4.18, 4.19a, 4.19b, 4.20 and 4.21

4   Clean the exterior of the caliper with brake cleaner or denatured alcohol. Never use gasoline, kerosene or petroleum-based cleaning solvents. Place the caliper on a clean workbench.
5   Position a wood block in the center of the caliper as a cushion, then use compressed air to remove the piston from the caliper (see illustration). Use only enough air to ease the piston out of the bore. If the piston is blown out, even with the cushion in place, it may be damaged. **Warning:** Never place your fingers in front of the piston in an attempt to catch or protect it when applying compressed air, as serious injury could occur.
6   Pull the dust boot out of the caliper bore (see illustrations).

9

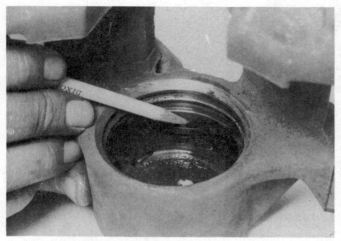

4.7　The piston seal should be removed with a plastic or wooden tool to avoid damage to the bore and seal groove (a pencil will do the job)

4.12　Grab the ends of the locating pin insulators and, using a twisting motion, push them through the caliper ears

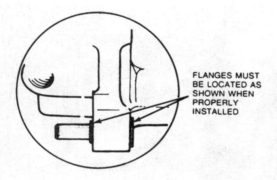

FLANGES MUST BE LOCATED AS SHOWN WHEN PROPERLY INSTALLED

4.14　Push the new insulators through the holes in the caliper ears, making sure they are installed all the way

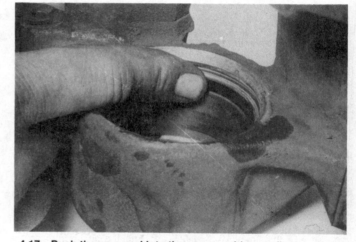

4.17　Push the new seal into the groove with your fingers, then check to see that it isn't twisted or kinked

4.18　Install the dust boot in the upper groove in the caliper bore, making sure it's completely seated

9　Check the caliper bore in a similar way. Light polishing with crocus cloth is permissible to remove light corrosion and stains.

10　Remove the bleeder valve and rubber cap.

11　Inspect the caliper locating pins for corrosion and damage. Replace them with new ones if necessary.

12　Remove the caliper locating pin insulators from the caliper ears **(see illustration)**.

13　Use clean brake fluid or denatured alcohol to clean all the parts. **Warning:** *Do not, under any circumstances, use petroleum-based solvents to clean brake parts. Allow all parts to dry, preferably using compressed air to blow out all passages. Make sure the compressed air is filtered, as a harmful lubricant residue or moisture may be present in unfiltered systems.*

14　Push the new locating pin insulators into place **(see illustration)**.

15　Check the fit of the piston in the bore by sliding it into the caliper. The piston should move easily.

16　Thread the bleeder valve into the caliper and tighten it securely. Install the rubber cap.

17　Lubricate the new piston seal and caliper bore with clean brake fluid. Position the seal in the caliper bore groove, making sure it doesn't twist **(see illustration)**.

18　Fit the new dust boot in the caliper bore upper groove, making sure it's seated **(see illustration)**.

7　Using a wood or plastic tool, remove the piston seal from the caliper bore **(see illustration)**. Metal tools may cause bore damage.

8　Carefully examine the piston for nicks, burrs, cracks, loss of plating, corrosion or any signs of damage. If surface defects are present, the parts must be replaced.

4.19a Lubricate the piston and bore with clean brake fluid, insert the piston into the dust boot (NOT the bore) at an angle, then, using a rotating motion, work the piston completely into the dust boot . . .

4.19b . . . and push it straight into the caliper as far as possible by hand

4.20 Use a C-clamp and a block of wood to bottom the piston in the caliper bore – make sure it goes in perfectly straight, or the sides of the piston may be damaged, rendering it useless

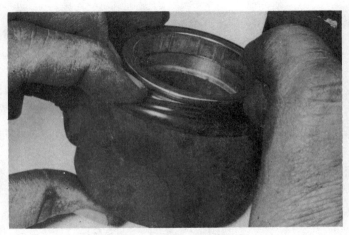

4.21 Install the lip of the dust boot in the groove on the caliper piston

5.5a Use a dial indicator to check disc runout – if the reading exceeds the maximum allowable runout limit, the rotor will have to be machined or replaced

19 Lubricate the caliper piston with clean brake fluid. Push the piston into the caliper, using a turning motion to roll the lip of the dust boot over the piston (see illustrations). Push the piston into the caliper by hand as far as possible.
20 Using a C-clamp and a block of wood, push the piston all the way to the bottom of the bore. Work slowly, keeping an eye on the side of the piston, making sure it enters the bore perfectly straight with no resistance (see illustration).
21 Seat the lip of the dust boot in the groove on the piston (see illustration).

Installation

22 Refer to Section 3 for the caliper installation procedure, as it is part of the brake pad replacement procedure.
23 Connect the brake hose to the caliper, using new sealing washers. Tighten the banjo bolt to the torque listed in this Chapter's Specifications.
24 Bleed the brakes as outlined in Section 12. This is not necessary if the banjo bolt was not loosened or removed.
25 Install the wheel and lower the vehicle. Tighten the lug nuts to the torque listed in the Chapter 1 Specifications.
26 Test the operation of the brakes before placing the vehicle into normal service.

5   Brake disc – inspection, removal and installation

Inspection

Refer to illustrations 5.5a, 5.5b, 5.6a, 5.6b and 5.7
Note: *This procedure applies to both front and rear disc brake assemblies.*
1   Loosen the wheel lug nuts, raise the vehicle and support it securely on jackstands. Remove the wheel.
2   Remove the brake caliper as outlined in Section 4 (front) or Section 7 (rear). It's not necessary to disconnect the brake hose. After removing the caliper bolts, suspend the caliper out of the way with a piece of wire. Don't let the caliper hang by the hose and don't stretch or twist the hose.
3   Reinstall two lug nuts to hold the disc against the hub.
4   Visually check the disc surface for score marks and other damage. Light scratches and shallow grooves are normal after use and may not always be detrimental to brake operation, but deep score marks – over 0.015-inch (0.38 mm) – require disc removal and refinishing by an automotive machine shop. Be sure to check both sides of the disc. If pulsating has been noticed during application of the brakes, suspect disc runout.
5   To check disc runout, place a dial indicator at a point about 1/2-inch from the outer edge of the disc (see illustration). Set the indicator to zero and turn the disc. The indicator reading should not exceed the specified allowable runout limit. If it does, the disc should be refinished by an auto

9

5.5b   Using a swirling motion, remove the glaze from the disc surface with emery cloth or sandpaper

5.6a   The minimum thickness limit is cast into the inside of the disc

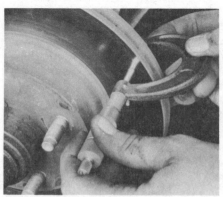

5.6b   Use a micrometer to measure disc thickness at several points near the edge

5.7   Lift the disc off the hub assembly

6.2   The brake hose bracket is located near the shock absorber

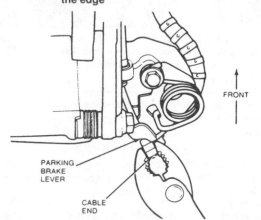

PARKING
BRAKE
LEVER

CABLE
END

FRONT

6.3   Using a pair of pliers, disconnect the parking brake cable from the parking brake lever on the caliper

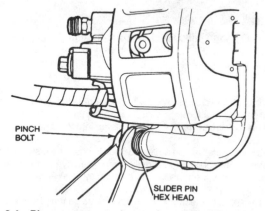

PINCH
BOLT

SLIDER PIN
HEX HEAD

6.4   Place an open end wrench on the slider pin hex head to prevent it from turning, then remove the upper caliper pinch bolt

motive machine shop. **Note:** *Professionals recommend resurfacing of brake discs regardless of the dial indicator reading (to produce a smooth, flat surface that will eliminate brake pedal pulsations and other undesirable symptoms related to questionable discs). At the very least, if you elect not to have the discs resurfaced, deglaze the brake pad surface with emery cloth or sandpaper (use a swirling motion to ensure a non-directional finish)* **(see illustration)**.

6   The disc must not be machined to a thickness less than the specified minimum refinish thickness. The minimum wear (or discard) thickness is cast into the inside of the disc **(see illustration)**. The disc thickness can be checked with a micrometer **(see illustration)**.

Removal

7   Remove the lug nuts that are temporarily holding the disc to the hub and lift the disc off **(see illustration)**.

Installation

8   Install the disc onto the hub assembly.

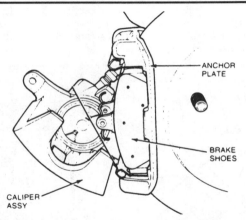

6.5 With the upper pinch bolt removed, swing the caliper back to gain access to the brake pads

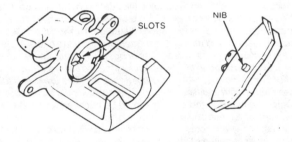

6.7   After the piston has been bottomed in the caliper, it may have to be turned the other way slightly to align a slot in the piston with the nib on the brake pad backing plate

9   Install the caliper and brake pad assembly over the disc and position it on the knuckle assembly (refer to Section 4 for the front caliper installation procedure), or on the anchor plate assembly (refer to Section 7 for the rear brake caliper installation procedure, if necessary). Tighten the caliper bolts to the torque listed in this Chapter's Specifications.

10   Install the wheel, then lower the vehicle to the ground. Depress the brake pedal a few times to bring the brake pads into contact with the rotor. Bleeding of the system will not be necessary unless the brake hose was disconnected from the caliper. Check the operation of the brakes carefully before placing the vehicle into normal service.

6   Rear brake pads – replacement

Refer to illustrations 6.2, 6.3, 6.4, 6.5 and 6.7

1   Block the front wheels. Loosen the wheel lug nuts, raise the rear of the vehicle and support it securely on jackstands. Remove the wheel.

2   Remove the brake hose bracket-to-shock absorber bracket screw **(see illustration)**.

3   Remove the parking brake cable retaining clip at the caliper. Using a pair of pliers, disconnect the cable end from the parking brake lever **(see illustration)**.

4   Hold the hex head portion of the caliper upper slider pin with an open end wrench to prevent it from turning, then remove the upper pinch bolt **(see illustration)**.

5   Rotate the top of the caliper away from the brake disc to gain access to the brake pads **(see illustration)**.

6   Lift the brake pads from the anchor plate.

7   Using a pair of needle-nose pliers, engage the tips of the pliers in the two slots in the caliper piston face. Turn the piston clockwise until it is completely seated in the caliper. Position the piston in such a way that one of the slots will be aligned with the locating nib on the brake pad when the caliper is installed **(see illustration)**.

8   Insert the brake pads into the anchor plate.

9   Swing the caliper into position, making sure the nib on the pad meshes with a slot in the caliper piston.

10   Apply Loctite to the threads of the pinch bolt. Insert the bolt through the caliper and into the slider pin. Tighten both pinch bolts to the torque listed in this Chapter's Specifications.

11   Connect the parking brake cable to the lever. Attach the cable retaining clip to the caliper.

12   Install the brake hose bracket screw.

13   Install the wheel, lower the vehicle and tighten the lug nuts to the torque listed in the Chapter 1 Specifications.

14   Depress the brake pedal a few times to bring the pads into contact with the rotor. Bleeding of the system will not be necessary unless the hose was disconnected from the caliper. Check the operation of the brakes carefully before placing the vehicle into normal service.

7   Rear brake caliper – removal and installation

Note: *Due to the relatively complex design of the rear brake caliper/parking brake actuator assembly, all service procedures requiring disassembly and reassembly should be left to a professional mechanic. The home mechanic can, however, remove the caliper and take it to a repair shop or Ford dealer service department for repair, thereby saving the cost of removal and installation.*

Removal

1   Refer to the first few steps of the previous Section, as it is necessary to partially remove the caliper to remove the rear brake pads.

2   Remove the lower slider pin pinch bolt.

3   Disconnect the brake hose from the caliper. Wrap a plastic bag tightly around the end of the hose to prevent fluid loss and contamination. If the caliper is being removed for access to other components only, removing the hose won't be necessary. If this is the case, hang the caliper out of the way with a piece of wire.

4   Lift the caliper away from the anchor plate.

Installation

5   Installation is the reverse of the removal procedure. Follow the procedure outlined in Section 6 to ensure correct installation of the caliper over the brake pads.

6   Bleed the brakes as outlined in Section 12.

8   Rear brake shoes – replacement

Refer to illustrations 8.4a through 8.4s and 8.5

Warning: *Drum brake shoes must be replaced on both wheels at the same time – never replace the shoes on only one wheel. Also, the dust created by the brake system contains asbestos, which is harmful to your health. Never blow it out with compressed air and don't inhale any of it. An approved filtering mask should be worn when working on the brakes. Do not, under any circumstances, use petroleum-based solvents to clean brake parts. Use brake cleaner or denatured alcohol only!*

Caution: *Whenever the brake shoes are replaced, the retractor and hold-down springs should also be replaced. Due to the continuous heating/cooling cycle that the springs are subjected to, they lose their tension over a period of time and may allow the shoes to drag on the drum and wear at a much faster rate than normal. When replacing the rear brake shoes, use only high quality nationally recognized brand-name parts.*

1   Loosen the wheel lug nuts, raise the rear of the vehicle and support it securely on jackstands. Block the front wheels to keep the vehicle from rolling.

2   Release the parking brake.

3   Remove the wheel. **Note:** *All four rear brake shoes must be replaced at the same time, but to avoid mixing up parts, work on only one brake assembly at a time.*

4   Follow the accompanying photos (illustrations 8.4a through 8.4s) for the inspection and replacement of the brake shoes. Be sure to stay in order and read the caption under each illustration. **Note:** *If the brake drum cannot be easily pulled off, pry the rubber plug from the backing plate inspection hole and insert a screwdriver or brake tool to rotate the adjusting screw and move the adjusting lever. This will cause the brake shoes to pull together. Spray the assembly with penetrating oil and allow the oil to soak in if the mechanism is difficult to turn. The drum should now come off.*

5   Before reinstalling the drum it should be checked for cracks, score marks, deep scratches and hard spots, which will appear as small discolored areas. If the hard spots cannot be removed with fine emery cloth or if any of the other conditions listed above exist, the drum must be taken to an automotive machine shop to have it turned. **Note:** *Professionals recommend resurfacing the drums whenever a brake job is done. Resurfacing will eliminate the possibility of out-of-round drums. If the drums are worn so much that they can't be resurfaced without exceeding the maximum allowable diameter (stamped into the drum), then new ones will be required* **(see illustration)**. *At the very least, if you elect not to have the drums resurfaced, remove the glazing from the surface with medium-grit emery cloth using a swirling motion.*

6   Install the brake drum on the hub.

7   Mount the wheel, install the lug nuts, then lower the vehicle.

8   Make a number of forward and reverse stops to adjust the brakes until satisfactory pedal action is obtained.

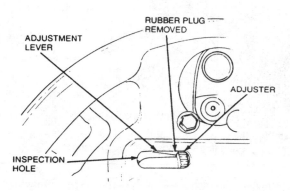

8.4a   View of the inspection hole from behind the backing plate

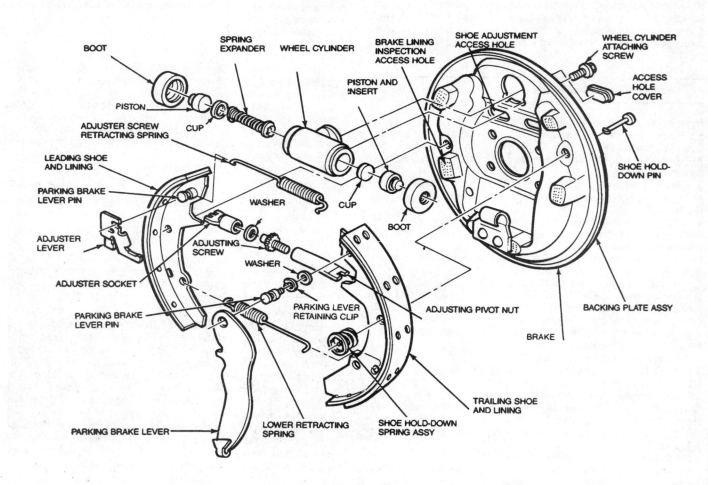

8.4b   Exploded view of the drum brake components (left side shown)

8.4c Before removing anything, clean the brake assembly with brake cleaner and allow it to dry – position a drain pan under the brake to catch the residue – DO NOT USE COMPRESSED AIR TO BLOW THE DUST FROM THE PARTS!

8.4d Use a pair of needle-nose pliers to remove the adjuster spring from the adjuster lever

8.4e Remove the adjuster lever by pulling it back and away from the alignment pin

8.4f Remove the adjuster screw

8.4g Remove the hold-down spring and pin from the leading shoe

8.4h Lift the leading shoe from the backing plate . . .

8.4i . . . then remove the lower retracting spring from the brake shoe

8.4j Remove the hold-down spring and pin from the trailing shoe

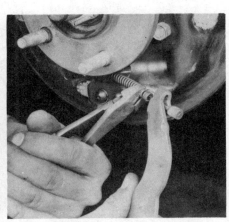

8.4k Use pliers to pull back the spring on the parking brake cable and remove the parking brake lever and the brake shoe from the vehicle

9

8.4l   Lubricate the brake shoe contact areas with high temperature grease

8.4m   Remove the parking brake lever from the brake shoe by forcing the clip off the clevis pin

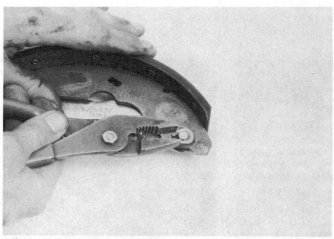

8.4n   After replacing the old shoe with a new one, install the parking brake lever to the trailing brake shoe using a new clip on the clevis pin

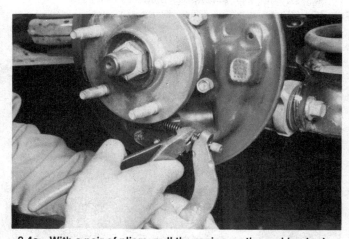

8.4o   With a pair of pliers, pull the spring on the parking brake cable back to make room for the parking brake lever – install the trailing shoe assembly

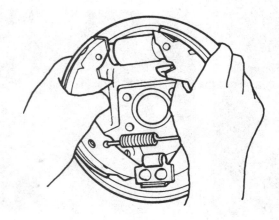

8.4p   Install the lower retracting spring to both shoes and spread the brake shoes over the guide slots of the wheel cylinder pistons

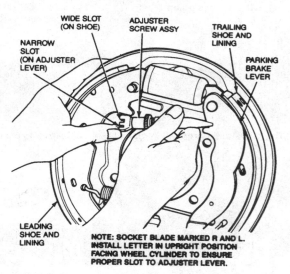

WIDE SLOT (ON SHOE)

NARROW SLOT (ON ADJUSTER LEVER)

ADJUSTER SCREW ASSY

TRAILING SHOE AND LINING

PARKING BRAKE LEVER

LEADING SHOE AND LINING

NOTE: SOCKET BLADE MARKED R AND L. INSTALL LETTER IN UPRIGHT POSITION FACING WHEEL CYLINDER TO ENSURE PROPER SLOT TO ADJUSTER LEVER.

8.4q   Install the adjuster assembly to the slots in the brake shoes – make sure the socket blade marked R or L is installed with the letters in the upright position to coincide with the proper slots in the brake shoe and the parking brake lever

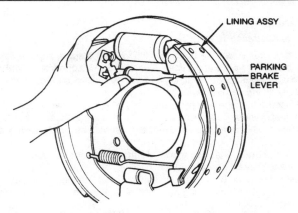

8.4r   Install the adjuster lever over the anchor pin, then install the hold-down springs and pins

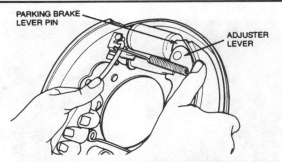

8.4s   Use a special tool or a screwdriver to install the upper retracting spring to the adjuster lever, then install the hold-down springs and pins – check to make sure the star wheel contacts the adjuster lever, and also wiggle the brake shoe assembly back and forth to make sure it's centered on the backing plate

9   Wheel cylinder – removal, overhaul and installation

Note: *If an overhaul is indicated (usually because of fluid leakage or sticky operation) explore all options before beginning the job. New wheel cylinders are available, which makes this job quite easy. If it's decided to rebuild the wheel cylinder, make sure that a rebuild kit is available before proceeding. Never overhaul only one wheel cylinder – always rebuild both of them at the same time.*

Removal

Refer to illustration 9.4

1   Raise the rear of the vehicle and support it securely on jackstands. Block the front wheels to keep the vehicle from rolling.
2   Remove the brake shoe assembly (see Section 8).
3   Remove all dirt and foreign material from around the wheel cylinder.

4   Disconnect the brake line **(see illustration)**. Don't pull the brake line away from the wheel cylinder.
5   Remove the wheel cylinder mounting bolts.
6   Detach the wheel cylinder from the brake backing plate and place it on a clean workbench. Immediately plug the brake line to prevent fluid loss and contamination.

Overhaul

Refer to illustration 9.7

7   Remove the bleeder screw, cups, pistons, boots and spring assembly from the wheel cylinder body **(see illustration)**.
8   Clean the wheel cylinder with brake fluid, denatured alcohol or brake system cleaner. **Warning:** *Do not, under any circumstances, use petroleum-based solvents to clean brake parts!*
9   Use compressed air to remove excess fluid from the wheel cylinder and to blow out the passages.

8.5   The maximum permissible diameter specification is cast into the brake drum

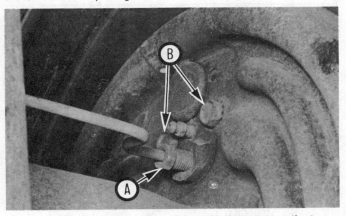

9.4   Disconnect the brake line fitting (A), then remove the two wheel cylinder bolts (B)

9

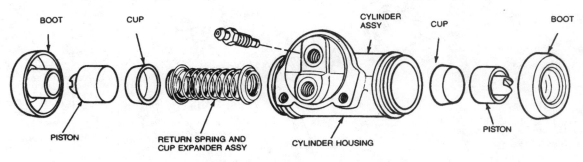

9.7   Exploded view of the rear wheel cylinder

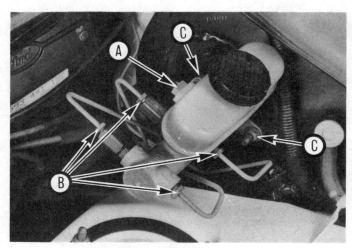

10.2 Disconnect the electrical connector (A), unscrew the hydraulic fitting tube nuts (B) then remove the two mounting nuts (C) and detach the master cylinder

10 Check the cylinder bore for corrosion and score marks. Crocus cloth can be used to remove light corrosion and stains, but the cylinder must be replaced with a new one if the defects cannot be removed easily, or if the bore is scored.

11 Lubricate the new cups with brake fluid.

12 Assemble the brake cylinder components. Make sure the cup lips face in.

Installation

13 Place the wheel cylinder in position and install the bolts.

14 Connect the brake line and install the brake shoe assembly.

15 Bleed the brakes (see Section 12).

---

10 Master cylinder – removal, overhaul and installation

Note: *If the vehicle is equipped with an Anti-Lock Brake (ABS) System, have the master cylinder rebuilt at a dealership service department. Also, before deciding to overhaul the master cylinder, check on the availability and cost of a new or factory rebuilt unit and also the availability of a rebuild kit.*

Removal

Refer to illustration 10.2

1 Place rags under the brake line fittings and prepare caps or plastic bags to cover the ends of the lines once they are disconnected. **Caution:** *Brake fluid will damage paint. Cover all body parts and be careful not to spill fluid during this procedure.*

2 Unscrew the tube nuts at the ends of the brake lines where they enter the master cylinder. To prevent rounding off the flats on these nuts, a flare-nut wrench, which wraps around the fitting, should be used **(see illustration)**.

3 Pull the brake lines away from the master cylinder slightly and plug the ends to prevent contamination.

4 Disconnect the brake warning light electrical connector, remove the two master cylinder mounting nuts, and detach the master cylinder from the vehicle.

5 Remove the reservoir cap, then discard any fluid remaining in the reservoir.

Overhaul

Refer to illustrations 10.7a, 10.7b, 10.8, 10.9, 10.10, 10.14 and 10.19

6 Mount the master cylinder in a vise with the vise jaws clamping on the mounting flange.

7 Remove the primary piston snap-ring by depressing the piston and extracting the ring with a pair of snap-ring pliers. **(see illustrations)**.

8 Remove the primary piston assembly from the cylinder bore **(see illustration)**.

9 Remove the secondary piston assembly from the cylinder bore. It may be necessary to remove the master cylinder from the vise and invert it, carefully tapping it against a block of wood to expel the piston **(see illustration)**.

10 If fluid has been leaking past the reservoir grommets, pry the reservoir from the cylinder body with a screwdriver **(see illustration)**. Remove the grommets.

11 Inspect the cylinder bore for corrosion and damage. If any corrosion or damage is found, replace the master cylinder body with a new one, as abrasives cannot be used on the bore.

12 Lubricate the new reservoir grommets with silicone lubricant and press them into the master cylinder body. Make sure they're properly seated.

13 Lay the reservoir on a hard surface and press the master cylinder body onto the reservoir, using a rocking motion.

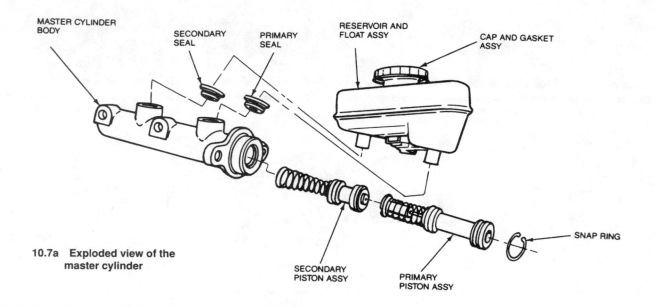

10.7a Exploded view of the master cylinder

MASTER CYLINDER BODY

SECONDARY SEAL

PRIMARY SEAL

RESERVOIR AND FLOAT ASSY

CAP AND GASKET ASSY

SNAP RING

SECONDARY PISTON ASSY

PRIMARY PISTON ASSY

10.7b   Use a Phillips head screwdriver to push the primary piston into the cylinder, then remove the snap-ring

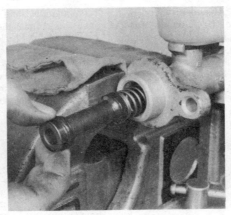

10.8   Remove the primary piston assembly from the cylinder

10.9   Tap the master cylinder against a block of wood to eject the secondary piston assembly

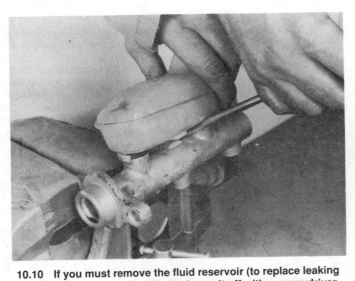

10.10   If you must remove the fluid reservoir (to replace leaking seals or a broken reservoir), gently pry it off with a screwdriver or prybar

10.14   Coat the secondary piston with clean brake fluid and install it in the master cylinder, spring end first

14   Lubricate the cylinder bore and primary and secondary piston assemblies with clean brake fluid. Insert the secondary piston assembly into the cylinder **(see illustration)**.

15   Install the primary piston assembly in the cylinder bore, depress it and install the snap-ring.

16   Inspect the reservoir cap and diaphragm for cracks and deformation. Replace any damaged parts with new ones and attach the diaphragm to the cap.

17   **Note:** *Whenever the master cylinder is removed, the complete hydraulic system must be bled. The time required to bleed the system can be reduced if the master cylinder is filled with fluid and bench bled (refer to Steps 18 through 23) before the master cylinder is installed on the vehicle.*

18   Insert threaded plugs of the correct size into the cylinder outlet holes and fill the reservoirs with brake fluid. The master cylinder should be supported in such a manner that brake fluid will not spill during the bench bleeding procedure.

19   Loosen one plug at a time, starting with the rear outlet port first, and push the piston assembly into the bore to force air from the master cylinder **(see illustration)**. To prevent air from being drawn back into the cylinder, the appropriate plug must be replaced before allowing the piston to return to its original position.

20   Stroke the piston three or four times for each outlet to ensure that all air has been expelled.

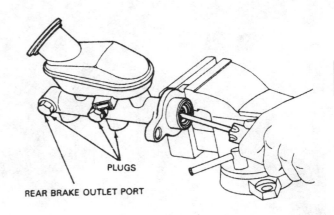

PLUGS

REAR BRAKE OUTLET PORT

10.19   When bench bleeding the master cylinder, start with the rear brake outlet port

9

21   Since high pressure is not involved in the bench bleeding procedure, an alternative to the removal and replacement of the plugs with each stroke of the piston assembly is available. Before pushing in on the piston assembly, remove one of the plugs completely. Before releasing the piston, however, instead of replacing the plug, simply put your finger tightly over the hole to keep air from being drawn back into the master cylinder. Wait several seconds for the brake fluid to be drawn from the reservoir to the piston bore, then repeat the procedure. When you push down on the piston it will force your finger off the hole, allowing the air inside to be expelled. When only brake fluid is being ejected from the hole, replace the plug and go on to the other port.

22   Refill the master cylinder reservoirs and install the diaphragm and cap assembly.

Installation

23   Carefully install the master cylinder by reversing the removal steps, then bleed the brakes (refer to Section 12).

---

11   Brake hoses and lines – inspection and replacement

Inspection

1   About every six months, with the vehicle raised and supported securely on jackstands, the rubber hoses which connect the steel brake lines with the front and rear brake assemblies should be inspected for cracks, chafing of the outer cover, leaks, blisters and other damage. These are important and vulnerable parts of the brake system and inspection should be complete. A light and mirror will be helpful for a thorough check. If a hose exhibits any of the above conditions, replace it with a new one.

Replacement

Flexible hose

Refer to illustration 11.2

2   Using a flare nut wrench, disconnect the brake line from the hose fitting, being careful not to bend the frame bracket or brake line (**see illustration**). If the fitting is extremely tight, hold the fitting block with a wrench to prevent the frame bracket from bending.

3   Detach the hose from the bracket and the body.

4   Remove the banjo bolt from the caliper and discard the sealing washers.

5   Connect the hose to the caliper, using new sealing washers. Tighten the banjo bolt to the torque listed in this Chapter's Specifications.

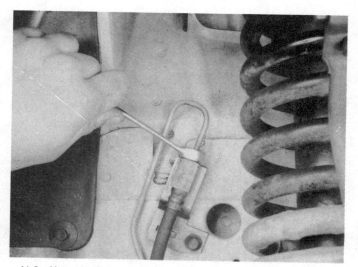

11.2   Use a flare nut wrench to remove the brake line from the bracket assembly

6   Without twisting the hose, connect the other end of the line to the chassis and install the bolt, but leave it a little loose for now.

7   Connect the brake line to the fitting block by hand, then tighten the fitting securely using a flare nut wrench. Tighten the bracket bolt securely.

8   When the brake hose installation is complete, there should be no kinks in the hose. Make sure the hose doesn't contact any part of the suspension. Check this by turning the wheels to the extreme left and right positions. If the hose makes contact, remove it and correct the installation as necessary.

Metal brake line

9   When replacing brake lines be sure to use the correct parts. Don't use copper tubing for any brake system components. Purchase steel brake lines from a dealer or auto parts store.

10   Prefabricated brake line, with the tube ends already flared and fittings installed, is available at auto parts stores and dealers. These lines are also bent to the proper shapes.

11   If prefabricated lines are not available, obtain the recommended steel tubing and fittings to match the line to be replaced. Determine the correct length by measuring the old brake line (a piece of string can usually be used for this) and cut the new tubing to length, allowing about 1/2-inch extra for flaring the ends.

12   Install the fitting over the cut tubing and flare the ends of the line with a flaring tool. A double-flare is the only acceptable type for automotive brake system applications.

13   If necessary, carefully bend the line to the proper shape. A tube bender is recommended for this. **Warning:** *Do not crimp or damage the line.*

14   When installing the new line make sure it's securely supported in the brackets and has plenty of clearance between moving or hot components.

15   After installation, check the master cylinder fluid level and add fluid as necessary. Bleed the brake system as outlined in the next Section and test the brakes carefully before driving the vehicle in traffic.

---

12   Brake hydraulic system – bleeding

Refer to illustration 12.8

Warning: *Wear eye protection when bleeding the brake system. If the fluid comes in contact with your eyes, immediately rinse them with water and seek medical attention.*

Note: *Bleeding the hydraulic system is necessary to remove any air that manages to find its way into the system when it's been opened during removal and installation of a hose, line, caliper or master cylinder.*

Conventional brakes (non-ABS)

1   It will probably be necessary to bleed the system at all four brakes if air has entered the system due to low fluid level, or if the brake lines have been disconnected at the master cylinder.

2   If a brake line was disconnected only at a wheel, then only that caliper or wheel cylinder must be bled.

3   If a brake line is disconnected at a fitting located between the master cylinder and any of the brakes, that part of the system served by the disconnected line must be bled.

4   Remove any residual vacuum from the brake power booster by applying the brake several times with the engine off.

5   Remove the master cylinder reservoir cover and fill the reservoir with brake fluid. Reinstall the cover. **Note:** *Check the fluid level often during the bleeding operation and add fluid as necessary to prevent the fluid level from falling low enough to allow air bubbles into the master cylinder.*

6   Have an assistant on hand, as well as a supply of new brake fluid, an empty clear plastic container, a length of 3/16-inch plastic, rubber or vinyl tubing to fit over the bleeder valve and a wrench to open and close the bleeder valve.

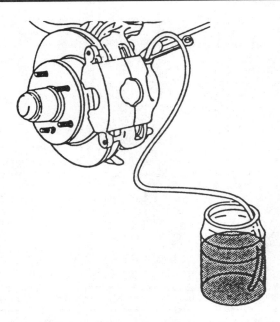

12.8   When bleeding the brakes, a hose is connected to the bleeder valve at the caliper or wheel cylinder and submerged in brake fluid – air will be seen as bubbles in the tube and container (when no more bubbles appear, the air has been purged from the caliper or wheel cylinder)

7   Beginning at the right rear wheel, loosen the bleeder valve slightly, then tighten it to a point where it is snug but can still be loosened quickly and easily.
8   Place one end of the tubing over the bleeder valve and submerge the other end in brake fluid in the container **(see illustration)**.
9   Have the assistant pump the brakes slowly a few times to get pressure in the system, then hold the pedal firmly depressed.
10   While the pedal is held depressed, open the bleeder valve just enough to allow a flow of fluid to leave the valve. Watch for air bubbles to exit the submerged end of the tube. When the fluid flow slows after a couple of seconds, close the valve and have your assistant release the pedal.
11   Repeat Steps 9 and 10 until no more air is seen leaving the tube, then tighten the bleeder valve and proceed to the left rear wheel, the right front wheel and the left front wheel, in that order, and perform the same procedure. Be sure to check the fluid in the master cylinder reservoir frequently.
12   Never use old brake fluid. It contains moisture which will deteriorate the brake system components.
13   Refill the master cylinder with fluid at the end of the operation.
14   Check the operation of the brakes. The pedal should feel solid when depressed, with no sponginess. If necessary, repeat the entire process. **Warning:** *Do not operate the vehicle if you are in doubt about the effectiveness of the brake system.*

Anti-lock brake system (ABS)

15   The rear calipers on ABS equipped vehicles require a slightly different bleeding procedure. Turn the ignition key to the On position, which will activate the hydraulic pump and charge up the accumulator.
16   Connect a length of tubing to the right rear caliper bleeder valve as shown in illustration 12.8. Place the other end of the tubing in a container partially filled with clean brake fluid.
17   Have an assistant depress the brake pedal and hold it in the applied position. SLOWLY loosen the bleeder valve and allow the fluid to flow for ten seconds, then close the valve. **Warning:** *the brake fluid in the rear calipers is under extremely high pressure, and careless opening of the bleeder valves may cause the fluid to shoot out with great force.*

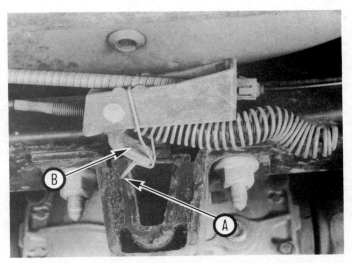

13.3   Remove the retaining clip (A) and pull the locking lever (B) down and the tensioner will remove any slack in the parking brake cable

18   Have the assistant pump the brakes several times then repeat the operation until the stream of fluid is free of air bubbles.
19   Check the fluid level in the reservoir, topping it up if necessary.
20   Repeat Steps 16 through 19 on the left rear caliper.
21   The front brakes may be bled using the standard brake bleeding procedure described in Steps 9 and 10.

13   Parking brake – adjustment

Refer to illustration 13.3
1   Raise the vehicle and support it securely on jackstands. Block the front wheels to prevent the vehicle from rolling.
2   Place the transmission in Neutral and fully release the parking brake.
3   From under the vehicle, remove the retaining clip and pull the locking lever down (away from the threaded rod) to engage the tensioner **(see illustration)**. The tensioner will automatically remove the slack in the cable. **Note:** *Do not pull excessively on the locking lever. The incorrect tension will stretch the cable.*
4   Lock the tensioner by releasing the locking lever and check to make sure the lever is secure by rotating it toward the threaded rod.
5   Lower the vehicle and check the operation of the parking brake.

14   Parking brake cables – replacement

1   Raise the vehicle and support it securely on jackstands. Release the parking brake completely.
2   Relieve the parking brake cable tension (see Section 13). **Note:** *Have an assistant depress the parking brake to the last notch when the tensioner is unlocked in order to attain the maximum amount of slack in the cable.* **Caution:** *Since the spring will have full tension, use wire to hold it in this position to prevent any accidents.*
3   Remove the tensioner.

Foot operated type
Front cable
Refer to illustrations 14.5a, 14.5b and 14.7
4   Disconnect the electrical connector from the parking brake warning switch.

9

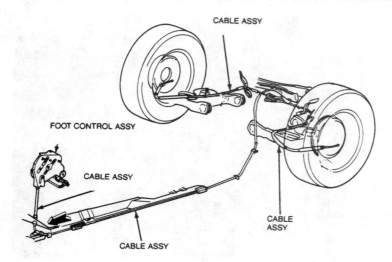

14.5a   Exploded view of the parking brake cables on the foot operated type

14.5b   The cable assembly and the foot control linkage

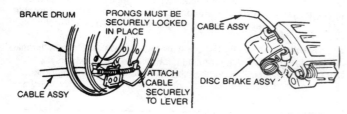

14.7   The intermediate (rear) cable connector (arrow) is located on the side of the chassis near the rear of the vehicle

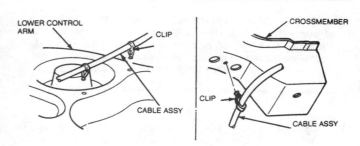

14.13   The cables are held to the frame and suspension with clips – use needle-nose pliers to pinch the underside of the clip to squeeze it through the opening

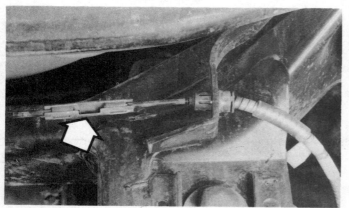

14.15   Detach the cable from the parking brake lever (drum and disc brake versions shown)

5   Remove the side trim panel and remove the cable end from the foot control assembly **(see illustrations)**.
6   With pliers, remove the control cable conduit retainer from the cable assembly. Squeeze the retainer enough to compress it through the opening in the bracket.
7   Disconnect the front cable from the intermediate cable at the connector **(see illustration)**.
8   Remove the intermediate cable conduit retainer from the cable bracket and let the cable hang down. The mechanism is released similar to the control cable conduit retainer (see Step 6).
9   Pull the cable and the grommet up through the floorpan.
10   Installation is the reverse of the removal procedure. Be sure to adjust the parking brake following the procedure in Section 13.

Rear cable(s)
Refer to illustrations 14.13 and 14.15

11   Remove the cable tension by releasing the cable tensioner (see Step 2). Remove the tensioner.
12   Disconnect the front cable from the intermediate cable (see Step 7).
13   Remove the cable routing clips from the body side rails and rear crossmember by squeezing the clip together with needle-nose pliers between the cable and the crossmember **(see illustration)**.
14   Remove the rear wheel and brake drum (if equipped). On drum brakes, remove the brake assembly as outlined in Section 8.
15   Disconnect the cable end from the parking brake lever **(see illustration)**.
16   On drum brake systems, using a pair of pliers, depress the tangs on the cable housing retainer and pull the cable and housing out through the backing plate.
17   Installation is the reverse of the removal procedure. Be sure to adjust the the parking brake following the procedure outlined in Section 13.

Hand operated type
Front cable
Refer to illustrations 14.21a and 14.21b

18   Disconnect the front cable from the rear cable at the cable connector.
19   Remove the cable routing clip from the body crossmember at the rear. Squeeze the clip with a pair of needle-nose pliers **(see illustration 14.13)**.
20   Working inside the vehicle, remove the rear seat, then remove the console.

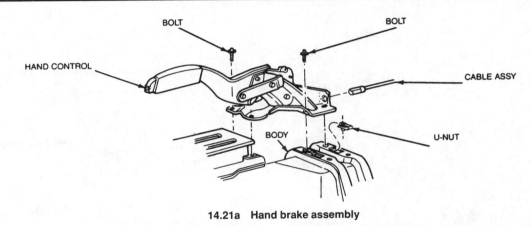

14.21a   Hand brake assembly

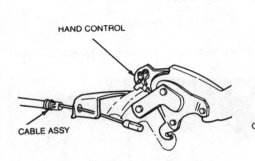

14.21b   The cable end is slotted to fit over the lever

15.4   Remove the bolts that retain the pedal assembly to the body

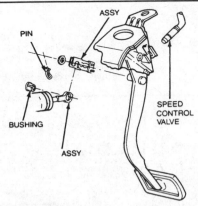

16.5   Details of the brake pedal and related components

21   Disconnect the cable from the hand control assembly **(see illustrations)**.
22   Pull the cable and grommet up through the rear floor and then pull the cable out from under the carpet.
23   Installation is the reverse of the removal procedure. Be sure to adjust the the parking brake following the procedure outlined in Section 13. **Note:** *The grommet must be fully inserted and seated in the floorpan hole to prevent water leakage.*

Rear cable

24   The rear cable(s) on the hand brake models are the same as the removal and installation of the cable(s) on the foot operated models. Refer to Steps 11 through 17.

---

15   Parking brake pedal – removal and installation

Refer to illustration 15.4
1   Release the parking brake completely.
2   Release the tension from the cables (see Section 13).
3   Follow Steps 1 through 6 of Section 14 to remove the front cable from the pedal assembly.
4   Remove the three pedal assembly mounting bolts **(see illustration)**.
5   Remove the bolt that holds the pedal assembly to the instrument panel.
6   Remove the pedal assembly.
7   To install the pedal assembly, reverse the removal procedure and adjust the parking brake cable as outlined in Section 13.

---

16   Power brake booster – removal, installation and adjustment

1   The power brake booster unit requires no special maintenance apart

from periodic inspection of the vacuum hose and the case.
2   Dismantling of the brake booster requires special tools and is not ordinarily done by the home mechanic. If a problem develops, install a new or factory rebuilt unit.

Removal

Refer to illustrations 16.5 and 16.6

3   Remove the nuts attaching the master cylinder to the booster and carefully pull the master cylinder forward until it clears the mounting studs. Use caution so as not to bend or kink the brake lines.
4   Disconnect the vacuum hose where it attaches to the power brake booster.
5   Working in the passenger compartment under the steering column, unplug the electrical connector from the brake light switch, then remove the pushrod retaining clip and nylon washer from the brake pedal pin. Slide the pushrod off the pin **(see illustration)**.
6   Also remove the nuts attaching the brake booster to the firewall **(see illustration)**.
7   Carefully detach the booster from the firewall and lift it out of the engine compartment.

Installation

8   Place the booster into position on the firewall and tighten the mounting nuts. Connect the pushrod and brake light switch to the brake pedal. Install the retaining clip in the brake pedal pin.
9   Install the master cylinder to the booster, tightening the nuts to the torque listed in this Chapter's Specifications.
10   Carefully check the operation of the brakes before driving the vehicle in traffic.

9

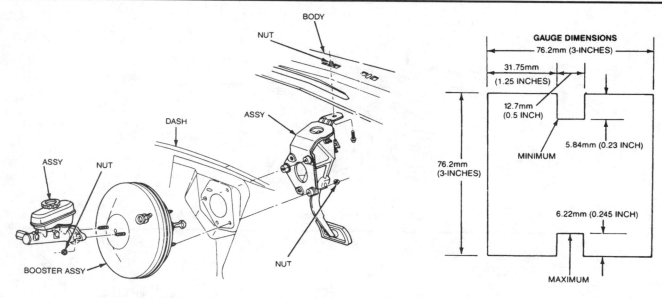

16.6   Power brake booster installation details

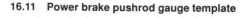

16.11   Power brake pushrod gauge template

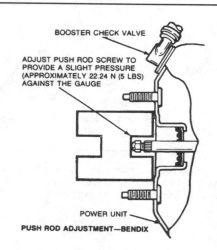

16.15   Checking the pushrod length (the pushrod is factory preset and most likely will never need adjusting)

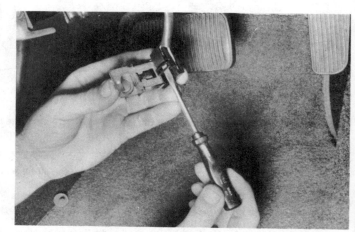

17.3   Use a small screwdriver to disengage the clip inside the electrical connector

Adjustment

Refer to illustrations 16.11 and 16.15

11   Some boosters feature an adjustable pushrod. They are matched to the booster at the factory and most likely will not require adjustment, but if a misadjusted pushrod is suspected, a gauge can be fabricated out of heavy gauge sheet metal using the accompanying template **(see illustration)**.

12   Some common symptoms caused by a misadjusted pushrod include dragging brakes (if the pushrod is too long) or excessive brake pedal travel accompanied by a groaning sound from the brake booster (if the pushrod is too short).

13   To check the pushrod length, unbolt the master cylinder from the booster and position it to one side. It isn't necessary to disconnect the hydraulic lines, but be careful not to bend them.

14   Block the front wheels, apply the parking brake and place the transaxle in Park or Neutral.

15   Start the engine and place the pushrod gauge against the end of the pushrod, exerting a force of approximately five pounds to seat the pushrod in the power unit **(see illustration)**. The rod measurement should fall somewhere between the minimum and maximum cutouts on the gauge. If

it doesn't, adjust it by holding the knurled portion of the pushrod with a pair of pliers and turning the end with a wrench.

16   When the adjustment is complete, reinstall the master cylinder and check for proper brake operation before driving the vehicle in traffic.

17   Brake light switch – removal and installation

Removal

Refer to illustration 17.3

1   Remove the under dash panel.

2   Locate the switch near the top of the brake pedal and disconnect the brake light switch assembly from the brake pedal by remove the retaining clip.

3   Use a screwdriver and disconnect the electrical connector from the brake light switch **(see illustration)**.

Installation

4   Install the switch to the electrical connector by snapping the clip into place.

5   Reconnect the assembly to the brake pedal.

6   Install the under dash panel.

7   Check the brake lights for proper operation.

Chapter 10
Suspension and steering systems

Contents

Specifications

Torque specifications	Ft-lbs
Front suspension	
Lower control arm-to-crossmember pivot bolts/nuts	96 to 110
Lower control arm balljoint-to-spindle nut*	100 to 118
Lower control arm-to-tension strut nut	103 to 118
Shock upper mount-to-body nuts	16 to 23
Shock-to-upper mount nut	37 to 45
Shock assembly-to-lower control arm	
1989 models	103 to 144
1990 models	148 to 162
Tie-rod end-to-spindle*	39 to 54
Upper control arm-to-body bolts/nuts	72 to 88
Upper control arm-to-spindle pinch bolt/nut	59 to 66
Rear suspension	
Upper control arm-to-frame pivot bolt/nut	50 to 70
Upper control arm-to-knuckle bolt/nut	118 to 148
Lower control arm-to-subframe pivot bolt/nut	
Front	184 to 229
Rear	25 to 170
Lower control arm-to-knuckle assembly	118 to 148
Lower control arm-to-toe compensator link	118 to 148
Shock-to-lower control arm	110 to 120
Shock-to-upper mount	27 to 35
Splash shield-to-knuckle bolts	45 to 59
Hub retainer nut	250
Steering system	
Tie-rod end-to-spindle arm nuts*	39 to 54
Steering gear mounting bolts/nuts	175 to 230
Intermediate shaft-to-steering gear bolt	20 to 30
Intermediate shaft-to-steering column shaft	
nut and bolt	30 to 40
Steering wheel bolt	23 to 33
Wheel lug nuts	See Chapter 1

Tighten to the minimum specified torque, then align the next castellation in the nut with the cotter pin hole.

1   General information

Refer to illustrations 1.1 and 1.2

Warning: *Whenever any of the suspension or steering fasteners are loosened or removed they must be inspected and if necessary, replaced with new ones of the same part number or of original equipment quality and design. Torque specifications must be followed for proper reassembly and component retention. Never attempt to heat, straighten or weld any suspension or steering component. Instead, replace any bent or damaged part with a new one.* **Note:** *These vehicles may use a combination of standard and metric fasteners on the various suspension and steering components, so it would be a good idea to have both types of tools available when beginning work.*

The front suspension is independent, allowing each wheel to compensate for road surface changes without appreciably affecting the other **(see illustration)**. Each wheel is connected to the frame by a spindle, balljoint, lower control arm, upper control arm and a shock absorber/coil spring assembly positioned vertically between the lower control arm and frame. Body side roll is controlled by a stabilizer bar.

The independent rear suspension consists of two coil springs, shock absorbers, a stabilizer bar, two lower and two upper control arms **(see illustration)**.

Some models are equipped with an Automatic Ride Control (ARC)

system. This feature automatically adjusts the suspension to suit road conditions and driving style by changing the shock absorber damping characteristics. The Automatic Ride Control will be described in greater detail in the next Section.

The steering system consists of the steering wheel, steering column, an articulated intermediate shaft, the steering gear, power steering pump and the tie-rods, which connect the steering gear to the spindles.

2   Automatic Ride Control (ARC) system – general information

Refer to illustration 2.2

The Automatic Ride Control system, installed on Super Coupe/XR7 models, automatically changes the shock absorber valving to firm-up the suspension to suit road conditions and driving style. The system incorporates a switch, mounted on the center console to the right of the driver's seat, which allows the driver to select either the "Auto" or "Firm" position. When in the "Auto" position, the suspension will maintain a smooth, soft ride during normal driving conditions, but when the system's computer detects harsh cornering, hard braking, rapid acceleration or high speed, it adjusts the shock absorber damping to improve vehicle handling and road feel. With the switch set in the "Firm" position, the shock damping will be firm no matter what driving conditions are present.

1.1 Underside view of the front suspension and steering components

1	Stabilizer bar	5	Spindle
2	Tension strut	6	Shock absorber/coil
3	Upper control arm		spring assembly
4	Tie-rod end	7	Lower control arm
		8	Tie-rod
		9	Steering gear boot
		10	Steering gear

1.2 Underside view of the rear suspension and related components

1	Stabilizer bar	3	Lower control arm	5	Halfshaft
2	Coil spring	4	Knuckle assembly	6	Differential

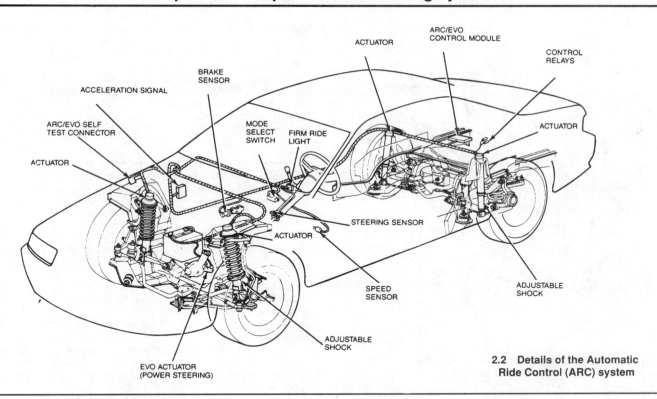

2.2 Details of the Automatic Ride Control (ARC) system

The system receives information from various information sensors located throughout the vehicle (see illustration). These sensors send inputs to the ARC control module, which in turn "decides" whether or not to adjust the shock absorbers. The system components and their functions are listed below:

a) Brake sensor – activated when brake system hydraulic pressure over 400 psi is detected.

b) Acceleration signal (ARC control module takes a reading, via the EEC-IV engine management computer) – the control module looks for large throttle openings.

c) Steering sensor – the steering sensor is a variable resistor assembly mounted to the steering column, which alters the voltage to the control module as the steering wheel is turned. The control module looks for a specific reading and, in conjunction with the vehicle speed reading, comes up with a lateral acceleration figure. Cornering forces above 0.35g will activate the "Firm" setting.

d) Speed sensor – the control module takes a reading from the speed sensor and adjusts the shock damping when speeds above 83 mph are attained.

e) Mode selector switch – when set in the "Firm" position, the shock absorber damping rates are increased, regardless of the above described parameters. When set in the "Auto" position, the control module assesses the information from the ARC sensors then selects either the "Firm" or "Soft" ride setting.

f) Control module – processes information from the above sensors and activates the ARC relays, which in turn control the power to the shock absorber actuators.

g) ARC relays – activated by the control module, the relays switch the polarity to the shock absorber actuators, placing the actuators in the proper positions.

h) Actuators – mounted to the top of the shock absorbers, the actuators change the damping rates by altering the internal valving of the shock absorber.

When any one of the required conditions are encountered, the "Firm" setting will automatically be selected, which will be evident by the green indicator light below the tachometer and the change in the vehicle's ride.

If the ARC control module detects any faults within the system, the indicator light will flash on and off. Sometimes a false or intermittent malfunction may exist, which may be able to be cleared by changing the ride control switch setting back and forth.

Due to the rather complex nature of the Automatic Ride Control system, all troubleshooting and repairs, with the exception of searching for loose connectors, wires and blown fuses, should be left to a qualified dealer service department technician.

3   Front stabilizer bar – removal and installation

Refer to illustrations 3.3 and 3.10

Removal

1 Remove the throttle body inlet tube (see Chapter 4).

2 Raise the vehicle and support it securely on jackstands. Apply the parking brake.

3 Remove the stabilizer bar link nuts and brackets, noting how the washers and bushings are positioned (see illustration).

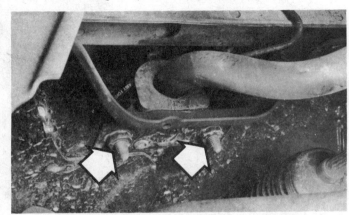

3.3 Clean the threads (arrows) with a wire brush before attempting to remove the stabilizer bracket bolts

10

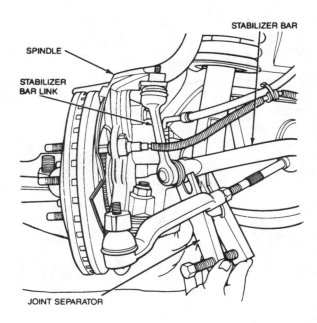

3.10   Separate the stabilizer bar from the stabilizer bar link with a special tool

4   Remove the serpentine drive belt (see Chapter 1).
5   Remove the front tires and wheels.
6   Remove the front crankshaft vibration damper (see Chapter 2B).
7   Separate the tie-rod ends from the spindle (see Section 16).
8   Remove the transmission oil cooler line bracket.
9   Remove the stabilizer bar-to-stabilizer bar link nuts.
10   Separate the stabilizer bar link from the stabilizer bar with a joint separator tool **(see illustration)**.
11   Remove the stabilizer bar by lifting it from the right side of the vehicle. Remove the stabilizer bushings. Inspect the bushings for cracks, harden-

ing and other signs of deterioration. If the bushings are damaged, cut them off the bar.

Installation

12   Lubricate the new stabilizer bar bushings with a rubber lubricant (such as a silicone spray) and slide the bushings onto the bar.
13   Push the brackets over the bushings and install the stabilizer bar. Tighten the bolts securely.
14   Installation is the reverse of removal.

---

4   Front shock absorber/coil spring assembly – removal and installation

---

Refer to illustrations 4.4, 4.5, 4.6a, 4.6b and 4.9

Removal

1   Loosen the front wheel lug nuts, raise the vehicle and support it securely on jackstands.
2   Remove the wheel.
3   Place a floor jack under the lower control arm and raise it slightly. The jack must remain in this position throughout the entire procedure.
4   On models equipped with Automatic Ride Control (ARC), remove the actuator retaining screws and lift the actuator from its mounting bracket **(see illustration)**.
5   Loosen the three upper mount-to-shock tower retaining nuts **(see illustration)** but do not remove them completely. If the upper mount is to be removed from the shock absorber/coil spring assembly, also loosen (but do not remove) the center nut at this time.
6   Remove the shock-to-lower control arm nut and bolt **(see illustrations)**.
7   Separate the shock absorber/coil spring assembly from the spindle.
8   Remove the stabilizer link upper mounting nut.
9   Separate the stabilizer link from the spindle **(see illustration)**.
10   Use the floor jack to raise the lower control arm to separate the stabilizer link from the spindle. Position the stabilizer link out of the way.
11   Disconnect the upper control arm from the spindle (see Section 7).
12   Lower the floor jack to separate the spindle from the upper control arm. Use wire to support the spindle by attaching it to the upper control arm. Lower the floor jack, remove the shock tower-to-upper mount nuts and remove the shock absorber/coil spring assembly from the vehicle.

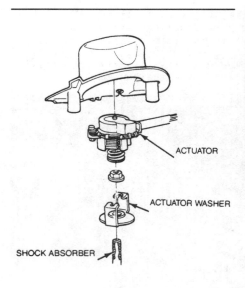

4.4   Mounting details of the ARC actuator

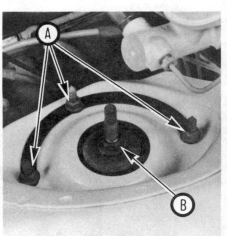

4.5   The upper mount of the shock absorber/coil spring assembly is retained to the body by three nuts (A) – if the upper mount is to be removed from the shock absorber/coil spring assembly, loosen (but do not remove) the center nut (B) first

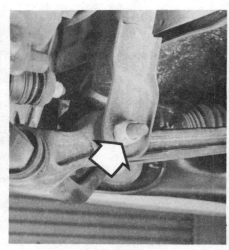

4.6a   Remove the shock-to-lower control arm bolt (arrow) – use a back-up wrench if necessary

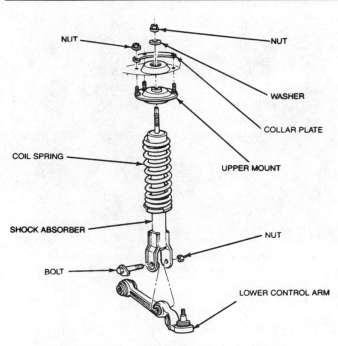

4.6b   Mounting details of the shock absorber/coil
spring assembly

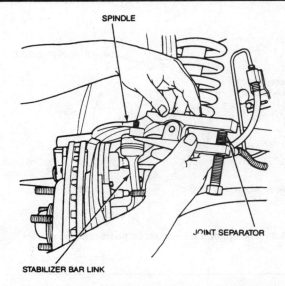

4.9   Use a special joint separating tool to disconnect
the stabilizer link

Installation

13   If the shock absorber/coil spring assembly was replaced and consequently the upper mount was removed, place it over the top of the new shock absorber/coil spring assembly and install the nut.

14   Guide the assembly into position in the wheel well, pushing the upper mount studs through the holes in the shock tower. Install the three nuts and tighten them to the torque listed in this Chapter's Specifications. **Note:** *The Ford Motor Company recommends that the nuts not be re-used – replace them with new ones.*

15   Remove the wire, insert the spindle into the upper control arm and install the nut and bolt. Again, it is recommended that new bolts and nuts be used. Install the nuts and tighten them to the torque listed in this Chapter's Specifications.

16   Attach the shock absorber/coil spring assembly to the lower control arm, tightening the nut securely.

17   Install the stabilizer link to the spindle.

18   Tighten the upper mount-to-shock assembly retaining nut to the torque listed in this Chapter's Specifications (if removed). Tighten the three upper mounting nuts securely.

19   On models equipped with Automatic Ride Control (ARC), attach the actuator to the mounting bracket, aligning the flats on the actuator rod with the slot in the shock absorber.

20   Remove the jack from under the lower control arm and install the disc brake caliper as outlined in Chapter 9.

21   Install the wheel, lower the vehicle and tighten the lug nuts to the torque listed in the Chapter 1 Specifications.

---

5   Front shock absorber/coil spring – replacement

Refer to illustrations 5.4 and 5.8

1   Remove the shock absorber/coil spring assembly from the vehicle (see Section 4).

2   Check the shock absorber for leaking fluid, dents, cracks or other obvious damage. Check the coil spring for chips or cracks which could cause premature failure and inspect the spring seats for hardness or general deterioration. Complete shock absorber/coil spring assemblies are available

on an exchange basis. This eliminates much time and work. So, before disassembling the shock absorber/coil spring assembly to replace individual components, check on the availability of parts and the price of a complete rebuilt unit. **Warning:** *Disassembling a shock absorber/coil spring assembly is a potentially dangerous undertaking and utmost attention must be directed to the job at hand, or serious injury may result. Use only a high quality spring compressor and carefully follow the manufacturer's instructions furnished with the tool. After removing the coil spring from the shock, set it aside in a safe, isolated area (a steel cabinet is preferred).*

3   Mount the shock absorber/coil spring assembly in a vise. Line the vise jaws with wood or rags to prevent damage to the unit and don't tighten the vise excessively.

4   Install a spring compressor in accordance with the tool manufacturer's instructions **(see illustration)**. (You can buy a spring compressor at most auto parts stores or rent one from most equipment yards on a daily basis.) Compress the spring far enough to relieve all pressure from the spring seat (if you can wiggle the spring, it's loose enough). **Note:** *The up-*

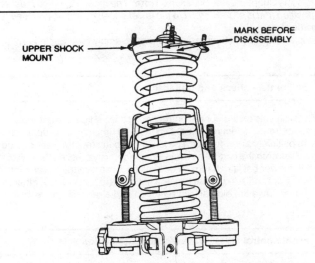

5.4   Mark the position of the upper mount to the coil spring –
also, make sure the spring compressor is securely attached and
the coil spring is compressed evenly

10

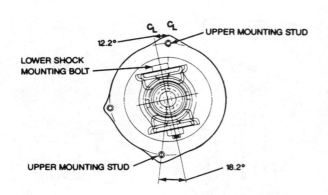

5.8 The upper mount must be positioned as shown

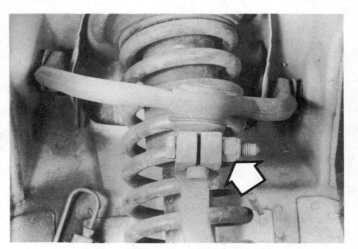

7.2 Remove the pinch bolt and nut (arrow) and detach the spindle from the upper control arm

per shock mount cannot rotate when the shock and the spring are assembled so it is very important to mark the position of the upper mount to the coil spring with chalk or paint before disassembly. If the upper mount is not in the proper position, the studs won't fit into the holes in the shock tower.

5   Place a box-end wrench on the damper rod nut, hold the damper rod with a wrench and remove the nut.

6   Disassemble the shock absorber/coil spring assembly. Carefully lift the compressed spring from the assembly and set it in a safe place, such as a steel cabinet. **Warning:** *Keep the ends of the spring facing away from your body!* Pay close attention to the order in which you remove the parts. It's a good idea to lay the parts out in their exact relationship to each other on the work bench because everything must be reassembled exactly the same way it came off.

7   Inspect the damper rod seal for leakage. Extend and retract the damper rod slowly, then quickly, through its full stroke. It should be smooth, quiet and offer resistance. If it's jerky, noisy or offers little or no resistance, replace the shock absorber. It's a sealed unit and can't be rebuilt.

8   Reassembly is the reverse of disassembly. Be sure to use a new damper rod nut. Tighten the damper rod (upper mount) nut to the torque listed in this Chapter's Specifications. **Note:** *The mounting studs must be in a position that is slightly offset to the lower shock mounting bolt* **(see illustration)**.

9   Install the shock absorber/coil spring assembly (see Section 4).

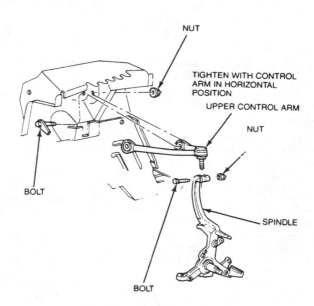

7.4 Upper control arm details

6   Balljoints – check and replacement

The balljoints on the upper control arm of this vehicle are not replaceable separately. The entire control arm must be replaced if the upper control arm balljoints are worn out. The lower balljoints require a special tool that clamps onto the control arm and simultaneously presses the balljoint out. If the lower balljoint needs to be replaced, remove the lower control arm (see Section 7) and take it to a dealer service department or other repair shop to have the old balljoint removed and a new one pressed in.

7   Front control arms – removal and installation

Removal

1   Loosen the wheel lug nuts, raise the vehicle and support it securely on jackstands. Remove the wheel.

Upper control arm
Refer to illustrations 7.2 and 7.4

2   Remove the upper balljoint-to-spindle bolt and nut **(see illustration)**. Separate the spindle from the upper control arm (it may be necessary to insert a screwdriver into the pinch joint and spread it slightly). Support the spindle with a piece of wire or rope. The Ford Motor Company recommends discarding the old bolt and nut and installing new ones.

3   Break off the tabs on the upper control arm pivot bolts.

4   Remove the upper control arm bolts **(see illustration)** and remove the control arm. **Note:** *Use a six-point socket to avoid rounding off the head of the bolt.* If the pivot bushings appear to be worn out or deteriorated, take the control arm to a dealer service department or other repair shop to have the old bushings pressed out and new ones pressed in.

Lower control arm
Refer to illustrations 7.5, 7.6, 7.7a and 7.7b

5   Loosen (but do not remove) the balljoint retaining nut **(see illustration)**, then separate the lower control arm from the spindle. Use a special balljoint separator tool (available at most auto parts stores). Also, it is a

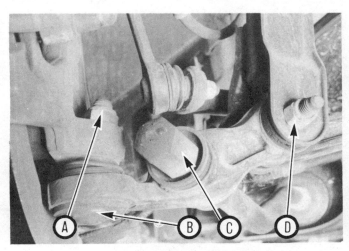

7.5 Lower control arm details

A   Balljoint retaining nut
B   Balljoint
C   Tension strut
D   Shock absorber
    lower mounting bolt
    and nut

good idea to use wire and support the spindle so the upper control arm does not sag excessively.

6   Mark the position of the camber adjustment cam to the chassis **(see illustration)**.

7   Remove the nut that attaches the tension strut to the control arm **(see illustration 7.5)**. **Note:** *Use a back-up wrench (open end) on the tension strut. Make sure only the flat side of the tension strut is used for leverage and place the wrench directly behind the lower control arm. Do not use the area near the bend in the strut or damage to the tension strut may occur* **(see illustrations)**.

8   Remove the shock absorber lower mounting bolt and nut.

9   Remove the pivot bolt and nut, then detach the control arm. If the pivot bushing appears to be worn out or deteriorated, take the control arm to a dealer service department or other repair shop to have the old bushings pressed out and new ones pressed in.

Installation

10   Installation is the reverse of the removal procedure, but don't tighten the pivot fasteners until the suspension is at normal ride height. This can be accomplished by positioning a floor jack under the lower control arm balljoint and raising it until the vehicle just raises off the jackstand. Be sure

7.6   Mark the position of the camber adjustment cam to the chassis

to tighten all of the fasteners to the torque values listed in this Chapter's Specifications.

11   Have the front end alignment checked at a dealer service department or alignment shop.

8   Spindle – removal and installation

Refer to illustration 8.7

Removal

1   Loosen the wheel lug nuts, apply the parking brake and raise the vehicle. Support it securely on jackstands placed under the frame. Remove the wheel.

2   Remove the brake caliper and secure it with wire so it doesn't interfere with the spindle. Slide the brake disc from the hub.

3   Remove the front hub and bearing assembly (see Section 9).

4   Remove the brake anti-lock sensor and position it out of the way (see Chapter 9).

5   Separate the tie-rod end from the spindle arm (see Section 16).

6   Remove the stabilizer bar link at the spindle using a special joint separating tool **(see illustration 4.9)**.

7.7a   Place the back-up wrench on the flat portion of the tension strut only

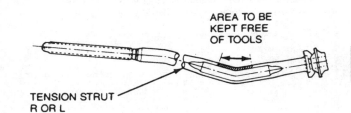

7.7b   The tension strut could be weakened if the bent area becomes nicked

10

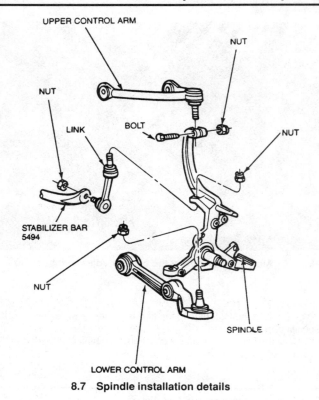

8.7   Spindle installation details

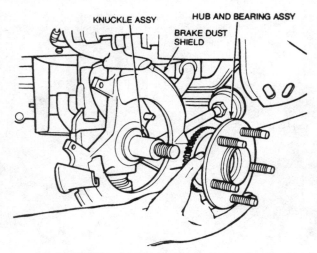

9.6   If the hub assembly is not easily removed by hand, use a puller.

7   Disconnect the lower balljoint from the spindle **(see illustration)**. Break the balljoint loose from the spindle using a balljoint separator tool or by rapping the spindle boss sharply with a hammer. **Note:** *A picklefork type balljoint separator may damage the balljoint seals.*
8   Remove and discard the spindle-to-upper control arm bolt and nut **(see illustration 7.2)**. Spread the slot in the connector slightly and remove the spindle from the vehicle.

Installation

9   Place the spindle onto the lower control arm balljoint.
10   Insert the top of the spindle into the upper control arm and install the bolt and nut. Tighten the nut to the torque listed in this Chapter's Specifications. **Note:** *The Ford Motor Company recommends that these bolts (and nuts) be replaced, not re-used.*
11   Tighten the lower control arm balljoint stud nut to the torque listed in this Chapter's Specifications.
12   Install the hub and bearing assembly (see Section 9).
13   Connect the tie-rod end to the spindle arm and tighten the nuts to the torque listed in this Chapter's Specifications. Be sure to use a new cotter pin.
14   Install the stabilizer link to the spindle.
15   Install the brake disc.
16   Install the brake caliper.
17   Install the wheel and lug nuts. Lower the vehicle and tighten the nuts to the torque listed in the Chapter 1 Specifications.

9   Front hub and bearing assembly – removal and installation

Refer to illustration 9.6

Note: *The front wheel bearings are a single unit hub design and are pre-greased, sealed and require no maintenance. The bearings are pre-set and cannot be adjusted. If a bearing replacement is required, the hub and bearing assembly must be replaced as an assembly.*

Removal

1   Loosen the wheel lug nuts, apply the parking brake and raise the vehicle. Support it securely on jackstands placed under the frame. Remove the wheel.
2   Remove the grease cap from the hub and discard it.
3   Remove the brake caliper (see Chapter 9) and secure it with wire so that it does not interfere with the spindle.
4   Remove the brake disc.
5   Remove the hub nut and discard it. **Warning:** *Never re-use the hub nut.*
6   Remove the hub and bearing assembly **(see illustration)**. **Note:** *If the assembly cannot be removed by hand, use a two-jaw puller. Don't immerse the hub unit in solvent. It is packed with grease at the factory and to do so would ruin it.*

Installation

7   Installation is the reverse of removal.
8   Tighten the hub nut to the torque listed in this Chapter's Specifications.

10   Steering wheel – removal and installation

Refer to illustrations 10.3 and 10.4

Removal

1   Disconnect the cable from the negative terminal of the battery.
2   Pull the horn pad from the steering wheel and disconnect the horn electrical connector. If equipped, disconnect the speed control switch wire from the contact plate terminal.
3   Remove the steering wheel retaining bolt, then mark the relationship of the steering shaft to the hub **(see illustration)** (if marks don't already exist or don't line up) to simplify installation and ensure correct steering wheel alignment.
4   Use a puller to detach the steering wheel from the shaft **(see illustration)**.

Installation

5   To install the wheel, align the mark on the steering wheel hub with the mark on the shaft and slip the wheel onto the shaft. Install the hub bolt and tighten it to the torque listed in this Chapter's Specifications.
6   Connect the horn electrical connector and install the horn pad.
7   Connect the negative battery cable.

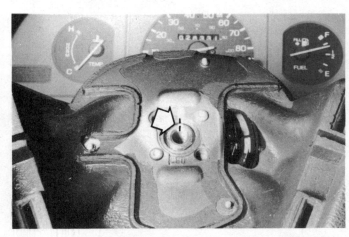

10.3   Mark the relationship of the steering wheel to the steering shaft to aid in alignment when reassembling

11   Intermediate shaft – removal and installation

Refer to illustrations 11.2a, 11.2b and 11.2c

1   Turn the front wheels to the straight ahead position.
2   Using a marking pen or white paint, place alignment marks on the intermediate shaft-to-steering shaft and the lower flexible coupling-to-steering gear input shaft joints **(see illustrations)**.
3   Remove the upper clamp bolt and lower flexible coupling pinch bolt **(see illustrations 11.2a and 11.2b)**. **Note:** *The Ford Motor Company recommends the replacement of the intermediate shaft fasteners once they have been removed (Use genuine Ford parts or equivalent quality fasteners only).*
4   Remove the intermediate shaft from the lower flexible coupling using a large screwdriver and then from the upper U-joint assembly.
5   Pull on the column end of the intermediate shaft toward the boot and into the vehicle, then pull the intermediate shaft out.
6   Installation is the reverse of the removal procedure. Be sure to align the marks and tighten the pinch bolts to the torque values listed in this Chapter's Specifications.

10.4   Remove the wheel from the shaft with a puller – DO NOT beat on the shaft

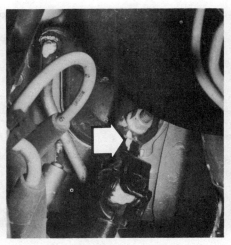

11.2a   Mark the upper end of the intermediate shaft and the steering column shaft . . .

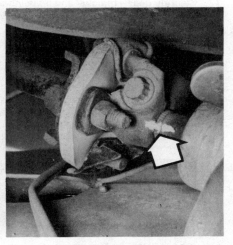

11.2b   . . . then mark the lower end of the intermediate shaft and the steering gear input shaft

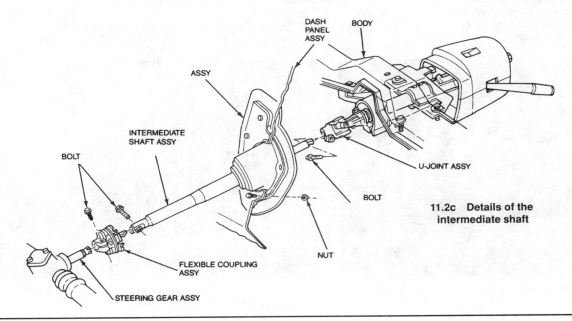

DASH PANEL ASSY

BODY

ASSY

INTERMEDIATE SHAFT ASSY

BOLT

U-JOINT ASSY

BOLT

NUT

FLEXIBLE COUPLING ASSY

STEERING GEAR ASSY

11.2c   Details of the intermediate shaft

10

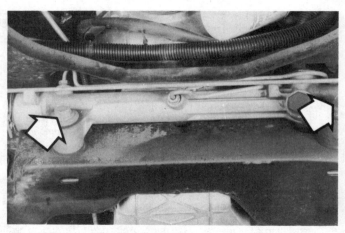

12.5a   Locations of the steering gear mounting bolts

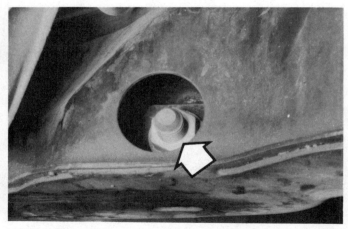

12.5b   The steering gear mounting nuts are accessible through holes in the rear of the crossmember

12   Steering gear – removal and installation

Refer to illustration 12.5a and 12.5b

Removal

1   Raise the front of the vehicle and support it securely on jackstands. Apply the parking brake.

2   Place a drain pan under the steering gear (power steering only). Remove the power steering pressure and return lines and cap the ends to prevent excessive fluid loss and contamination.

3   Mark the relationship of the intermediate shaft flexible coupling to the steering gear input shaft. Remove the pinch bolt **(see illustration 11.2b)**.

4   Separate the tie-rod ends from the spindle arms (see Section 16).

5   Support the steering gear and remove the steering gear-to-frame mounting nuts and bolts **(see illustration)**. The nuts are accessible through the hole in rear of the crossmember **(see illustration)**. Lower the unit, separate the intermediate shaft from the steering gear input shaft and remove the steering gear from the vehicle.

Installation

6   Raise the steering gear into position and connect the intermediate shaft, aligning the marks.

7   Install the mounting bolts and washers and tighten the nuts to the torque listed in this Chapter's Specifications.

8   Connect the tie-rod ends to the spindle arms (see Section 16)

9   Install the intermediate shaft pinch bolt and tighten it to the torque listed in this Chapter's Specifications.

10   Connect the power steering pressure and return hoses to the steering gear and fill the power steering pump reservoir with the recommended fluid (see Chapter 1).

11   Lower the vehicle and bleed the steering system as outlined in Section 15.

13   Power steering pump – removal and installation

Refer to illustrations 13.3 and 13.5

Removal

Note: *If you are working on a supercharged model, the intercooler and intercooler tubes must be removed to gain access to the pump (see Chapter 4).*

1   Disconnect the cable from the negative terminal of the battery.

2   Place a drain pan under the power steering pump. Remove the drivebelt (see Chapter 1).

3   Using a special power steering pump pulley remover, remove the pulley from the pump **(see illustration)**.

4   Remove the pressure and return hoses from the backside of the pump and allow the fluid to drain. Plug the hoses to prevent contaminants from entering.

5   Remove the pump mounting bolts **(see illustration)** and lift the pump from the vehicle, taking care not to spill fluid on the painted surfaces.

13.3   A special puller is required to remove the power steering pump pulley

13.5   First remove the pump bracket bolts and the bracket, then remove the power steering pump bolts

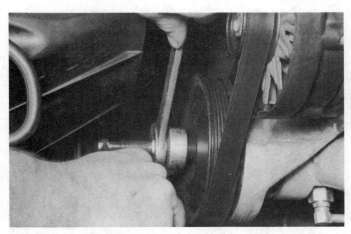

13.8 A special pulley-installer tool (available at tool and auto parts stores) is needed to push the pulley onto the pump shaft – under no circumstances should the pulley be hammered onto the shaft, as this would damage the pump!

Installation

Refer to illustration 13.8

6   Position the pump in the mounting bracket and install the bolts. Tighten the bolts securely.

7   Connect the hoses to the pump. Tighten the fittings securely.

8   Press the pulley onto the pump shaft using a special pulley installer tool **(see illustration)**. Push the pulley onto the shaft until the front of the hub is flush with the end of the shaft, but no further.

9   Install the drivebelt.

10 Fill the power steering reservoir with the recommended fluid and bleed the system following the procedure described in Section 15.

---

14   Variable Assist Power Steering (EVO) – general information

Refer to illustrations 14.3

1   The EVO system is designed to vary the flow from the power steering pump in relation to the vehicle's speed and steering wheel rotation, thereby delivering different rates of assistance to the system. The EVO system provides full power steering assist at low vehicle speeds for easy parking effort and a minimum assist at high speed for directional stability and enhanced road feel. Full power steering is returned for difficult road maneuvers.

2   A Fail Safe feature is designed into the EVO system. In the event of an electrical circuit failure, open circuit, malfunctioning controller or some component problem the actuator will provide full power steering assist during these failure modes. Have the system diagnosed by a dealer service department or other repair shop as soon as possible.

3   The system is composed of an EVO Actuator Assembly, steering wheel rotation sensor, vehicle speed sensor, service diagnostic connector and a control module **(see illustration)**. Diagnosing the EVO system is beyond the scope of the home mechanic, due to the special equipment required. If the system becomes defective, have the vehicle diagnosed by a dealer service department or other repair shop.

---

15   Power steering system – bleeding

1   Following any operation in which the power steering fluid lines have been disconnected, the power steering system must be bled to remove all air and obtain proper steering performance.

2   With the front wheels in the straight ahead position, check the power steering fluid level and, if low, add fluid until it reaches the Cold mark on the dipstick.

3   Start the engine and allow it to run at fast idle. Recheck the fluid level and add more if necessary to reach the Cold mark on the dipstick.

4   Bleed the system by turning the wheels from side-to-side, without hitting the stops. This will work the air out of the system. Keep the reservoir full of fluid as this is done.

5   When the air is worked out of the system, return the wheels to the straight ahead position and leave the vehicle running for several more minutes before shutting it off.

6   Road test the vehicle to be sure the steering system is functioning normally and noise free.

7   Recheck the fluid level to be sure it is up to the Hot mark on the dipstick while the engine is at normal operating temperature. Add fluid if necessary (see Chapter 1).

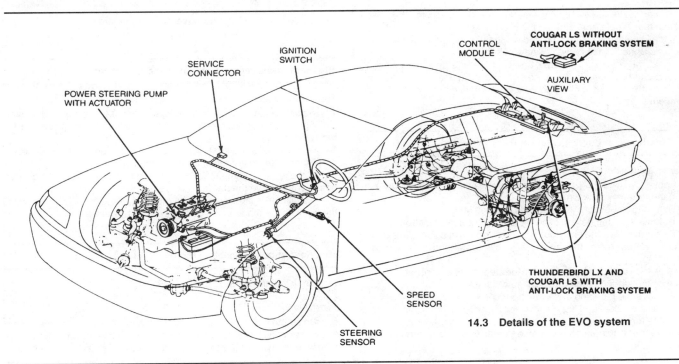

14.3   Details of the EVO system

10

16.2a Hold the tie-rod end with a wrench and loosen the jam nut

16.2b Mark the position of the tie-rod end on the tie-rod

16.4 Use a two jaw puller to separate the tie-rod end from the spindle arm (notice the nut has been loosened, but not removed – this will prevent the components from separating violently)

16   Tie-rod ends – removal and installation

Refer to illustrations 16.2a, 16.2b and 16.4

Removal

1   Loosen the wheel lug nuts. Block the rear wheels and set the parking brake. Raise the front of the vehicle and support it securely on jackstands. Remove the front wheel.
2   Hold the tie-rod end with a wrench and loosen the jam nut enough to mark the position of the tie-rod end in relation to the threads **(see illustrations)**.
3   Remove the cotter pin and loosen the nut on the tie-rod end stud.
4   Disconnect the tie-rod from the spindle arm with a puller **(see illustration)**. Remove the nut and separate the tie-rod.
5   Unscrew the tie-rod end from the tie-rod.

Installation

6   Thread the tie-rod end onto the marked position and insert the tie-rod stud into the spindle arm. Tighten the jam nut securely.
7   Install a new nut on the stud and tighten it to the torque listed in this Chapter's Specifications. Install a new cotter pin.
8   Install the wheel and lug nuts. Lower the vehicle and tighten the lug nuts to the torque listed in the Chapter 1 Specifications.
9   Have the alignment checked by a dealer service department or an alignment shop.

17   Steering gear boots – replacement

Refer to illustration 17.3

1   Loosen the wheel lug nuts, raise the vehicle and support it securely on jackstands. Remove the wheel.
2   Referring to Section 16, remove the tie-rod end.
3   Remove the clamps and slide the boot off **(see illustrations)**.
4   Before installing the new boot, wrap the threads and serrations on the end of the steering rod with a layer of tape so the small end of the new boot isn't damaged.
5   Slide the new boot into position on the steering gear until it seats in the groove in the steering rod and install new clamps.
6   Remove the tape and install the tie-rod end (see Section 16).
7   Install the wheel and lug nuts. Lower the vehicle and tighten the lug nuts to the torque listed in Chapter 1.
8   Have the alignment checked by a dealer service department or an alignment shop.

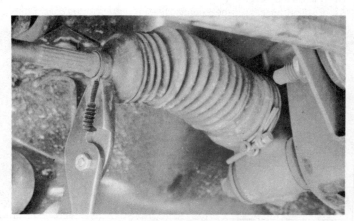

17.3 Remove the boot clamps

18   Rear stabilizer bar – removal and installation

Refer to illustration 18.2

1   Raise the rear of the vehicle and support it securely on jackstands.
2   Remove the stabilizer bar-to-stabilizer bar link attaching bolts **(see illustration)**.
3   Remove the stabilizer bar bracket bolts and remove the brackets.
4   Remove the rear muffler hanger retaining bolts.
5   Make a mark on the stabilizer bar and chassis for reassembly purposes and remove the bar from the vehicle.
6   Installation is the reverse of the removal procedure. Be sure to install the bar with the mark on the correct side of the vehicle.

19   Rear shock absorber – removal and installation

Refer to illustrations 19.4, 19.5 and 19.6

Removal

1   Raise the rear of the vehicle and support it securely on jackstands.
2   Support the lower control arm with a floor jack to prevent it from dropping when the shock absorber is disconnected. The jack must remain in

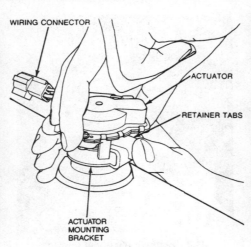

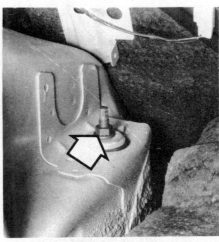

18.2   Remove the bolt and nut (arrow) from the stabilizer bar link

19.4   The rear shock absorber ARC actuator can be removed from the shock by pinching the retainer tabs and lifting it off

19.5   Location of the upper mounting nut of the rear shock absorber (standard suspension shown) – note the hex area at the top for using a wrench in case the rod turns when the nut is removed

this position throughout the entire procedure.
3   Open the rear compartment and remove the side trim panel.
4   On models equipped with ARC (Automatic Ride Control), remove the cover, disconnect the ARC actuator electrical connector, squeeze the retaining tabs and lift the actuator from the top of the shock absorber **(see illustration)**.
5   Remove the upper mounting nut from the shock absorber rod **(see illustration)**. It may be necessary to prevent the rod from turning by holding it with a wrench or locking pliers.
6   Remove the lower mounting bolt and nut **(see illustration)**, pull the bottom of the shock absorber out of the mounting bracket and remove it from the vehicle.

Installation

7   Place the inner washer and rubber insulator on the shock rod and insert the rod through the upper mounting hole. Push up on the shock absorber to align the lower shock eye in the mounting bracket and install the bolt and nut, tightening them securely.
8   Install the upper mounting rubber insulator and the dished washer on the shock rod. Install the nut and tighten it securely.
9   On models equipped with ARC, install the ARC actuator and recon-

nect the electrical connector.
10   Install the side trim panel inside the trunk.

20   Rear coil spring – removal and installation

Refer to illustrations 20.4 and 20.6

Removal

1   Loosen the wheel lug nuts, raise the rear of the vehicle and support it securely on jackstands placed under the frame. Remove the wheel and block the front wheels.
2   Remove the rear stabilizer bar (see Section 18) if the vehicle is equipped with one.
3   Disconnect the parking brake cables at the rear brake caliper or drum (see Chapter 9).
4   Install three rear spring compressors (Ford tool number 086-00031) to the coil spring **(see illustration)**. **Note:** *Be sure to stagger the three compressing tools at 120-degrees to each other.*
5   Position a floor jack under the lower control arm of the side being disassembled.

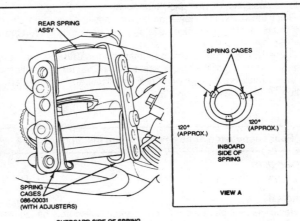

19.6   Location of the shock lower mounting bolt and nut

20.4   Position the coil spring compressor tools as shown

10

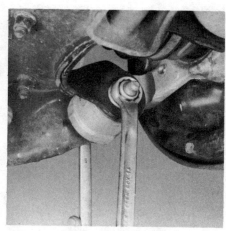

20.6   Remove the lower control arm-to-knuckle bolts

21.3   Remove the upper control arm-to-knuckle assembly bolt and nut (A) then the inner control arm-to-sub-frame bolt and nut (B)

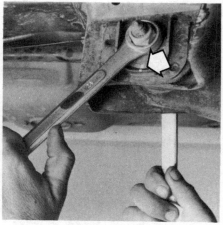

21.11   Be sure to mark the relationship of the camber adjusting washer to the subframe before removing the lower control arm pivot bolts and nuts

6   Remove the nuts and bolts from the lower control arm-to-knuckle assembly **(see illustration)**.

7   Support the rear knuckle and caliper assembly by wiring the upper control arm to the body.

8   Remove the shock absorber lower mounting bolt and nut (see Section 19).

9   Mark the position of the lower control arm cam to keep the toe adjustment correct for reassembly. Loosen but do not remove the lower control arm pivot bolts.

10   Slowly lower the jack until the spring can be removed.

11   Remove the coil spring and insulators from between the suspension arm and the spring upper seat. **Note:** *Make a note to remember the position of the pigtail (or the end of the coil spring) and the chassis to aid in reassembly.* **Note:** *If the coil springs must be replaced with new ones, carefully separate the compressing tools from the coil spring using Ford special tool number D78P-5310-A or equivalent.*

Installation

12   Set the upper insulator on top of the spring, using tape to hold it in place, if necessary.

13   Place the lower insulator on the lower suspension arm.

14   Install the coil spring compressor (see Step 11) if the coil springs are being replaced with new ones.

15   Place the spring between the suspension arm and the frame, so that the pigtail (the end of the spring) on the suspension lower arm is in the exact same position as it was prior to removal.

16   Raise the suspension lower arm up into position and install the pivot bolts and nuts into the knuckle assembly, but don't fully tighten the nuts yet.

17   Raise the lower control arm to simulate a normal ride height and tighten the pivot bolt nut to the torque listed in this Chapter's Specifications.

18   If the vehicle is equipped with a rear stabilizer bar, install it, referring to Section 18 if necessary.

---

21   Rear suspension arms – removal and installation

Upper arm

Refer to illustration 21.3

Removal

1   Raise the rear of the vehicle and support it securely on jackstands placed beneath the frame rails. Block the front wheels.

2   Support the knuckle and hub assembly with wire so that it cannot swing outward when disconnected from the upper control arm. Place a floor jack under the lower arm and raise it slightly. It must remain in this position throughout the entire procedure.

3   Remove the upper arm-to-knuckle bolt and nut **(see illustration)**.

4   Remove the upper arm-to-frame pivot bolt and nut and remove the upper control arm from the vehicle.

Installation

Note: *The Ford Motor Company recommends installing new fasteners when reassembling suspension components.*

5   Position the control arm in its mounting bosses and install the pivot bolts and nuts.

6   Raise the floor jack until the vehicle just raises off the jackstand. Tighten the nuts to the torque listed in this Chapter's Specifications.

7   Install the rear wheels and tighten the lug nuts to the torque listed in the Chapter 1 Specifications. Have the alignment checked at a dealer service department or other repair shop.

Lower arm

Refer to illustration 21.11

Removal

8   Loosen the wheel lug nuts, raise the rear of the vehicle and support it securely on jackstands placed under the frame rails. Block the front wheels and remove the rear wheel.

9   Remove the coil spring following the procedure outlined in Section 20.

10   Remove the toe compensating link from the lower control arm.

11   Mark the position of the camber adjustment washer on the pivot bolt to the subframe. Remove the lower arm-to-frame pivot bolts and nuts **(see illustration)**, then remove the arm from the vehicle.

Installation

Note: *The Ford Motor Company recommends installing new fasteners when reassembling the suspension components.*

12   Inspect the large nut used at the inner front arm attachment. If the plastic cap is cracked, replace it with a new one. Install the lower control arm but do not tighten the nuts completely at this time. Align the match-marks made on the camber adjustment washer and subframe.

13   Install the toe compensating link to the control arm and the sub-frame.

14   Install the coil spring and connect the outer end of the control arm to the knuckle assembly. Position a floor jack under the lower arm and raise it until the vehicle just lifts off the jackstand, then tighten the nuts to the torque values listed in this Chapter's Specifications.

15   Install the wheel and lug nuts. Lower the vehicle and tighten the lug nuts to the torque listed in the Chapter 1 Specifications.

16   Have the alignment checked at a dealer service department or other repair shop.

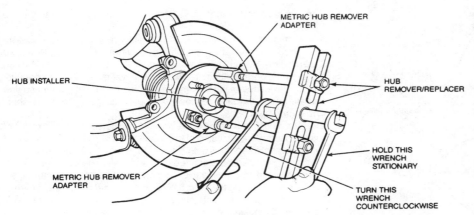

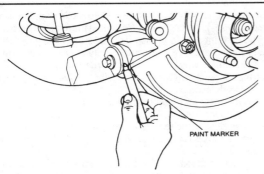

22.10   Use a special tool to push the halfshaft from the hub assembly

22.13   Remove the lower control arm-to-knuckle assembly bolts (arrows)

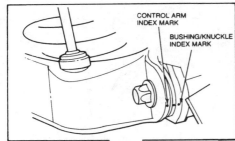

22.11   Mark the position of the bushings to keep proper alignment with the lower control arm

22   Rear suspension knuckle – removal and installation

Refer to illustrations 22.10, 22.11 and 22.13
Note: *The Ford Motor Company recommends the replacement of the hub retainer nut once it has been removed.*

Removal

1   Loosen the rear wheel lug nuts, raise the rear of the vehicle and support it securely on jackstands. Block the front wheels.
2   Remove the wheel.
3   Remove the parking brake cable from the rear calipers or drums (see Chapter 9).
4   Remove the caliper (if equipped) (see Chapter 9).
5   Wire the caliper out of the way. **Note:** *Be careful not to twist or kink the brake hose assembly.*
6   Remove the brake disc or drum (see Chapter 9).
7   On disc brake models, remove the three bolts that retain the splash shield to the knuckle and remove the splash shield.
8   On drum brakes, disconnect the brake line from the wheel cylinder (see Chapter 9).
9   Remove the upper control arm nut and bolt.

10   Use Ford special tool number T81P-1104-C or equivalent, and push the halfshaft from the hub **(see illustration)**. If this tool isn't available, a two-jaw puller can be used.
11   Mark the position of the lower control arm to the knuckle with the bushings in a relaxed position **(see illustration)**. **Note:** *when the upper control arm bolt is removed from the knuckle, the lower arm bushings return to the relaxed position. Correct position of the bushings is very important in order to avoid incorrect ride height and premature tire wear.*
12   If the knuckle is to be replaced, note the angle of the knuckle in the relaxed position by measuring the distance from the upper bushing to the vehicle body. Write the measurement down for future reference.
13   Remove the lower control arm-to-knuckle bolts and nuts **(see illustration)**.
14   Remove the knuckle from the driveshaft.

Installation

15   Place the knuckle assembly on the driveshaft splines and install the lower control arm-to-knuckle assembly bolts and nuts. Position the knuckle assembly so that the index marks on the bushing (see Step 11) line up with the marks on the control arm. If a new knuckle is being installed, set the assembly in the approximate angle as noted before removal (see Step 12).
16   Push the knuckle assembly onto the halfshaft and into the upper control arm connection. Install the upper control arm nut and bolt.
17   Install a new hub nut onto the halfshaft and temporarily tighten it hand tight.
18   Install the splash shield (disc brake models) onto the hub assembly and tighten the three bolts to the torque listed in this Chapter's Specifications.

10

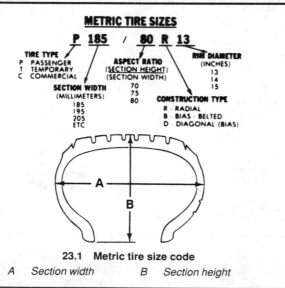

23.1   Metric tire size code

A   Section width   B   Section height

19   Attach the brake line to the wheel cylinder (drum brake models) and attach the parking brake cables (see Chapter 9).
20   Install the brake drums or disc.
21   Install the rear brake calipers (see Chapter 9).
22   Install the parking brake cable onto the calipers (disc brake models).
23   Adjust the parking brake (see Chapter 9).
24   On drum brake models, bleed the brakes (see Chapter 9).
25   Install the rear wheels. Set the parking brake and tighten the hub nut to the torque listed in this Chapter's Specifications.
26   Tighten the lug nuts to the torque listed in the Chapter 1 Specifications. Install the hub caps.

23   Wheels and tires – general information

Refer to illustration 23.1

All vehicles covered by this manual are equipped with metric-sized fiberglass or steel belted radial tires **(see illustration)**. Use of other size or type of tires may affect the ride and handling of the vehicle. Don't mix different types of tires, such as radials and bias belted, on the same vehicle as handling may be seriously affected. It's recommended that tires be replaced in pairs on the same axle, but if only one tire is being replaced, be sure it's the same size, structure and tread design as the other.

Because tire pressure has a substantial effect on handling and wear, the pressure on all tires should be checked at least once a month or before any extended trips (see Chapter 1).

Wheels must be replaced if they are bent, dented, leak air, have elongated bolt holes, are heavily rusted, out of vertical symmetry or if the lug nuts won't stay tight. Wheel repairs that use welding or peening are not recommended.

Tire and wheel balance affects the overall handling, braking and performance of the vehicle. Unbalanced wheels can adversely affect handling and ride characteristics as well as tire life. Whenever a tire is installed on a wheel, the tire and wheel should be balanced by a shop with the proper equipment.

24   Wheel alignment – general information

Refer to illustration 24.1

A wheel alignment refers to the adjustments made to the suspension so the wheels are in proper angular relationship to the suspension and the ground. Wheels that are out of proper alignment not only affect steering control, but also increase tire wear. The front end may be adjusted for cast-

er, camber and toe-in **(see illustration)**. The rear end may only be adjusted for camber and toe.

Getting the proper wheel alignment is a very exacting process, one in which complicated and expensive machines are necessary to perform the job properly. Because of this, you should have a technician with the proper equipment perform these tasks. We will, however, use this space to give you a basic idea of what is involved with front end alignment so you can better understand the process and deal intelligently with the shop that does the work.

Toe-in is the turning in of the wheels. The purpose of a toe specification is to ensure parallel rolling of the wheels. In a vehicle with zero toe-in, the distance between the front edges of the wheels will be the same as the distance between the rear edges of the wheels. The actual amount of toe-in is normally only a fraction of an inch. Front toe-in is adjusted by the tie-rod end position on the tie-rod. Rear toe-in is set by turning a cam bolt at the lower arm inner pivot. Incorrect toe-in will cause the tires to wear improperly by making them scrub against the road surface.

Camber is the tilting of the wheels from the vertical when viewed from the end of the vehicle. When the wheels tilt out at the top, the camber is said to be positive (+). When the wheels tilt in at the top the camber is negative (-). The amount of tilt is measured in degrees from the vertical and this measurement is called the camber angle. This angle affects the amount of tire tread which contacts the road and compensates for changes in the suspension geometry when the vehicle is cornering or travelling over an undulating surface.

Front and rear camber is adjusted by rotating a cam bolt at the respective lower arm inner pivot.

Caster is the tilting of the top of the front steering axis from the vertical. A tilt toward the rear is positive caster and a tilt toward the front is negative caster.

Front caster is adjusted by moving the tension strut relative to the front subframe. Rear caster is not adjustable.

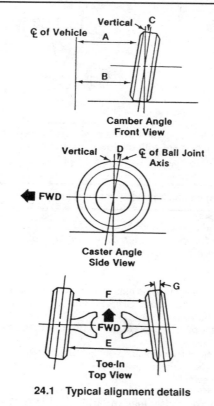

24.1   Typical alignment details

A minus B = C (degrees camber)
D = caster (measured in degrees)
E minus F = toe-in (measured in inches)
G = toe-in (expressed in degrees)

Chapter 11   Body

Contents

1   General information

These models feature a "unibody" layout, using a floor pan with front and rear frame side rails which support the body components, front and rear suspension systems and other mechanical components.

Certain components are particularly vulnerable to accident damage and can be unbolted and repaired or replaced. Among these parts are the body moldings, bumpers, the hood and trunk lids and all glass.

Only general body maintenance practices and body panel repair procedures within the scope of the do-it-yourselfer are included in this Chapter.

2   Body – maintenance

1   The condition of your vehicle's body is very important, because the resale value depends a great deal on it. It's much more difficult to repair a neglected or damaged body than it is to repair mechanical components. The hidden areas of the body, such as the wheel wells, the frame and the engine compartment, are equally important, although they don't require as frequent attention as the rest of the body.

2   Once a year, or every 12,000 miles, it's a good idea to have the under-side of the body steam cleaned. All traces of dirt and oil will be removed and the area can then be inspected carefully for rust, damaged brake lines, frayed electrical wires, damaged cables and other problems. The front suspension components should be greased after completion of this job.

3   At the same time, clean the engine and the engine compartment with a steam cleaner or water soluble degreaser.

4   The wheel wells should be given close attention, since undercoating can peel away and stones and dirt thrown up by the tires can cause the paint to chip and flake, allowing rust to set in. If rust is found, clean down to the bare metal and apply an anti-rust paint.

5   The body should be washed about once a week. Wet the vehicle thoroughly to soften the dirt, then wash it down with a soft sponge and plenty of clean soapy water. If the surplus dirt is not washed off very carefully, it can wear down the paint.

6   Spots of tar or asphalt thrown up from the road should be removed with a cloth soaked in solvent.

11

7   Once every six months, wax the body and chrome trim. If a chrome cleaner is used to remove rust from any of the vehicle's plated parts, remember that the cleaner also removes part of the chrome, so use it sparingly.

3   Vinyl trim – maintenance

Don't clean vinyl trim with detergents, caustic soap or petroleum-based cleaners. Plain soap and water works just fine, with a soft brush to clean dirt that may be ingrained. Wash the vinyl as frequently as the rest of the vehicle.

After cleaning, application of a high quality rubber and vinyl protectant will help prevent oxidation and cracks. The protectant can also be applied to weatherstripping, vacuum lines and rubber hoses, which often fail as a result of chemical degradation, and to the tires.

4   Upholstery and carpets – maintenance

1   Every three months remove the carpets or mats and clean the interior of the vehicle (more frequently if necessary). Vacuum the upholstery and carpets to remove loose dirt and dust.
2   Leather upholstery requires special care. Stains should be removed with warm water and a very mild soap solution. Use a clean, damp cloth to remove the soap, then wipe again with a dry cloth. Never use alcohol, gasoline, nail polish remover or thinner to clean leather upholstery.
3   After cleaning, regularly treat leather upholstery with a leather wax. Never use car wax on leather upholstery.
4   In areas where the interior of the vehicle is subject to bright sunlight, cover leather seats with a sheet if the vehicle is to be left out for any length of time.

5   Body repair – minor damage

See color photo sequence

Repair of minor scratches

1   If the scratch is superficial and does not penetrate to the metal of the body, repair is very simple. Lightly rub the scratched area with a fine rubbing compound to remove loose paint and built up wax. Rinse the area with clean water.
2   Apply touch-up paint to the scratch, using a small brush. Continue to apply thin layers of paint until the surface of the paint in the scratch is level with the surrounding paint. Allow the new paint at least two weeks to harden, then blend it into the surrounding paint by rubbing with a very fine rubbing compound. Finally, apply a coat of wax to the scratch area.
3   If the scratch has penetrated the paint and exposed the metal of the body, causing the metal to rust, a different repair technique is required. Remove all loose rust from the bottom of the scratch with a pocket knife, then apply rust inhibiting paint to prevent the formation of rust in the future. Using a rubber or nylon applicator, coat the scratched area with glaze-type filler. If required, the filler can be mixed with thinner to provide a very thin paste, which is ideal for filling narrow scratches. Before the glaze filler in the scratch hardens, wrap a piece of smooth cotton cloth around the tip of a finger. Dip the cloth in thinner and then quickly wipe it along the surface of the scratch. This will ensure that the surface of the filler is slightly hollow. The scratch can now be painted over as described earlier in this section.

Repair of dents

4   When repairing dents, the first job is to pull the dent out until the affected area is as close as possible to its original shape. There is no point in trying to restore the original shape completely as the metal in the damaged area will have stretched on impact and cannot be restored to its original contours. It is better to bring the level of the dent up to a point which is about 1/8-inch below the level of the surrounding metal. In cases where the dent is very shallow, it is not worth trying to pull it out at all.
5   If the back side of the dent is accessible, it can be hammered out gently from behind using a soft-face hammer. While doing this, hold a block of wood firmly against the opposite side of the metal to absorb the hammer blows and prevent the metal from being stretched.
6   If the dent is in a section of the body which has double layers, or some other factor makes it inaccessible from behind, a different technique is required. Drill several small holes through the metal inside the damaged area, particularly in the deeper sections. Screw long, self tapping screws into the holes just enough for them to get a good grip in the metal. Now the dent can be pulled out by pulling on the protruding heads of the screws with locking pliers.
7   The next stage of repair is the removal of paint from the damaged area and from an inch or so of the surrounding metal. This is easily done with a wire brush or sanding disk in a drill motor, although it can be done just as effectively by hand with sandpaper. To complete the preparation for filling, score the surface of the bare metal with a screwdriver or the tang of a file or drill small holes in the affected area. This will provide a good grip for the filler material. To complete the repair, see the Section on filling and painting.

Repair of rust holes or gashes

8   Remove all paint from the affected area and from an inch or so of the surrounding metal using a sanding disk or wire brush mounted in a drill motor. If these are not available, a few sheets of sandpaper will do the job just as effectively.
9   With the paint removed, you will be able to determine the severity of the corrosion and decide whether to replace the whole panel, if possible, or repair the affected area. New body panels are not as expensive as most people think and it is often quicker to install a new panel than to repair large areas of rust.
10   Remove all trim pieces from the affected area except those which will act as a guide to the original shape of the damaged body, such as headlight shells, etc. Using metal snips or a hacksaw blade, remove all loose metal and any other metal that is badly affected by rust. Hammer the edges of the hole inward to create a slight depression for the filler material.
11   Wire brush the affected area to remove the powdery rust from the surface of the metal. If the back of the rusted area is accessible, treat it with rust inhibiting paint.
12   Before filling is done, block the hole in some way. This can be done with sheet metal riveted or screwed into place, or by stuffing the hole with wire mesh.
13   Once the hole is blocked off, the affected area can be filled and painted. See the following subsection on filling and painting.

Filling and painting

14   Many types of body fillers are available, but generally speaking, body repair kits which contain filler paste and a tube of resin hardener are best for this type of repair work. A wide, flexible plastic or nylon applicator will be necessary for imparting a smooth and contoured finish to the surface of the filler material. Mix up a small amount of filler on a clean piece of wood or cardboard (use the hardener sparingly). Follow the manufacturer's instructions on the package, otherwise the filler will set incorrectly.
15   Using the applicator, apply the filler paste to the prepared area. Draw the applicator across the surface of the filler to achieve the desired contour and to level the filler surface. As soon as a contour that approximates the original one is achieved, stop working the paste. If you continue, the paste will begin to stick to the applicator. Continue to add thin layers of paste at 20-minute intervals until the level of the filler is just above the surrounding metal.
16   Once the filler has hardened, the excess can be removed with a body file. From then on, progressively finer grades of sandpaper should be used, starting with a 180-grit paper and finishing with 600-grit wet-or-dry paper. Always wrap the sandpaper around a flat rubber or wooden block, otherwise the surface of the filler will not be completely flat. During the sanding of the filler surface, the wet-or-dry paper should be periodically rinsed in water. This will ensure that a very smooth finish is produced in the final stage.

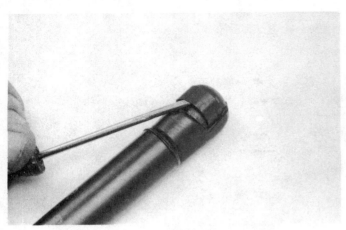

9.3a Insert a small screwdriver under the clip and pry up to detach the support strut from the hood

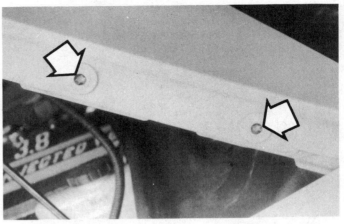

9.3b Use a Torx driver to remove the special hood screws

17 At this point, the repair area should be surrounded by a ring of bare metal, which in turn should be encircled by the finely feathered edge of good paint. Rinse the repair area with clean water until all of the dust produced by the sanding operation is gone.

18 Spray the entire area with a light coat of primer. This will reveal any imperfections in the surface of the filler. Repair the imperfections with fresh filler paste or glaze filler and once more smooth the surface with sandpaper. Repeat this spray-and-repair procedure until you are satisfied that the surface of the filler and the feathered edge of the paint are perfect. Rinse the area with clean water and allow it to dry completely.

19 The repair area is now ready for painting. Spray painting must be carried out in a warm, dry, windless and dust free atmosphere. These conditions can be created if you have access to a large indoor work area, but if you are forced to work in the open, you will have to pick the day very carefully. If you are working indoors, dousing the floor in the work area with water will help settle the dust which would otherwise be in the air. If the repair area is confined to one body panel, mask off the surrounding panels. This will help minimize the effects of a slight mismatch in paint color. Trim pieces such as chrome strips, door handles, etc., will also need to be masked off or removed. Use masking tape and several thicknesses of newspaper for the masking operations.

20 Before spraying, shake the paint can thoroughly, then spray a test area until the spray painting technique is mastered. Cover the repair area with a thick coat of primer. The thickness should be built up using several thin layers of primer rather than one thick one. Using 600-grit wet-or-dry sandpaper, rub down the surface of the primer until it is very smooth. While doing this, the work area should be thoroughly rinsed with water and the wet-or-dry sandpaper periodically rinsed as well. Allow the primer to dry before spraying additional coats.

21 Spray on the top coat, again building up the thickness by using several thin layers of paint. Begin spraying in the center of the repair area and then, using a circular motion, work out until the whole repair area and about two inches of the surrounding original paint is covered. Remove all masking material 10 to 15 minutes after spraying on the final coat of paint. Allow the new paint at least two weeks to harden, then use a very fine rubbing compound to blend the edges of the new paint into the existing paint. Finally, apply a coat of wax.

6   Body repair – major damage

1 Major damage must be repaired by an auto body shop specifically equipped to perform unibody repairs. These shops have the specialized equipment required to do the job properly.

2 If the damage is extensive, the body must be checked for proper alignment or the vehicle's handling characteristics may be adversely affected and other components may wear at an accelerated rate.

3 Due to the fact that all of the major body components (hood, fenders, etc.) are separate and replaceable units, any seriously damaged components should be replaced rather than repaired. Sometimes the components can be found in a wrecking yard that specializes in used vehicle components, often at considerable savings over the cost of new parts.

7   Hinges and locks – maintenance

Once every 3000 miles, or every three months, the hinges and latch assemblies on the doors, hood and trunk should be given a few drops of light oil or lock lubricant. The door latch strikers should also be lubricated with a thin coat of grease to reduce wear and ensure free movement. Lubricate the door and trunk locks with spray-on graphite lubricant.

8   Fixed glass – replacement

Replacement of the windshield and fixed glass requires the use of special fast-setting adhesive/caulk materials and some specialized tools and techniques. These operations should be left to a dealer service department or a shop specializing in glass work.

9   Hood – removal, installation and adjustment

Refer to illustrations 9.3a, 9.3b, 9.8 and 9.9
Note: *The hood is heavy and somewhat awkward to remove and install – at least two people should perform this procedure.*

Removal and installation

1 Use blankets or pads to cover the cowl area of the body and the fenders. This will protect the body and paint as the hood is lifted off.

2 Disconnect any cables or wire harnesses which will interfere with removal.

3 Have an assistant support the weight of the hood. Disconnect the upper ends of the hood support struts, using a small screwdriver **(see illustration)**. Remove the hinge bracket-to-hood bolts **(see illustration)**.

4 Lift off the hood.

5 Installation is the reverse of removal.

Adjustment

6 Fore-and-aft and side-to-side adjustment of the hood is done by moving the hinge plate in relation to the inner fender panel after loosening the bolts.

7 Scribe a line around the entire hinge plate so you can judge the amount of movement.

11

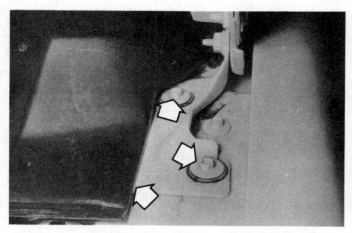

9.8   Scribe around the hinge plate and loosen the three bolts (arrows) to adjust the hood position

9.9   Loosen the two bolts (arrows) to adjust the hood latch position

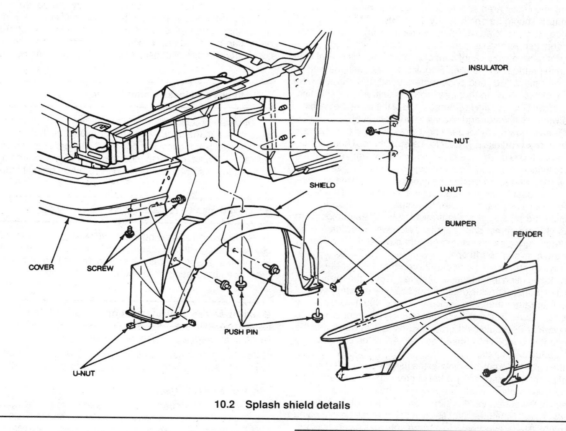

10.2   Splash shield details

8   Loosen the bolts and move the hood into correct alignment **(see illustration)**. Move it only a little at a time. Tighten the hinge bolts or nuts and carefully lower the hood to check the alignment.

9   If necessary after installation, the entire hood latch assembly can be adjusted up-and-down as well as from side-to-side on the radiator support so the hood closes securely and is flush with the fenders. To do this, scribe a line around the hood latch mounting bolts to provide a reference point. Then loosen the bolts and reposition the latch assembly as necessary. Following adjustment, retighten the mounting bolts **(see illustration)**.

10   Finally, adjust the hood bumpers on the radiator support so the hood, when closed, is flush with the fenders.

11   The hood latch assembly, as well as the hinges, should be periodically lubricated with white lithium-base grease to prevent sticking and wear.

10   Front fender and splash shield – removal and installation

Splash shield

Refer to illustration 10.2

1   Raise the vehicle, support it securely on jackstands and remove the front wheel.

2   Remove the plastic push pins retaining the splash shield to the body. This is accomplished by pulling out the centers of the pins with pliers to unlock them, then grasping the body of the pin with the pliers to pull it from the fender **(see illustration)**.

3   Remove the bolts and nuts and detach the splash shield and insulator from the fender and body.

4   Installation is the reverse of removal.

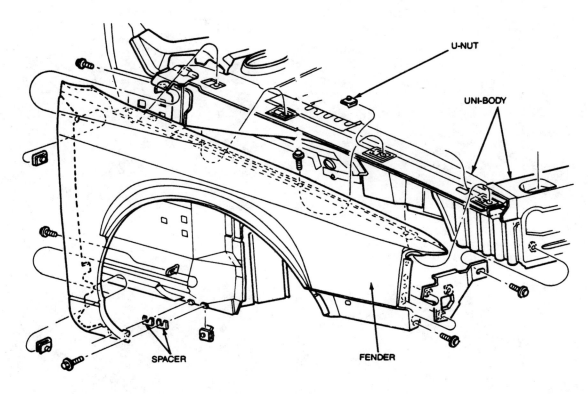

10.7   Front fender details

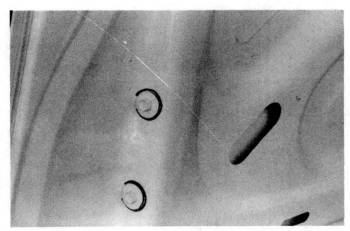

11.3   Scribe around the trunk lid mounting bolts with a pencil or marker to ensure the reinstallation to the same position

Fender

Refer to illustration 10.7

5   Remove the splash shield.
6   Disconnect the antenna and all light bulb wiring harness connectors and other components that would interfere with fender removal.
7   Remove the fender mounting bolts **(see illustration)**.
8   Detach the fender. It is a good idea to have an assistant support the fender while it's being moved away from the vehicle to prevent damage to the surrounding body panels.

9   Installation is the reverse of removal.
10   Tighten all nuts, bolts and screws securely.

11   Trunk lid – removal, installation and adjustment

Refer to illustration 11.3

Removal

1   Open the trunk lid and cover the edges of the trunk compartment with pads or cloths to protect the painted surfaces when the lid is removed.
2   Disconnect any cables or wire harness connectors attached to the trunk lid that would interfere with removal. Trace the wiring harness to the electrical connector, located under the rear window ledge.
3   Scribe or paint alignment marks around the hinge bolt mounting flanges **(see illustration)**.
4   While an assistant supports the trunk lid, remove the hinge bolts from both sides and lift it off.

Installation and adjustment

5   Installation is the reverse of removal. **Note:** *When reinstalling the trunk lid, align the hinge bolt flanges with the marks made during removal.*
6   After installation, close the lid and see if it's in proper alignment with the surrounding panels. Fore-and-aft and side-to-side adjustments of the lid are controlled by the position of the hinge bolts in the slots. To adjust it, loosen the hinge bolts, reposition the lid and retighten the bolts.
7   The height of the lid in relation to the surrounding body panels when closed can be adjusted by loosening the lock striker bolts, repositioning the striker and retightening the bolts.

11

These photos illustrate a method of repairing simple dents. They are intended to supplement *Body repair - minor damage* in this Chapter and should not be used as the sole instructions for body repair on these vehicles.

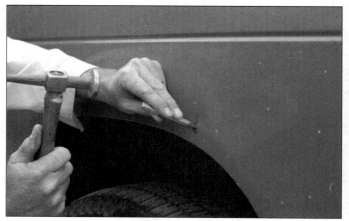

1   If you can't access the backside of the body panel to hammer out the dent, pull it out with a slide-hammer-type dent puller. In the deepest portion of the dent or along the crease line, drill or punch hole(s) at least one inch apart . . .

2   . . . then screw the slide-hammer into the hole and operate it. Tap with a hammer near the edge of the dent to help 'pop' the metal back to its original shape. When you're finished, the dent area should be close to its original contour and about 1/8-inch below the surface of the surrounding metal

3   Using coarse-grit sandpaper, remove the paint down to the bare metal. Hand sanding works fine, but the disc sander shown here makes the job faster. Use finer (about 320-grit) sandpaper to feather-edge the paint at least one inch around the dent area

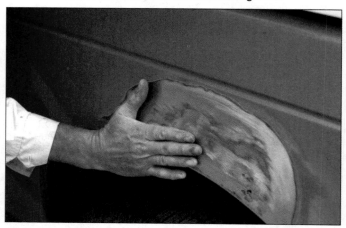

4   When the paint is removed, touch will probably be more helpful than sight for telling if the metal is straight. Hammer down the high spots or raise the low spots as necessary. Clean the repair area with wax/silicone remover

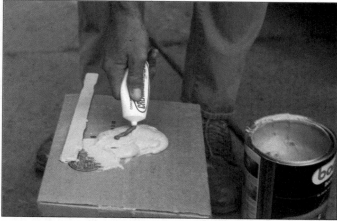

5   Following label instructions, mix up a batch of plastic filler and hardener. The ratio of filler to hardener is critical, and, if you mix it incorrectly, it will either not cure properly or cure too quickly (you won't have time to file and sand it into shape)

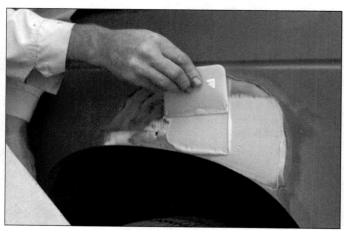

6   Working quickly so the filler doesn't harden, use a plastic applicator to press the body filler firmly into the metal, assuring it bonds completely. Work the filler until it matches the original contour and is slightly above the surrounding metal

7   Let the filler harden until you can just dent it with your fingernail. Use a body file or Surform tool (shown here) to rough-shape the filler

8   Use coarse-grit sandpaper and a sanding board or block to work the filler down until it's smooth and even. Work down to finer grits of sandpaper - always using a board or block - ending up with 360 or 400 grit

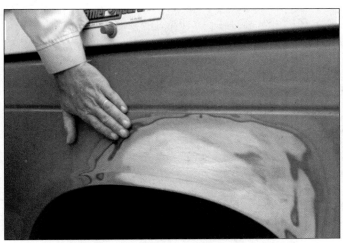

9   You shouldn't be able to feel any ridge at the transition from the filler to the bare metal or from the bare metal to the old paint. As soon as the repair is flat and uniform, remove the dust and mask off the adjacent panels or trim pieces

10   Apply several layers of primer to the area. Don't spray the primer on too heavy, so it sags or runs, and make sure each coat is dry before you spray on the next one. A professional-type spray gun is being used here, but aerosol spray primer is available inexpensively from auto parts stores

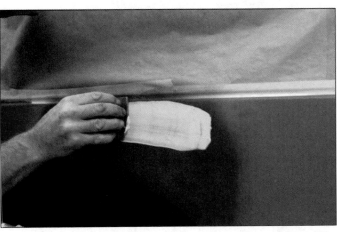

11   The primer will help reveal imperfections or scratches. Fill these with glazing compound. Follow the label instructions and sand it with 360 or 400-grit sandpaper until it's smooth. Repeat the glazing, sanding and respraying until the primer reveals a perfectly smooth surface

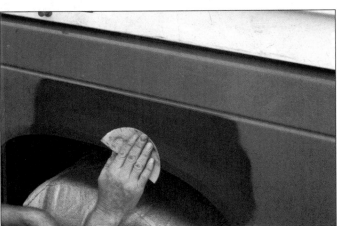

12   Finish sand the primer with very fine sandpaper (400 or 600-grit) to remove the primer overspray. Clean the area with water and allow it to dry. Use a tack rag to remove any dust, then apply the finish coat. Don't attempt to rub out or wax the repair area until the paint has dried completely (at least two weeks)

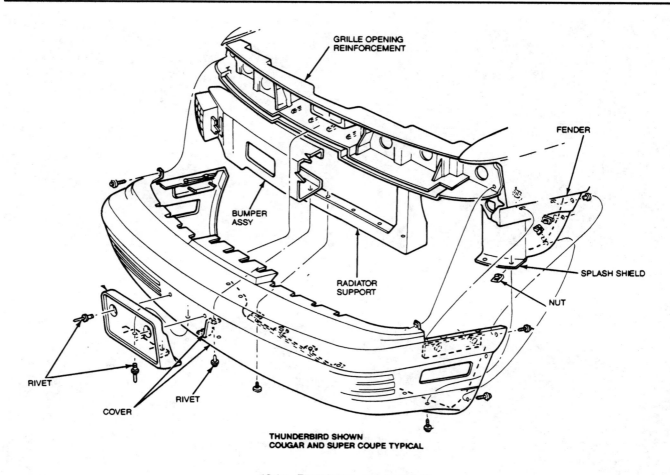

12.1a   Front bumper cover details

Removal

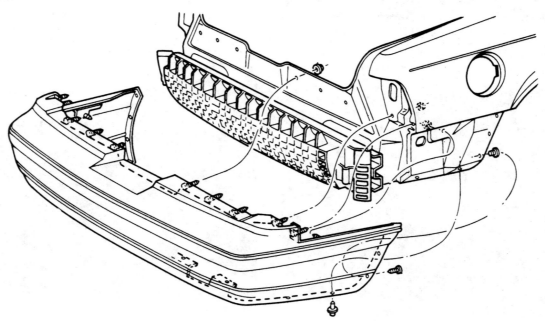

12.1b   Rear bumper cover details

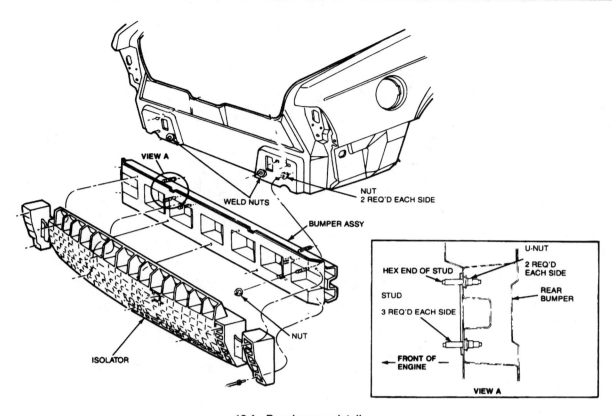

12.4   Rear bumper details

12   Bumpers – removal and installation

Refer to illustrations 12.1a, 12.1b and 12.4

Removal

1   Detach the bumper covers **(see illustrations)**. The front bumper assembly is welded to the unibody structure and removal and installation should be left to a body shop.
2   Disconnect any wiring or other components that would interfere with bumper removal.
3   Support the bumper with a jack or jackstand. Alternatively, have an assistant support the bumper as the bolts are removed.
4   Remove the retaining bolts and detach the bumper (rear only)**(see illustration)**.

Installation

5   Installation is the reverse of removal.
6   Tighten the retaining bolts securely.
7   Install the bumper cover and any other components that were removed.

13   Door – removal, installation and adjustment

Refer to illustration 13.4

Removal

1   Remove the door trim panel (see Section 14). Disconnect any wire harness connectors and push them through the door opening so they won't interfere with door removal.
2   Place a jack or jackstand under the door or have an assistant on hand to support it when the hinge bolts are removed. **Note:** *If a jack or jackstand*
is used, place a rag between it and the door to protect the door's painted surfaces.
3   Scribe around the door hinges.
4   Remove the hinge-to-door bolts and carefully lift off the door **(see illustration)**.

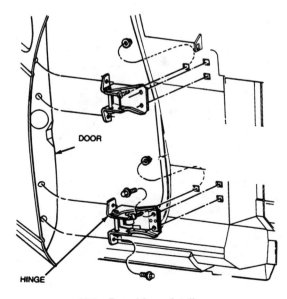

13.4   Door hinge details

11

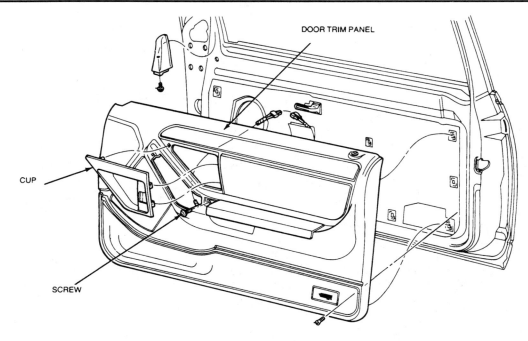

14.2 Door trim panel details

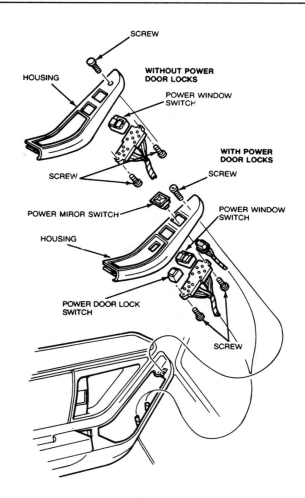

14.3 Switch housing details

Installation and adjustment

5   Installation is the reverse of removal.

6   Following installation of the door, check the alignment and adjust it if necessary as follows:

   a) Up-and-down and forward-and-backward adjustments are made by loosening the hinge-to-body bolts and moving the door as necessary.

   b) The door lock striker can also be adjusted both up-and-down and sideways to provide positive engagement with the lock mechanism. This is done by loosening the striker pin with a Torx-head tool moving the pin as necessary.

---

14   Door trim panel – removal and installation

Refer to illustrations 14.2, 14.3, 14.4 and 14.5

Removal

1   Disconnect the negative cable from the battery.

2   Remove all door trim panel retaining screws and door pull/armrest assemblies **(see illustration)**.

3   On manual window regulator equipped models, remove the window crank. On power regulator models, remove the switch housing screw, pry out the housing and unplug the switch **(see illustration)**.

4   Dislodge the clips at the bottom edge, grasp the trim panel and rotate the bottom edge out, then lift the panel up to detach it from the door **(see illustration)**. Unplug any wire harness connectors and remove the trim panel from the vehicle.

5   For access to the inner door, carefully peel back the plastic watershield **(see illustration)**.

Installation

6   Prior to installation of the door panel, be sure to reinstall any clips in the panel which may have come out during the removal procedure and remain in the door itself.

7   Plug in the wire harness connectors and place the panel in position in window glass opening at the top of door, then rotate it down into position and seat the clips at the bottom, then install the armrest/door pulls. Install the manual regulator window crank or power window switch assembly.

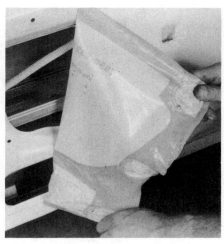

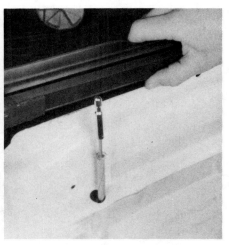

14.4   Rotate the bottom of the trim panel out, then lift it up out of the glass opening at the top of the door

14.5   Peel the watershield carefully off the door, so that it isn't torn or distorted

15.2   Remove the screw and lift the weatherstrip out of the door glass opening

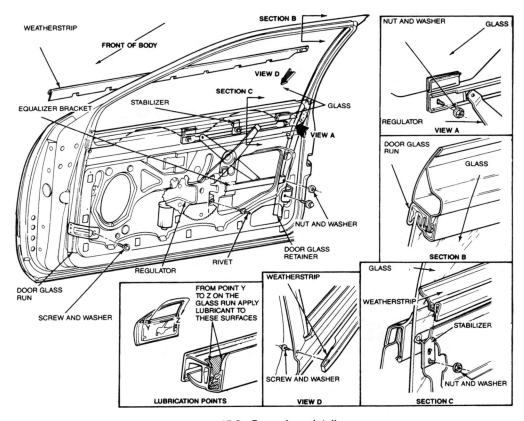

15.3   Door glass details

15   Door window glass – removal, installation and adjustment

Refer to illustrations 15.2 and 15.3

Removal

1   Remove the door trim panel and watershield (see Section 14).
2   Remove the inside door belt weatherstrip **(see illustration)**.
3   Lower the glass until the two retaining nuts are accessible through the holes in the inner door panel. Remove the two nuts, then loosen the stabilizer nut and washer **(see illustration)**.
4   Remove the glass from the door by tipping it forward, then lifting it up and out of the opening at the top of the door, toward the outside.

Installation

5   Lower the glass into position, making sure it is set between the front and rear glass run retainers.

11

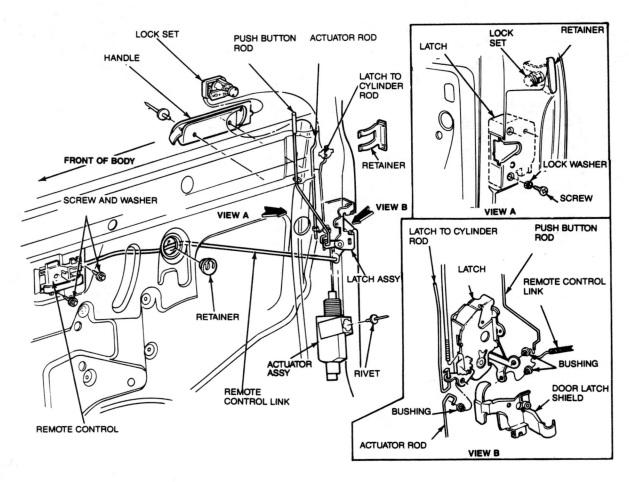

16.2   Door lock and remote control component layout

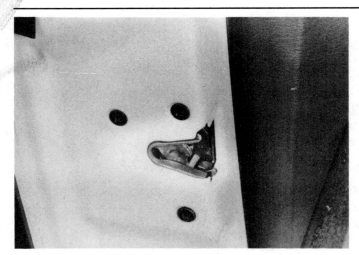

16.4   The three door latch retaining screws are accessible with the door open

6   Place the glass in position in the bracket, install the two nuts and tighten them securely.
7   Install the door belt weatherstrip.

Adjustment

8   Raise the glass to within three inches of the top of the door.
9   Make sure the stabilizer nut and washer are loose, then with door open, seat the glass in the rear glass run (B pillar).
10   Press down on the equalizer bracket and tighten the nut and washer securely.
11   Set the glass stabilizer so that it touches the glass slightly and tighten the nut and washer securely.
12   Cycle the glass several times to make sure it is properly adjusted.

16   Door lock and remote controls – removal and installation

Refer to illustrations 16.2 and 16.4

1   Remove the door trim panel and peel the watershield back (see Section 14).
2   Remove the remote control assembly and disconnect the rod at the control and the lock cylinder **(see illustration)**.
3   Disconnect the push button rod and handle from the latch.
4   Remove the three screws located in the end of the door and detach the latch **(see illustration)**.
5   Installation is the reverse of removal.

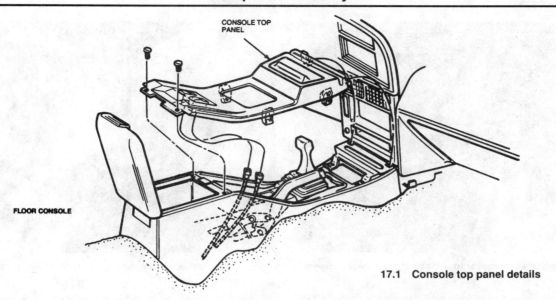

17.1   Console top panel details

17.2   Press the automatic transmission detent button, then pull up sharply and detach the shift knob

17   Center console – removal and installation

Console top panel
Refer to illustrations 17.1 and 17.2

1   Open the console lid for access and remove the two retaining screws **(see illustration)**.
2   Remove the shift lever knob. On manual models this is accomplished by removing the two screws and detaching the upper part of the lever. On automatic models, push the detent button in and hold it, then pull up sharply to detach the knob from the lever **(see illustration)**.
3   Rotate the rear of the panel forward, disconnect the electrical connectors, then detach the clips at the front edge and lift the panel from the vehicle.

Console housing
Refer to illustration 17.4

4   Remove the top panel and the stereo tape container or mat **(see illustration)**.

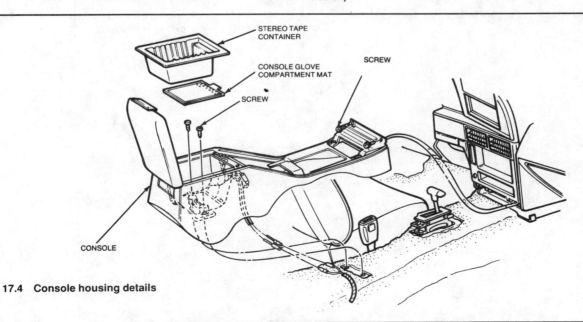

17.4   Console housing details

11

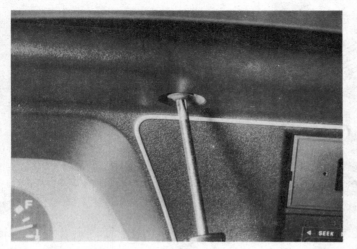

18.1   **Use a Phillips screwdriver to remove the two bezel screws**

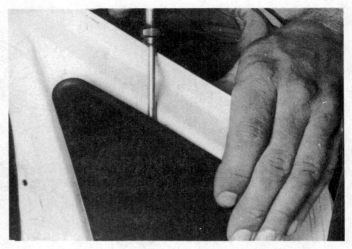

19.3   **Use a screwdriver to pry the access cover off**

5   Remove the screws, lift the housing up, disconnect the electrical connectors, then remove the housing.
6   Installation is the reverse of removal.

18   Instrument cluster bezel – removal and installation

Refer to illustration 18.1
1   Remove the two screws along the top of the bezel **(see illustration)**.
2   Remove the headlight switch (see Chapter 12).
3   Detach the bezel and remove it from the instrument panel.
4   Installation is the reverse of removal.

19   Outside mirror – removal and installation

Refer to illustrations 19.3 and 19.4
1   On power mirror models, disconnect the negative battery cable.
2   Remove the door trim panel (see Section 14).
3   Pry off the mirror access hole cover **(see illustration)**.
4   Remove the three nuts and detach the mirror from the door **(see illustration)**.
5   On power models, unplug the electrical connector.
6   Installation is the reverse of removal.

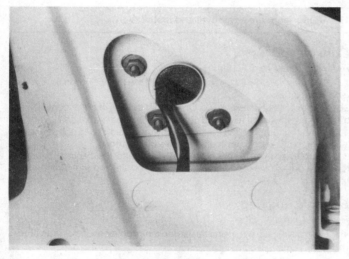

19.4   **The mirror is held in place by three nuts**

Chapter 12 Chassis electrical system

Contents

1 General information

The electrical system is a 12-volt, negative ground type. Power for the lights and all electrical accessories is supplied by a lead/acid-type battery which is charged by the alternator.

This Chapter covers repair and service procedures for the various electrical components not associated with the engine.

Information on the battery, alternator, distributor and starter motor can be found in Chapter 5.

It should be noted that when portions of the electrical system are serviced, the negative battery cable should be disconnected from the battery to prevent electrical shorts and/or fires.

2 Electrical troubleshooting – general information

A typical electrical circuit consists of an electrical component, any switches, relays, motors, fuses, fusible links or circuit breakers related to that component and the wiring and connectors that link the component to both the battery and the chassis. To help you pinpoint an electrical circuit problem, wiring diagrams are included at the end of this book.

Before tackling any troublesome electrical circuit, first study the appropriate wiring diagrams to get a complete understanding of what makes up that individual circuit. Trouble spots, for instance, can often be narrowed down by noting if other components related to the circuit are operating properly. If several components or circuits fail at one time, chances are the

12

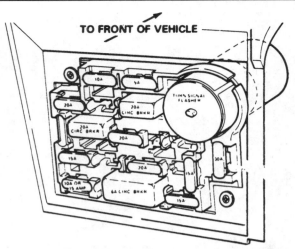

3.1a   The standard fuse block is located under the left side of the instrument panel, behind a cover

3.1b   The high current fuse block is next to the battery in the engine compartment

problem is in a fuse or ground connection, because several circuits are often routed through the same fuse and ground connections.

Electrical problems usually stem from simple causes, such as loose or corroded connections, a blown fuse, a melted fusible link or a bad relay. Visually inspect the condition of all fuses, wires and connections in a problem circuit before troubleshooting it.

If testing instruments are going to be utilized, use the diagrams to plan ahead of time where you will make the necessary connections in order to accurately pinpoint the trouble spot.

The basic tools needed for electrical troubleshooting include a circuit tester or voltmeter (a 12-volt bulb with a set of test leads can also be used), a continuity tester, which includes a bulb, battery and set of test leads, and a jumper wire, preferably with a circuit breaker incorporated, which can be used to bypass electrical components. Before attempting to locate a problem with test instruments, use the wiring diagram(s) to decide where to make the connections.

Voltage checks

Voltage checks should be performed if a circuit is not functioning properly. Connect one lead of a circuit tester to either the negative battery terminal or a known good ground. Connect the other lead to a connector in the circuit being tested, preferably nearest to the battery or fuse. If the bulb of the tester lights, voltage is present, which means that the part of the circuit between the connector and the battery is problem free. Continue checking the rest of the circuit in the same fashion. When you reach a point at which no voltage is present, the problem lies between that point and the last test point with voltage. Most of the time the problem can be traced to a loose connection. **Note:** *Keep in mind that some circuits receive voltage only when the ignition key is in the Accessory or Run position.*

Finding a short

One method of finding shorts in a circuit is to remove the fuse and connect a test light or voltmeter in its place to the fuse terminals. There should be no voltage present in the circuit. Move the wiring harness from side-to-side while watching the test light. If the bulb goes on, there is a short to ground somewhere in that area, probably where the insulation has rubbed through. The same test can be performed on each component in the circuit, even a switch.

Ground check

Perform a ground test to check whether a component is properly grounded. Disconnect the battery and connect one lead of a selfpowered test light, known as a continuity tester, to a known good ground. Connect the other lead to the wire or ground connection being tested. If the bulb goes on, the ground is good. If the bulb does not go on, the ground is not good.

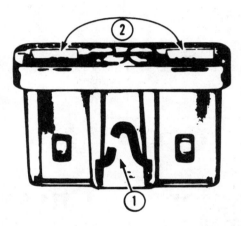

3.2   To test for a blown fuse, pull it out and inspect it for an open (1), then, with the circuit activated, use a test light across the terminals (2)

Continuity check

A continuity check is done to determine if there are any breaks in a circuit – if it is passing electricity properly. With the circuit off (no power in the circuit), a self-powered continuity tester can be used to check the circuit. Connect the test leads to both ends of the circuit (or to the "power" end and a good ground), and if the test light comes on the circuit is passing current properly. If the light doesn't come on, there is a break somewhere in the circuit. The same procedure can be used to test a switch, by connecting the continuity tester to the switch terminals. With the switch turned On, the test light should come on.

Finding an open circuit

When diagnosing for possible open circuits, it is often difficult to locate them by sight because oxidation or terminal misalignment are hidden by the connectors. Merely wiggling a connector on a sensor or in the wiring harness may correct the open circuit condition. Remember this when an open circuit is indicated when troubleshooting a circuit. Intermittent problems may also be caused by oxidized or loose connections.

Electrical troubleshooting is simple if you keep in mind that all electrical circuits are basically electricity running from the battery, through the wires, switches, relays, fuses and fusible links to each electrical component (light bulb, motor, etc.) and to ground, from which it is passed back to the battery. Any electrical problem is an interruption in the flow of electricity to and from the battery.

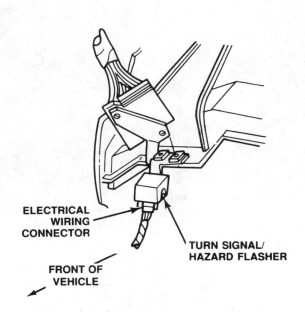

ELECTRICAL WIRING CONNECTOR

TURN SIGNAL/ HAZARD FLASHER

FRONT OF VEHICLE

7.1   The turn signal/hazard flasher is located to the right of the steering column

3   Fuses – general information

Refer to illustrations 3.1a, 3.1b and 3.2

The electrical circuits of the vehicle are protected by a combination of fuses, circuit breakers and fusible links. These models have two fuse blocks, one for standard fused located under the instrument panel on the left side of the dashboard and one for high current fuses in the engine compartment, adjacent to the battery **(see illustrations)**. Disconnect the battery negative cable before replacing high current fuses. **Note:** *The manufacturer recommends that high capacity fuses be replaced by a dealer or qualified electrical technician.*

Miniaturized fuses are employed in the fuse block in the passenger compartment. These compact fuses, with blade terminal design, allow fingertip removal and replacement. If an electrical component fails, always check the fuse first. A blown fuse is easily identified through the clear plastic body. Visually inspect the element for evidence of damage **(see illustration)**. If a continuity check is called for, the blade terminal tips are exposed in the fuse body.

Be sure to replace blown fuses with the correct type. Fuses of different ratings are physically interchangeable, but only fuses of the proper rating should be used. Replacing a fuse with one of a higher or lower value than specified is not recommended. Each electrical circuit needs a specific amount of protection. The amperage value of each fuse is molded into the fuse body.

If the replacement fuse immediately fails, don't replace it again until the cause of the problem is isolated and corrected. In most cases, the cause will be a short circuit in the wiring caused by a broken or deteriorated wire.

4   Fusible links – general information

Some circuits are protected by fusible links. The links are used in circuits which are not ordinarily fused, such as the ignition circuit.

In addition to the conventional type of fusible link described below (located in the wiring harness), cartridge fusible links, similar to a large fuses, are used on some models. Cartridge fusible links are located in the engine compartment fuse block and, after disconnecting the negative battery cable, are simply unplugged and replaced by a unit of the same amperage.

Some cartridge fusible links are held in place by bolts which must be loosened before removing the link.

Fusible links cannot be repaired, but a new link of the same size wire can be put in its place. The procedure is as follows:
a) Disconnect the negative cable from the battery.
b) Disconnect the fusible link from the wiring harness.
c) Cut the damaged fusible link out of the wiring just behind the connector.
d) Strip the insulation back approximately 1/2-inch.
e) Position the connector on the new fusible link and crimp it into place.
f) Use rosin core solder at each end of the new link to obtain a good solder joint.
g) Use plenty of electrical tape around the soldered joint. No wires should be exposed.
h) Connect the battery ground cable. Test the circuit for proper operation.

5   Circuit breakers – general information

Circuit breakers protect components such as power windows, power door locks and headlights. Some circuit breakers are located in the fuse box.

On some models the circuit breaker resets itself automatically, so an electrical overload in a circuit breaker protected system will cause the circuit to fail momentarily, then come back on. If the circuit does not come back on, check it immediately. Once the condition is corrected, the circuit breaker will resume its normal function.

6   Relays – general information

Several electrical accessories in the vehicle use relays to transmit the electrical signal to the component. If the relay is defective, that component will not operate properly.

The various relays are grouped together in several locations.

If a faulty relay is suspected, it can be removed and tested by a dealer service department or a repair shop. Defective relays must be replaced as a unit.

7   Turn signal/hazard flasher – check and replacement

Refer to illustration 7.1

1   The turn signal/hazard flasher, a small rectangular-shaped unit located in a clip on a bracket to the right of the steering column, flashes the turn signals or hazard flasher **(see illustration)**.
2   When the flasher unit is functioning properly, an audible click can be heard during its operation. If the turn signals fail on one side or the other and the flasher unit does not make its characteristic clicking sound, a faulty turn signal bulb is indicated.
3   If both turn signals fail to blink, the problem may be due to a blown fuse, a faulty flasher unit, a broken switch or a loose or open connection. If a quick check of the fuse box indicates that the turn signal fuse has blown, check the wiring for a short before installing a new fuse.
4   To replace the flasher, simply pull it out of the clip on the steering column.
5   Make sure that the replacement unit is identical to the original. Compare the old one to the new one before installing it.
6   Installation is the reverse of removal.

8   Multi-function switch – removal and installation

Refer to illustrations 8.3a and 8.3b

1   Disconnect the negative cable from the battery.
2   Remove the steering column cover.

12

8.3a   Remove the two multi-function switch bolts (arrows)

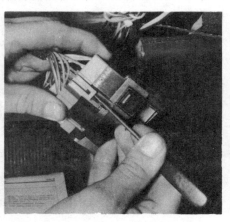

8.3b   Use a small screwdriver to release the latch so the electrical connector can be unplugged

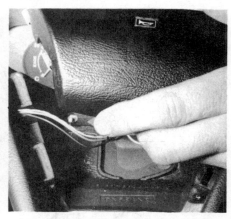

9.2a   Grasp the horn pad securely and pull it off the steering wheel

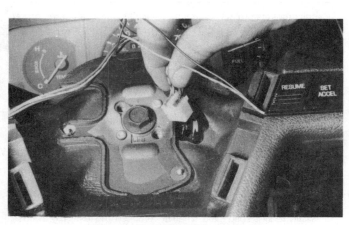

9.2b   Unplug the switch connector

3   Remove the two retaining bolts, pull the switch out, unplug the connector and withdraw the switch assembly from the steering column (**see illustrations**).
4   Plug in the electrical connector, place the switch in position and install the screws. Tighten the bolts securely.
5   Install the steering column cover.
6   Connect the negative battery cable.

9   Steering wheel switches – removal and installation

Refer to illustrations 9.2a and 9.2b
1   Disconnect the negative cable from the battery.
2   Grasp the horn pad securely and detach it from the steering wheel (**see illustrations**).
3   Unplug the electrical connector, use a small screwdriver to gently pry the switch from the steering wheel and remove it.
4   Installation is the reverse of removal.

10   Ignition switch – removal and installation

Refer to illustration 10.9

Removal

1   Disconnect the negative cable from the battery.
2   Remove the screws and detach the lower steering column cover.

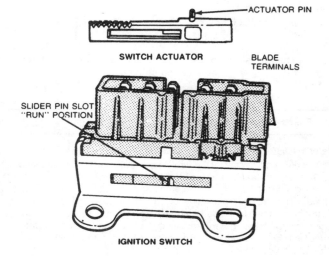

10.9   The switch actuator pin slot must be in the Run position when the switch is installed

3   Remove the four nuts retaining the steering column to the bracket and lower the column for access to the switch screws.
4   Remove the upper steering column cover.
5   Unplug the ignition switch electrical connector.
6   Turn the ignition key lock cylinder to the Run position.
7   Remove the two switch retaining screws.
8   Disengage the ignition switch from the actuator pin.

Installation

9   Make sure the actuator pin slot in the new ignition switch is in the Run position (**see illustration**). **Note:** *A new replacement switch assembly will be set in this position.*
10   Place the new switch in position on the actuator pin and install the retaining screws. It may be necessary to move the switch back and forth to line up the screw holes.
11   Plug the electrical connector into the switch.
12   Install the upper steering column cover.
13   Raise the steering column into position and install the retaining nuts. Tighten the nuts securely. **Note:** *If there are any clips on the steering column studs, remove them before installing the nuts.*
14   Install the steering lower column cover.
15   Connect the negative battery cable.

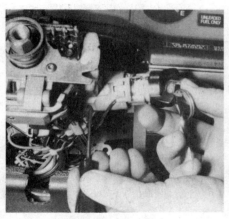

11.7   With the lock cylinder in the Run position, depress the release lever with a punch or screwdriver and pull the cylinder out

12.3   Use a screwdriver to hold the retaining clip out of the way and slide the electrical connector off the bulb holder

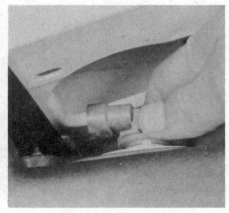

12.4   Rotate the bulb holder counterclockwise and pull it out of the housing

11   Ignition lock cylinder – removal and installation

Refer to illustration 11.7

Removal

1   Disconnect the negative cable from the battery.
2   Remove the steering wheel (see Chapter 10).
3   If your vehicle is equipped with a tilt column, remove the steering column upper cover.
4   Remove the retaining screws and detach the column cover.
5   Locate the electrical lead for the key warning buzzer (the insulated single wire coming out of the key lock cylinder housing), trace it back to the pigtail connector near the multi-terminal connector for the ignition switch and unplug it.
6   Turn the ignition switch to the Run position.
7   Place a 1/8-inch punch in the hole in the casting surrounding the lock cylinder. Depress the punch while pulling out on the lock cylinder to remove it from the column housing **(see illustration)**.

Installation

8   Install the lock cylinder by turning it to the Run position and depressing the retaining pin. Insert the lock cylinder into the lock cylinder housing. Make sure the cylinder is completely seated and aligned in the interlocking washer before turning the key to the Off position. This will permit the retaining pin to extend into the hole.
9   Turn the lock to ensure that operation is correct in all positions.
10   The remainder of installation is the reverse of removal.

12   Headlight bulbs – replacement

Refer to illustrations 12.3 and 12.4
Warning: *Halogen gas filled bulbs are under pressure and may shatter if the surface is scratched or the bulb is dropped. Wear eye protection and handle the bulbs carefully, grasping only the base whenever possible. Do not touch the surface of the bulb with your fingers because the oil from your skin could cause it to overheat and fail prematurely. If you do touch the bulb surface, clean it with rubbing alcohol.*

1   Disconnect the negative cable from the battery.
2   Open the hood.
3   Reach behind the headlight assembly and unplug the electrical connector, using a screwdriver to hold the clip out of the way **(see illustration)**.
4   Grasp the bulb holder and turn it counterclockwise to remove it **(see illustration)**. Lift the holder assembly out for access to the bulb.
5   Push in and rotate the bulb counterclockwise to remove it.

13.1   The adjustment screws (arrows) are accessible from the back of the headlight housing

6   Insert the new bulb into the holder and rotate it clockwise to seat it in the holder.
7   Install the bulb holder in the headlight assembly.

13   Headlights – adjustment

Refer to illustration 13.1
Note: *The headlights must be aimed correctly. If adjusted incorrectly they could blind the driver of an oncoming vehicle and cause a serious accident or seriously reduce your ability to see the road. The headlights should be checked for proper aim every 12 months and any time a new headlight is installed or front end body work is performed. It should be emphasized that the following procedure is only an interim step which will provide temporary adjustment until the headlights can be adjusted by a properly equipped shop.*

1   Headlights have two spring loaded adjusting screws, one on the top controlling up-and-down movement and one on the side controlling left-and-right movement **(see illustration)**.
2   There are several methods of adjusting the headlights. The simplest method requires a blank wall 25 feet in front of the vehicle and a level floor.
3   Position masking tape vertically on the wall in reference to the vehicle centerline and the centerlines of both headlights.
4   Position a horizontal tape line in reference to the centerline of all the headlights. **Note:** *It may be easier to position the tape on the wall with the vehicle parked only a few inches away.*

12

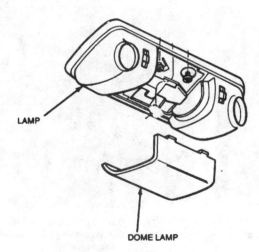

14.2 The dome lamp can be replaced after prying off the lens

5 Adjustment should be made with the vehicle sitting level, the gas tank half-full and no unusually heavy load in the vehicle.
6 Starting with the low beam adjustment, position the high intensity zone so it is two inches below the horizontal line and two inches to the right of the headlight vertical line. Adjustment is made by turning the top adjusting screw clockwise to raise the beam and counterclockwise to lower the beam. The adjusting screw on the side should be used in the same manner to move the beam left or right.
7 With the high beams on, the high intensity zone should be vertically centered with the exact center just below the horizontal line. **Note:** *It may not be possible to position the headlight aim exactly for both high and low beams. If a compromise must be made, keep in mind that the low beams are the most used and have the greatest effect on safety.*
8 Have the headlights adjusted by a dealer service department or service station at the earliest opportunity.

14 Bulb replacement

Refer to illustrations 14.2, 14.3a, 14.3b and 14.4
1 The lenses of many lights are held in place by screws, which makes it a simple procedure to gain access to the bulbs.
2 On some lights the lenses are held in place by clips. The lenses can be removed either by unsnapping them or by using a small screwdriver to pry them off **(see illustration)**.
3 Several types of bulbs are used. Some are removed by pushing in and turning them counterclockwise **(see illustration)**. Others can simply be unclipped from the terminals or pulled straight out of the socket **(see illustration)**.
4 To gain access to the instrument panel lights, the instrument cluster will have to be removed first **(see illustration)**.

15 Radio/CD player and speakers – removal and installation

1 Disconnect the negative cable from the battery.

Radio/CD player
Refer to illustration 15.4
Removal
2 Remove the instrument cluster bezel (Chapter 11).
3 For theft protection, the radio receiver and CD player assemblies are retained in the instrument panel by special clips. Releasing these clips requires the use of two Ford removal tools T87P-19061-A, or two short lengths of coathanger wire bent into U-shapes. Insert the tools into the holes at the corners of the radio/CD player assembly until you feel the internal clips release.
4 With the clips released, flex outward simultaneously on both tools and pull the assembly out instrument panel, disconnect the antenna and electrical connectors and remove it from the vehicle **(see illustration)**.
Installation
5 Plug in the electrical connectors and slide the radio or CD player along the track and into the instrument panel until the clips can be felt snapping in place.

Speakers
Door mounted
Refer to illustrations 15.7a and 15.7b
6 Remove the door trim panel (see Chapter 11).
7 Remove the mounting screws, withdraw the speaker, unplug the electrical connector and remove the speaker from the vehicle **(see illustrations)**.
8 Installation is the reverse of removal.
Rear quarter panel mounted
Refer to illustration 15.10
9 Pry off the speaker grille.
10 Remove the retaining screws, withdraw the speaker, unplug the electrical connector and remove the speaker from the vehicle **(see illustration)**.
11 Installation is the reverse of removal

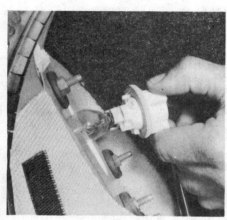

14.3a Turn the bulb housing for the taillight counterclockwise, lift it out, then remove the bulb by turning it counterclockwise

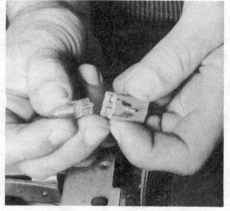

14.3b The center console bulb simply pulls straight out from the socket

14.4 Turn the instrument cluster bulb holders counterclockwise, then lift them out

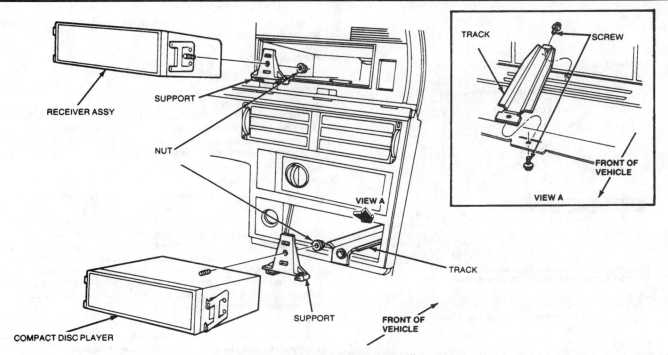

15.4   Radio and CD player details

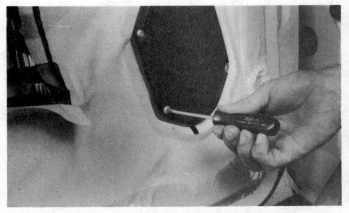

15.7a   Remove the speaker screws with a Phillips screwdriver

15.7b   Pull the speaker out and use a flat bladed screwdriver to detach the electrical connector

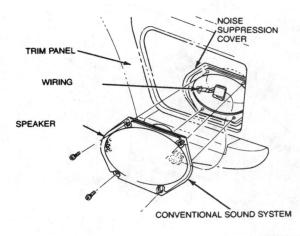

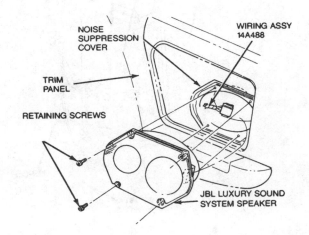

15.10   Details of the rear quarter panel mounted speaker

12

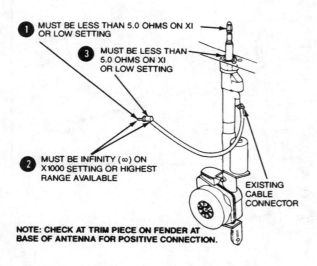

① MUST BE LESS THAN 5.0 OHMS ON XI OR LOW SETTING

③ MUST BE LESS THAN 5.0 OHMS ON XI OR LOW SETTING

② MUST BE INFINITY (∞) ON X1000 SETTING OR HIGHEST RANGE AVAILABLE

EXISTING CABLE CONNECTOR

NOTE: CHECK AT TRIM PIECE ON FENDER AT BASE OF ANTENNA FOR POSITIVE CONNECTION.

16.1   Antenna resistance check

16   Radio antenna – check and replacement

Refer to illustrations 16.1, 16.4, 16.9 and 16.11

Resistance check

1   With the antenna cable installed on the vehicle and the cable unplugged from the radio, check the antenna with an ohmmeter at the points shown in the accompanying illustration (**see illustration**). If any readings are not as specified, replace the antenna and cable assembly.

Replacement

2   Disconnect the negative battery cable.

Power antenna

3   Lower the antenna.
4   Remove the rear screws from the right side front splash shield for access and remove the lower antenna bolt (**see illustration**).
5   Remove the nut at the top of the antenna stanchion and remove the antenna through the fender opening.
6   Installation is the reverse of removal.

Manual antenna

7   Detach the holding straps from the instrument panel and lower the glove compartment.
8   Remove the screws and detach the right cowl side trim panel.
9   Unplug the cable from the radio (**see illustration**).
10   Disengage the antenna cable from the clips and retainers along the top of the heater/air conditioning assembly (**see illustration 16.9**).
11   Remove the radio antenna base cap, remove the mounting screws, pull the base and cable assembly out through the holes in the door hinge pillar and remove the assembly from the vehicle (**see illustration**).
12   Installation is the reverse of removal.

17   Instrument cluster – removal and installation

Refer to illustration 17.5

1   Disconnect the negative battery cable.
2   Remove the instrument cluster bezel (see Chapter 11).
3   Remove the four instrument cluster retaining screws.
4   Pull the cluster out and unplug the electrical connectors. On supercharged models, disconnect the boost gauge vacuum hose.
5   Swing the bottom of the cluster out to clear the top of the steering column cover and remove it from the instrument panel (**see illustration**).

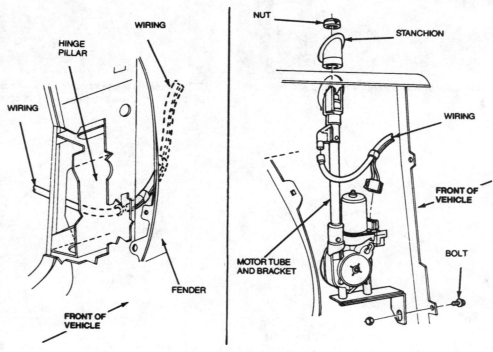

16.4   Power antenna details

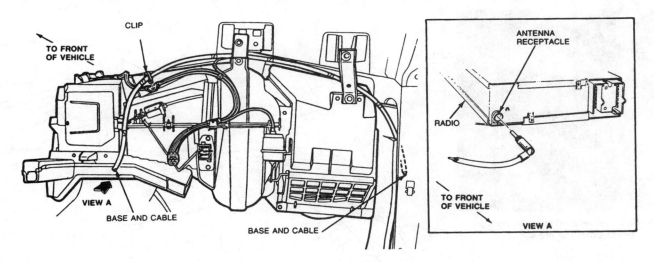

16.9 Antenna cable routing details

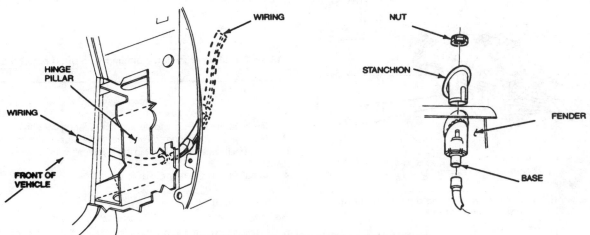

16.11 Antenna fender attachment and cable details

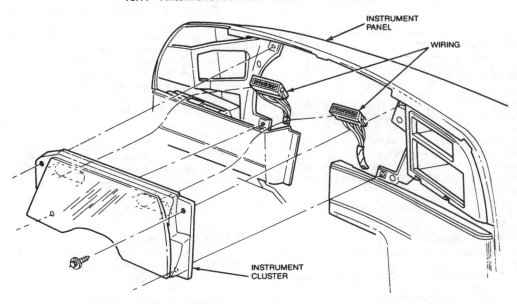

17.5 Remove the screws, rotate the bottom edge clear of the steering column, then pull the cluster out of the instrument panel

18.2   Push the release lever in, then pull the knob out of the switch

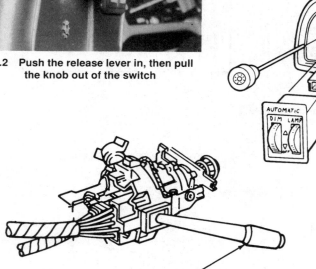

19.3   The windshield wiper switch is held on the steering column by two screws

6   Installation is the reverse of removal.

18   Headlight switch – replacement

Refer to illustrations 18.2 and 18.3

1   Disconnect the negative cable from the battery.
2   Detach the headlight switch knob by inserting a pointed tool into the release hole at its base and then pulling the knob out of the switch housing **(see illustration)**.
3   Pry the dimmer switch (if equipped) out of the bezel, unplug the electrical connector, then remove it **(see illustration)**.
4   Remove the screws and detach the instrument panel bezel.
5   Remove the nut, lower the switch, unplug the connector and remove the switch from the vehicle.
6   Installation is the reverse of removal.

19   Windshield wiper/washer switch and motor – removal and installation

1   Disconnect the negative cable from the battery.

Wiper/washer switch

Refer to illustration 19.3

18.3   The dimmer switch can simply be pried out of the bezel

2   Remove the screws and detach the steering column cover.
3   Remove the mounting screws and lift the wiper switch off the steering column **(see illustration)**. Unplug the electrical connector and remove the switch.
4   Installation is the reverse of removal.

Wiper motor

Refer to illustrations 19.6, 19.7 and 19.8

5   Use a screwdriver to pry the windshield wiper arm release lever out and lift the wiper arm off.
6   Remove the left cowl vent screen **(see illustration)**.
7   Remove the vacuum manifold connectors from the wiper module assembly, unplug the electrical connectors, then remove the five screws and one nut and lift the wiper module out as an assembly **(see illustration)**.
8   Remove the clip from the wiper motor and disconnect the wiper linkage drive arm from the motor **(see illustration)**.
9   Remove the retaining nuts and lift the wiper motor from the wiper module.
10   Installation is the reverse of removal.

20   Rear window defogger – check and repair

Refer to illustrations 20.9 and 20.19

Check

1   Use a strong light inside the vehicle. Visually inspect the wire grid from the outside. A broken grid wire will appear as a brown spot.
2   Run the engine at idle. Set the control switch to On. The indicator light should come on.
3   Working inside the vehicle with a voltmeter, contact the broad red/brown strips (the "bus") on the sides of the rear window. The meter should read 10-to-13 volts. A lower voltage reading indicates a loose ground wire (pigtail) connection at the grounded side of the glass.

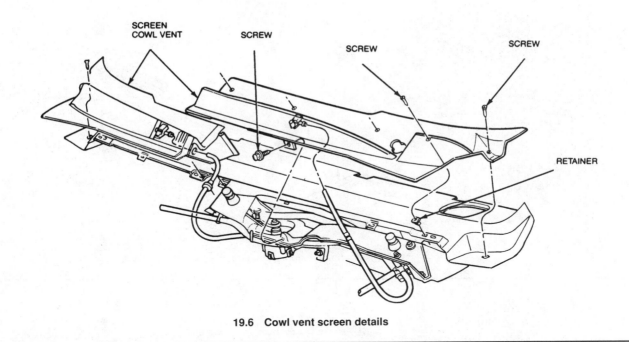

19.6   Cowl vent screen details

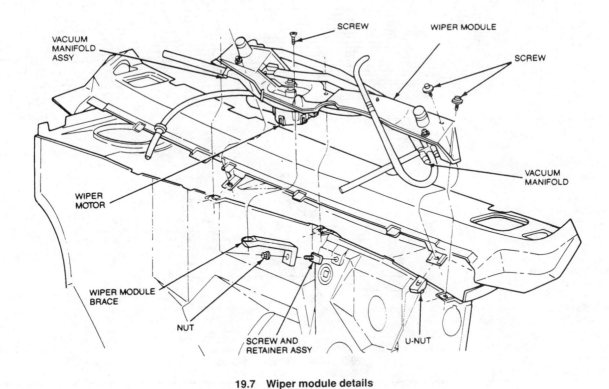

19.7   Wiper module details

4   Contact a good ground point with the negative lead of the meter. The voltage reading should not change.

5   With the negative lead of the meter grounded, touch each grid line of the heated rear window at its midpoint with the positive lead:

   a) A reading of approximately 6-volts indicates that the line is good.

   b) A reading of 0-volts indicates that the line is broken between the mid-point and the positive side of the grid line.

   c) A reading of 12-volts indicates that the circuit is broken between the mid-point of the grid and ground.

Repair

Note: *Any break in the grid longer than one inch cannot be repaired. The rear window must be replaced. For breaks less than one inch in length, use*

12

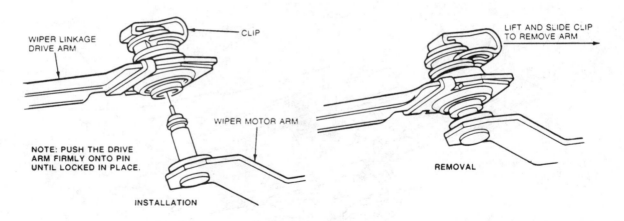

19.8   Wiper linkage connection details

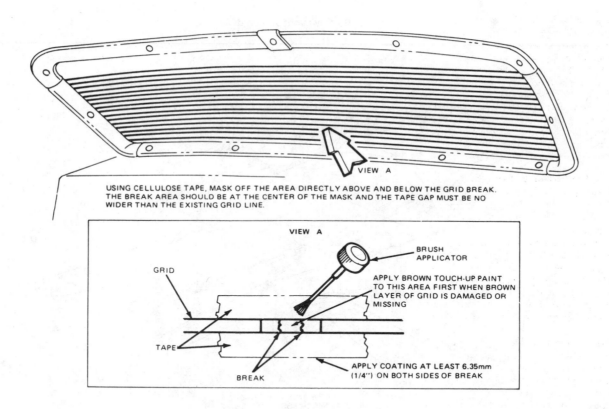

20.9   Grid wire repair details

the following procedure. You will need to obtain grid repair compound and brown touch-up paint from a Ford dealer.

6   Bring the vehicle inside and allow it to reach room temperature, which should be 60-degrees F or above.

7   Clean the entire grid line repair area with glass cleaner or a suitable cleaning solvent. Remove all dirt, wax, grease, oil or other foreign matter. The repair area must be clean and dry.

8   Mark the location of the break on the outside of the window.

9   Using cellulose tape, mask off the area directly above and below the grid break. The break area should be at the center of the mask and the tape gap must be no wider than the existing grid line (see illustration).

10   If both the brown and silver layers of the grid are broken or missing, apply a coating of the brown touch-up paint across the break area first. Two coats may be necessary to obtain the proper color. Allow the touch-up paint to dry.

11   Apply three coats of the silver grid repair compound. Allow three to five minutes drying time between coats. The coating of the silver grid repair compound should extend at least 1/4-inch on both sides of the break.

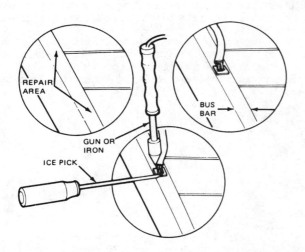

20.19   Bus bar repair details

Note: *If the brown layer of the grid is not broken or missing, apply only the silver grid repair compound to the break. Allow the compound to dry for five minutes, then remove the mask.*

12   After removing the mask, check the outside appearance of the grid repair. If the silver repair compound is visible above or below the grid, this excess should be removed. This can be done by placing a single edge razor blade on the glass parallel to the grid and scraping gently towards the grid. **Caution:** *Be careful not to damage the grid line with the razor blade.*
13   The repair coating will air dry in about one minute and can be energized within three to five minutes. Optimum hardness and adhesion occurs after approximately 24 hours. At that time, the repair area may be cleaned with a mild window cleaner.

Lead wire terminal service

14   Allow the rear window to warm up to room temperature for a half hour to an hour.
15   Clean the bus bar in the area to be repaired using fine steel wool (3/O to 4/O grade).
16   Restore the area where the bus bar terminal was originally attached by applying three coats of grid repair compound. Allow approximately ten minutes drying time between coats.
17   Working as quickly as possible to avoid overheating the glass, tin the bus bar with solder in the area where the terminal will be reattached.
18   Using a heat gun or heat lamp, pre-heat the glass in the solder area to between 120-degrees and 150-degrees F just prior to soldering the terminal on.
19   Position the terminal on the bus bar in the area that was tinned and hold it in place with an ice pick or screwdriver **(see illustration)**.
20   Apply soldering heat to the pad of the terminal until the solder flows. **Note:** *To avoid damaging the bus bar, remove the soldering gun or iron as soon as the solder flows.*
21   Start the vehicle, turn the heated rear window on and leave it on for five minutes.

21   Cruise control system – description and check

The cruise control system maintains vehicle speed with a vacuum actuated servo motor located in the engine compartment, which is connected to the throttle linkage by a cable. The system consists of the servo motor, clutch switch, brake switch, control switches, a relay and associated vacuum hoses.
Because of the complexity of the cruise control system and the special tools and techniques required for diagnosis, repair should be left to a dealer service department or a repair shop. However, it is possible for the home mechanic to make simple checks of the wiring and vacuum connections for minor faults which can be easily repaired. These include:
   a) Inspect the cruise control actuating switches for broken wires and loose connections.
   b) Check the cruise control fuse.
   c) The cruise control system is operated by vacuum so it's critical that all vacuum switches, hoses and connections are secure.
Check the hoses in the engine compartment for tight connections, cracks and obvious vacuum leaks.

22   Power window system – description and check

The power window system operates the electric motors mounted in the doors which lower and raise the windows. The system consists of the control switches, the motors (regulators), glass mechanisms and associated wiring.
Because of the complexity of the power window system and the special tools and techniques required for diagnosis, repair should be left to a dealer service department or a repair shop. However, it is possible for the home mechanic to make simple checks of the wiring connections and motors for minor faults which can be easily repaired. These include:
   a) Inspect the power window actuating switches for broken wires and loose connections.
   b) Check the power window fuse/and or circuit breaker.
   c) Remove the door panel(s) and check the power window motor wires to see if they're loose or damaged. Inspect the glass mechanisms for damage which could cause binding.

23   Power door lock system – description and check

The power door lock system operates the door lock actuators mounted in each door. The system consists of the switches, actuators and associated wiring. Since special tools and techniques are required to diagnose the system, it should be left to a dealer service department or a repair shop. However, it is possible for the home mechanic to make simple checks of the wiring connections and actuators for minor faults which can be easily repaired. These include:
   a) Check the system fuse and/or circuit breaker.
   b) Check the switch wires for damage and loose connections. Check the switches for continuity.
   c) Remove the door panel(s) and check the actuator wiring connections to see if they're loose or damaged. Inspect the actuator rods (if equipped) to make sure they aren't bent or damaged. Inspect the actuator wiring for damaged or loose connections. The actuator can be checked by applying battery power momentarily. A discernible click indicates that the solenoid is operating properly.

BK	Black	O	Orange
BR	Brown	PK	Pink
DB	Dark Blue	P	Purple
DG	Dark Green	R	Red
GY	Gray	T	Tan
LB	Light Blue	W	White
LG	Light Green	Y	Yellow
N	Natural		

12

24.4   Wiring color codes

24   Wiring diagrams – general information

Since it isn't possible to include all wiring diagrams for every year covered by this manual, the following diagrams are those that are typical and most commonly needed.

Prior to troubleshooting any circuits, check the fuse and circuit breakers (if equipped) to make sure they're in good condition. Make sure the battery is properly charged and check the cable connections (see Chapter 1).

When checking a circuit, make sure that all connectors are clean, with no broken or loose terminals. When unplugging a connector, do not pull on the wires. Pull only on the connector housings themselves.

Refer to the accompanying table for the wire color codes applicable to your vehicle.

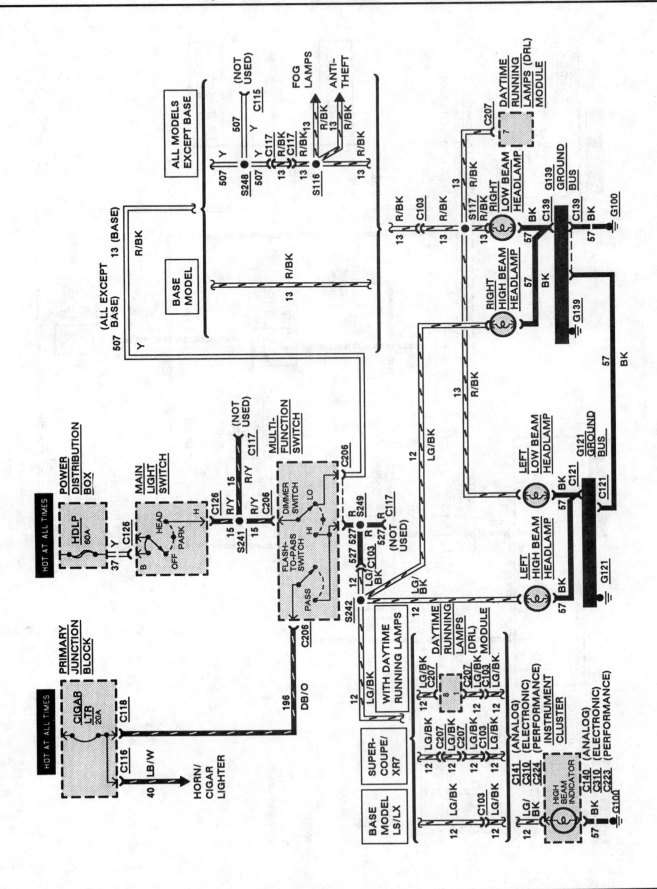

Typical headlight circuit

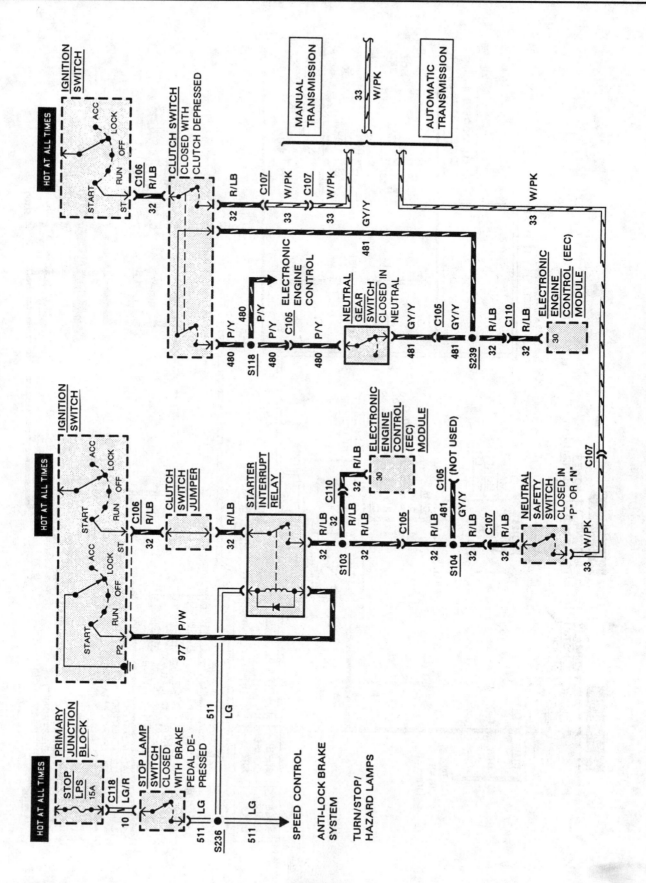

Start/ignition circuit – non-supercharged models (1 of 3)

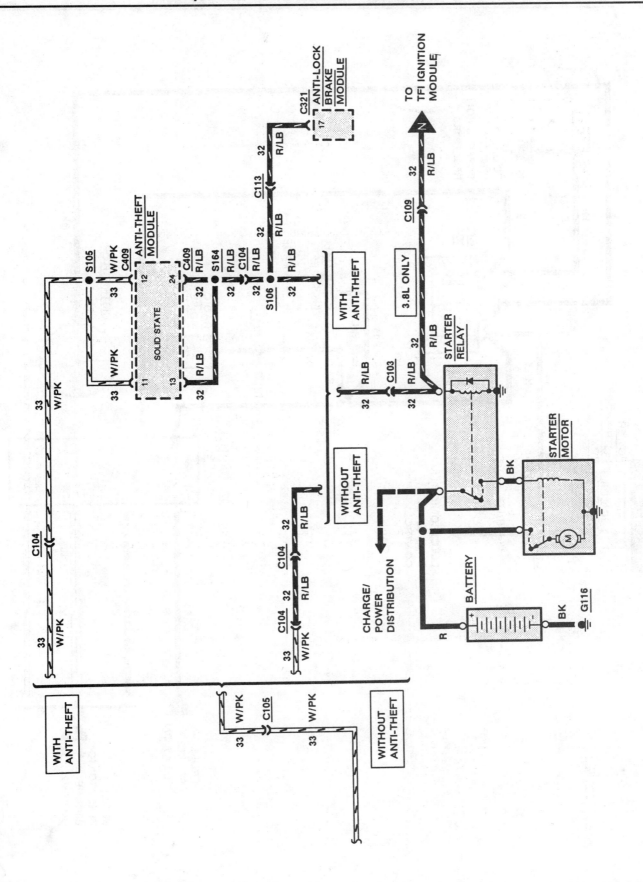

Start/ignition circuit – non-supercharged models (2 of 3)

12

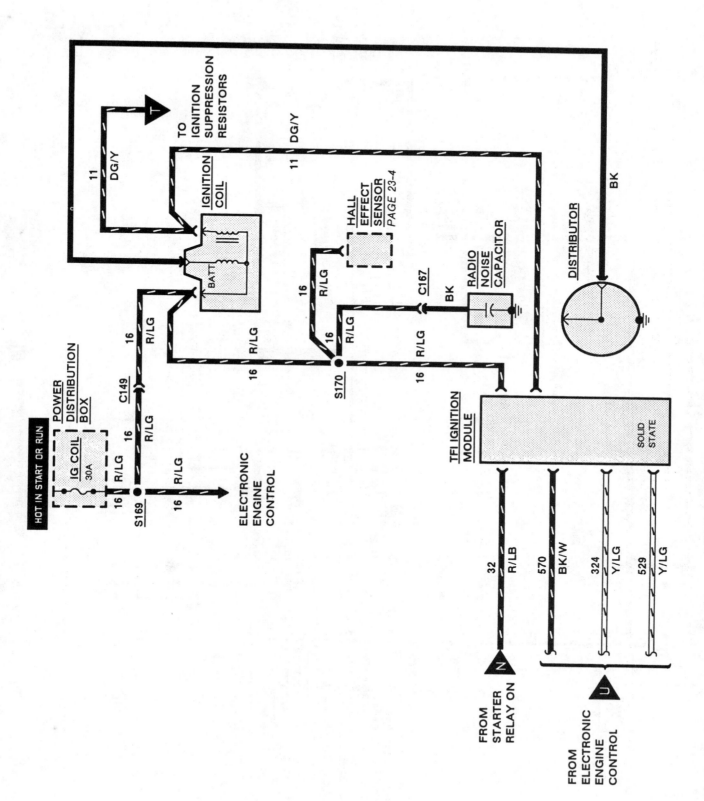

Start/ignition circuit – non-supercharged models (3 of 3)

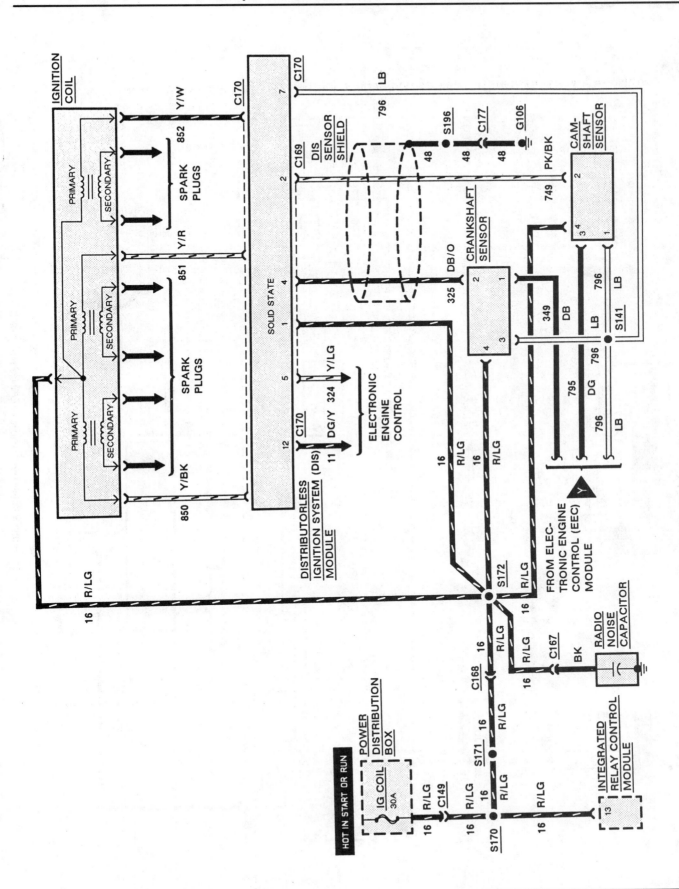

Ignition circuit – supercharged models

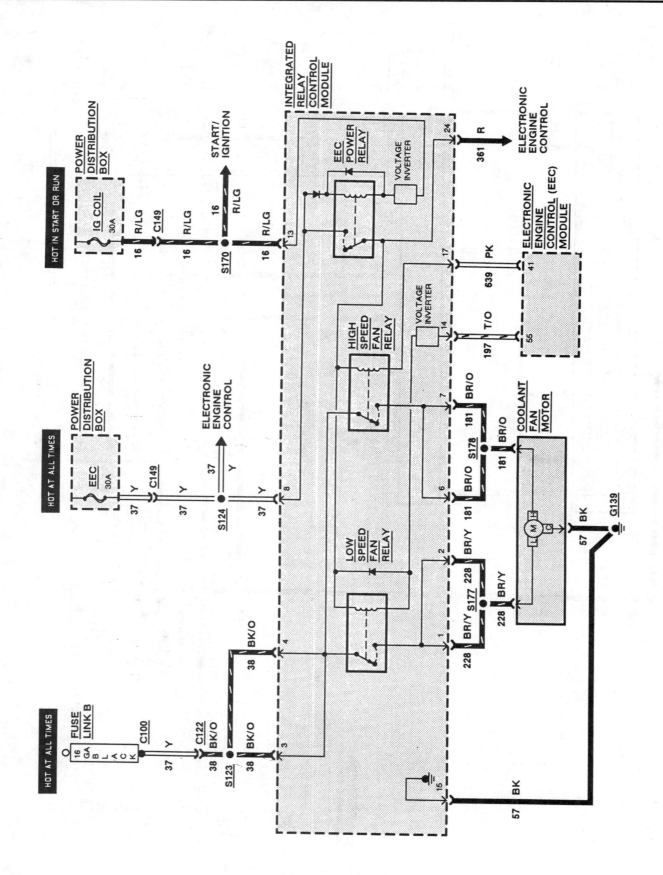

Cooling fan circuit – supercharged models

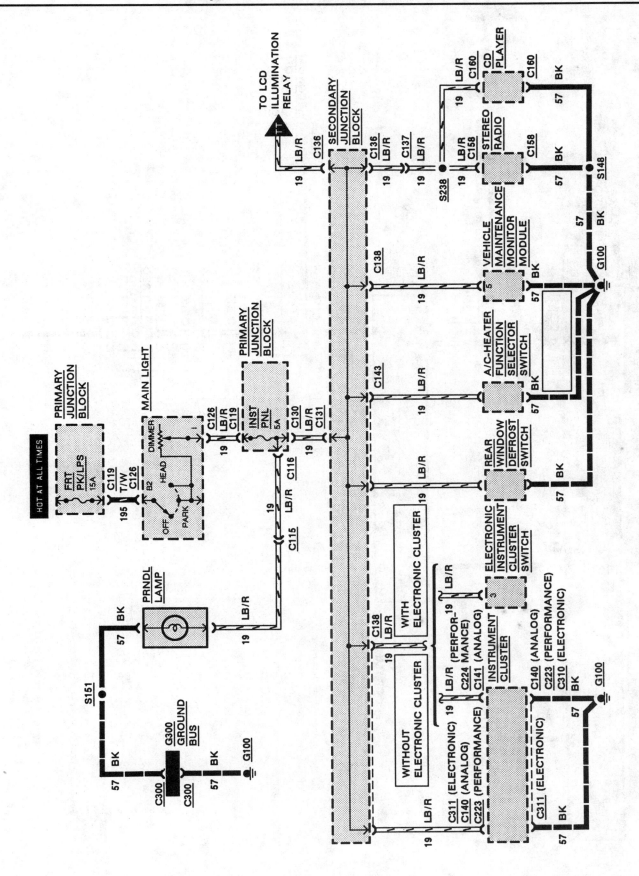

Instrument panel lighting circuit (1 of 2)

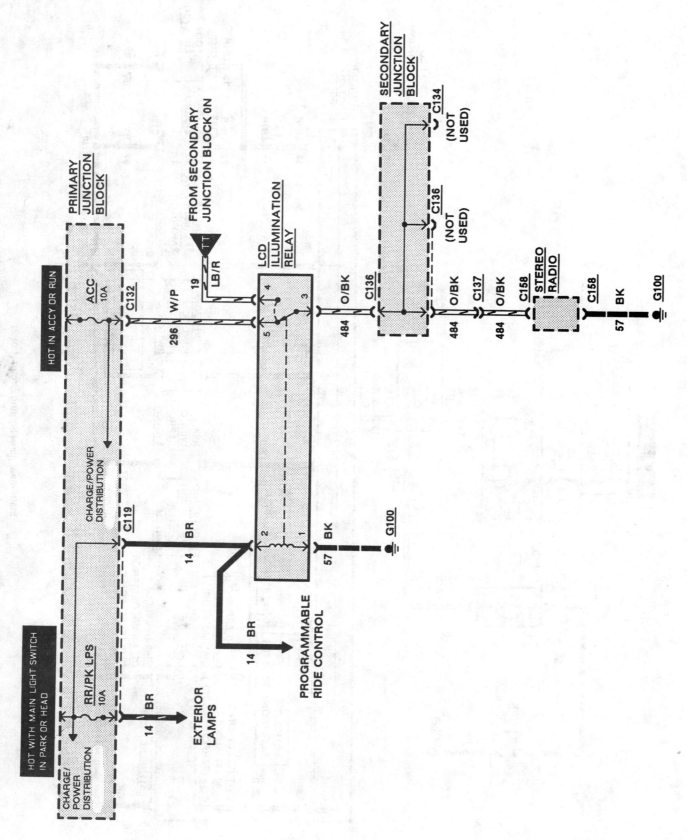

Instrument panel lighting circuit (2 of 2)

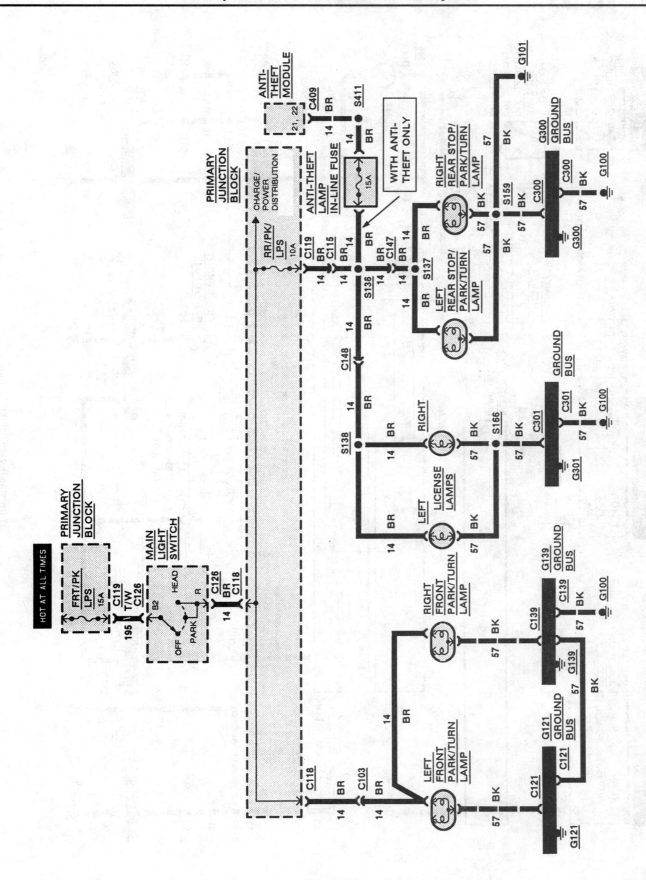

Exterior lighting circuit

12

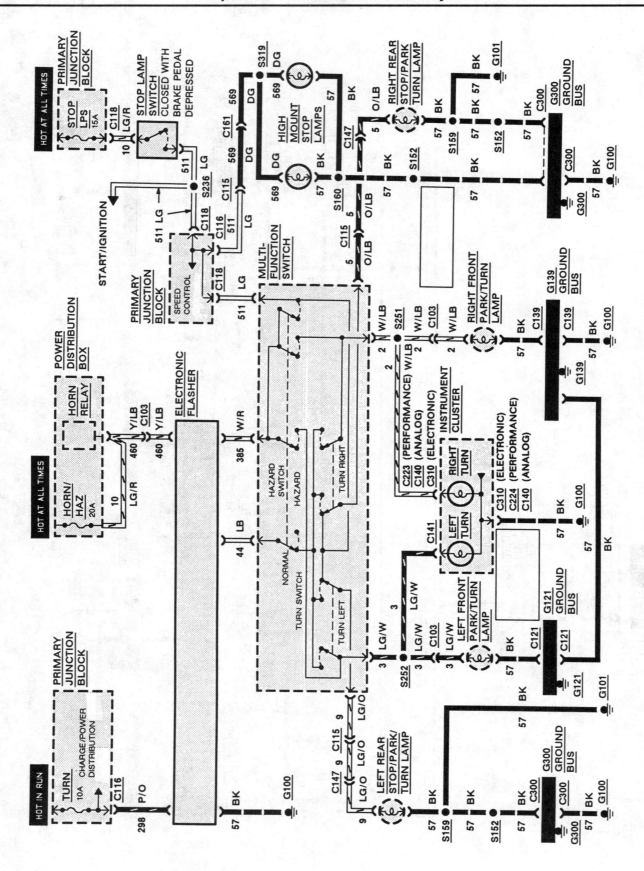

Turn/stop/hazard lighting circuit

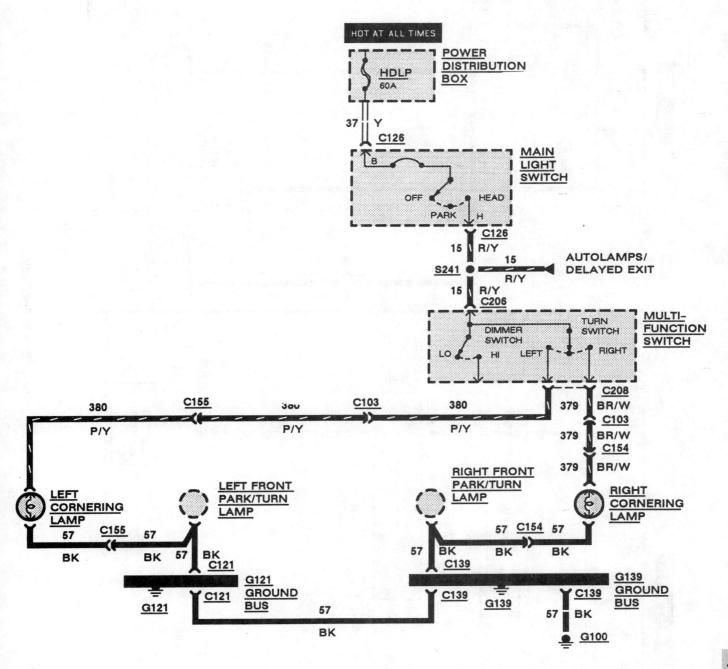

Cornering light circuit

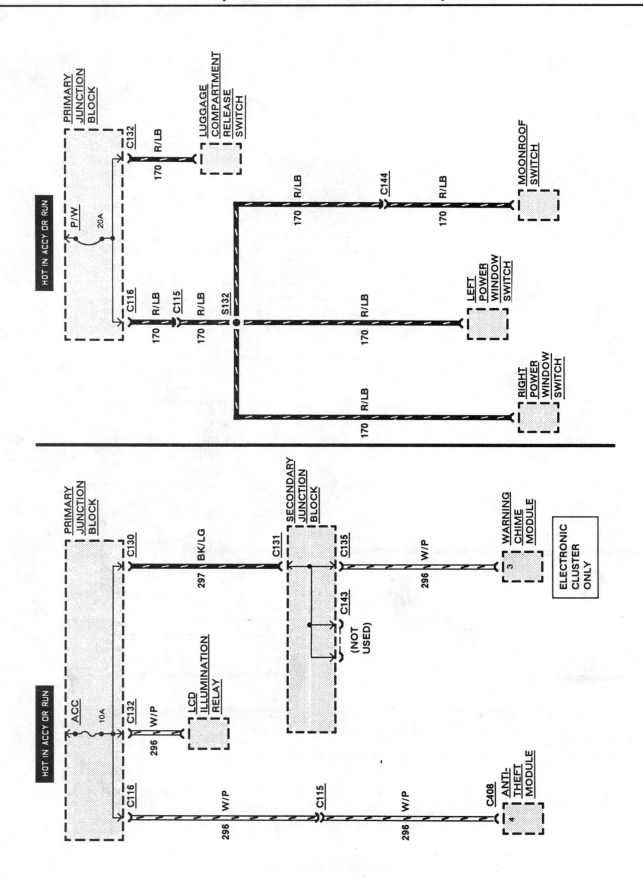

Power window circuit

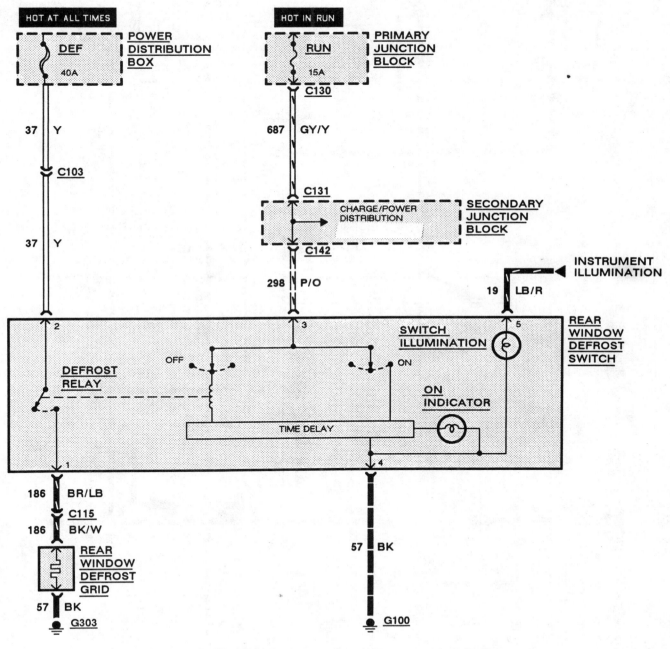

Rear window defogger circuit

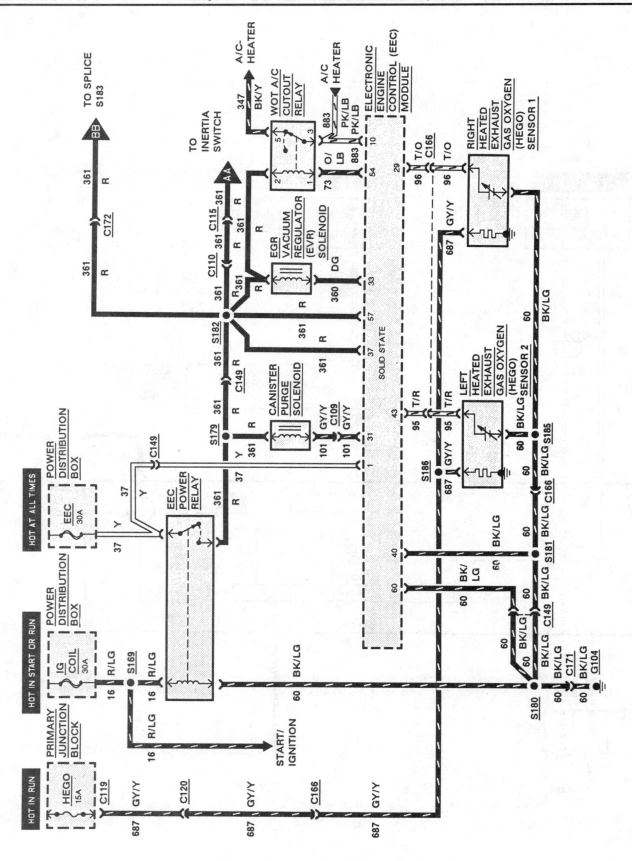

Electronic engine control systems – non-supercharged models (1 of 4)

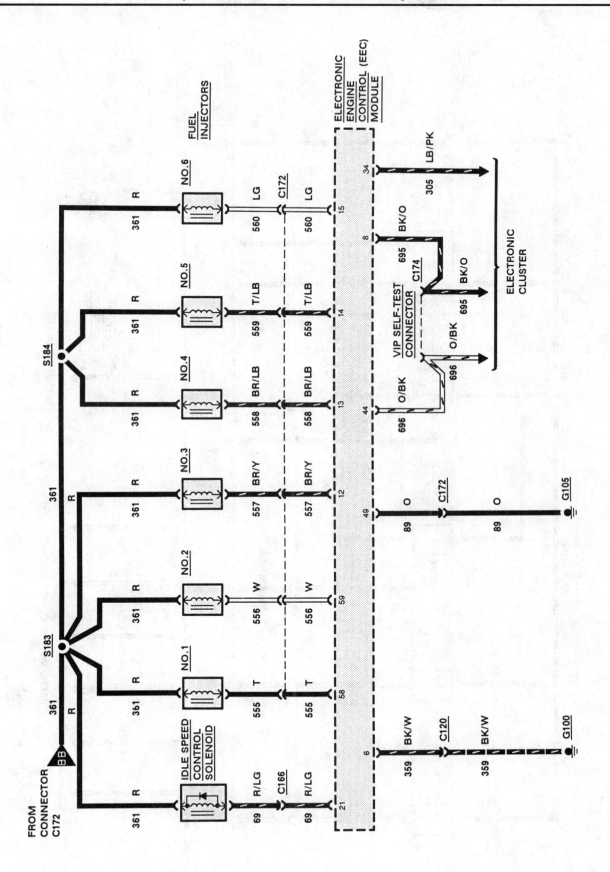

Electronic engine control systems – non-supercharged models (2 of 4)

12

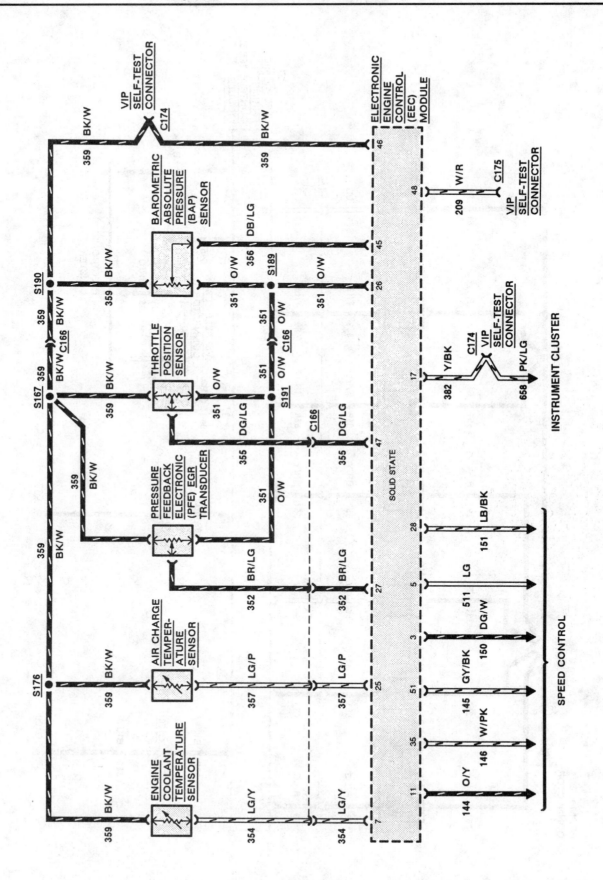

Electronic engine control systems – non-supercharged models (3 of 4)

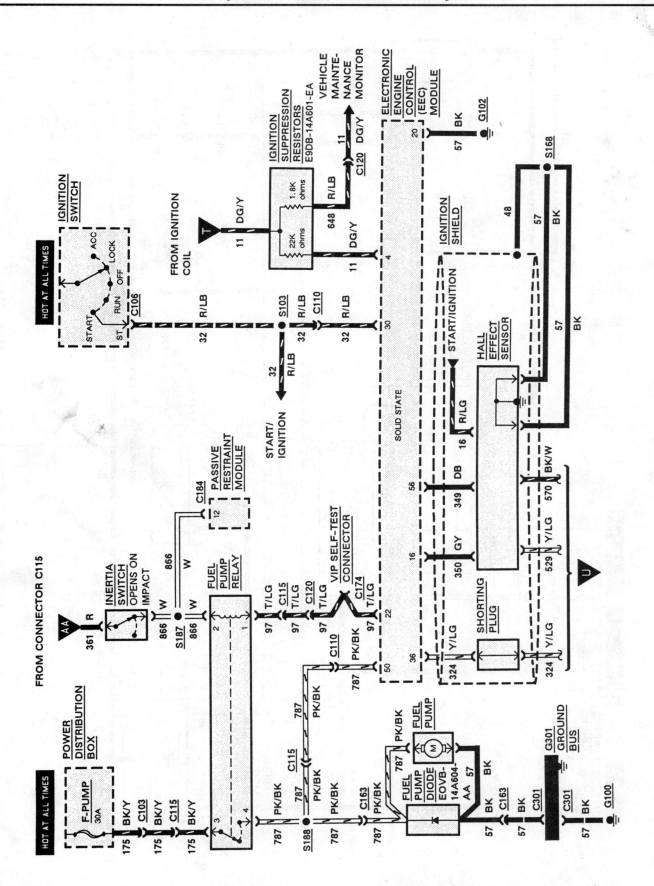

Electronic engine control systems – non-supercharged models (4 of 4)

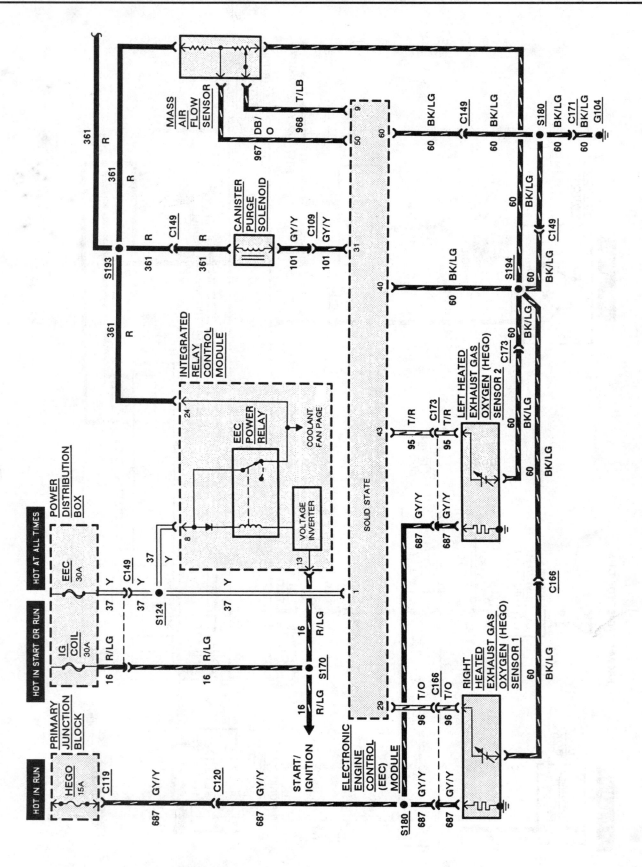

Electronic engine control systems – supercharged models (1 of 4)

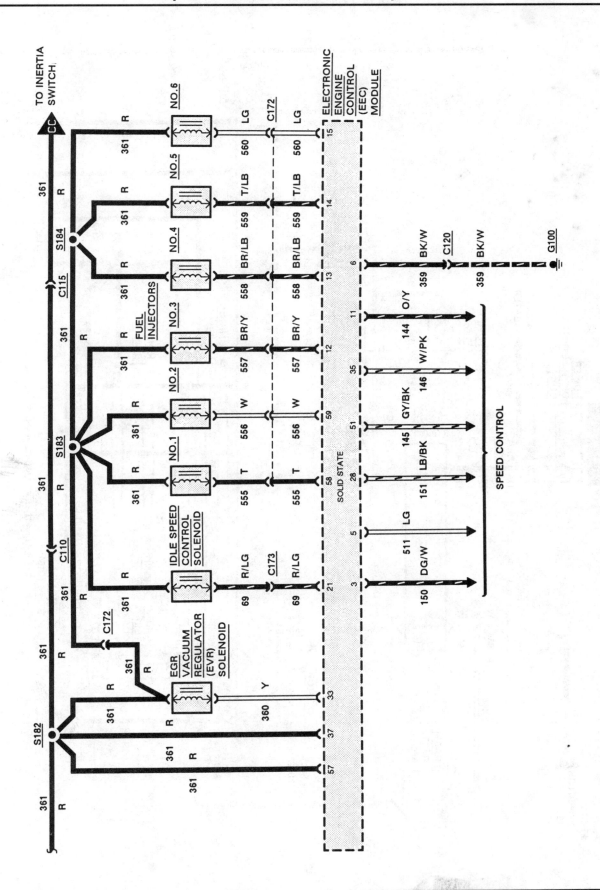

Electronic engine control systems – supercharged models (2 of 4)

12

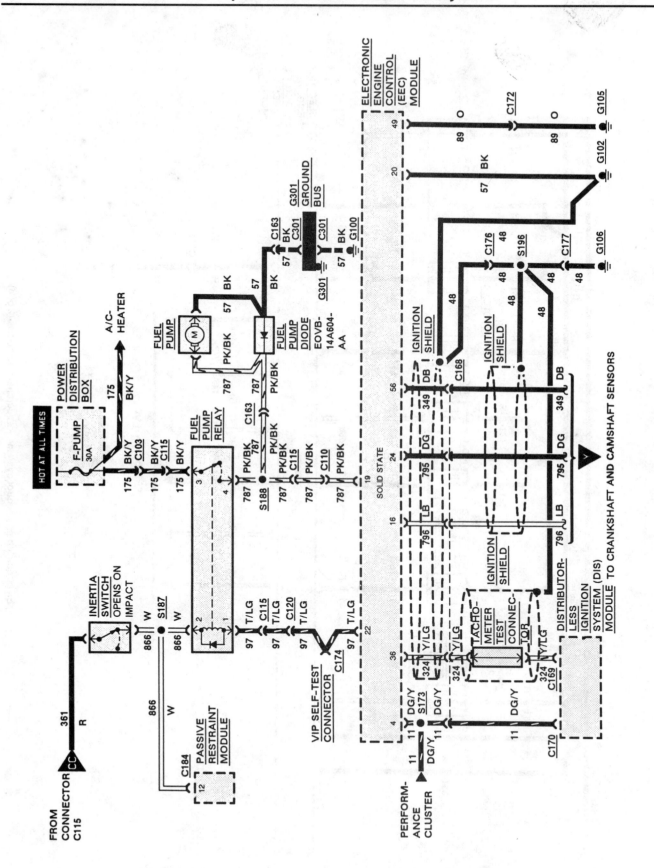

Electronic engine control systems – supercharged models (3 of 4)

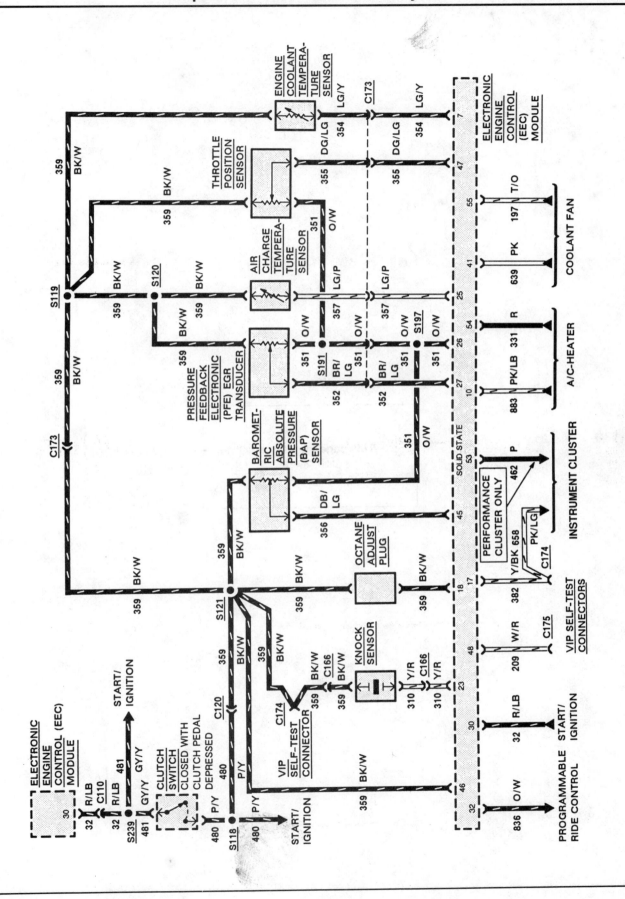

Electronic engine control systems – supercharged models (4 of 4)

This page intentionally
left blank

Index

HAYNES AUTOMOTIVE MANUALS

NOTE: New manuals are added to this list on a periodic basis. If you do not see a listing for your vehicle, consult your local Haynes dealer for the latest product information.

ACURA
1776   **Integra & Legend** '86 thru '90

AMC
    Jeep CJ – see JEEP (412)
694   **Mid-size models,** Concord, Hornet, Gremlin & Spirit '70 thru '83
934   **(Renault) Alliance & Encore** all models '83 thru '87

AUDI
615   **4000** all models '80 thru '87
428   **5000** all models '77 thru '83
1117   **5000** all models '84 thru '88

AUSTIN
    Healey Sprite – see MG Midget Roadster (265)

BMW
276   **320i** all 4 cyl models '75 thru '83
632   **528i & 530i** all models '75 thru '80
240   **1500 thru 2002** all models except Turbo '59 thru '77
348   **2500, 2800, 3.0 & Bavaria** '69 thru '76

BUICK
    Century (front wheel drive) – see GENERAL MOTORS A-Cars (829)
*1627   **Buick, Oldsmobile & Pontiac Full-size (Front wheel drive)** all models '85 thru '93
    Buick Electra, LeSabre and Park Avenue; **Oldsmobile** Delta 88 Royale, Ninety Eight and Regency; **Pontiac** Bonneville
*1551   **Buick Oldsmobile & Pontiac Full-size (Rear wheel drive)**
    Buick Electra '70 thru '84, Estate '70 thru '90, LeSabre '70 thru '79
    Oldsmobile Custom Cruiser '70 thru '90, Delta 88 '70 thru '85, Ninety-eight '70 thru '84
    Pontiac Bonneville '70 thru '81, Catalina '70 thru '81, Grandville '70 thru '75, Parisienne '84 thru '86
627   **Mid-size** all rear-drive **Regal & Century** models with V6, V8 and Turbo '74 thru '87
    Regal – see GENERAL MOTORS (1671)
    Skyhawk – see GENERAL MOTORS J-Cars (766)
552   **Skylark** all X-car models '80 thru '85

CADILLAC
*751   **Cadillac Rear Wheel Drive** all gasoline models '70 thru '90
    Cimarron – see GENERAL MOTORS J-Cars (766)

CAPRI
296   **2000 MK I Coupe** all models '71 thru '75
205   **2600 & 2800** V6 Coupe '71 thru '75
375   **2800 Mk II** V6 Coupe '75 thru '78
    Mercury Capri – see FORD Mustang (654)

CHEVROLET
*1477   **Astro & GMC Safari Mini-vans** all models '85 thru '91
554   **Camaro** V8 all models '70 thru '81
*866   **Camaro** all models '82 thru '91
    Cavalier – see GENERAL MOTORS J-Cars (766)
    Celebrity – see GENERAL MOTORS A-Cars (829)
625   **Chevelle, Malibu & El Camino** all V6 & V8 models '69 thru '87
449   **Chevette & Pontiac T1000** all models '76 thru '87
550   **Citation** all models '80 thru '85
*1628   **Corsica/Beretta** all models '87 thru '92
274   **Corvette** all V8 models '68 thru '82
*1336   **Corvette** all models '84 thru '91

704   **Full-size Sedans** Caprice, Impala, Biscayne, Bel Air & Wagons, all V6 & V8 models '69 thru '90
    Lumina – see GENERAL MOTORS (1671)
    Lumina APV – see GENERAL MOTORS (2035)
319   **Luv Pick-up** all 2WD & 4WD models '72 thru '82
626   **Monte Carlo** all V6, V8 & Turbo models '70 thru '88
241   **Nova** all V8 models '69 thru '79
*1642   **Nova and Geo Prizm** all front wheel drive models '85 thru '90
*420   **Pick-ups '67 thru '87** – Chevrolet & GMC, all full-size models '67 thru '87; Suburban, Blazer & Jimmy '67 thru '91
*1664   **Pick-ups '88 thru '92** – Chevrolet & GMC, all full-size (C and K) models, '88 thru '92
*1727   **Sprint & Geo Metro** '85 thru '92
*831   **S-10 & GMC S-15 Pick-ups** all models '82 thru '92
*345   **Vans** – Chevrolet & GMC, V8 & in-line 6 cyl models '68 thru '92

CHRYSLER
*1337   **Chrysler & Plymouth Mid-size** front wheel drive '82 thru '89
    K-Cars – see DODGE Aries (723)
    Laser – see DODGE Daytona (1140)

DATSUN
402   **200SX** all models '77 thru '79
647   **200SX** all models '80 thru '83
228   **B-210** all models '73 thru '78
525   **210** all models '78 thru '82
206   **240Z, 260Z & 280Z** Coupe & 2+2 '70 thru '78
563   **280ZX** Coupe & 2+2 '79 thru '83
    300ZX – see NISSAN (1137)
679   **310** all models '78 thru '82
123   **510 & PL521 Pick-up** '68 thru '73
430   **510** all models '78 thru '81
372   **610** all models '72 thru '76
277   **620 Series Pick-up** all models '73 thru '79
    720 Series Pick-up – see NISSAN Pick-ups (771)
376   **810/Maxima** all gasoline models '77 thru '84
124   **1200** all models '70 thru '73
368   **F10** all models '76 thru '79
    Pulsar – see NISSAN (876)
    Sentra – see NISSAN (982)
    Stanza – see NISSAN (981)

DODGE
*723   **Aries & Plymouth Reliant** all models '81 thru '89
*1231   **Caravan & Plymouth Voyager Mini-Vans** all models '84 thru '91
699   **Challenger & Plymouth Saporro** all models '78 thru '83
236   **Colt** all models '71 thru '77
610   **Colt & Plymouth Champ (front wheel drive)** all models '78 thru '87
*556   **D50/Ram 50/Plymouth Arrow Pick-ups & Raider** '79 thru '91
*1668   **Dakota Pick-up** all models '87 thru '90
234   **Dart & Plymouth Valiant** all 6 cyl models '67 thru '76
*1140   **Daytona & Chrysler Laser** all models '84 thru '89
*545   **Omni & Plymouth Horizon** all models '78 thru '90
*912   **Pick-ups** all full-size models '74 thru '91
*1726   **Shadow & Plymouth Sundance** '87 thru '91
*1779   **Spirit & Plymouth Acclaim** '89 thru '92
*349   **Vans** – Dodge & Plymouth V8 & 6 cyl models '71 thru '91

FIAT
094   **124 Sport Coupe & Spider** '68 thru '78

479   **Strada** all models '79 thru '82
273   **X1/9** all models '74 thru '80

FORD
*1476   **Aerostar Mini-vans** all models '86 thru '92
788   **Bronco and Pick-ups** '73 thru '79
*880   **Bronco and Pick-ups** '80 thru '91
268   **Courier Pick-up** all models '72 thru '82
789   **Escort & Mercury Lynx** all models '81 thru '90
*2046   **Escort & Mercury Tracer** all models '91 thru '93
*2021   **Explorer & Mazda Navajo** '91 thru '92
560   **Fairmont & Mercury Zephyr** all in-line & V8 models '78 thru '83
334   **Fiesta** all models '77 thru '80
754   **Ford & Mercury Full-size,** Ford LTD & Mercury Marquis ('75 thru '82); Ford Custom 500, Country Squire, Crown Victoria & Mercury Colony Park ('75 thru '87); Ford LTD Crown Victoria & Mercury Gran Marquis ('83 thru '87)
359   **Granada & Mercury Monarch** all in-line, 6 cyl & V8 models '75 thru '80
773   **Ford & Mercury Mid-size,** Ford Thunderbird & Mercury Cougar ('75 thru '82); Ford LTD & Mercury Marquis ('83 thru '86); Ford Torino, Gran Torino, Elite, Ranchero pick-up, LTD II, Mercury Montego, Comet, XR-7 & Lincoln Versailles ('75 thru '86)
*654   **Mustang & Mercury Capri** all models including Turbo '79 thru '92
357   **Mustang V8** all models '64-1/2 thru '73
231   **Mustang II** all 4 cyl, V6 & V8 models '74 thru '78
649   **Pinto & Mercury Bobcat** all models '75 thru '80
*1670   **Probe** all models '89 thru '92
*1026   **Ranger & Bronco II** all gasoline models '83 thru '92
*1421   **Taurus & Mercury Sable** '86 thru '92
*1418   **Tempo & Mercury Topaz** all gasoline models '84 thru '91
1338   **Thunderbird & Mercury Cougar/XR7** '83 thru '88
*1725   **Thunderbird & Mercury Cougar** '89 and '90
*344   **Vans** all V8 Econoline models '69 thru '91

GENERAL MOTORS
*829   **A-Cars** – Chevrolet Celebrity, Buick Century, Pontiac 6000 & Oldsmobile Cutlass Ciera all models '82 thru '90
*766   **J-Cars** – Chevrolet Cavalier, Pontiac J-2000, Oldsmobile Firenza, Buick Skyhawk & Cadillac Cimarron all models '82 thru '92
*1420   **N-Cars** – Buick Somerset '85 thru '87; Pontiac Grand Am and Oldsmobile Calais '85 thru '91; Buick Skylark '86 thru '91
*1671   **GM:** Buick Regal, Chevrolet Lumina, Oldsmobile Cutlass Supreme, Pontiac Grand Prix, all front wheel drive models '88 thru '90
*2035   **GM:** Chevrolet Lumina APV, Oldsmobile Silhouette, Pontiac Trans Sport '90 thru '92

GEO
    Metro – see CHEVROLET Sprint (1727)
    Prizm – see CHEVROLET Nova (1642)
    Tracker – see SUZUKI Samurai (1626)

GMC
    Safari – see CHEVROLET ASTRO (1477)
    Vans & Pick-ups – see CHEVROLET (420, 831, 345, 1664)

(continued on next page)

---

* Listings shown with an asterisk (*) indicate model coverage as of this printing. These titles will be periodically updated to include later model years – consult your Haynes dealer for more information.

Haynes North America, Inc., 861 Lawrence Drive, Newbury Park, CA 91320 • (805) 498-6703

HAYNES AUTOMOTIVE MANUALS

(continued from previous page)

NOTE: New manuals are added to this list on a periodic basis. If you do not see a listing for your vehicle, consult your local Haynes dealer for the latest product information.

HONDA

351	**Accord CVCC** all models '76 thru '83
*1221	**Accord** all models '84 thru '89
160	**Civic 1200** all models '73 thru '79
633	**Civic 1300 & 1500 CVCC** all models '80 thru '83
297	**Civic 1500 CVCC** all models '75 thru '79
*1227	**Civic** all models '84 thru '91
*601	**Prelude CVCC** all models '79 thru '89

HYUNDAI

*1552	**Excel** all models '86 thru '91

ISUZU

*1641	**Trooper & Pick-up**, all gasoline models '81 thru '91

JAGUAR

*242	**XJ6** all 6 cyl models '68 thru '86
*478	**XJ12 & XJS** all 12 cyl models '72 thru '85

JEEP

*1553	**Cherokee, Comanche & Wagoneer Limited** all models '84 thru '91
412	**CJ** all models '49 thru '86
*1777	**Wrangler** all models '87 thru '92

LADA

*413	**1200, 1300, 1500 & 1600** all models including Riva '74 thru '86

MAZDA

648	**626 Sedan & Coupe (rear wheel drive)** all models '79 thru '82
1082	**626 & MX-6 (front wheel drive)** all models '83 thru '92
370	**GLC Hatchback (rear wheel drive)** all models '77 thru '83
757	**GLC (front wheel drive)** all models '81 thru '86
*2047	**MPV** '89 thru '93
	Navajo – see FORD Explorer (2021)
*267	**Pick-ups** '72 thru '92
460	**RX-7** all models '79 thru '85
*1419	**RX-7** all models '86 thru '91

MERCEDES-BENZ

*1643	**190 Series** all four-cylinder gasoline models, '84 thru '88
346	**230, 250 & 280** Sedan, Coupe & Roadster all 6 cyl sohc models '68 thru '72
983	**280 123 Series** all gasoline models '77 thru '81
698	**350 & 450** Sedan, Coupe & Roadster all models '71 thru '80
697	**Diesel 123 Series** 200D, 220D, 240D, 240TD, 300D, 300CD, 300TD, 4- & 5-cyl incl. Turbo '76 thru '85

MERCURY

For all PLYMOUTH titles see FORD Listing

MG

111	**MGB** Roadster & GT Coupe all models '62 thru '80
265	**MG Midget & Austin Healey Sprite** Roadster '58 thru '80

MITSUBISHI

*1669	**Cordia, Tredia, Galant, Precis & Mirage** '83 thru '90
*2022	**Pick-ups & Montero** '83 thru '91

MORRIS

074	**(Austin) Marina 1.8** all models '71 thru '80
024	**Minor 1000** sedan & wagon '56 thru '71

NISSAN

1137	**300ZX** all Turbo & non-Turbo models '84 thru '89

*1341	**Maxima** all models '85 thru '91
*771	**Pick-ups/Pathfinder** gas models '80 thru '91
*876	**Pulsar** all models '83 thru '86
*982	**Sentra** all models '82 thru '90
*981	**Stanza** all models '82 thru '90

OLDSMOBILE

	Custom Cruiser – see BUICK Full-size (1551)
658	**Cutlass** all standard gasoline V6 & V8 models '74 thru '88
	Cutlass Ciera – see GENERAL MOTORS A-Cars (829)
	Cutlass Supreme – see GENERAL MOTORS (1671)
	Firenza – see GENERAL MOTORS J-Cars (766)
	Ninety-eight – see BUICK Full-size (1551)
	Omega – see PONTIAC Phoenix & Omega (551)
	Silhouette – see GENERAL MOTORS (2035)

PEUGEOT

663	**504** all diesel models '74 thru '83

PLYMOUTH

For all PLYMOUTH titles, see DODGE listing.

PONTIAC

	T1000 – see CHEVROLET Chevette (449)
	J-2000 – see GENERAL MOTORS J-Cars (766)
	6000 – see GENERAL MOTORS A-Cars (829)
1232	**Fiero** all models '84 thru '88
555	**Firebird** all V8 models except Turbo '70 thru '81
*867	**Firebird** all models '82 thru '91
	Full-size Rear Wheel Drive – see Buick, Oldsmobile, Pontiac Full-size (1551)
	Grand Prix – see GENERAL MOTORS (1671)
551	**Phoenix & Oldsmobile Omega** all X-car models '80 thru '84
	Trans Sport – see GENERAL MOTORS (2035)

PORSCHE

*264	**911** all Coupe & Targa models except Turbo & Carrera 4 '65 thru '89
239	**914** all 4 cyl models '69 thru '76
397	**924** all models including Turbo '76 thru '82
*1027	**944** all models including Turbo '83 thru '89

RENAULT

141	**5 Le Car** all models '76 thru '83
079	**8 & 10** all models with 58.4 cu in engines '62 thru '72
097	**12 Saloon & Estate** all models 1289 cc engines '70 thru '80
768	**15 & 17** all models '73 thru '79
081	**16** all models 89.7 cu in & 95.5 cu in engines '65 thru '72
	Alliance & Encore – see AMC (934)

SAAB

247	**99** all models including Turbo '69 thru '80
*980	**900** all models including Turbo '79 thru '88

SUBARU

237	**1100, 1300, 1400 & 1600** all models '71 thru '79
*681	**1600 & 1800** 2WD & 4WD all models '80 thru '89

SUZUKI

*1626	**Samurai/Sidekick and Geo Tracker** all models '86 thru '91

TOYOTA

*1023	**Camry** all models '83 thru '91
150	**Carina Sedan** all models '71 thru '74
*2038	**Celica Front Wheel Drive** '86 thru '92
935	**Celica Rear Wheel Drive** '71 thru '85
*1139	**Celica Supra** '79 thru '92
361	**Corolla** all models '75 thru '79
961	**Corolla** all models (rear wheel drive) '80 thru '87
*1025	**Corolla** all models (front wheel drive) '84 thru '91
*636	**Corolla Tercel** all models '80 thru '82
230	**Corona & MK II** all 4 cyl sohc models '69 thru '74
360	**Corona** all models '74 thru '82
*532	**Cressida** all models '78 thru '82
313	**Land Cruiser** all models '68 thru '82
200	**MK II** all 6 cyl models '72 thru '76
*1339	**MR2** all models '85 thru '87
304	**Pick-up** all models '69 thru '78
*656	**Pick-up** all models '79 thru '92

TRIUMPH

112	**GT6 & Vitesse** all models '62 thru '74
113	**Spitfire** all models '62 thru '81
322	**TR7** all models '75 thru '81

VW

159	**Beetle & Karmann Ghia** all models '54 thru '79
238	**Dasher** all gasoline models '74 thru '81
*884	**Rabbit, Jetta, Scirocco, & Pick-up** all gasoline models '74 thru '91 & Convertible '80 thru '91
451	**Rabbit, Jetta & Pick-up** all diesel models '77 thru '84
082	**Transporter 1600** all models '68 thru '79
226	**Transporter 1700, 1800 & 2000** all models '72 thru '79
084	**Type 3 1500 & 1600** all models '63 thru '73
1029	**Vanagon** all air-cooled models '80 thru '83

VOLVO

203	**120, 130 Series & 1800 Sports** '61 thru '73
129	**140 Series** all models '66 thru '74
*270	**240 Series** all models '74 thru '90
400	**260 Series** all models '75 thru '82
*1550	**740 & 760 Series** all models '82 thru '88

SPECIAL MANUALS

1479	**Automotive Body Repair & Painting Manual**
1654	**Automotive Electrical Manual**
1480	**Automotive Heating & Air Conditioning Manual**
1762	**Chevrolet Engine Overhaul Manual**
1736	**Diesel Engine Repair Manual**
1667	**Emission Control Manual**
1763	**Ford Engine Overhaul Manual**
482	**Fuel Injection Manual**
1666	**Small Engine Repair Manual**
299	**SU Carburetors** thru '88
393	**Weber Carburetors** thru '79
300	**Zenith/Stromberg CD Carburetors** thru '76

See your dealer for other available titles

---

* Listings shown with an asterisk (*) indicate model coverage as of this printing. These titles will be periodically updated to include later model years – consult your Haynes dealer for more information.

Over 100 Haynes motorcycle manuals also available

1-93

Haynes North America, Inc., 861 Lawrence Drive, Newbury Park, CA 91320 • (805) 498-6703